A Grammar of Paraguayan Guaraní

GRAMMARS OF WORLD AND MINORITY LANGUAGES

Series Editors
Lily Kahn and Riitta-Liisa Valijärvi

This series consists of accessible yet thorough open-access grammars of world and minority languages. The volumes are intended for a broad audience, including the scholarly community, students and the general public. The series is devoted to less commonly taught, regional, minority and endangered languages. Each volume includes a historical and sociolinguistic introduction to the language followed by sections on phonology, orthography, morphology, syntax and lexis, as well as additional material, such as text samples. The series aims to promote and support the study, teaching and, in some cases, revitalisation of languages worldwide.

Lily Kahn is Reader in Hebrew and Jewish Languages at UCL.

Riitta-Liisa Valijärvi is Principal Teaching Fellow in Finnish and Minority Languages at UCL and Senior Lecturer in Finno-Ugric Languages at Uppsala University, Sweden.

A Grammar of Paraguayan Guarani

Bruno Estigarribia

First published in 2020 by
UCL Press
University College London
Gower Street
London WC1E 6BT

Available to download free: www.uclpress.co.uk

Text © Bruno Estigarribia, 2020
Images © Author and copyright holders named in captions, 2020

Bruno Estigarribia has asserted his right under the Copyright, Designs and Patents Act 1988 to be identified as author of this work.

A CIP catalogue record for this book is available from The British Library.

This book is published under a Creative Commons 4.0 International licence (CC BY 4.0). This licence allows you to share, copy, distribute and transmit the work; to adapt the work and to make commercial use of the work providing attribution is made to the authors (but not in any way that suggests that they endorse you or your use of the work). Attribution should include the following information:

Estigarribia, B. 2020. *A Grammar of Paraguayan Guarani*. London, UCL Press.
https://doi.org/10.14324/111.9781787352872

Further details about Creative Commons licences are available at
http://creativecommons.org/licenses/

Any third-party material in this book is published under the book's Creative Commons licence unless indicated otherwise in the credit line to the material. If you would like to re-use any third-party material not covered by the book's Creative Commons licence, you will need to obtain permission directly from the copyright holder.

ISBN: 978-1-78735-322-0 (Hbk)
ISBN: 978-1-78735-292-6 (Pbk)
ISBN: 978-1-78735-287-2 (PDF)
DOI: https://doi.org/10.14324/111.9781787352872

Contents

List of figures   xi
Preface   xii
Acknowledgments   xv
Note on the presentation of language examples   xvii

1. Introduction   1
   1.1. Overview of the language   1
   1.2. Brief history since the European colonization of the region   3
   1.3. Sociolinguistic information   6
   1.4. Basic pronunciation summary   8
   1.5. Typological information   9
   1.6. Contact with Spanish and other languages   16
   1.7. Guarani as a second or foreign language   20
   1.8. Pointers for students   21

2. Phonology and orthography: the sound system and its written representation   26
   2.1. Sound inventory and pronunciation (segmental phonology)   26
      2.1.1. Vowels and diphthongs   26
      2.1.2. Consonants   30
   2.2. Suprasegmental phonology   34
      2.2.1. Syllable structure   35
      2.2.2. Stress   36
      2.2.3. Nasal harmony   39
      2.2.4. Prosody sketch: practical considerations for pronunciation   45
   2.3. The alphabet or *achegety* and modern orthographic conventions in Paraguay   46
      2.3.1. History of orthographic conventions   46
      2.3.2. Recommended orthography   46

- 3. Nominals — 57
  - 3.1. Nouns — 57
    - 3.1.1. Plural marking — 59
    - 3.1.2. Gender marking — 62
    - 3.1.3. Relational (multiform) nominal roots — 63
    - 3.1.4. Functions of noun phrases in a sentence — 69
  - 3.2. Forming nouns from other words — 70
    - 3.2.1. Nominalizations — 71
      - 3.2.1.1. Nominalizing suffixes — 71
        - 3.2.1.1.1. General nominalizer *-ha* — 71
        - 3.2.1.1.2. Passive *-py* — 73
        - 3.2.1.1.3. Adjectival *-va* — 74
        - 3.2.1.1.4. Abstract *-kue* — 75
      - 3.2.1.2. Nominalizing prefixes — 77
        - 3.2.1.2.1. Resultative/instrumental *t-embi-* — 77
        - 3.2.1.2.2. Reflexive/passive/impersonal *je-* — 79
        - 3.2.1.2.3. Reciprocal *jo-* — 80
        - 3.2.1.2.4. Abstract *t-eko-* — 81
        - 3.2.1.2.5. Abstract *mba'e-* — 82
      - 3.2.1.3. Noun compounds — 82
    - 3.2.2. Nominal/adjectival negation — 85
    - 3.2.3. Diminutives and attenuatives — 86
  - 3.3. Adjectival modifiers of the noun — 87
  - 3.4. Determiners — 89
    - 3.4.1. Articles — 90
    - 3.4.2. Demonstratives — 94
    - 3.4.3. Numerals and quantifiers — 99
  - 3.5. Pronouns — 105
    - 3.5.1 Personal pronouns — 105
    - 3.5.2 Interrogative pronouns — 111
    - 3.5.3 Indefinite and negative pronouns — 113
    - 3.5.4 Demonstrative pronouns — 115
    - 3.5.5 Possessive pronouns — 116
  - 3.6. Possessive noun phrases — 117
  - 3.7. Nominal temporal-aspectual markers — 121

- 4. Verbs — 126
  - 4.1 Intransitive verbs — 127
    - 4.1.1. Active verbs — 128
    - 4.1.2. Inactive verbs — 130

4.2.	Transitive verbs	132
4.3.	Ditransitive verbs	140
4.4.	Postpositional complement verbs	141
4.5.	Irregular verbs	146
4.6.	Relational (multiform) verbs	148
4.7.	Verbs with increments	150
4.8.	Verbs with loss of initial consonant	152
4.9.	Verbal negation	154
4.10.	Expressing properties of events: tense, aspect, mood/modality, evidentiality	157
	4.10.1 Tense	157
	4.10.2 Aspect	163
	4.10.3 Mood and modality	170
	4.10.3.1. Expressing commands	170
	4.10.3.1.1 Basic imperative mood	170
	4.10.3.1.2 Imperative modalizers	172
	4.10.3.1.3 Prohibitive mood	176
	4.10.3.2. Expressing possibility and ability	178
	4.10.3.3. Expressing obligation and permission	180
	4.10.3.4. Expressing desire and volition	181
	4.10.3.4.1 Volitive mood	181
	4.10.3.4.2 Hortative and optative mood	183
	4.10.3.5. Expressing negative evaluations	186
4.11.	Verbalizations	188
4.12.	Modifiers of the verb	190
4.13.	Verb compounds	192

5. Postpositions — 194
   5.1. Postpositions marking a predicate's complements — 194
   5.2. Postpositions of place — 197
   5.3. Postpositions of time — 198
   5.4. Other postpositions — 200

6. Voice — 203
   6.1. Active voice — 203
   6.2. Inactive voice — 204
   6.3. Passive/reflexive/impersonal voice — 207
       6.3.1. With intransitive verbs: generic and impersonal interpretations — 208
       6.3.2. With transitive verbs: passive and reflexive interpretations — 209

6.4.	Reciprocal voice	211
6.5.	Antipassive voice	213
6.6.	Causative voice	215
	6.6.1. Causative voice for intransitive verbs	215
	6.6.2. Sociative causative	218
	6.6.3. Causative voice for transitive verbs	220
7.	Evidentiality	223
7.1.	Emphatic and veridical markers	223
7.2.	Markers of hearsay	225
7.3.	Markers of direct evidence	226
7.4.	Markers of reasoned evidence	227
8.	Basic clauses	230
8.1.	Word order in simple clauses	230
8.2.	Predicative and equative clauses	231
8.3.	Location and existence clauses	232
8.4.	Sentences expressing possession	235
	8.4.1. Non-verbal possessive sentences	235
	8.4.2. Verbal possessive sentences	236
8.5.	Questions	237
9.	Quantification	241
10.	Degree expressions	246
10.1.	Comparatives	246
10.2.	Superlatives	249
11.	Noun incorporation into the verb	255
12.	Complex sentences	259
12.1.	Coordinated clauses	259
12.2.	Subordinate clauses	263
	12.2.1. Relative clauses	263
	12.2.2. Complement clauses	267
	12.2.3. Adverbial clauses	271
	12.2.3.1. Purposive	271
	12.2.3.2. Concessive	272
	12.2.3.3. Causal	273

12.2.3.4.	Conditional	274
12.2.3.5.	Manner	276
12.2.3.6.	Temporal	277
12.2.3.7.	Locative	278

13. Information structure — 280
   13.1. Focus — 280
   13.2. Topic — 283

14. Order of affixes, clitics and other particles in the predicate — 285

15. Common vocabulary — 290
   15.1. Food — 290
   15.2. Body parts — 291
   15.3. Senses — 293
   15.4. Numbers — 293
   15.5. Kinship terms — 293
   15.6. Animals — 294
   15.7. Time — 295
   15.8. Dwelling — 297
   15.9. Colours — 298

16. Text samples — 299
   16.1. Interview — 299
   16.2. Narrative — 302
   16.3. Poem — 304
   16.4. Theatre — 305
   16.5. Newspaper article — 308

17. Paradigms — 309
   17.1. List of circumfixes — 309
   17.2. List of prefixes — 309
   17.3. List of postpositional particles — 310
   17.4. List of morphemes with consonant allomorphs conditioned by nasal harmony — 313
       17.4.1. Affixes and clitics — 313
       17.4.2. Roots — 314
   17.5. List of relational roots and morphemes — 316
   17.6. List of aireal verbs — 320

18. Common phrases and expressions	321
References	327
Data sources	327
Suggested resources	328
General introductions	328
Phrasebooks	328
Textbooks and online courses	328
Dictionaries	329
Grammars	329
Linguistic overviews	330
Online resources	330
Online bookshops	330
Academic works consulted	330
Glossary	333
Index	359

List of figures

Figure 1.1   Putative Proto-Tupian homeland (Tupian Urheimat)   4
Figure 1.2   Reconstructed migrations yielding the current
              Tupi-Guarani spread   5
Figure 4.1   Main classes of verbs   127

Preface

The purpose of this work is to provide an up-to-date reference of the grammar of Modern Paraguayan Guarani that is comprehensive in scope yet accessible to non-linguists, primarily students and teachers, while remaining useful to foster further research by scholars of the language. It is not intended as a language course book, with lessons progressing in difficulty or with exercises for the reader. Rather, it is aimed at furnishing a systematic presentation of the main features of the grammar of Guarani as it is used today in speech, print and other visual and social media. Because of this, this grammar is not necessarily to be read chapter by chapter in order. The table of contents and the detailed index (together with the last section on grammatical paradigms and the glossary of technical terms at the end) can guide readers to the sections they are most interested in. Frequent cross-referencing of chapters and sections in the text further ensures that the reader can locate all the important information about a given grammatical item.

Consistent with this goal, my approach is resolutely descriptive: my aim is to give a representative picture of the language that a variety of speakers are likely to use and understand, and not necessarily to adjudicate between different linguistic forms, perceived sometimes as more or less "correct". This is, of course, a fundamental tenet of modern linguistics, but it is all the more crucial in the case of Paraguayan Guarani. Due to extensive contact with Spanish since the sixteenth century and to high rates of variable individual bilingualism and multilingualism, the occurrence of mostly non-mixed, "pure" Guarani in Paraguay is limited to colloquial use in monolingual-leaning rural areas, or conversely to formal academic contexts where the use of Guarani is required. When the 1992 Paraguayan constitution declared Guarani an official language, and concomitantly mandated full availability of public education in Guarani, the normative issue of whether to adopt the contact-influenced urban spoken Guarani, or a de-Hispanicized, restandardized form of the language became the subject of much (still ongoing) debate. This book does not aim to take sides on this issue. I will try to present general aspects of the grammar without attaching value judgments to them. My goal is to give as much useful information as possible, in an accessible and compact way, to facilitate further study and research on the language. Clearly, some of the issues treated here could (and should) be the object of deeper scrutiny, or at least argued for in more detail. But, given the goal of remaining accessible and useful to a broader audience, I will try to minimize linguistic explanation and analysis. Technical terms (useful for linguist readers) will be given in boldface with an accompanying explanation (and recapped in the **Glossary**).

The examples in this book come from a variety of sources, reflecting the diversity of individual and social functions a living language serves. Many examples come from creative works, such as novels, short stories, myths, poetry and film (a list is given under Data sources in the **References**). I have also consulted sources of **naturalistic data**, sometimes hailed as a gold standard for linguistic data because it is assumed to be truly representative and authentic, free of observer interference or goals that are extraneous to non-pre-planned speech or edited language. These include:

- online content
  - social media content, such as posts and comments on Facebook, Twitter, blogs or publicly available videos and audio (for example, from YouTube)
  - newspaper articles
  - Vikipetã (Guarani Wikipedia) entries
  - Bible translations and other religious texts from the internet
- naturalistic interactions with family and friends where I was a participant during fieldwork visits.

For particular aspects of the grammar without published analyses or whose published analyses I considered unsatisfactory, I have elicited controlled data from the following sources:

- **sociolinguistic interviews** and narratives I collected with the Paraguayan expatriate community in Buenos Aires (the largest in the world, with over half a million immigrants, according to the 2010 Argentinian census) in 2013
- an **elicitation questionnaire** from fieldwork in Asunción and Encarnación, Paraguay, in 2018, and further elicitations with Guarani speakers in the USA in 2019.

A few examples come from scholarly data; from published grammars and dictionaries of the language, research articles and textbooks (also listed in the **References**, under Academic works consulted). The use of examples from research or scholarly sources will be explicitly identified in footnotes. Finally, some examples were created by myself specifically for exemplification purposes (which I have generally avoided doing for the more subtle or debatable phenomena).

As a result of the use of such varied sources, the language represented in this work contains a high degree of variation, from more academic writing to more informal, colloquial styles. The conscious choice was made here not to avoid this variation by presenting an artificially standardized and homogeneous view of Guarani, but rather to expose readers to the most representative tableau of the Guarani they will encounter in real life, across different situations. This is most visible in the variable use of the letter <g̃>, which represents the nasal sound at the end of the English word 'king' (International Phonetic Alphabet symbol: /ŋ/). Some very frequent words like *ko'ág̃a* 'now' or *g̃uahẽ* 'to arrive' can be found with spellings that mark the nasality of the word on a different letter, for example *ko'ãga* or *guahẽ*. Readers should bear in mind that this variation has been retained to facilitate their engagement with authentic written sources.

In fact, the standardization of Guarani is relatively recent and actually still vigorously under way. By way of example, the Paraguayan Academy of the Guarani Language (Guarani Ñe'ẽ Rerekuapavẽ) published its first official grammar only very recently, in August of 2018. Because of this, many different orthographic conventions are found in written sources (including in social media data). Again, I felt it was important to reflect this natural variation in writing in this book, since such inconsistencies will be encountered by readers further continuing their study of the language. Occasionally I have chosen to modify naturally occurring examples to better conform to the orthography recommended in Estigarribia (2017), mainly in order to make the structure and/or pronunciation of some examples clearer.

Lastly, I will refer to the language as *Guarani* throughout, so a few clarifications are in order. First, although this is a name currently used by native speakers to refer to the language, the original **endonym** (that is, the name originally used inside the linguistic community of speakers) is *avañe'ẽ* 'language of man'. Second, the spelling *Guaraní* is often found in the literature, following Spanish orthographic conventions, but I use *Guarani* here, in keeping with the modern standard rules of Guarani for written stress (see **2.2.2**). Third, and perhaps most importantly, *Guarani* is a term that encompasses many different varieties – including indigenous varieties such as Mbyá Guarani or Avá Guarani – that are different from Paraguayan Guarani. The use of *Guarani* to refer exclusively to the latter variety here is purely a matter of simplicity and should not be construed as a judgment on the relative worth of different Guarani languages.

Acknowledgments

I am deeply indebted to the many individuals and organizations that have made the content and preparation of this book possible. First and foremost, this work would not have been possible without the support of the United States' National Endowment for the Humanities (NEH Fellowship Award #FEL-257415, January 2018 to December 2018). The University of North Carolina (UNC) and Duke University Consortium in Latin American and Caribbean Studies funded the early stages of this project through UNC's Institute for the Study of the Americas. I also received support from the Buchan Excellence Fund administered by my home department, Romance Studies, and from a Schwab Excellence Award from UNC's College of Arts and Sciences.

I want to also acknowledge the invaluable assistance with Guarani data of my colleagues Ernesto López Almada and Shaw Gynan, and of the participants of the Facebook groups Avañe'ẽ and Avañe'ẽ porã (Group for Guarani and Tupi-Guarani Studies). My colleague Justin Pinta provided careful reading and insightful comments on a first version of this manuscript. I would also like to thank Wolf Lustig, Alexandre Pereira Martins, Gilbert Ramirez and Kirill Tolpygo for generously working under time constraints to provide continuous access to Professor Lustig's outstanding Interactive Guarani Dictionary at a critical juncture in this project.[1]

I would like to thank my colleagues in the Department of Romance Studies at UNC Chapel Hill for their support and collegiality over the years. Special thanks go to my colleague Lamar Graham for some very timely discussions about the possible classifications of types of clauses.

It would be remiss of me not to acknowledge here the role of the foreign language course publisher ASSiMiL in teaching me for many years how to write to facilitate the self-study of a foreign language. Much of what I learned working for ASSiMiL a couple of decades ago permeates my approach here, especially in Chapters 1 and 2. I am, unfortunately,

---

[1] Dr Lustig's Interactive Guarani Dictionary can be accessed at http://www.unimainz.de/cgi-bin/guarani2/dictionary.pl.

not as good as they are, so I will have to ask the reader to be patient with me.

I am forever indebted to the series editors, Dr Riitta-Liisa Valijärvi and Dr Lily Kahn, for giving me the opportunity to work on this grammar and publish it in such an important venue, and for making the process so enjoyable.

Finally, to my family, the absolute best thing that ever happened to me:

> *down-home*
> *You honour your origins*
> *You are a daughter of your old Missouri*
> *and I am an urban product*
> *unrooted and rooted here and there.*
>
> *But we met*
> *and when we met*
> *it was like coming home to us.*
> *Up and down went home*
> *Home is where we start*
> *and home is what we found.*

Note on the presentation of language examples

Exemplifying a language's properties in the clearest and most informative way is crucial in any reference grammar. The need for full linguistic information (especially for linguist readers) needs to be balanced against the need to achieve readability and usability by a broad audience, readers who perhaps do not need as much detail as a linguist. For that reason, I have decided to treat language examples as follows:

- First of all, grammar points will be exemplified wherever possible with single words or simple phrases first and then in full sentences to provide contexts of use.
- All examples contain at least four lines.
  - The first line is the example as found in a primary source or my own creation. It is in italics and is the same size font as the running text. The punctuation and spelling usually follow the format of the original source (for example, if an example is part of a longer sentence found in a source, no capitals or end-sentence punctuation may appear). Generally, whatever part of the example is the most relevant to what is being explained will appear in boldface.
  - The fourth line contains a free, idiomatic translation into English. It is also in regular-sized font but enclosed in single quotation marks. Generally, I will underline the English part of the translation that corresponds to what is being exemplified (in boldface) in the Guarani line, to facilitate comparison.
  - The second and third lines are mostly technical. They are both given in smaller font, so that readers not interested in details of how an example is constructed morphologically and syntactically can skip these lines easily and concentrate instead on the example on the first line and the free translation on the fourth. Nevertheless, I must note from the outset that trying to understand how a Guarani sentence relates to the English translation is difficult without the help of these two technical intermediate lines. This is because single Guarani words with many attached parts often correspond to multiple separate English words.

- The second line contains a division in **morphemes** (that is, words or parts of words that each contribute an identifiable meaning to a whole word or sentence). This is very useful in helping to understand how the meaning of particular words, phrases and sentences is constructed from the meanings of their parts. Since the orthography of Guarani is not fully fixed, this line may differ slightly from the first line, especially when it comes to writing morphemes together in one word or separately in different words. This should not present insurmountable problems to readers. Bear in mind that the way this second line is segmented is a result of my own choices on how to analyse the language, the justification of which is outside the scope of this book. (See Academic works consulted for technical texts that contain more developed linguistic analyses.)
- The third line contains a more technical **gloss**, often using technical abbreviations set off in SMALL CAPS. It is aligned with the second line word for word. For this third line, examples are glossed following the Leipzig conventions for interlinear morpheme-by-morpheme glossing, but in as simple a way as possible.[2] For example, I will sometimes prefer to gloss morphemes with words from English rather than with technical abbreviations, even though the English words are often not precise matches for the Guarani morphemes. Needless to say, glossing Guarani morphemes with English terms should not be construed as a claim that the Guarani morphemes in question have the same morphological or syntactic properties as their English glosses (for example, that they are distinct words or even lexical words). Since sometimes using a technical term is the only sensible option to satisfy both clarity and accuracy, below I list the technical abbreviations used (with comparisons to English words or affixes where possible). The more casual reader may not need to refer to this line for every example.
- In Chapter **2**, where the sound system is discussed, many examples will have an added second line with a **phonetic transcription** to clarify the specifics of pronunciation that are being explained. Again, a more casual reader may not need to refer to this line for every example.
- Finally, boldface, small caps and underlining can have special and often varying uses depending on the focus of the chapter.

---

[2] For the Leipzig conventions, see https://www.eva.mpg.de/lingua/resources/glossing-rules.php, accessed 22 December 2019.

Technical abbreviations used

1,2,3	First, second, third person (cf. English 'I/we, you, s/he/it/they')
ACT	Active (cf. English active voice)
ADJZ	Adjectivizer (cf. English '-y' in 'room-y')
AGD	Agent-demoting voice
ALMOST	Quasi-eventive / Frustrative aspect
ATT	Attenuative suffix (cf. English '-ish' in 'green-ish')
DES	Desiderative mood (cf. English 'I wish that …')
DEST	Destinative aspect / Nominal future tense
DET	Determiner (cf. English 'the')
DIM	Diminutive (cf. English '-ling' in 'duck-ling')
DIR.PAST	Direct evidence past
DIST	Distal demonstrative (cf. English 'that over there')
DIST.EV	Distal demonstrative for removed events
DIST.IND	Distal demonstrative without speaker direct knowledge
DIST.PER	Distal demonstrative for removed persons
DUB	Dubitative future
EMPH	Emphatic
EXCL	Exclusive of the addressee(s)
FORCE	Forceful imperative
FUT	Verbal future tense / Prospective aspect (cf. English 'will' in 'I will go')
FUT.NEG	Negation of the verbal future tense (cf. English 'won't')
IMP	Imperative
INACT	Inactive
INCL	Inclusive of the addressee(s)
INTERM	Intermittent aspect
LONG.INF	Distant past inferential
MAKE1	Causative voice for intransitive verbs (cf. English 'make')
MAKE2	Causative voice for transitive verbs (cf. English 'make')
MAKE.SOC	Sociative causative voice
MED	Medial demonstrative (cf. English 'that here')
NEG	Negation (cf. English 'not')

NMLZ	General nominalizer suffix (cf. English '-ness', '-ship', and so on)
NMLZ.ABS.P	Abstract nominalizer prefix
NMLZ.ABS.S	Abstract nominalizer suffix
NMLZ.AG	Agentive nominalizer (cf. English '-er' as in 'do-er' or '-or' in 'advis-or')
NMLZ.LOC	Locative nominalizer
NMLZ.PASS	Passive nominalizer
NMLZ.QUAL	Abstract nominalizer for qualities
NMLZ.REL	Relational nominalizer
NPOSSM	Non-possessed form of relational roots
NPROX.PL	General non-proximal plural demonstrative (cf. English 'those')
OPT	Optative mood (cf. English 'may it …!' or 'let it …!')
PAST	Past tense (cf. English '-ed' in 'walk-ed')
PEOPLE	Antipassive voice (referring to an implicit human patient)
PL	Plural (cf. English '-s' in 'cat-s')
PLEAD	Pleading imperative
POSSM	Possessed form of relational roots (for non-third-person pronominal possessor)
POSSM3	Possessed form of relational roots (for third-person pronominal possessor)
POST	Post-stative aspect / Nominal past tense
PRIV	Privative (cf. English '-less' in 'hair-less')
PROG	Progressive (or continuous) aspect (cf. English '-ing' in 'walk-ing')
PROX	Proximal demonstrative (cf. English 'this right here')
RECENT.INF	Recent inferential
RECP	Reciprocal (cf. English 'each other' or 'one another')
REMOVE	Resultative denominal verbalizer (meaning 'remove')
REQ	Requestative suffix
SG	Singular
SUBJ	Subject
SUP	Superlative (cf. English '-est' in 'high-est')
TH	Ordinal number marker (cf. English '-th' in 'four-th')

THING	Antipassive voice (referring to an implicit non-human patient)
UNCERTAIN	Uncertainty marker
URG	Urging imperative
VERD	Veridical emphatic

1
Introduction

1.1 Overview of the language

Modern Paraguayan Guarani (henceforth *Guarani*; ISO 639-3 code 'gug', **endonym** *avañe'ẽ* 'language of men', from *ava* 'man, person; Guarani person', *ñe'ẽ* 'language') is a member of the Tupi-Guarani family belonging to a posited Tupian stock comprising between 60 and 70 different languages. Tupian languages are found in the Americas from approximately 4° latitude in the North to 30° latitude in the South. The closest families to Tupi-Guarani are Aweti and Satere-Mawe, with other families in this stock being Arikemic, Monde, Mundurukuic, Purubora-Ramarama, Tuparic and Yuruna. Brazil has the largest concentration of Tupian languages, but they are also found in Argentina, Bolivia, French Guiana, Paraguay and Peru. The Tupi-Guarani family itself is the largest in the Tupian stock. It includes around 40–50 languages, present in all these countries. With its approximately 6 million speakers (extrapolating figures from the 2012 Paraguayan census, the 2014 Permanent Survey of Homes and the estimated number of Paraguayan expatriates), Guarani is the Tupi-Guarani language with the most speakers. It is, in fact, among the top three Amerindian languages by number of speakers, and the only one that is spoken by a large majority that is not exclusively indigenous (see **1.3**).

Despite extensive migration and the resulting geographical spread, the Tupi-Guarani family is morphologically and typologically remarkably consistent. The name of the family is derived from the denominations of the two language groups most prominent in the period of Portuguese and Spanish colonization of the area: the Tupinambá, who lived along the coast in the present-day Brazilian states of São Paulo, Rio de Janeiro and Espírito Santo, whose extinct language is known as Tupinambá, Old Tupi, Brasilica language or Brasiliano, and who had contact mainly with Portuguese colonists; and the Guarani, who lived south of present-day

São Paulo, whose language is referred to as Old Guarani, and who had contact mainly with Spanish colonists.

Guarani presents several traits characteristic of this family:

- At the level of the sound system (**phonology**):
  - an opposition between **oral vowels** (that is, produced without nasalization, not allowing air to pass through the nose) and **nasal vowels** (that is, produced allowing the passage of air through the nose)
  - the presence of **nasal harmony** (the fact that sounds that are close to one another tend to all be oral or all be nasal)
  - **fixed stress** at the word level (most often at the end of a word).
- At the level of word formation (**morphology**):
  - most meanings are built into a word as parts of it, as affixes or other particles (**agglutinative** morphology)
  - remnants of an extensive **polysynthetic** behaviour; that is, the fact that most words are composed of many parts, each with its own meaning to contribute to the whole. This is often noticeable in the fact that what would otherwise be a whole sentence in English is a single word in polysynthetic languages
  - two first-person plural pronouns, one that includes the addressees and one that excludes them (**clusivity**)
  - specific prefixes that simultaneously represent a first-person agent acting on a second-person patient (**portmanteau person prefixes**)
  - two kinds of intransitive verb whose subjects look different, a phenomenon called **split intransitivity** (also called **active/stative split**)
  - a class of words that take different prefixes when they are in the same phrase with other words (**relational prefixes**)
  - three ways to indicate events where a participant makes another participant do something (three different **morphological causatives**)
  - instead of prepositions that come before a noun phrase, an extensive system of **postpositions** that come at the end of a noun phrase to indicate its relation to a predicate
  - verbs and other predicates are negated by a **circumfix**, that is, a negation that has two parts: a prefix that comes before the verb and a suffix that comes after
  - finally, nouns take suffixes that indicate past or future, among other interpretations (**nominal temporal-aspectual inflection**).

Guarani has, however, lost other Tupi-Guarani traits:

- Words used to require a specific suffix to function as nouns (a **nominal case marking suffix**).
- When an adverb or a temporal phrase would begin a sentence, verbs used to take a different form, but not anymore.
- Generally, Guarani has innovated a push towards a more fixed word order for the main sentence constituents (Subject-Verb-Object/Complement, or **SVO**) and less reliance on polysynthesis, but more on constructions using clearly separate words (**analytic constructions**).

The latter two traits have clearly been lost due to contact with Spanish, which has also lent Guarani several grammatical morphemes (see **1.6**). The lexicon has also been influenced by Spanish, even in the most Guarani-oriented registers, as attested by the numerous integrated loans (see **1.6**). However, these lexical borrowings stop well short of supplanting most of the lexical items of the language (**relexification**, common in creole languages, and actually very common in Correntinean Guarani, spoken in Corrientes, Argentina). In fact, most of the basic lexicon is still of Tupi-Guarani extraction.

1.2 Brief history since the European colonization of the region

The history of Guarani is a history of resilience. After centuries of colonization and linguistic pressure from Spanish, Guarani has become the only indigenous language in the Americas that has been adopted as a native language by a mostly non-indigenous population. Figure 1.1 shows the approximative original homeland of putative Proto-Tupian speakers (their **urheimat**), which is assumed to have been in the Madeira River basin between the Guaporé and Aripuanã rivers in today's Brazilian state of Rondônia. The Guaporé river marks part of the border between Bolivia and Brazil. In Bolivia it is known as the Iténez River. The Aripuanã River meets the larger Madeira at Novo Aripuanã, about 150 miles south of Manaus in the Brazilian state of Amazonas. This hypothesized urheimat is based on the fact that half of the languages in the Tupian stock are located there. Extensive migrations, depicted in Figure 1.2, enabled the Tupi-Guarani languages to cover a much larger area in South America.

Figure 1.1 Putative Proto-Tupian homeland (Tupian Urheimat)
Source: Author (created using Scribble Maps (scribblemaps.com), based on Google Maps data).

Because of its relevance in explaining Guaraní's survival and flourishing under extreme colonizing pressures, Paraguay's linguistic history is reviewed in almost every publication on Guaraní. (A helpful summary can be found in Gómez Rendón 2017; see Suggested resources.) Asunción was founded on the eastern banks of the Paraguay River in 1537 and remained the only Spanish outpost in eastern South America for decades. Extremely isolated geographically, the Paraguayan territory has been marked by a predominantly mestizo population since the late sixteenth century. Due to a negligible influx of Spaniards after foundation, there were no European elites and mestizos quickly became part of the ruling classes. The relatively few Spanish males married Guarani women whose children spoke Guarani. Crucially, and contrary to other colonized

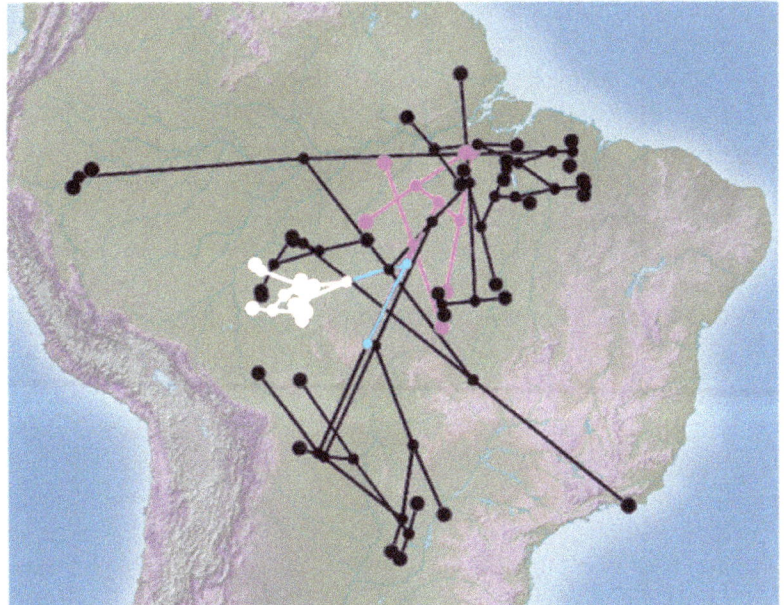

Figure 1.2 Reconstructed migrations yielding the current Tupi-Guarani spread
Note: The smaller central white area is the Tupi early migration; the magenta area to its north-east, the second expansion; the larger number of black lines correspond to Tupi-Guarani later migratory waves; finally, the two small cyan lines represent a later Tupi-Guarani return to their homeland.
Source: Original figure from Walker *et al.* (2012), recoloured for colour-blind accessibility.

territories in the Americas, these creole elites were Guarani-Spanish bilinguals, providing the indigenous language with a strong foothold in Paraguayan society. The general assumption is that Guarani survived in the non-indigenous population because Spain did not put in place a full administrative apparatus with its concomitant larger presence of Spanish speakers. The survival of Guarani was also fostered by the Jesuits (present in the area in the period 1609–1768), who evangelized in Guarani, and wrote its first textbooks, dictionaries and grammars – for example, the works of Jesuits Joseph de Anchieta (1595), Alonso de Aragona (1625/1629), Antonio Ruiz de Montoya (1639/1640) and Paulo Restivo (1729). This opinion, however, has been questioned by some scholars who claim that it is more likely that the Guarani from the Jesuit missions

INTRODUCTION 5

never joined the nascent urban society but rather returned to live in jungle areas, and that as a consequence, their Guarani (now lost) would have had little influence on the survival of modern Guarani.

Later, the identification of Guarani as the defining Paraguayan language (as opposed to Spanish) was cemented by its use as a nationalistic rallying cry during the formation of the modern Paraguayan state (1811–1842), and in the wars Paraguay fought against its non-Guarani speaking neighbours: the catastrophic Triple Alliance War (1865–1870), when Paraguay came under attack from Argentina, Brazil and Uruguay, and the Chaco War (1932–1935) against Bolivia. Hence, by the mid-twentieth century, the majority of the Paraguayan population, crucially often including the dominant elites, was either bilingual in Guarani and Spanish or still monolingual in Guarani. In recognition of this long-standing attachment of Paraguayans to the original indigenous language, Guarani was first declared a national language in the 1967 Paraguayan constitution. In 1992, the new constitution further declared it an official language (Article 140), and mandated access to education in Guarani for Guarani-dominant children (Article 77). These almost five centuries of intense coexistence have changed the linguistic landscapes of both Guarani and Spanish in Paraguay, to yield the current language contact situation that I will summarize in **1.6**.

1.3 Sociolinguistic information

Paraguay's *Dirección General de Estadística, Encuestas y Censos* (DGEEC, Paraguay's census and national statistics body)[3] estimates Paraguay's total population as of 2018 at 7,052,983 (the most recent figures available at the time of writing). Considering that the 2012 census found that 46.3 per cent of homes used both Guarani and Spanish, and 34 per cent only Guarani, we can extrapolate to assume Guarani is spoken to some degree by around 80 per cent of the population; that is, between 5.5 and 6 million Paraguayans. Functionally monolingual or quasi-monolingual Guarani speakers may even form the majority of the population in rural areas. In urban areas there is a greater concentration of bilingual and Spanish monolingual speakers, although Guarani is spoken there by many Paraguayans, with varying degrees of fluency. To these figures one should add the between half a million to a million Paraguayan expatriates in Argentina, and thus arrive at a figure of 6 to 7 million speakers

---

[3] See http://www.dgeec.gov.py/.

of this particular variety. This probably makes Guarani the most widely spoken indigenous language in the Americas. Remember that here *Guarani* refers exclusively to Paraguayan Guarani. Quechua and Mayan are languages that are usually considered to have more than 6 or 7 million speakers, but that number is arrived at by collapsing many dialects that are actually not mutually intelligible. Whatever the actual numbers, one should rejoice in the fact that these three languages have such a vibrant presence in a modern world that has been rather hostile to them.

In its 1967 constitution Paraguay declared Guarani a national language, with Spanish remaining the official language of administration and schooling. This situation changed with the 1992 constitution when Guarani was finally recognized as an official language alongside Spanish. However, and in spite of the oft-repeated classification of Paraguay as bilingual, Paraguay is a multilingual country, with many Amerindian and non-Amerindian language families represented in its territory. Yet only Guarani and Spanish are official, and hence schooling is guaranteed only in those two languages.

Importantly, Guarani is the only indigenous official language of MERCOSUR, an economic and political agreement among Argentina, Bolivia (in the process of admission as of December 2019), Brazil, Paraguay, Uruguay and Venezuela (suspended as of December 2019). (A closely related variety, Correntinean Guarani, is co-official with Spanish in the province of Corrientes, Argentina.) Guarani is, therefore, not an endangered language, but shows rather exceptional vibrancy and viability. It is the only indigenous language of the Americas that has been widely adopted by speakers that are not of exclusive indigenous ancestry, namely, speakers of European or mixed Amerindian-European ancestry. Many of these speakers of mixed descent would consider themselves indigenous, since they are the descendants of the indigenous population and are in every other sense "locals". That is why I have refrained from saying that Guarani is mostly spoken by non-indigenous people. This can only be true if we considered indigenous solely the inhabitants belonging to ethnic Guarani tribes in Paraguay, although I do feel compelled to note that there are both linguistic and great socio-economic and cultural differences between these two types of indigenous Paraguayan populations.

Furthermore, the intergenerational transmission of Guarani is not threatened, since it is learned as a first language by many Paraguayan children and enjoys some measure of support from the Paraguayan state. It must be noted that although Guarani is in a disadvantageous position relative to the more overtly prestigious Spanish, it still enjoys considerable **covert prestige** (that is, speakers' positive evaluation of and orientation towards the language), with Paraguayans maintaining it as a means of constructing and supporting their national identity.

1.4 Basic pronunciation summary

At this point, it is useful to give a basic pronunciation summary to read the examples in the sections that follow (see **2** for more details):

- Words should be stressed on the vowel that carries an acute stress mark (´) or a nasal tilde (˜). If the word is not marked, pronounce it with stress on the last syllable.
- Vowels and consonants are reasonably similar to those you may know from Spanish. Single vowels never have off-glides as they do in English (cf. Spanish 'no' versus English 'no'). The only difference is that Guarani has nasal vowels, like Portuguese, French or Polish, for example.[4]
- Articulation of consonants and vowels is much more relaxed than it is in English. Languages like English or French generally produce their sounds with more tension in the articulators in the mouth (tongue, lips), whereas languages like Spanish and Guarani generally have less tense vowels and consonants.
- Unlike English, vowels in unstressed syllables do not get reduced to **schwas** (the mid-central vowel [ə], like the first vowel in English 'ago'). Pronounce each vowel with the same quality as you would in a stressed syllable.
- Pay attention to nasal sounds: not only do they differentiate words, but nasality also tends to spread within a word. If you listen closely to Guarani speakers, you can hear long spans of nasal sounds alternating with long spans of oral sounds.

---

[4] I understand that using Spanish (the colonizing language) to reference properties of Guarani (the autochthonous language) is problematic for a variety of reasons. However, this is dictated purely by practical considerations: Spanish is the second most widely spoken language in the world in terms of native speakers and is rather well known in English-speaking countries. Of course, the grammar of Guarani is independent of Spanish and should not be described by reference to it. The same goes for references to Portuguese (the other major European colonizing language in the Guarani-speaking region), and to other languages. They are provided here only to aid readers in grasping aspects of the pronunciation and grammar of Guarani.

1.5 Typological information

This section is mostly of use to researchers in linguistics. Other readers may skip directly to **1.6** and return to this section later, after having read a less succinct version of the phenomena mentioned here.

From the viewpoint of the system of sounds, Guarani is a language with a cross-linguistically moderately small inventory of 15 consonants, and a cross-linguistically large inventory of 12 vowels (for a very low resulting consonant/vowel ratio of 1.25). These should be understood as 15 consonant **phonemes** and 12 vowel **phonemes**; that is, sounds that, when exchanged, generate different words, and are not simply pronunciation variants (**allophones**). Phonemes are generally thought of as abstract mental categories, and are always represented between forward slashes, as in /a/, whereas the pronunciations associated with them or **phones** are represented between square brackets, as in [a]. See **2.1** for more explanation of the sounds and their **IPA** symbols (International Phonetic Alphabet).

Changing an oral vowel for a nasal vowel generates a different word (oral and nasal vowels are different phonemes; see **2.1.1**), so one needs to exercise care in pronouncing both sets of vowels correctly and distinctly. Voiced stops such as /b/, /d/, /g/ are absent from the language, as is common in the Tupi-Guarani family; Guarani has instead the series of consonants /ᵐb/, /ⁿd/, /ᵑg/, which begin with a brief nasal phase and end in an oral phase. I call these **nasal-oral stops**, but they are most commonly called **prenasalized**, or sometimes **postoralized**, in linguistics papers and grammars. If C represents any consonant and V any vowel, the permissible syllable structure is (C)(V)V(V), where the parentheses indicate optional sounds. (But see **2.2.1** for changes to this underlying structure in the pronunciation.) For single lexical words (that is, noun, verb, adjective or adverb **roots** with no added affixes), stress is nearly fixed, falling almost always on the last syllable (but see **2.2.2**). The language does not use tone to differentiate words. Lastly, like most other Tupi-Guarani languages, Guarani presents **nasal harmony**; that is, the tendency for sounds in a word to have the same nasal/non-nasal value as their neighbours (see **2.2.3**).

From the viewpoint of classical **morphological typology** (that is, the classification of languages in terms of how they form words and sentences), Guarani is a **concatenative** language; that is, it forms words by taking one (or occasionally two) roots and adding "parts" with additional meanings to it (these parts are called **morphemes**, although the roots are morphemes too), to form a linear chain. Think about how English, although mostly concatenative, occasionally has non-concatenative morphology. For example, the verb 'sing' forms its past tense, not by concatenating morphemes, but by changing the root's shape: 'sang'. This option does not exist in Guarani, which is fully concatenative.

We classify Guarani also as **agglutinative**, which means that the morphemes that make up a complex word can usually be neatly separated from one another and do not change shape unpredictably with different bases (a **base** is simply whatever you add a morpheme to: it can be a single root or a root plus other morphemes; for example, in the English sequence of derivations where the root 'act' can go to 'act-ion' and this in turn to 'act-ion-able', 'act' is the base of '-ion', and 'action' is the base of '-able'). The morphemes that are always added to some base because they cannot appear by themselves are **affixes** (when they attach to words, like English plural '-s' in 'cat-s' or English third-person singular '-s' in 'sing-s') or **clitics** (when they attach to whole phrases, like English genitive '='s' in 'my old friend's car'). Clitics do have some properties of independent words, but they are always pronounced attached to a host. For example, the English article 'the' is thought of as a word, but it can be considered a (pro)clitic, since it always needs a host to the right. English genitive '='s' is an enclitic, since it needs a host to its left. In the glosses, a dash (-) indicates the addition of an affix to a base, whereas an equals sign (=) indicates the addition of a clitic to a host. (This difference is only relevant to the more linguistically inclined readers and, in the examples, can generally be safely ignored by non-linguists.)

Even though Guarani is still considered by some authors a **polysynthetic** language, this is hard to justify. Indeed, what characterizes polysynthetic languages is the frequent occurrence of single words that include multiple roots and are equivalent to whole sentences in other languages, but polysynthesis has been much reduced since Old Guarani.

The following examples are given to clarify these concepts. Full analysis in constituent morphemes and glosses appears in smaller font on lines 2 and 3, to exemplify more clearly how the meanings of the different parts of the words/sentences make up the meaning of the whole.

Concatenation/agglutination

Reporomoñombo'e.
re-poro-mo-ño-mbo'e
2SG.ACT-PEOPLE-MAKE1-RECP-teach
'You (sg.) make people teach one another.'

ikakuaa'iruguekuérape
i-kakuaa+'irũ-ngue=kuéra=pe
3.INACT-grow.up+friend-POST=PL=in
'to his/her/their childhood friends'[5]

ojehepyme'ẽkuaágui
o-je-h-epy+me'ẽ+kuaa=gui
3.ACT-AGD-POSSM3-price+give+know=from
'because of knowing how to get paid (for it)'

Note how in all three examples one or two roots are "augmented" with morphemes to their left and right, as is typical of concatenation. Moreover, as is typical of agglutination, these morphemes have single identifiable meanings (unlike, for example, English '-s' in 'runs', which means third-person, singular and present at the same time).

Polysynthetic construction (noun/object incorporation)

Ajepohéita.
a-je-po+(jo)héi-ta
1SG.ACT-AGD-hand+wash-FUT
'I will wash my hands.'

Note that in this example, the roots *po* 'hand' and *(jo)héi* 'wash' are joined and together with the remaining morphemes form a single word that is equivalent to a complete English sentence. We call it **noun incorporation** or **object incorporation** because the noun *po* forms a unit with the verb *johéi* to designate a single event (similar to 'hand-washing' in English). Polysynthetic Guarani constructions often have analytic paraphrases in the modern language that keep the words separate and are more frequently used by speakers.[6]

---

[5] Often a word or morpheme in Guarani does not make as many distinctions as the corresponding items in English. For example, here *i-* is third-person, but does not mark gender or number. In that case, the English translation will indicate all possible options separated by forward slashes. For naturalistic examples (that is, real examples found "in the wild"), the option that was intended in the context is usually kept in the translation.

[6] The following examples are from de Canese and Acosta Alcaraz (2007, 170).

Polysynthetic construction (noun/object incorporation)

Ojurumboty.
o-juru+mboty
3.ACT-mouth+close
'S/he closes/closed his/her mouth.'

Analytic construction

Omboty ijuru.
o-mboty   i-juru
3.ACT-close 3.INACT-mouth
'S/he closes/closed his/her mouth.'

Guarani does not have cases that identify the function of nouns as subject, object and so on. Instead, the function and interpretation of noun phrases is carried out by **postpositions** that are placed at the end of the noun, pronoun or noun phrase.

*Aha Luque**gui** Paraguay**pe***
a-ha   Luque=gui   Paraguay=pe
1SG.ACT-go Luque=from   Asunción=in
'I go/went from Luque to Asunción' (=*gui* identifies a noun phrase as designating a location from where movement starts; =*pe* identifies a noun phrase as designating a location to where movement proceeds)

*Che aikuaa amo kuñá**me***
che ai-kuaa   amo   kuña=me
I   1SG.ACT-know DIST.SG woman=in
'I know that woman' (=*pe* marks a human participant as direct object)

*Chemandu'áta nde**rehe***
che-mandu'a-ta   nde=rehe
1SG.INACT-remember-FUT   2SG.INACT=at
'I will remember you' (=*rehe* marks the object of the predicate *mandu'a*)

Postpositions appear with the noun phrases that depend on a predicate. This is called **dependent-marking**. Guarani also displays two other kinds of marking: **head-marking**, that is, grammatical marking directly on predicates, and **no marking**, that is, the absence of any affixes, clitics, particles or words to clarify the relationship between two words or phrases.

Head-marking

The examples below show how the main participant in an event is referenced directly on a predicate. This is a case of head-marking because the verb is the **head** (or **nucleus**) of the predicate phrase, and it receives a prefix to mark its main participant.

*re*ho
re-ho
2SG.ACT-go
'you (sg.) go/went'

*nde*katupyry
nde-katupyry
2SG.INACT-efficient
'you (sg.) are efficient'

No marking

The example below, showing a possessive phrase with a noun (*María*) as possessor, is a case of no marking because the relationship between the nouns is not marked explicitly on either of them. Note that there is no morpheme in the gloss that indicates the possessive relationship.

María ajaka
María   ajaka
María   basket
'María's basket'

A verb is **intransitive** if it only takes one participant or **argument**: its subject (often referred to as the **S argument**). The two head-marking examples given above (repeated here for convenience) show two different intransitive verbs. Note that in each example the second-person singular subject is referenced with a different prefix: *re-* in the first example (from a series of **active** prefixes; see **4.1.1**), *nde-* in the second (from a series of **inactive** prefixes; see **4.1.2**). (To get an idea of how this works, imagine English used 'I go' but *'me live', with the subjects of 'go' and 'live' taking different pronouns.)

*re*ho
re-ho
2SG.ACT-go
'you (sg.) go/went'

*nde*katupyry
nde-katupyry
2SG.INACT-efficient
'you (sg.) are efficient'

The examination of these patterns of subject (and object) marking is called **morphosyntactic alignment**. We say that Guarani is a **split intransitive** language, because intransitive predicates are "split" into two different classes, one that takes active prefixes for subjects, and the other that takes inactive prefixes for subjects (for this reason, such languages are sometimes called **active-stative** languages). Note again that no such thing occurs in English, as shown by the fact that both translations use the same second-person pronoun 'you'.

Furthermore, looking at transitive verbs this time, Guarani has properties of languages with **direct-inverse systems** (see 6). The person prefixes *a-* and *che-* are both first-person, that is, they both refer to the speaker, meaning 'I'. The examples below illustrate that the prefix used on the predicate is active (*a-*) when the first-person agent acts on a third person (**direct** scenario), but that the prefix used is inactive (*che-*) when the first person is acted upon by a second- or third-person agent (**inverse** scenario). This would be the case if English speakers said 'I hit him' but *'Me hit he', instead of 'He hit me'. Of course, this difference in pronoun use does not happen in English, but it is obligatory in Guarani, so the learner must be careful to pay attention to it.

Direct configuration: first-person agent acts
on third-person patient

ajuka **ichupe**
a-juka   ichupe
1SG.ACT-kill to.him/her
'I kill(ed) him/her'

Inverse configuration: first-person patient is acted upon by
second- or third-person agent

chejuka (nde)
che-juka   (nde)
1SG.INACT-kill (you.SG)
'you kill(ed) me'

*che**juka (ha'e)***
che-juka	(ha'e)
1SG.INACT-kill	((s)he)

'<u>s/he</u> killed/kills <u>me</u>'

In Guarani neither subjects nor objects are obligatory in a sentence. They can be left out if they can be understood from the context (this is generally impossible in English). Sentences without a subject noun phrase or pronoun (**subject drop**) are extremely common in connected discourse. Sentences without an object noun phrase or object pronoun (**object drop**) also occur, albeit a little less frequently. Hence, the most frequent word order for sentences in Guarani is simply V (verb) or VO (verb-object). If a noun phrase or pronoun subject is used, it can come before or after the verb, since the order of phrases in a sentence is rather flexible (see **8**).

Finally, a note on **word classes** (also called **parts of speech**) is in order. We know lexical word classes such as nouns, verbs, adjectives and adverbs from English. In Guarani the main division is simply between **nouns** and **verbs** (although even this difference is not accepted by some scholars). Little evidence exists for recognizing a lexical category of **adjectives** different from nouns or verbs (see **3.3**), and even less for an **adverb** category (see **4.12**). In fact, it is very common for a root to function as a member of different word classes depending on the sentence context:

Root

tuicha
(adjective) 'big, tall'; (adverb) 'much'

Adjectival use

*ko yvyra **tuicha***
ko	yvyra	tuicha
this	tree	big

'this <u>tall</u> tree'

Adverbial use

*Upéva **tuicha** orepytyvõ.*
upe-va   tuicha   ore-pytyvõ
MED.SG-ADJZ big   1PL.INACT.EXCL-help
'That helped us a lot.'

Verbal/Predicative use

*Che **tuicha**.*
che   tuicha
I   big
'I am big.'

Cases like these where a root can switch word classes without changes in form are called **conversion** or **zero derivation**. It is possible, in fact, to claim that Guarani only has roots that do not belong inherently to any part of speech, but can function as nouns, verbs, adjectives or adverbs depending on the sentence context. However, for the sake of clarity in exposition, in this work I will present two main lexical classes: nouns (including adjectives as their modifiers) and verbs (including adverbs as their modifiers).

1.6 Contact with Spanish and other languages

Guarani (as I mentioned in **1.3**) is spoken by between 5.5 and 6 million Paraguayans. Of particular importance for the learner or researcher is the fact that, due to a long history of language contact, today's Guarani can show varied degrees of mixing with Spanish. This depends both on the relative competence of the speaker in each language (that is, whether they are dominant in Guarani or in Spanish), as well as on which language is required by the specific communicative situation (Guarani historically has tended to be used in the private, intimate sphere, and Spanish in the public sphere).

Paraguayans have a name for this mixing: *Jopara* (meaning 'mixed'). They use this term to refer to any sentences that mix Guarani and Spanish, independently of whether they are mostly Guarani with Spanish elements or mostly Spanish mixed with Guarani elements. By way of an example, all four of the sentences below can be used in Paraguay today to convey the meaning 'help me please', going from Guaraniete (literally, 'true Guarani'; that is, as free of Spanish influence as possible) to Paraguayan

Spanish. "Guarañol" usually refers to a Jopara mixture mostly based on Guarani, whereas "Castení" is an academic neologism that can be used to refer to a mostly Spanish-based Jopara. In the examples, Guarani is in regular font, and Spanish in boldface.

Guaraniete

Chepytyvõmína.
che-pytyvõ-mi-na
1SG.INACT-help-PLEAD-REQ
'Help me, please.'

Guarañol

*Che**ayuda**mína.*
che-ayuda-mi-na
1SG.INACT-help-PLEAD-REQ
'Help me, please.'

Castení

Ayudámena.
ayuda=me-na
help=me-REQ
'Help me, please.'

Paraguayan Spanish

Ayudame, por favor.
ayuda=me   por favor
help=me   by favor
'Help me, please.'

In the course of the almost five centuries of contact between the languages, Guarani has adopted many Spanish words. A small sample (not exhaustive!) of Spanish loanwords in common use in Guarani is given in the table below. Some of these we call **integrated loanwords** because they function like native Guarani terms phonologically and in the lexicon and are often not recognized by speakers as foreign words. Other loans have a lesser degree of integration and/or are more easily recognized by speakers as being of Spanish origin (usually because they are more recent loans). In the examples in this book, loanwords will not be distinguished in any way from Guarani **patrimonial** words (except in **16**), because they occur naturally in Guarani discourse.

Word	Meaning	Original Spanish word
agarra	'to grab'	agarrar
ajuda	'to help'	ayudar
algúno	'some'	alguno
aramboha	'pillow'	almohada
aramirõ	'starch'	almidón
arriéro	'peasant; man'	arriero
entéro	'all'	entero
gusta	'please'	gustar
havõ	'soap'	jabón
kamiõ	'truck'	camión
kamisa	'shirt'	camisa
kavaju	'horse'	caballo
kavara	'goat'	cabra
kesu	'cheese'	queso
Kirito	'Christ'	Cristo
kora	'pen (enclosure for animals)'	corral
korasõ	'heart'	corazón
kosina	'kitchen'	cocina
krivi, ehkrivi	'to write'	escribir
kurusu	'cross'	cruz
lee	'to read'	leer
limõ	'lemon'	limón
malisia	'to suspect'	maliciar
merõ	'melon'	melón
mesa	'table'	mesa
ntende	'to understand'	entender
ovecha	'sheep'	oveja
ovetã	'window'	ventana
péro	'but'	pero
pórke	'because'	porque
sapatu	'shoe'	zapato
topa	'to meet'	topar(se)
vaka	'cow'	vaca
vale	'to be worth'	valer
vende	'to sell'	vender
vosa	'bag'	bolsa
votõ	'button'	botón

Conversely, Spanish has also been influenced by Guarani. Some of the Guarani grammatical morphemes in common use in today's Paraguayan Spanish are listed in the table below (again, not an exhaustive list!).

Guarani morpheme	Meaning
=pa	interrogative enclitic
=pi(k)o	interrogative enclitic
=(ni)ko, =(ni)ngo	veridical emphatic enclitic
-na	requestative imperative suffix
-ke	forceful imperative suffix
-py	urging imperative suffix
-(e)te, -(i)te	intensifier suffix
-mi, -'i	diminutive suffix
=kuéra	plural enclitic
-kue	post-stative suffix
che-	first-person singular (inactive) prefix

Points to note:
- Most numbers are also loans, since Spanish numbers are commonly used beyond 3 or 4. This applies to days of the week and names of the months as well (see **15.7**).

Although Paraguay is most often called a bilingual country, it is actually multilingual.[7] Guarani is also in contact with languages other than Spanish, but current knowledge of the structural and sociolinguistic characteristics of these multilingual communities is cursory. Of the other languages spoken in Paraguay, Portuguese is the most widely used. Portuguese contact with local Tupi-Guarani languages was immediate upon the arrival of the Europeans to the coasts of modern-day Brazil. Both Spanish and Portuguese missionaries and government officials used Tupinambá as a sort of lingua franca (in Portuguese, *Lingua Geral*, 'general language') in the region. These contacts are reflected in the abundance of Old Tupi borrowings in Portuguese, Spanish and even English (for example, 'cougar', 'jaguar', 'manioc', 'maracas', 'tapioca'). According to the last Paraguayan national census (2012), almost 7 per cent of the population is Portuguese-speaking (mostly in the departments of Canindeyú and

---

[7] See statements to that effect on the website of the Foundation Yvy Marãe'ỹ at http://www.yvymaraey.org.

Alto Paraná, but also in Amambay, Caaguazú, Caazapá and Itapúa); 70 per cent of Portuguese speakers in Paraguay are trilingual Guarani-Portuguese-Spanish. German is another important language (especially in rural areas in the Chaco region, due to historical Mennonite settlements), with 0.7 per cent of households speaking it. Finally, 1.2 per cent of households speak other indigenous languages, mostly in rural areas. These indigenous languages are:

- Tupi-Guarani family: Kaiwá, Ache, Pã'i tavyterã, Mbyá, Ava chiripa, Guarayo/Chiriguano/Guaraní Occidental and Tapiete/Ñandéva
- Mataco Mataguayo family: Maká, Manjui and Nivaclé/Chulupí
- Zamuco family: Chamacoco Ybytoso, Chamacoco Tomarãho and Ayoreo
- Guaicurú family: Toba Qom
- Enlhet/Maskoy family: Enlhet, Enxet, Toba Maskoy, Angaité, Sanapaná, Toba and Guaná.

As previously mentioned, better data on the extent and types of multilingualism for these communities are unfortunately not available.

1.7 Guarani as a second or foreign language

Guarani is learned in Paraguay as a foreign language by many visitors or immigrants to the country (the US Missionaries and Peace Corps Volunteers, for example), and as a second language by Paraguayans who are Spanish-dominant or Spanish-monolingual. There is important research on language attitudes and language planning in Paraguay, including teacher education, but there are no quantitative data on the populations of foreign- and second-language learners. Here, I will limit myself then to mentioning some places that offer courses on Guarani as a second or foreign language in Paraguay and in Argentina (there are also university courses in Brazil and Bolivia, but they teach varieties of Guarani that are different from Paraguayan):

Paraguay:

- Ateneo de Lengua y Cultura Guarani
- El Granel
- IDIPAR (Idiomas en Paraguay)
- CELPE (Centro de enseñanza de lenguas para extranjeros)
- private tutoring

Argentina:

- Laboratorio de idiomas, Facultad de Filosofía y Letras, Universidad de Buenos Aires
- Centro Universitario de Idiomas, Buenos Aires
- Universidad Nacional del Nordeste, Corrientes
- Universidad Nacional Arturo Jauretche, Buenos Aires
- Facultad de Humanidades y Ciencias de la Educación de la Universidad Nacional de La Plata
- Cátedra de Pueblos Originarios y la Secretaría de Extensión, Universidad Nacional de la Patagonia San Juan Bosco, Comodoro Rivadavia
- Municipalidad de Posadas, Misiones
- Municipio de Ituzaingó, Corrientes
- Secretaría de Turismo y Cultura, Gobierno de Entre Ríos, Museo Antonio Serrano, Paraná
- Universidad Autónoma de Entre Ríos, Concepción del Uruguay
- Asociación Civil Casa Paraguaya CABA, Buenos Aires
- Centro Social y Cultural Paraguayo Silvio Morínigo, San Justo

There are also some courses available online, but their quality varies greatly.

1.8 Pointers for students

Speaking a language involves four basic skills that, although interrelated, are somewhat independent of one another and therefore must each be practised using different techniques: spoken production, oral comprehension, written production and written comprehension. The table below shows which language-related activity mainly exercises each basic skill.

	Production (expressive language)	Comprehension (receptive language)
Speech	Talking practice	Listening practice
Literacy	Writing practice	Reading practice

In what follows, I will try to give some general pointers for anybody trying to learn Guarani as a foreign language. First of all, one of the most important activities you can dedicate your time to when studying is listening to as much Guarani as you can. This exercises oral comprehension. Many of us foreign-language learners have had the experience of trying to strike up a conversation with a native speaker only to realize we cannot understand the answers. This is incredibly frustrating and generates avoidance on the part of the learner ('why am I going to make an effort speaking if I cannot understand what people are saying to me?'). I call this the "conversation guide effect". To avoid this, you must listen to as much naturally occurring language as you can. YouTube is a great place to start finding clips in your target language. Although there is very little (relatively speaking) in Guarani, look for content on the channels ayvuguarani, cafeterambarete, Guarani Ñe'ẽ or Paraguay TV. Pay attention to whether you are listening to native speakers or non-native speakers: YouTube contains many videos of non-Paraguayans (missionaries, researchers, and so on) speaking the language. Whereas their efforts are certainly commendable, and can help you in your learning, you should strive to hear natively spoken examples if at all possible.

To help with listening practice, a new app called ArandukApp was released in November 2018. It was created with the support of Paraguay's Secretariat of Linguistic Policy and contains short stories, myths, legends and poetry read by Guarani native speakers. I highly recommend it to begin to develop an ear for how the language sounds. When listening, do not only pay attention to the individual sounds: make an effort to recognize and remember the different intonation patterns. The pitch goes up or down in Guarani in ways that are different from both English and Spanish.

Reading is an activity that will increase your vocabulary and your ability to decode complex phrases and sentences (although not necessarily in real time, as is needed for oral comprehension in real dialogue). You can find many texts in Guarani online, for example, the newspaper *ABC* has a section called ABC Remiandu in Guarani.[8] You can compare the texts of news articles in Guarani with the text in Spanish. There are also blogs on and in Guarani: Ñane Ñe'ẽ Guarani,[9] David Galeano Olivera's blog Guarani Ñe'ẽ,[10] and even Facebook groups dedicated to the language, such as Avañe'ẽ and Avañe'ẽ porã (Group for Guarani and Tupi-Guarani Studies). You can also post questions to native speakers and researchers on those groups (although many of them read and understand Guarani and Spanish, but not English). You can practise writing on these blogs and Facebook pages too. You must beware, however: many

---

[8] See http://www.abc.com.py/especiales/remiandu/.
[9] See http://guaraniete.blogspot.com.
[10] See https://dgaleanolivera.wordpress.com.

native speakers are not formally educated in Guarani and therefore will not follow necessarily the standard orthographic conventions.

<u>Talking</u> is perhaps the hardest skill to practise. Most speakers of (Paraguayan) Guarani live in Paraguay or Argentina. It may be very hard for you to find a local conversation partner or native research consultant. On a trip to Paraguay you may also find that Paraguayans tend to speak Spanish to foreigners, not Guarani. That is why you must absolutely take advantage of any and all possibilities you have to speak, even if it is in front of a mirror at your home, reading and "acting" plays written in Guarani (there are many!), or shadowing videos or movies.

There is a Guarani/Jopara course on Duolingo, but I do not recommend it as your sole or even main go-to strategy. As of 2019 it was seemingly in a development phase and had many inconsistencies. Sure, it can be a low-key complement to your learning, but it will not magically teach you the language, and you have to take what you see there with a grain of salt (there are good reviews of Duolingo online by experienced language learners and tutors). The Guaranglish app can also be judiciously used as flashcards to support the limited goal of vocabulary learning. The more complete Peace Corps Guarani basic course is a little dated, but it is good, and it is also available online. Its main drawback is that it is in a more academic format, which requires a good amount of motivation and effort to follow. (See Suggested resources.)

Lastly, when you listen to Paraguayans speak, unless they are in an academic or formal context that requires the use of Guarani, you will most likely hear a version of *Jopara*, which is the Guarani-Spanish mixed variety in common use in Paraguay (see **1.6**). Jopara can have varying degrees of mixing with Spanish, going from mostly Guarani with some Spanish loans, to mostly Paraguayan Spanish with some Guarani words and particles mixed in. Although this reference grammar will eschew Jopara variants as much as possible, it is crucial to note that this mixed code has been part of the normal repertoire of Paraguayans probably since the sixteenth and seventeenth centuries and it is part of regular use of the language today. Therefore, many of the examples in this book that were taken from authentic sources will actually be in Jopara rather than academic Guarani (Guaraniete).

What is easier and what is more difficult for English-speaking learners of Guarani?

- Easier:
  - The order of the major constituents in a sentence tends to be (Subject)-Verb-Object(s), or (S)VO, similar to English, but it is also relatively free, similar to Spanish.

- There is no gender agreement, and there is very little number agreement (usually optional) in nouns.
- No cases are used to mark the function of noun phrases (contrary to languages with cases like Latin, German, Finnish, and so on).
- It has relatively simple morphology, without long paradigms of verbal inflections, contrary to the morphology of Romance languages like Spanish, French or Italian, for example.
- There is no familiar/formal distinction (like 'tú-vos/usted' in Spanish, or 'tu/vous' in French), or honorific systems as in Japanese or Korean.
- There are no obligatory copular verbs (like English 'to be', or Spanish 'ser/estar').
- It has a simple system to mark possession in possessive noun phrases by juxtaposition.
• More difficult:
  - In comprehension, the real-time parsing of words with many parts/morphemes is a challenge at the beginning. However, the inherent regularity of agglutinative languages helps, the more practice the learner has with listening.
  - A good strategy for understanding agglutinating forms quickly is to try to learn the meaning of complex forms as a whole, without trying to analyse their parts. For example, learning that *oñembohasa* means 'it is/was translated' without trying each time to analyse it in real time into its constituent parts *o-ñe-mbo-h-asa* (3.ACT-AGD-MAKE1-POSSM3-pass; literally, 'it was made to pass/cross'). Too much early reliance on analysing forms fully reduces fluency and speed in understanding spoken language on the fly. It may also increase frustration in trying to use the language in conversational contexts.
  - Becoming fluent with a system of postpositions (found at the end of a noun phrase) instead of prepositions (found at the beginning of a noun phrase). See **4.4** and **5**.
  - Accurate pronunciation can be hard for an English speaker (although it is a bit easier for Spanish speakers). See especially **2.1** for the pronunciation of vowels and consonants.
  - In speech, attention must be paid to the two first-person plural pronouns and person prefixes, one that includes the addressees (**inclusive**), another that excludes them (**exclusive**). Languages that make this distinction are said to have the linguistic property of **clusivity** in the pronominal system. See **3.5.1** and **4.1**.

- Depending on the verb, on its subject and on its object, different verb prefixes have to be used. See **4.1** and **4.2**.
- Some roots change their initial consonant in different sentence contexts (**relational roots**). See **3.1.3** and **4.6**.
- There are several different types of negation for whole sentences.
- There is an extensive system of verb suffixes, enclitics and particles that indicate from what source a speaker knows the content he or she is communicating, and also their degree of certainty about this content (**evidentials**). See **7**.
- There are different affixes to express the general notion of 'making someone do something' for intransitive and transitive verbs, as well as for different configurations of subjects and objects in a sentence (**causative** affixes). See **6.6**.
- There are two main ways to express possession in a sentence, one without a verb and one with a verb. See **8.4**.
- For questions, Guarani does not use interrogative intonation or changes in word order, as in English. Rather, it uses interrogative enclitics attached to the end of the phrase being questioned. See **8.5**.

2
Phonology and orthography: the sound system and its written representation

In this chapter I present the sounds of Guarani, how they are pronounced, how they are represented in writing and their organization in a system of consonants and vowels that forms the distinct words in the language. The study of these properties is called **segmental phonology**, because consonants and vowels are the segments of the linear speech chain. I also briefly present some speech properties that involve entire syllables, words or phrases (**suprasegmental phonology**).

2.1 Sound inventory and pronunciation (segmental phonology)

2.1.1 Vowels and diphthongs

Vowels
Guarani has 6 oral vowels and 6 corresponding nasal vowels, for a total of 12 vowel sounds. This count abstracts away from variations in pronunciation due to the vowels' environment in a word or to individual speaker or regional differences. By convention, these abstractions (called **phonemes**) are always indicated by double slashes (//), while their pronunciation variants appear within square brackets ([ ]). The vowels themselves are represented with symbols from the International Phonetic Alphabet (IPA).[11]

---

[11] The IPA is available online at http://www.internationalphoneticalphabet.org/ipa-sounds/ipa-chart-with-sounds/.

Vowels are described according to three dimensions. First, the height of the vowel, determined by the height of the lower jaw, can be **close** (lower jaw in high position; for example, English 'beat', 'fool'), **mid** (lower jaw in mid position; for example, English 'bread', 'fur') or **open** (lower jaw in low position; for example, English 'father'). Vowels can also be called **high**, **mid** and **low** for this reason.

Second, the position of the tongue body is important. Vowels are **front** when the tongue is advanced in the mouth towards the teeth (for example, English 'beat', 'met'), **back** when the tongue body is retracted away from the teeth, towards the throat (for example, English 'fool', 'boss'), or **central** when the tongue is more neutral in the mouth, neither advanced nor retracted (for example, English 'fur', 'ago').

Third, **nasal** vowels have a lowered velum that allows the passage of air through the nose and gives these vowels their nasal quality (for example, English 'man'). **Oral** vowels do not allow the passage of air through the nose (for example, English 'bad'). If you cannot hear the difference between the vowels in 'man' and 'bad' in English, do not worry; that is perfectly normal since English does not use the difference between those vowels to create different words. But if you lengthen both vowels and place your finger on the side of your nose, you will feel vibration during the vowel of 'man' but no vibration during the vowel of 'bad'. That is the difference between a nasal and an oral vowel.

The nasal vowels are otherwise identical in every respect to the oral vowels (that is, in the shape of the lips, the height of the lower jaw, the placement of the tongue, the relative tension of the articulators, their length). In the table below, the current official orthography is given between chevrons (< >).

	Front		Central		Back	
	Oral	Nasal	Oral	Nasal	Oral	Nasal
Close	/i/ <i>	/ĩ/ <ĩ>	/ɨ/ <y>	/ɨ̃/ <ỹ>	/u/ <u>	/ũ/ <ũ>
Mid	/e/ <e>	/ẽ/ <ẽ>			/o/ <o>	/õ/ <õ>
Open			/a/ <a>	/ã/ <ã>		

The following pairs of words show that whether you have an oral or a nasal vowel in the stressed syllable of a word is crucial in Guarani. Indeed, such a difference changes the meaning of words. (We say, therefore, that the contrast between an oral vowel and a nasal vowel is **phonological**; that is, it serves to create different words as opposed to alternative pronunciations of the same word.) The pairs constructed below to show this are called **minimal pairs**, and the contrastive sounds in each pair are **phonemes** of Guarani.

aka 'quarrel' / *akã* 'head'
oke 's/he sleeps' / *okẽ* 'door'
piri 'fibre mat' / *pirĩ* 'chill, shiver'
kói 'farm' / *kõi* 'pair; twin'
pytu 'breath' / *pytũ* 'dark'
aky 'green; tender' / *akỹ* 'wet'

Some pointers for pronunciation:

- All of these vowels (especially /e/ and /o/) are pure vowels; they do not have final glides into /i/ or /u/ as in English. They are very similar to Spanish vowels, except for /ɨ/ <y>.
- The **open** (or **low**) **central oral vowel** /a/ <a> can be produced by starting with the back vowel in 'f<u>a</u>ther' and slowly fronting the tongue body to say the word 'f<u>a</u>t'. The Guarani /a/ sound is in between, exactly like the Spanish sound.
- Correct pronunciation of the **close** (or **high**) **central oral unrounded vowel** /ɨ/ <y> can be achieved by positioning the mouth to pronounce /i/ and, <u>without rounding the lips or opening the jaw</u>, moving the tongue body (not the tip of the tongue!) backwards in the mouth as if to pronounce /u/. Alternatively, one can start by positioning the mouth as if to pronounce /u/ and then, <u>without moving the tongue or opening the jaw</u>, spreading (that is, un-rounding) the lips as if to pronounce /i/. Similar vowel sounds are found in other widely spoken languages such as Mandarin (Pinyin <i>), Russian (<ы>) and Turkish (<ı>).
- Pronunciation of the nasal vowels is achieved by adding nasalization to the corresponding oral vowel, without changing any other articulator in the mouth. A way of training oneself to do this is to pronounce the English word 'singing'. In some pronunciations, the middle <g> is not produced, which makes both vowels fully nasal. The learner can then maintain those vowel sounds to identify what nasalization sounds like and feels like in the mouth. The word 'king' can also help detect the moment when the velum lowers to allow the passage of air through the nasal cavity, hence nasalizing the vowel. The learner can also touch the tip of their finger to the side of their nose and pronounce "nnnnnn" and then "sssssss" to feel the air making the nose vibrate in the first case, but not in the second. This vibration should always be felt in nasal vowels because it is a sign that air is indeed exiting through the nose.

Diphthongs

A **diphthong** is a sequence of two vowels that belong to the same syllable. When one of them is more closed than the other, it is pronounced as a semivowel or **glide** (it is shorter and carries less weight; think, for example, of <y> in the English word 'say'). Guarani is similar to English (and so, different from Spanish), in that adjacent vowels have a greater tendency to be pronounced in two separate syllables (**hiatus**). In the table below, diphthongs are illustrated with oral and nasal vowels where possible. The separation between syllables is indicated with a full point. Diphthongs given in parentheses are less frequent or rare.

	Diphthong	IPA	Examples
With final /i/:	yi, ỹi	[ɨʲ], [ɨ̃ʲ]	*ve.v**yi*** 'light (=not heavy)', *ta.h**yi*** 'ant', *ra.'**ỹi*** 'seed'
	ui, uĩ	[uʲ], [ʷi], [ʷ̃ĩ]	*ve.v**úi*** 'light (=not heavy)', *á.**gui*** 'from here', *a.**guĩ*** 'close by'
	ei	[eʲ]	*u.p**éi*** 'after, later'
	oi, õi	[oʲ], [õʲ]	*he.n**ói*** 'call', *mo.k**õi*** 'two'
	ai, ãi	[aʲ], [ãʲ]	*s**ái*** 'skirt', *t**ãi*** 'tooth'
With final /ɨ/:	uy	[ʷɨ] or [ʷⁱ]	*a.g**uy**.je* 'thanks'
	ay	[aⁱ]	*p**áy*** 'awake'
With final /u/:	(eu)	[eʷ]	***éu*** 'vomit'
	(au)	[aʷ]	*a.ma.nd**áu*** 'hail (precipitation)'
With final /e/:	(ye)	[ⁱe]	*t**ye*** 'abdomen'
	ue	[ʷe]	*ka.ng**ue*** 'bone'
With final /o/:	(io)	[ʲo]	*p**io*** (interrogative enclitic)
With final /a/:	(ia)	[ʲa]	*je.ro.v**ia*** 'belief, trust'
	ya	[ⁱa]	*p**ya**.'e* 'fast'
	ua, uã	[ʷa], [ʷ̃ã]	*k**ua*** 'hole', *k**uã*** 'finger'

Points to note:

- Guarani diphthongs must include at least one unstressed high vowel as a glide (represented here as [ʲ], [ⁱ], [ʷ]).
- The most common diphthongs are those which end in a high front vowel, either oral /i/ or nasal /ĩ/, and those that begin with the oral high back vowel /u/.

- The diphthongs that begin with the oral high back vowel /u/ all have velar consonants that precede them in the onset of the syllable.
- The lack of other lexical diphthongs not given in this table is presumably accidental. Note that some of them can appear in words composed of more than one morpheme. For example, *ẽi* [ẽʲ] in *nañe'ẽi* 'I did not talk' (n-a-ñe'ẽ-i, NEG-1SG.ACT-word-NEG).
- In some cases, speakers pronounce /ɨ/ as closer to [i] in diphthongs; for example, *hayhu* 'love' > *haihu*; *pyahu* 'new' > *piahu*; *aguyje* 'thanks' > *aguije*.
- Many vowel sequences that look like diphthongs are in fact to be pronounced in two syllables as a hiatus: *a.o* 'clothes', *ha.i* 'line', *a.ve.i* 'also'. These vowels do not belong to the same syllable.
- Triphthongs (sequences of three vowels in the same syllable) are also found in Guarani, with high vowels at both ends as glides and /a/ or /e/ as focal vowels. Some examples are: *pyáu* 'hoarse'; *hi.kuái* 'they'; *kuãi.rũ* 'ring'; *guéi* 'ox'; *juay.hu* 'mutual love'.

2.1.2 Consonants

The following table shows the consonants of Guarani represented by their symbols from the International Phonetic Alphabet (IPA).

By convention, the columns group the consonants with the same **place of articulation** (indicating where in the mouth the flow of air is modified by the tongue or lips). The rows group the consonants with the same **manner of articulation** (indicating how much the flow of air is modified by the tongue or lips, and how the air escapes). In each column, voiceless sounds are on the left, voiced sounds on the right.

	Labial	Coronal	Dorsal	Velar	Glottal
Voiceless stops	p	t		k	ʔ
Nasal	m	n	ɲ	ŋ	
Nasal-oral	ᵐb	ⁿd		ŋg	
Fricative		s	ʃ ʝ		h
Approximant	ʋ			ɰ	
Flap		ɾ			
Lateral		l			

In the table on p.31, I give the closest English equivalents for each consonant, to aid in pronunciation. (Alternative letter representations are given in parentheses.)

Description	IPA	Closest English equivalent	Letter representation	Example
Voiceless bilabial stop	p	spot, spin	p	*popo* 'jump'
Voiceless dental stop	t	stain, start	t	*tatu* 'armadillo'
Voiceless velar stop	k	school, skin	k	*kakuaa* 'grow (intransitive)'
Voiceless glottal stop	ʔ	uh-oh; (Cockney pronunciation of) butter	' (-)	*mba'e* 'thing'
Voiced bilabial nasal	m	my	m	*meme* 'continuously'
Voiced dental nasal	n	no	n	*nune* 'maybe'
Voiced palatal nasal	ɲ	(in some dialects) onion; like Spanish ñ	ñ	*ñyñýi* 'wither'
Voiced velar nasal	ŋ	singer	g̃ (often just g)	*hag̃uã* 'for'
Voiced nasal-oral bilabial	ᵐb	amber	mb	*mbarakaja* 'cat'
Voiced nasal-oral dental	ⁿd	undoubtedly	nd	*nde* 'you (sg.)'
Voiced nasal-oral velar	ⁿg	angle	ng	*ngotyo* 'towards'
Voiceless alveolar fricative	s	so	s	*sy* 'mother'
Voiceless postalveolar fricative	ʃ	share	ch (x)	*che* 'I'
Voiced palatal fricative	ʝ	(No English equivalent, but close to) jay, leisure	j (y)	*juka* 'to kill'
Voiceless glottal fricative	h	hi	h (j, jh)	*ha* 'and'
Voiced labiodental approximant	ʋ	(Indian English) wet, vet	v (b)	*vevúi* 'to float'

Description	IPA	Closest English equivalent	Letter representation	Example
Voiced velar approximant	ɰ	(No English equivalent, but close to) **w**ok (without any lip protrusion or rounding)	g	ó**g**a 'house'
Voiced alveolar flap	ɾ	American English a**t**om ("flapped" pronunciation)	r	**r**i**r**e 'after'
Voiced alveolar lateral	l	English **l**it	l	**l**a**l**a 'complain'

Points to note:

- These two tables contain an inventory of basic consonant phones. These are the ones native speakers intuitively think of as different from one another and the ones that are written differently in the orthography. They do not include all possible pronunciation variants for consonants, but only those that are generated by nasal harmony rules (see **2.2.3**).
- The table above gives the current official orthography. Other possible **graphemes** (that is, letters and combinations of letters) are given in parentheses. Familiarity with them is paramount for understanding older texts, for example, but also to understand modern texts that do not conform to the official orthography.
- **Voiceless** sounds are those that do not involve vibration of the vocal cords. In the table, they appear to the left in each column.
- **Voiced** sounds are produced with accompanying vibration of the vocal cords. They appear to the right in each column.
- Practise how to produce voicing and devoicing by pronouncing the voiceless and voiced English consonants given as examples in the table. You can detect voicing or lack thereof by either putting your hand on your throat or covering both your ears and listening for a "buzz" (its presence indicates voicing).
- Like Spanish voiceless stops, Guarani voiceless stops never have an aspiration or puff of air at the end (they are **unaspirated**). This can be detected in English by comparing the aspirated <t> in 'top' (non-existent in Guarani) with the unaspirated <t> in 'stop'. (Put a paper towel in front of your mouth if you have trouble perceiving

a difference: it will move more when you pronounce 'top' because of the added explosion of air at the end of *t*.) The only context in which the English pronunciation of voiceless stops approximates the ones in Guarani is after /s/ at the beginning of an English word.

- The **glottal stop** /ʔ/ is represented by an apostrophe in the orthography. This grapheme is called in Guarani *puso*. It is the "catch in the throat" that occurs before each vowel of 'uh-oh' in English. It can be learned by practising a very quiet cough. This glottal stop is often completely elided in rapid speech and for very frequent words; for example, *mba'e* 'thing' can be pronounced [ᵐbaʔe] or [ᵐbae].

- The **voiceless postalveolar fricative** /ʃ/ is often actually pronounced with the front half of the tongue flat and raised, following closely the upper surface of the mouth, from the teeth to the hard palate (that is, the strongly palatalized, higher-pitched and sharp alveolo-palatal consonant [ɕ]) This sound can be approximated somewhat by pronouncing the English sequence 'wi<u>sh y</u>ou'.

- The **voiced palatal fricative** /ʝ/ can be pronounced as a voiced palatal stop [ɟ] or as a voiced palatal affricate [ɟ͡ʝ] in more careful speech.[12] Another possible pronunciation is a voiced alveopalatal fricative [d͡ʒ], similar to the sound for 'jay' in English, but perhaps less tense. Using the sound for 'jay', while non-native, will not cause any problems for comprehension and is the easiest solution for English speakers.

- The **voiceless glottal fricative** /h/ is usually pronounced as an English <h> but it can be pronounced more strongly as [x] by some speakers, similar to the "harder" pronunciation of the letter <j> in many varieties of Spanish.

- The **voiced labiodental approximant** /ʋ/ is a sound commonly heard, for example, in native Indian varieties of English: it is articulated like [v] but without full contact of lips and teeth (hence the label "approximant"). It can be completely elided in frequent words, for example: *kóva* 'this thing', *péva* 'that thing', *túva* 'father' and *jevy* 'again' are commonly pronounced *kóa*, *péa*, *túa*, *jey*, respectively. Written evidence for its approximant articulation (instead of fully fricative like English [v]) is that in older texts it appears written as <b> (which is the approximant [β] in Spanish) or <w>.

- The **voiced velar approximant** /ɰ/ appears almost exclusively in the sequence <gu>, where it can be pronounced as [ɣʷ] or even

---

[12] These pronunciations have no equivalent in English but can be heard online, for example, at https://en.wikipedia.org/wiki/Voiced_palatal_stop and https://en.wikipedia.org/wiki/Voiced_palatal_affricate.

[w]. The only frequent word where it appears before a vowel that is not /u/ is óga 'house', where it is pronounced like a very relaxed version of English <g>, akin to Spanish <g> in most dialects. Other, less frequent words where /ɰ/ appears before a vowel that is not /u/ are techagi 'neglect' and techaga'u 'nostalgia'.
- The letter <r> never represents a trill (like Spanish <rr>) in Guarani. It is always pronounced with a single tap of the tip of the tongue, as in Italian *Roma*, for example (think of the American English pronunciation of <tt> in 'butter', 'better').
- The /r/ trill (<rr>) in Spanish loanwords that originally contain it gives rise to the rare, marginal phoneme /ʐ/. This is a voiced retroflex sibilant consonant. **Retroflex** means that the tip of the tongue curves inwards to meet the roof of the palate. **Sibilants** are consonants that make a hissing sound by directing air towards the teeth. This particular [ʐ] sound is very similar to the <g> in English '**g**enre'.
- The **voiced alveolar lateral** /l/ is never "dark" (that is, velarized by retracting the tongue) as in American English 'pool'. It is always pronounced with the body of the tongue in a more central or anterior position, as in Spanish. It is not originally a Guarani phoneme. It was incorporated in the system from Spanish loanwords (for example, *vale* 'to be worth', *lee* 'to read', *limõ* 'lemon', *lája* 'character'; see **1.6**).

There are no voiced stops /b/, /d/, /g/ in the language. The nasal and nasal-oral (or prenasalized) segments are usually variants of each other, their appearance depending on what other nasal sounds may be in the word (see **2.2.3**). Typically, no consonants can end a syllable in Guarani, with the exception of nasals in cases of **resyllabification** (see **2.2.1**).

2.2 Suprasegmental phonology

Suprasegmental features involve entire syllables, words or phrases. These usually belong in the domain of the study of **prosody**. I will first describe the better-known prosodic characteristics of Guarani, namely syllable structure, stress placement in words and nasal harmony. Then, I will end with a sketch of further prosodic properties that have not been thoroughly investigated.

2.2.1 Syllable structure

Syllables in native Guarani words are overwhelmingly frequently formed by an initial consonant followed by a single vowel (put somewhat more technically but more succinctly, they are CV, that is, a consonantal **onset** plus a vowel **nucleus**). Other types of syllables found are V (syllable with a single vowel in the nucleus without a consonant onset), VV (syllable with a composite nucleus including one **focal** vowel and one **glide**), and CVV (syllable with consonant onset plus composite nucleus); CVVV (syllable with onset plus composite nucleus with two glides) are also found. No **codas** (consonants that end a syllable) are found in native words. Remember from **2.1.1** that a word's separation in syllables is customarily indicated with a full point in the phonetic transcription.

V	*y*	'water'
VV	*éu*	'vomit'
CV	*sy*	'mother'
CVV	*tãi*	'tooth'
CVVV	*pyáu*	'hoarse'

Points to note:

- It is rare for a syllable to begin with a stop /p/, /t/, or /k/ followed by /l/ or /ɾ/, but clusters in onsets do occur occasionally due to a number of Spanish loans in the modern language (for example, *plíki* 'clumsy'). When words with original clusters like these were borrowed earlier in the history of contact with Spanish, they were changed to fit the Guarani phonological system. For example, Spanish *cruz* 'cross' gave Guarani *kurusu*, with a helping vowel /u/ breaking the consonant cluster and another /u/ at the end to avoid having a consonant end the syllable in the coda. Hence, the original syllable CCVC (*cruz*) yielded a word with three syllables, with the structure CV.CV.CV (*ku.ru.su*), in conformity with Guarani syllable structure.
- The glottal stop is always present in pronunciation at the beginning of vowel-initial words. (The same is true in English though native speakers are usually not aware of this.) The orthography does not require that initial glottal stops in isolated words be written. Nevertheless, some authors indicate that one must differentiate words that begin with a vowel from those that begin with a glottal stop, because this glottal stop is written whenever an affix

or another root is added. For example, *ára* 'time' without an initial < ' >, but *hi'ára* 'his/her/its time'.
- Although consonant codas did not exist in classical Guarani before contact with Spanish, they do exist today. First, the nasal-oral consonants produce codas in the pronunciation. For example, a word like *me.**mb**y* 'child (of a woman)' is actually separated in syllables by speakers as *mem.by* (this is called **resyllabification**). Furthermore, some loanwords from Spanish have been integrated with codas: *ar.he**l*** 'unfriendly'.

2.2.2 Stress

Stress is the relative prominence of a syllable with respect to others in the word, indicated by higher volume, higher pitch, longer duration or a combination of these (although Guarani does not seem to use duration for this). It is indicated in a phonetic transcription by a raised vertical line at the beginning of the stressed syllable: ['].

Guarani morphemes can have their own stress or can be inherently unstressed. Knowing whether a given morpheme has inherent stress or not is very important, since it impacts on the pronunciation of words in which the morpheme in question is used. For that reason, in this book I will always indicate whether a morpheme is stressed or unstressed when first introduced.

Native Guarani lexical roots (nouns, verbs, adjectives, adverbs) always have inherent stress, in the vast majority of cases on the last vowel.

*a.**sy***	'pain'
*mo.ro.**tĩ***	'white'
*ñan.**du***	'spider'
*gua.**ta***	'to walk'

Prefixes are always unstressed. Suffixes and phrasal enclitics can be inherently stressed or inherently unstressed. The rule for stressing words with more than one morpheme is that the last inherently stressed morpheme will carry the word's primary stress. The examples below contain the root *guata* 'to walk', inherently stressed on its final syllable, the (unstressed) first-person active prefix *a-*, the inherently stressed suffixes *-se* 'want' and *-ve* 'more', the unstressed negation **circumfix** *nd-...-i* and the unstressed suffix *-ma* 'already'. Note how the stress seems to "move to the right" in each example that adds an inherently stressed suffix but stops moving when unstressed affixes are added.

aguata [a.ɰʷa.ˈta]
a-guata
1SG.ACT-walk
'I walk(ed)'

aguatase [a.ɰʷa.ta.ˈse]
a-guata-se
1SG.ACT-walk-want
'I want to walk'

aguataseve [a.ɰʷa.ta.se.ˈʋe]
a-guata-se-ve
1SG.ACT-walk-want-more
'I want to walk more'

ndaguatasevéi [ⁿda.ɰʷa.ta.se.ˈʋeʲ]
nd-a-guata-se-ve-i
NEG-1SG.ACT-walk-want-more-NEG
'I do not want to walk more'

ndaguatasevéima [ⁿda.ɰʷa.ta.se.ˈʋeʲ.ma]
nd-a-guata-se-ve-i-ma
NEG-1SG.ACT-walk-want-more-NEG-already
'I already do not want to walk more'

A few morphemes however, be they roots, suffixes (marked with a dash) or clitics (marked with an equal sign), are stressed on the penultimate syllable. Others can also be stressed on the antepenultimate syllable, albeit more rarely. Since these morphemes violate the common stress pattern, their stressed vowels are marked in the standard orthography with an acute stress mark (´) if the vowel is oral, or with a nasal tilde (˜) if the vowel is nasal (see **2.3.2**).

ajúra	'neck'
áke (also *háke*, *cháke*)	'careful!'
ánga	'soul'
ára	'day'
=ári	'upon'
atĩa	'sneeze'
áva	'hair'
eíra	'honey'

=guýpe	'below'
háime	'almost'
-hára	agentive nominalizer
hikóni	frequentative aspect
hína	progressive aspect
jára	'master, lord, owner'
káma	'scabies'
karácha	'breast; nipple'
káso	'short story'
káva	'wasp'
kéra	'sleep, dream'
kuára	'hole'
=kuéra	plural
lája	'character'
liméta	'bottle'
mamóne	'papaya'
máramo	'never'
máva	'who'
ména	'husband'
nahániri	'no'
ne'ĩra	'yet'
óga	'house'
okára	'countryside, interior; courtyard'
póra	'spirit'
syrýky	'all of a sudden'
tãimbíra	'gingiva, gum'
tajýra	'daughter'
táva	'city, town'
ta'ýra	'son'
téra	'name'
tẽra	'or'
túva	'father'
týra	'breads to accompany a meal'
výro	'stupid'
ýva	'handle'
yvága	'sky'
yvypóra (ypóra)	'human being, person' (that is, 'spirit of the earth' or 'spirit of the water')

Points to note:

- Many of these words stressed on the penultimate syllable end in /a/. They come from earlier forms that ended in consonants and were followed by the suffix -*a* when used as nouns. Such forms are now fossilized (that is, the noun marker -*a* does not have a recognizable function anymore). Many of these are kinship terms.
- Other cases also come originally from a combination of two forms: Proto Tupi-Guarani *ár + i* > Guarani =*ári* 'upon'; Proto Tupi-Guarani *wýr-pe* > Guarani =*guýpe* 'below'.

Native speakers of Guarani can pronounce and perceive one or several **secondary stresses** (underlined in the examples below) preceding the final primary stress (boldfaced). This often happens in words that are compounds of two roots, but not exclusively.

*pir<u>a</u>pir**e***
pira+pire
fish+leather
'money'

*oñemb<u>o</u>pir<u>a</u>pirev**é**ta*
o-ñe-mbo-pira+pire-ve-ta
3.ACT-AGD-MAKE1-fish+leather-more-FUT
's/he will become richer'

*ch<u>e</u>py'ait<u>e</u>guiv**é**ma*
che-py'a-ite-guive-ma
1SG.INACT-heart-very-since-already
'from the very core of my being'

2.2.3 Nasal harmony

Nasal harmony (also often referred to as **nasal spread** or **nasalization**) is a very distinctive feature of Guarani and of Tupi-Guarani and Tupian languages more generally. This section gives a very basic understanding of nasal harmony, perforce glossing over many complications that arise in the application of these rules (the interested reader can refer to Estigarribia (2017)).

The main thing to know is that, in Guarani, when a nasal vowel or a nasal consonant appears in a root, it spreads nasalization to other sounds in the same morphological word. These nasal vowels and consonants are called **triggers** (boxed in the following examples for clarity). The affected sounds are called **targets** (boldfaced).

This nasal spread is very important for Guarani morphology. For example, the (non-exhaustive) table below shows that some prefixes and suffixes can have different forms (**allomorphs**) depending on whether and how they are affected by the spread of nasalization. (See **17.4** for a fuller table containing morphemes with consonant allomorphs conditioned by nasal harmony.)

Meaning or gloss	Non-nasal allomorph	Nasal allomorph
Prefixes		
First person plural active, inclusive	*ja-*	*ña-*
Second person singular inactive	*nde-*	*ne-*
Negation	*nd-*...*-i*	*n-*...*-i*
Agent-demoting voice	*je-*	*ñe-*
Reciprocal	*jo-*	*ño-*
Causative ('make')	*mbo-, mby-, mbu-*	*mo-, my-, mu-*
Suffixes and enclitics		
'in, on, at, to'	=*pe*	=*me*
Plural	=*kuéra*	=*nguéra*
Post-stative aspect/ Nominal past tense	-*kue*	-*ngue*

Below I give some examples of these alternations, which are the main way in which students of the language first encounter nasal harmony. On the left I show the oral versions of the affixes, used when the root has no nasal sounds. On the right I show the nasal versions, used when the root has a nasal sound. For every example, a line of phonetic transcription is added that reflects the pronunciation.

Note in the examples that nasalization spreads to most sounds in the words, but that this is indicated by a change in spelling only for a few of them (<mb> → <m>; <nd> → <n>; <j> → <ñ>; sometimes <p> → <mb> or <m>, <k> → <ng> and <g> → <g̃> as well). Note also that voiceless sounds are **transparent**; that is, they are not affected by nasalization that spreads to the left, neither do they stop its spread (see [k] and [t] below in *kytĩ* [kɨ̃tĩ], for example). Hence, although only the nasalization of nasal-oral segments to nasal segments is marked in the spelling, all segments except the voiceless stops are assumed to be pronounced as nasal.

ndakarúi
[ⁿda.ka.ˈruʲ]
nd-a-karu-i
NEG-1SG.ACT-eat(intransitive)-NEG
'I don't/didn't eat'

nasẽ̃i
[nã.ˈsẽʲ]
n-a-sẽ-i
NEG-1SG.ACT-go.out-NEG
'I don't/didn't go out'

ndaikuaái
[ⁿdaʲ.kʷa.ˈaʲ]
nd-ai-kuaa-i
NEG-1SG.ACT-know-NEG
'I don't/didn't know'

namondái
[nã.mõ.ˈⁿdaʲ]
n-a-monda-i
NEG-1SG.ACT-steal-NEG
'I don't/didn't steal'

ojekuaa
[o.ɟe.kʷa.ˈa]
o-je-kuaa
3.ACT-AGD-know
'it is known'

oñenupã̃
[õ.ɲẽ.nũ.ˈpã]
o-ñe-nupã
3.ACT-AGD-beat.up
's/he/it is punished'

ojohayhu
[o.ɟo.haⁱ.ˈhu]
o-jo-h-ayhu
3.ACT-RECP-POSSM3-love
'they love each other'

oñohenói
[õ.ɲõ.hẽ.ˈnõʲ]
o-ño-h-enói
3.ACT-RECP-POSSM3-call
'they call each other'

Ja'u ndeso'o.
[ɟa.ˈʔu.ⁿde.so.ˈʔo]
ja-'u   nde-so'o
1PL.INCL.ACT-eat   2SG.INACT-meat
'Let's eat your meat.'

Ñakytĩ̃ neanaña.
[ɲã.kɨ̃.ˈtĩ.nẽ.ã.nã.ˈnã]
ña-kytĩ
1PL.INCL.ACT-cut
ne-anana
2SG.INACT-pineapple
'Let's cut your pineapple.'

pendekotýpe
[pẽ.ⁿde.ko.ˈtɨ.pe]
pende-kotý=pe
2PL.INACT-room=in
'in/to your (pl.) room(s)'

peneakãme
[pẽ.nẽ.ã.ˈkã.mẽ]
pene-akã=me
2PL.INACT-head=in
'in/to your (pl.) head(s)'

PHONOLOGY AND ORTHOGRAPHY   41

jaguakuéra
[ɟa.ɰʷa.'kʷe.ɾa]
jagua=kuéra
dog=PL
'dogs'

mitãnguéra
[mĩ.tã.'ᵑgʷe.ɾa]
mitã=nguéra
child=PL
'children'

jaha
[ɟa.'ha]
ja-ha
1PL.INCL.ACT-go
'we (and you) go/went'

ñag̃uahẽ
[ɲã.ŋʷã.'hẽ]
ña-g̃uahẽ
1PL.INCL.ACT-arrive
'we (and you) arrive(d)'

The examples above show that nasalization mostly works leftward; that is, **regressively**. This leftward spread of nasalization diminishes with distance from the trigger. It is difficult to give a hard and fast rule, but it is generally accepted that nasalization is not perceptible more than three syllables away from the trigger.

In Guarani nasalization also has a limited rightward, or **progressive**, spread to subsequent segments (usually the next syllable only), whether the subsequent syllable is part of the root or is an added oral suffix or enclitic. Voiceless sounds are not transparent to this kind of nasalization (they are affected by it).

pakovaty
[pa.ko.ʋa.'tɨ]
pakova-ty
banana-collective
'banana grove'

*ñana**ndy***
[ɲã.nã.'ⁿdɨ]
ñana-ndy
weed-collective
'scrubland'

tupa'ópe
[tu.pa.ʔo.pe]
tupa'o=pe
church=in
'at church'

guaraníme
[ɰʷã.ɾ̃ã.'nĩ.mẽ]
guarani=me
Guarani=in
'in Guarani'

Notably, nasal-oral consonants only trigger regressive nasal assimilation. This makes sense because the second half of a nasal-oral consonant, being oral, cannot spread nasality forward.

neme̅mb̅ykuéra
[nẽ.mẽ.ᵐbɨ.ˈkʷe.ɾa]
ne-memby=kuéra
2SG.INACT-child.of.woman=PL
'your (sg.) children' (said to a woman; *memby* is the term used for 'child of a woman')

Even though roots are the most common sources of nasalization, prefixes containing nasal or nasal-oral consonants also create nasal spans to their left (that is, away from the direction of the root).

ñañe̅mb̅otavy
[ɲã.ɲẽ.ᵐbo.taˈʋɨ]
ña-ñe-mbo-tavy
1PL.INCL.ACT-AGD-MAKE1-stupid
'we (and you) fool ourselves'

Exceptionally, the causative prefix *mbo-* can nasalize the first voiceless stop of a root and become nasalized to *mo-* in turn (see **6.6.1** and **17.4.2**).

mongaru (from the root *karu* 'eat (intransitive)')
[mõ.ᵑgaˈɾu]
mo-ngaru
MAKE1-eat(intransitive)
'feed'

Suffixes (whether stressed or unstressed) and enclitics do not create nasal spans to their left (that is, in the direction of the root). In the examples below, the suffixes *-mi* (diminutive, stressed), *-nte* ('only', unstressed), *-ma* ('already', unstressed) and *-na* (requestative, unstressed) all have nasal consonants, yet they do not cause nasalization of the roots they attach to or other suffixes to their left, as the following examples show:

*cherajy**mi*** (not *cherañymi)
[ʃe.ɾa.ɟɨˈmĩ]
che-r-ajy-mi
1SG.INACT-POSSM-daughter.of.man-DIM
'my little daughter'

*ime**mbý**nte* (not *imemýnte)
[ĩ.mẽ.ˈᵐbɨ.ⁿte]
i-memby-nte
3.INACT-child.of.woman-only
'only her child'

*a**ñ**a**nd**úma* (not *añanúma)
[ã.ɲa.ⁿdu.ma]
a-ñandu-ma
1SG.ACT-feel-already
'I already feel/felt (it)'

*ehe**nd**úke**n**a* (not *ehenúngena)
[ẽ.hẽ.ⁿdu.ke.nã]
e-h-endu-ke-na
IMP-POSSM3-listen-FORCE-REQ
'please, do listen'

Furthermore, regressive nasalization cannot cross a boundary between compound roots.

jaikoporã̃ (not *ñaikoporã)
[ʝaʲ.ko.põ.ˈrã]
ja-iko+porã
1PL.INCL.ACT-be+well
'we (and you) get along'

The learner should be aware that, under conditions that are not well understood, some speakers fail to use consistently the nasal variants expected from nasal harmony, especially in the case of suffixes and enclitics. For example, it is common to hear *mitakuéra* 'children', instead of *mitãnguéra*. Nasal harmony may be gradually disappearing, perhaps through contact with Spanish, but our current research is inconclusive.

To summarize, Guarani roots can be nasal (if they contain a stressed nasal vowel or a nasal consonant), nasal-oral (if they contain a nasal-oral consonant) or oral (if they do not contain any nasal segments). Excluding words with stressed nasal suffixes, all words are either oral (containing oral segments and voiceless stops), nasal (nasal segments and voiceless stops) or nasal-oral in that order (containing a nasal-oral consonant at the boundary between the nasal portion and the oral portion).

2.2.4 Prosody sketch: practical considerations for pronunciation

In this section I have described syllable structure (**2.2.1**), stress (**2.2.2**) and nasal harmony (**2.2.3**). Here I will provide a rough sketch of other prosodic characteristics, which will unfortunately be largely impressionistic due to the lack of research in this area.

Guarani is a language with fixed stress and no lexical **tone** (that is, variations in pitch and pitch contour that can differentiate words, like in most varieties of Chinese, Thai, Punjabi, Norwegian, Navajo, and Yucatec Mayan, to name a few languages that use tone productively). The primary stress of roots almost always falls on the last syllable. In words of more than one morpheme it still tends towards the end, although this depends on the presence or absence of unstressed suffixes. Impressionistically, stressed syllables have noticeably more intensity/volume (more so than in English or Spanish) and a higher pitch than the rest of the word, but are not necessarily longer, and they often sound clipped, especially at the end of an **utterance**.

A language property that can influence the ease with which a foreign speaker and native speaker can understand one another is **rhythm**. The major difference between Guarani and English is that in English, vowels in unstressed syllables become reduced and therefore the stressed syllables are much more important in the rhythm of phrases. In Guarani, on the other hand, there is no vowel reduction in unstressed syllables. Each syllable must be pronounced with a full vowel and take the same time as a stressed syllable.

Declarative sentences (statements) have a final fall in pitch (like in English). It is often said that interrogative sentences have no special prosody in Guarani, and are pronounced with a final fall just like statements (in English they usually have a final rise in pitch). However, we do not have good phonetic studies to back this contention up (see **8.5**).

Inside sentences we can find notable **pitch rises** at the end of phrases, often accompanied by **lengthening** the duration of the vowel in the last syllable. These are present in the prosody used in conversation and are even more marked when speakers are reading. There can be vowel lengthening and rise-fall peaking contours during a hesitation or before a pause. Finally, some **fillers** used are *eeh*, *pero* and *bueno* (from Spanish). (Fillers are sounds or small words or phrases that are used during hesitations to signal that the speaker is not done talking. Common filler words in English are 'um', 'uh', 'er', 'like', 'you know'.) **Backchanneling** (that is, responses that are used mainly to signal the hearer's attention or agreement without interrupting a speaker's turn) can be accomplished by the use of *hmm*, much like in English or Spanish.

2.3 The alphabet or *achegety* and modern orthographic conventions in Paraguay

2.3.1 History of orthographic conventions

Before contact with Spanish (and Portuguese) Guarani was an oral language and had no written form. After the Spanish colonization, the Jesuit missionaries devised ad hoc writing systems based on the Roman alphabet, which allowed them to write the first grammars and dictionaries. Widespread standardization of the orthography first occurred in 1950, and the system proposed then is (with a few changes) the one that is in use today. Guarani is written horizontally, from left to right, like English. The Guarani **graphemes** (letters and letter combinations) are organized in an alphabet called *achegety*, from the names of the first three letters, *a*, *che*, *ge*, and the collective plural suffix *-ty* (*achegety*, then, means something like 'set of the *a*, *che*, *ge*'s').

A major advantage of this system is that each grapheme (be it a letter or a **digraph** composed of two letters) corresponds to one basic phone of the language (unlike in English). Two **diacritic marks** are used: the acute stress mark (´) to identify an oral vowel that bears the primary stress of a morphological word but is not the last vowel of that word; and the nasal tilde (˜) to identify phonologically nasal vowels (that is, vowels that are inherently nasal, not vowels that are nasal due to nasal harmony).

Achegety: a – ã – ch – e – ẽ – g – g̃ – h – i – ĩ – j – k – l – m – mb – n – nd – ng – nt – ñ – o – õ – p – r – rr – s – t – u – ũ – v – y – ỹ – '

When reciting the *achegety*, vowels are simply pronounced as they would be in a word. Consonant names end in /e/ (for example, <ch> /ʃe/, <mb> /ᵐbe/, <r> /ɾe/). The only exception is the grapheme <'> for the glottal stop, which is called *puso* (from *pu* 'sound' and *so* 'cut').

2.3.2 Recommended orthography

Even though a standardized orthography now exists, the learner and/or researcher needs to be prepared to find many deviations from these conventions. Older texts use varying spellings, and even modern texts differ in their degree of adherence to the recommendations by the Paraguayan Academy of the Guarani Language which are not always completely systematic. The orthography used in this book generally follows the recommendations in Penner and Bobadilla de Cazal (2010) and Estigarribia (2017). Here, I list the main orthographic rules (noting aspects in which the orthography I have adopted in this book differs from the officially recommended one).

- *Achegety*:
  - I have chosen to use the grapheme <g̃> even though its status as a necessary letter is debatable (in this, I depart from Penner and Bobadilla de Cazal (2010) and Estigarribia (2017) who do not recommend its use). This letter can only occur in nasal words and is therefore predictably nasal (see **2.2.3**): it represents [ŋ]. This can be thought of as a variant of /ɡ/ in nasal words and for this reason <g> is often used instead in texts. By way of an example, the word *hag̃uã* 'for' has a stressed nasal vowel *ã*. This vowel causes nasalization of the whole word, which is pronounced [hãŋw̃ã]. For this reason, it is also found spelled as *haguã* or even *hanguã* or *hag̃ua*. Similar spelling variants are found for some very frequent words, including *koʼág̃a* 'now' (also found as *koʼãga* or *koʼaga*), the root *g̃uahẽ* 'arrive' (also spelled *guahẽ* or *guãhẽ*) and the postposition *g̃uarã* 'for' (also spelled *guarã*). The reader will find variation in the spelling of these words in this book, because I generally chose to maintain the orthography found in the original sources in the examples. This is important because any reader of Guarani will find different spellings of these words and needs to be able to recognize them as the same word.
  - Relatedly, the word *tẽra* 'or' is also found as *térã* in texts.
- Stress:
  - Remember that modern orthographic norms require a morphological word (a root plus all attached affixes and particles) to bear a stress mark only when it is not stressed on its final vowel, or if it is, when it ends in a diphthong or triphthong with a glide at the end. The following are examples of roots with stress marked orthographically.

  ména 'husband'
  nahániri 'no'
  purahéi 'song'
  karáu 'sprain, dislocation'

  Since Guarani has both stress-bearing and non-stress-bearing suffixes and enclitics, stress in words with more than one morpheme falls (and is marked on) the last stress-bearing morpheme (if not nasal). The following are examples of stress marking for words with more than one morpheme:

nahendusevéima
n-a-h-endu-se-ve-i-ma
NEG-1SG.ACT-POSSM3-hear-want-more-NEG-already
'I already do not want to hear more'

chembopukákena
che-mbo-puka-ke-na
1SG.INACT-MAKE1-laugh-FORCE-REQ
'please, do make me laugh'

- Nasality:
  - For each nasal morpheme, nasality is marked on the stressed syllable and no stress mark is used.

    porã 'beautiful; good; well'
    karãu 'ibis'
    ne'ĩra 'not yet'

The same rule applies if the word is composed of more than one morpheme.

osẽta
o-sẽ-ta
3.ACT-go.out-FUT
's/he/it will go out'

- Inherently nasal morphemes always keep their nasal marking, even if there is more than one in a word and even if they do not bear the primary accent of the morphological word.

    mitãkaria'y (stressed on *'y*)
    mitã-karia'y
    child-young.man
    'youngster'

    mitãpytã (stressed on the second *tã*)
    mitã-pytã
    child-red
    '(a) new-born'

iporãite (stressed on *te*)
i-porã-ite
3.INACT-beautiful-very
's/he/it is very beautiful' / 'great!'

- Prefixes preceding nouns and verbs:
  - Free personal pronouns and inactive person prefixes (see **3.5.1** and **4.1.2**) are almost always pronounced identically (they are **homophonous**) and hence, in the standard academic spelling, both are written separate from the predicate. In this book, I write the free personal pronouns as independent, separate words but attach the person prefixes to their base. This more accurately reflects the morphosyntactic differences of words versus prefixes. More generally, since prefixes are unstressed, they should be attached to their base. On the other hand, free pronouns, demonstratives and numerals, being generally able to be stressed, should be written separately from the noun or verb.

    Personal pronoun:

    Che *apuka.*
    che   a-puka
    I   1SG.ACT-laugh
    'I laugh.'

    Nde *ndetuja.*
    nde   nde-tuja
    you.SG   2SG.INACT-old
    'You, you are old.'

    Person prefix:

    che*nupã* (Academy orthography: *che nupã*)
    che-nupã
    1SG.INACT-hit
    's/he/they hit me'

    *Nde **nde***tuja.
    nde   nde-tuja
    you.SG   2SG.INACT-old
    'You, you are old.'

Demonstratives:

***ko** kururu*
ko   kururu
PROX.SG frog
'<u>this</u> frog'

***umi** mitã*
umi   mitã
NPROX.PL child
'<u>those</u> children'

Numerals:

***peteĩ** añai*
peteĩ añai
one   frontier
'<u>a/one</u> frontier'

***mokõi** mitã*
mokõi mitã
two   child
'<u>two</u> children'

***mbohapy** jakapu*
mbohapy jakapu
three   explosion
'<u>three</u> explosions'

***irundy** yvu*
irundy yvu
four   spring
'<u>four</u> springs (=water sources)'

- Postpositions, enclitics and suffixes that follow nouns, verbs and phrases:
  ○ Traditionally, monosyllabic postpositions are written attached to the word they follow, and postpositions of more than one syllable separate from it:

Perúpe
Peru=pe
Peru=in
'to Pedro'

Peru rehe
Peru   rehe
Peru   at
'at Pedro'

The reasons for this convention are not clear, since many bisyllabic postpositions have monosyllabic variants (for example, *rehe = re* 'at').

In this work, I will generally attach all postpositions to the word they follow. This, in practical terms, includes almost all grammatical particles that follow a noun or verb they modify. Writing all postpositions attached to their stem better reflects that they are part of the same phonological word (they are pronounced as a single word together with the base they attach to). Then it becomes possible to differentiate in writing, for example:

aháramo	from	*aharamo*
a-ha=ramo		a-ha=ramo
1SG.ACT-go=if		1SG.ACT-go=recently
'if I go/went'		'I just went'

ahárire	from	*aharire*
a-ha=rire		a-ha=rire
1SG.ACT-go=if		1SG.ACT-go=after
'if I go/went'		'after I go/went'

In the Academy's standard orthography, both members of these pairs are written *aha ramo* and *aha rire*. This does not represent accurately the fact that the pronunciations are different because the stress patterns are different, as indicated by the stress marks in the examples. (Note that this is not necessarily a big problem for native speakers, who can easily disambiguate by context.)

- Compound words:
  ◦ No spaces will be used between roots in a compound word.

uvãkangue
uvã+kangue
thigh+bone
'femur'

hyakuãvu
hyakuã+vu
smell+ferment
'strong smell'

arayvoty
ára+yvoty
day+flower
'(the) spring' (literally, 'flower time')

avañe'ẽ
ava+ñe'ẽ
person+speak
'Guarani (language)'

karaiñe'ẽ
karai+ñe'ẽ
gentleman+speak
'Spanish (language)'

tovamokõi
t-ova+mokõi
NPOSSM-face+two
'hypocrisy'

- **Reduplications** are rendered as one word or two words depending on the original source (they are marked with a tilde ~ in the gloss).

mokõimokõi
mokõi~mokõi
two~two
'in pairs; in groups of two; two for each'

overavera or *overa vera*
o-vera~vera
3.ACT-flash~flash
'it is flashing lightning'

oñepyrũ ombotambota
o-ñepyrũ   o-mbota~mbota
3.ACT-begin   3.ACT-knock~knock
's/he began to knock and knock (on the door)'

- For compound words, nasal tildes are kept for each nasal morpheme, even though only one of the nasal vowels bears the primary stress:

kuãirũ
kuã+irũ
finger+friend
'ring'

mitãporã
mitã+porã
child+beautiful
'pretty child'

If stress falls on a non-nasal vowel, it is marked only if it is not the last syllable:

mitãrusu
mitã+rusu
child+grown
'adolescent'

mitãnguéra
mitã=nguéra
child=PL
'children'

- Loanwords:
  - The graphemes <l>, <ll>, <f>, <b> (do not confuse with the digraph <mb>!), <d> (do not confuse with the digraph <nd>!) do not belong to the Guarani *achegety*, but can be used for Spanish loans.

*l**é**i* 'law' (from Spanish *ley*)

*ll*antenkokue (from Spanish *llantén*)
llanten+kokue
broadleaf.plantain+farm
'farm broadleaf plantain'

o*farrea hikuái* (from Spanish *farrear* 'to party')
o-farrea   hikuái
3.ACT-party   they
'they party/partied'

*nde **b**obo* (from Spanish *bobo* 'silly')
nde   bobo
you.SG   dumb
'you idiot'

o*reaju**d**ami* (from Spanish *ayudar* 'to help')
ore-ajuda-mi
1PL.EXCL.INACT-help-PLEAD
'help us a bit'

- Likewise, the grapheme <rr> can be used for Spanish loans when they conserve the **trill** pronunciation /r/:

***rr**éi* 'king' (from Spanish *rey* 'king')

***rr**ósa* 'rose' (from Spanish *rosa* 'rose')

*pa**rr**ókia* 'parish' (from Spanish *parroquia* 'parish')

*ka**rr**éta sã* (from Spanish *carreta* 'wagon')
karréta   sã
cart   rope
'cart rope'

- A dash can be used to separate a Spanish root, word or phrase from an attached Guarani morpheme (as long as the Spanish item is not an integrated loan). In the example below, the integrated loan *Hyãsia* 'France' could have been used (fully adapted as a Guarani word), but instead the Spanish word *Francia* was used. This **code-switch** can then be identified with a dash.

Francia-pe
Francia=pe
Francia=in
'in/to France'

- Questions
  - Since most interrogative sentences contain one of a set of interrogative enclitic markers (=*pa*, =*piko* and, less frequently, others), a closing interrogative mark (?) is used only if none of these markers appear.

Mba'e ere? Eremi jey pe ere vaekue?
mba'e   ere   ere-mi   jey   pe   ere   va'ekue
what   2SG.ACT.say   2SG.ACT.say-PLEAD   again   that   2SG.ACT.say   PAST
'What did you say? Say again what you said?'

Sometimes an opening interrogative mark (¿) is used, similar to the convention for Spanish.

¿Ha moõ rupi ñambopila?
ha   moõ=rupi   ña-mbo-pila
and   where=through   1PL.INCL.ACT-MAKE1-battery
'And where does one put the batteries?'

The inconsistencies found in the orthographic rendering of Guarani from different texts can be challenging unless one has a substantial familiarity with the language. To help learners and scholars engage with a broad range of materials, the following table summarizes the most common discrepancies between the orthography used in this book and that found in other sources.

Deviations from the norms adopted in this book	Non-standard example found in other texts	Normalized example
Use of <x> instead of <ch>	*xe* 'I'	*che*
Use of <j> instead of <h>	*ja* 'and'	*ha*
Use of <jh> instead of <h>	*jha* 'and'	*ha*
Use of <y> instead of <j>	*yuka* 'to kill'	*juka*

Use of \<b> instead of \<v>	aba 'indigenous man, person'	ava
Use of \<w> instead of \<v>	howy 'blue'	hovy
Use of \<c> instead of \<k>	añangareco 'I take care of'	añangareko
Use of \<c> instead of \<s>	tacê 'cry'	tasẽ
Use of \<ç> instead of \<s>	guaçu 'big'	guasu
Use of \<ĭ> instead of \<y>	guĭpe 'under'	guype
Use of \< - > instead of \< ' >	ka-i 'monkey'	ka'i
Use of \< ˆ > instead of \< ˜ >	aguî 'near'	aguĩ
Use of \< ¨ > instead of \< ˜ >	'ÿ 'without'	'ỹ
Use of \<˘> instead of \< ˜ >	tĭ 'nose'	tĩ
Use of \<gü> instead of \<gu>	ichugüi 'from him/her'	ichugui
Use of \<gw> instead of \<gu>	gwarani 'from him/her'	guarani
Use of \<qu> instead of \<ku>	quarepotitĩ 'silver'	kuarepotitĩ
Use of \<qu> instead of \<k>	aque 'I sleep'	ake
Redundant use of \<g̃> and \<ã>	hag̃uã 'for'	haguã or hag̃ua
Overmarking of nasality	põrã 'good'	porã
	ãguĩ / ag̃uĩ 'near'	aguĩ
Unattached person prefixes	che kane'õ 'I am tired'	chekane'õ
	nde juka 'he killed you'	ndejuka
Unattached bisyllabic postpositions / enclitics	che ndive 'with me'	chendive
	mymba kuéra '(domesticated) animals'	mymbakuéra
Use of Spanish stress marking conventions	che aiporuva pe kysé 'I am in the habit of using that knife'	che aiporúva pe kyse

3
Nominals

This chapter introduces Guarani nouns, their modifiers (for example, adjectives) and their determiners (for example, articles, numerals, quantifiers, demonstratives). We must note that whereas there is clear evidence for distinguishing a class of nouns separate from a class of verbs, most roots have very flexible behaviour, being able to function as different word classes depending on the sentence context in which they appear.

3.1 Nouns

Nouns are often defined as words that identify people, places or things. As mentioned in **1.5**, most roots can function as different word classes, so that a word like *karu* can mean 'food' (and therefore would be a noun), but it can also mean 'to eat' (in which case it would be a verb), or 'gluttonous' (in which case it would be an adjective). It is therefore of utmost importance to try to define the class of nouns independently from what a particular root refers to, but rather based on what kinds of morphemes it can combine with and how it can function in a sentence. Guarani nouns do not have different declension classes. Since Guarani is an agglutinative language that does not mark gender or number obligatorily, nouns do not have extensive inflectional paradigms that can help identify them either.

Given this, we will consider a Guarani root to be a noun if it can:

1. appear with the plural enclitic =*kuéra* (***koty**kuéra* 'rooms') or the multitudinal enclitic =*eta*/=*ita* that serves to pluralize uncountable nouns (***kamby**eta* 'lots of milk')
2. appear with the nominal tense/aspect markers -*kue* (past tense/post-stative aspect; ***koty**kue* 'former room') and -*rã* (future tense/destinative aspect; ***koty**rã* 'future room'; ***mena**rã* 'boyfriend, fiancé (literally, 'future husband')')

3. appear with inactive personal markers to express a relation of possession inside the noun phrase (*che**koty*** 'my room')
4. be the main word (**head**) in the complement of a postposition (***koty*** *guasúpe* 'in the big room')
5. appear with the derivational suffix *-'o* that creates verbs (***pire'****o* 'to skin').

Noun phrases are constituents of the sentence whose **head** (or **nucleus**; that is, the obligatory element that everything else in the phrase relates to) is a noun. Noun phrases in Guarani can consist of a single noun, or of a noun accompanied by **determiners** (demonstratives, numerals, and so on) and **modifiers** (adjectives, relative clauses). The noun can also appear with attached affixes or enclitics.

***Kuarahy** overa ko'ãga.*
kuarahy	o-vera	ko'ãga
sun	3.ACT-shine	now

'The sun is shining now.'

***Pe karai** ome'ẽ **so'o** itajýrape.*
pe	karai	o-me'ẽ	so'o	i-tajýra=pe
that	gentleman	3.ACT-give	meat	3.INACT-daughter.of.man=in

'That gentleman gives meat to his daughter.'

*Chegustaite **la yvoty regueruva'ekue** chéve.*
che-gusta-ite	la	yvoty	re-gueru-va'e-kue	chéve
1SG.INACT-please-very	DET.SG	flower	2SG.ACT-bring-ADJZ-POST	to.me

'I like a lot the flower that you brought (to) me.'

Generally, the order of the constituents of the noun phrase is as follows. Since all of the elements, except the head noun, are optional, they are indicated within parentheses.

(determiner/demonstrative/numeral/quantifier) + (possessor) + head noun + (modifying adjective) + (modifying relative clause)

Note in particular that the order **possessor-possessum** (that is, the noun that possesses comes before the noun that is possessed) and the order noun-relative clause are the same in Guarani as in English. The noun-adjective order in Guarani, however, is the reverse to English.

ko jagua ñarõ (demonstrative + head noun + adjective)
ko　　　　jagua　ñarõ
PROX.SG　dog　ferocious
'this ferocious dog'

mayma kuña oikuaáva (quantifier + head noun + relative clause)
mayma　kuña　　oi-kuaa-va
every　　woman　3.ACT-know-ADJZ
'all the women that know (it)'

mitã'i po ky'a (possessor + head noun + adjective)
mitã-'i　　po　　ky'a
child-DIM　hand　dirty
'the small child's dirty hand(s)'

*Che areko **ko'ã mbohapy kuatiañe'ẽ puku rehaiva'ekue**.*
(demonstrative + numeral + head noun + adjective + relative clause)
che　a-reko　　　　ko'ã　　mbohapy　kuatia+ñe'ẽ　　puku
I　　1SG.ACT-have　PROX.PL　three　　　paper+language　long
re-h-ai-va'e-kue
2SG.ACT-POSSM3-write-ADJZ-POST
'I have these three letters that you wrote.'

3.1.1 Plural marking

The marking of number, specifically plural number, is less frequent in Guarani than it is in English. Countable nouns can be made plural by the enclitic =*kuéra* (with nasal variant =*nguéra* if it attaches to a nasal word). This is usually done mostly for animate nouns (referring to people or animals) or when it is crucial to indicate plurality; otherwise, plural marking can generally be omitted.

*arai**kuéra** ha mbyja**kuéra***
arai=kuéra　ha　　mbyja=kuéra
cloud=PL　　and　star=PL
'(the) clouds and (the) stars'

*oremenarã**nguéra** tẽra penerembirekorã**nguéra***
ore-mena-rã=nguéra　　　　　　　　tẽra　pene-r-embireko-rã=nguéra
1PL.EXCL.INACT-husband-DEST=PL　or　　2PL.INACT-POSSM-wife-DEST=PL
'our fiancés or your fiancées'

kuña mbarete
kuña   mbarete
woman   strong
'(a) strong woman' or 'strong women'

Kuña imbarete.
kuña   i-mbarete
woman   3.INACT-strong
'The woman is strong.' / 'Women are strong.'

Plural number is generally not marked when the noun is accompanied by a numeral or by a determiner that already indicates plurality, but it is sometimes used by speakers, even when not necessary.

mokõi jyva
mokõi   jyva
two   arm
'two arms'

ko'ã óga
ko'ã   óga
PROX.PL   house
'these houses'

heta mymba
h-eta   mymba
POSSM3-numerous   domesticated.animal
'many (farm) animals'

*ko'ã ta'anga**kuéra***
ko'ã   t-a'anga=kuéra
PROX.PL   NPOSSM-image=PL
'these image<u>s</u>'

The stressed multitudinal plural enclitic =*eta* (the variant used when the previous vowel is closed) or =*ita* (the variant used when the previous vowel is mid or open) indicates a substantial number of the type of individual that is indicated by the noun. It can also be used to make uncountable nouns plural.

panambieta
panambi=eta
butterfly=multitude
'(a great) many butterflies'

kypy'yeta
kypy'y=eta
younger.sister.of.a.woman=multitude
'(a great) many younger sisters (of a woman)'

yvoty morotĩeta, yvoty pytãita
yvoty   morotĩ=eta   yvoty   pytã=ita
flower white=multitude flower red=multitude
'(a great) many white flowers, (a great) many red flowers'

kambyeta
kamby=eta
milk=multitude
'lots of milk'

Guarani has two collective plural suffixes that indicate a place where something is abundant: stressed *-ty* (*-ndy* with nasal bases) to indicate abundance of plants, minerals or objects in general, and stressed *-kua* to indicate abundance of animals and people. This latter, however, seems to survive mostly in place names (**toponyms**), and is not in general use in the modern language.

pakovaty   *ñanandy*
pakova-ty   ñana-ndy
banana-collective weed-collective
'banana grove'   'scrubland'

avatity   *yvaty*
avati-ty   yva-ty
corn-collective   fruit-collective
'cornfield'   'orchard'

aoty   *yvotyty*
ao-ty   yvoty-ty
clothes-collective   flower-collective
'a bunch of clothes, a set of clothes'   'garden, park'

*petỹ**ndy*   *kuaa**ty*
petỹ-ndy   kuaa-ty
tobacco-collective know-collective
'tobacco field'   'science'

*jaguarete**kua*   *guasu**kua*
jaguarete-kua   guasu-kua
jaguar-group   deer-group
'a place with many jaguars' 'a place with many deer'

3.1.2 Gender marking

Like English nouns, Guarani nouns do not have inherent gender. When necessary, gender can be marked by adding *kuña* 'woman' or *kuimba'e* 'man' to a noun.

*memby**kuña*
memby+kuña
child.of.woman+woman
'daughter (of a woman)'

*jagua**kuña*
jagua+kuña
dog+woman
'<u>female</u> dog'

*oĩmboyve yvy ape'ári **ava kuimba'e**, ndaipóri avei **ava kuña***
oĩ=mboyve   yvy   ape='ári   ava   kuimba'e ndaipóri
there.is=before Earth surface=upon person man   there.is.not
avei ava   kuña
also person woman
'before there were <u>men</u> on the Earth, or <u>women</u> either'

Given the lack of obligatory number and gender marking, compared to other languages like English or Spanish, nouns in Guarani are largely invariable. However, in **3.1.3** I will introduce an important class that is an exception to this.

3.1.3 Relational (multiform) nominal roots

An interesting particularity of Tupi-Guarani languages is that they have lexical roots (by and large nouns, but also some verbs and adjectives) whose initial consonant changes. This change depends on whether they enter into a relation with another word in the sentence or with a prefix. I call these **relational roots**. (In traditional scholastic grammars one will find them called "oscillating roots", "triform roots", "aspirated roots" or "roots with varying initial".) The initial consonant of these roots is itself a prefix that varies between *t-*, *h-* and *r-*.

For nouns the *t-* form is used when the noun is not preceded by another noun that indicates its possessor. It is the **absolute** or **non-possessed** form (glossed in examples as NPOSSM).

tayhu** váicha arandu, peteĩha **tayhu
t-ayhu   váicha arandu peteĩ-ha t-ayhu
NPOSSM-love seems wisdom one-TH NPOSSM-love
'<u>love</u> (that is) like wisdom, first <u>love</u>'

*Ndepa nandegustái ko **ta'anga**.*
nde=pa   na-nde-gusta-i   ko   t-a'anga
you.SG=Q NEG-2SG.INACT-please-NEG PROX.SG NPOSSM-image
'You don't like this <u>photo</u>?'

*añorairõ **tymba** ñarõndive*
a-ño-rairõ   t-ymba   ñarõ=ndive
1SG.ACT-RECP-attack NPOSSM-animal wild=with
'I fight/fought with wild animals'

The other two forms are used when the noun is a possessum (that is, understood as being possessed). The *h-* form (glossed in examples as POSSM3) functions like 'his', 'her', 'its' or 'their' in English; that is, it indicates a pronominal third-person possessor, singular or plural.

***Hesa** iporãiterei.*
h-esa   i-porã-iterei
POSSM3-eye 3.INACT-beautiful-very.much
'<u>His/Her/Its/Their eyes</u> are really beautiful.'

Héra ha'e Susána.
h-éra ha'e Susána
POSSM3-name be Susana
'Her name is Susana.'

Che aikuaa hembirekópe.
che ai-kuaa h-embireko=pe
I 1SG.ACT-know POSSM3-wife=in
'Me, I know his wife.'

omombaretehaguã hetekuéra
o-mo-mbarete=haguã h-ete=kuéra
3.ACT-MAKE1-strong=for 3.INACT-body=PL
'in order to make his/her/its/their body stronger'

The remaining form, the *r*- form (glossed POSSM in the examples), is used in all other cases. Notably, it is used with possessors that are full noun phrases and with first and second person inactive prefixes that indicate possession.

Lili rague
Lili r-ague
Lili POSSM-hair
'Lili's hair'

Ndahejaséi cheretã.
nd-a-h-eja-se-i che-r-etã
NEG-1SG.ACT-POSSM3-leave-want-NEG 1SG.INACT-POSSM-country
'I do not want to leave my country.'

nderajy ratypy
nde-r-ajy r-atypy
2SG.INACT-POSSM-daughter.of.man POSSM-cheek
'your daughter's cheeks' (said to a man)

Note how all three forms differ in use and meaning in the following example:

Henda niko tayhu renda.
h-enda niko t-ayhu r-enda
POSSM3-place VERD NPOSSM-love POSSM-place
'(I tell you) His/Her/Their place is the place of love.'

Another particularly clear example of the importance of using these relational prefixes appropriately is provided by the name for the creator of the world in the Mbyá Guarani cosmogony and mythology, *Ñanderu Tenonde*, meaning 'Our Father, the first'. Note that the use of the *t-* non-relational prefix indicates that *tenonde* 'the first' is in apposition to *ñanderu* 'our father'. If *renonde* had been used, the interpretation would have been that *-enonde* 'front' functions as a modifier or a possessed noun.

*Ñanderu **T**enonde*
ñande-r-u   t-enonde
1PL.INCL.INACT-POSSM-father   NPOSSM-front
'Our Father, the first'

*Ñanderu **r**enonde*
ñande-r-u   r-enonde
1PL.INCL.INACT-POSSM-father   POSSM-front
'Our Father's front' / 'in front of our father'

The following table summarizes the alternations for this most common pattern of relational nouns.

t-	h-	r-
tetyma '(a/the) leg'	*hetyma* 'his/her/its leg'	*che**r**etyma* 'my leg'
		*María **r**etyma* 'María's leg'
tupa '(a/the) bed'	*hupa* 'his/her/its bed'	*nde**r**upa* 'your bed'
		*chesy **r**upa* 'my mom's bed'
tesa '(an/the) eye(s)'	*hesa* 'his/her/its eye(s)'	*ñande**r**esa* 'our eyes'
		*mbo'ehára **r**esa* 'the teacher's eyes'
tova '(a/the) face'	*hova* 'his/her/its face'	*ore**r**ova* 'our face(s)'
		*hembireko **r**ova* 'his wife's face'

Points to note:

- Even though a great number of nouns beginning with *t, h* or *r* are relational, not all of them are (for example, the very frequent words *táva* 'town' or *ryguasu* 'hen, chicken' and the word *haru* 'spoil, damage' are not relational). It is not possible to predict from the meaning or shape of nouns which are relational, and which are not.
- Some verbs, adjectives, postpositions and even prefixes can also be triform (be on the lookout for examples in the relevant sections).

NOMINALS   65

- When some prefixes are added to these roots, the initial consonant is lost (for example, *t-aku* 'heat' > *mby-aku* 'to heat something'). This clearly indicates that the initial consonant is not part of the root but functions like a removable prefix.
- A few relational roots lack a prefix for non-possessed, absolute uses:

    óga/hóga/róga 'house' (not **tóga*)
    ovetã/hovetã/rovetã 'window' (not **tovetã*)
    okẽ/hokẽ/rokẽ 'door' (not **tokẽ*)
- Some kinship terms have the following different paradigm, often called "biform", instead of the regular "triform" pattern:

Non-possessed	Third-person pronominal possessor	First-/second-person possessor or noun phrase possessor	
túva	*itúva* (not **húva*)	*ru* (not **rúva*)	'father'
ta'ýra	*ita'ýra* (not **ha'ýra*)	*ra'y* (not **ra'ýra*)	'son (of a father)'
tajýra	*itajýra* (not **hajýra*)	*rajy* (not **rajýra*)	'daughter (of a father)'

- This pattern is called "biform" because there are two forms, *túva* and *ru*, with the remaining form being obtained by regular prefixation of the third-person inactive prefix *i-* (see **3.6** for more details of how this works).
- A small number of relational roots have four forms. For example, for the root *-o'o*, the triform set denotes **inalienably possessed** flesh (that is, the flesh in someone's or some animal's body); the "extra", irregular form *so'o* denotes **alienably possessed** flesh; that is, meat bought for consumption, for example.

ho'o
h-o'o
POSSM3-flesh
'his/her/its flesh'

vaka ro'o
vaka r-o'o
cow   POSSM-flesh
'cow's meat; beef'

to'o
t-o'o
NPOSSM-flesh
'flesh (in a body)'

so'o
so'o
meat
'meat (for consumption)'

Similarly, for the root *-ymba,* the triform set denotes an animal in general, whereas the "extra", irregular form *mymba* denotes domesticated animals. Another example is the root *-enimbo*. The triform set is used when the creator of a thread is referenced or alluded to, or is understood to be relevant in the discourse (for example, a thread understood as a spider's thread); the "extra", irregular form *inimbo* does not reference the creator of the thread.

henimbo
h-enimbo
POSSM3-thread
'his/her/its thread'

ñandu renimbo
ñandu   r-enimbo
spider   POSSM3-thread
'(a) spider's web'

tenimbo
t-enimbo
NPOSSM-thread
'thread' (as created by someone or something)

inimbo
inimbo
thread
'thread' (without reference, even implicit, to the creator of the thread)

The difference between *tenimbo* and *inimbo* in the last series of examples is difficult to grasp. The reader may want to refer to

3.2.1.2.1, where the difference between the prefix *t-embi-* and the suffix *-py* to form nouns is discussed, since there is a certain similarity to this case.

- The nouns related by the *r-* prefix are usually in a possessor-possessum relation, but this need not be the case, since the relationship can be different from what we consider strict possession. For example, the relationship can be "origin" or "source":

hetyma ry'ái
h-etyma   r-y'ái
POSSM3-leg POSSM-sweat
'perspiration <u>from</u> his/her leg'

The relationship between the nouns can be "whole-part":

tupa retyma
t-upa   r-etyma
NPOSSM-bed POSSM-leg
'a/the bed'<u>s</u> leg(s)'

The relationship between the nouns can also be "habitat":

ka'aguy rymba tẽra óga rymba
ka'aguy   r-ymba   tẽra óga   r-ymba
forest   POSSM-animal or   house POSSM-animal
'forest animal(s) or house animal(s)'

In fact, for any relation that can be expressed by juxtaposition of nouns, if the second noun is relational, it will be marked by *r-*. For example, when a noun root is used as an adjective to modify another noun, it will appear with *r-*.

yvága rovy
yvága r-ovy
sky   POSSM-blue
'(a/the) blue sky'

jasy renyhẽ
jasy   r-enyhẽ
moon   POSSM-full
'(a/the) full moon'

> *kuñataĩ rory*
> kuñataĩ r-ory
> young.girl POSSM-joy
> '(a/the) joyous girl'

A fuller list of relational roots and morphemes is given in **17.5** for completeness and ease of reference.

3.1.4 Functions of noun phrases in a sentence

Noun phrases can have one of the following functions in a sentence:

Subject of a predicate
Subjects require no special marking or special position in Guarani. They can come before or after the main verb.

> ***Tahyikuéra** omanomba.*
> tahyi=kuéra o-mano-mba
> ant=PL 3.ACT-die-all
> 'The ants all died.'

> *Ñandejukapa **pe ñati'ũ**.*
> ñande-juka-pa pe ñati'ũ
> 1PL.INCL.INACT-kill-all MED.SG mosquito
> 'That mosquito will kill us all.'

> *¿Mba'épa oguerekóne **pe jagua** iñapytu'ũme?*
> mba'e=pa o-guereko-ne pe jagua iñ-apytu'ũ=me
> what=Q 3.ACT-have-DUB MED.SG dog 3.INACT-mind=in
> 'What can that dog be thinking . . . ?' (literally, 'What does that dog have in its mind?')

Direct object of a predicate
Direct objects do not require special marking either, except when they refer to a human participant. In that case they are marked with the enclitic postposition =*pe/=me* (see **5.1**).

> *Cheru ojukapáta **tahyikuéra**.*
> che-r-u o-juka-pa-ta tahýi=kuéra
> 1SG.INACT-POSSM-father 3.ACT-kill-all-FUT ant=PL
> 'My father will kill all the ants.'

*Cheru ohayhu **chesýpe***.
che-r-u　　　　　　　　o-h-ayhu　　　　　　　che-sy=pe
1SG.INACT-POSSM-father　3.ACT-POSSM3-love　1SG.INACT-mother=in
'My father loves <u>my mother</u>.'

Complement of a postposition

Relationships that are indicated in English by means of prepositions, are usually indicated in Guarani by **postpositions**; that is, morphemes coming after a noun phrase. The noun phrases in these cases are the complement of the postposition (see **5** for more details).

*Oñangareko hikuái **nderógare***.
o-ñangareko　　　　　hikuái　nde-r-óga=re
3.ACT-take.care.of　they　　2SG.INACT-POSSM-house=at
'They take care of <u>your house</u>.'

*Eho **Peru jarýindive***.
e-ho　　Peru　jarýi=ndive
IMP-go　Peru　grandmother=with
'Go (you.sg) with <u>Pedro's grandmother</u>.'

Possessor

Noun phrases without any special marking can refer to possessors of another noun that follows. The juxtaposition of noun phrases is enough to ensure this relationship (see **3.6**).

***ko auto tuja** ovetã*
ko　　　　　auto　tuja　ovetã
PROX.SG　car　　old　　window
'<u>this old car's</u> window'

***tupão** okẽ*
tupão　　okẽ
church　door
'(a/the) <u>church</u> door'

3.2 Forming nouns from other words

Languages have devices to form words that are linked to other words in the language in a family of words (think of English 'act' > 'action' > 'actionable', or 'dog' > 'doggie'). These devices are part of a language's

derivational morphology (so called because the related words are derived from existing words). In this section I first look at how to convert a verb or adjective into a related noun (**nominalizations**). Then I show how to obtain **antonyms** (opposites) and **diminutives** of nouns.

3.2.1 Nominalizations

In order to allow a phrase that is not nominal to fulfil one of the noun phrase functions shown in **3.1.4**, Guarani uses **nominalizations**. **Lexical nominalizations** are nouns derived from non-nominal words or expressions. **Sentential nominalizations** (that is, mechanisms to make a sentence function as a noun) create relative and complement clauses and will be examined in **12.2**.

Guarani only has two clearly defined lexical parts of speech, nouns and verbs, and a very small class of adjectives (see **3.3**), so nominalizations in Guarani are mostly obtained from verbs. These are called **deverbal nouns** and are obtained using suffixes (**3.2.1.1**) or prefixes (**3.2.1.2**), depending on the meaning of the resulting noun. There are many different nominalizers in Guarani, as we will see in the following sections.

3.2.1.1 Nominalizing suffixes

3.2.1.1.1 General nominalizer -ha

This stressed nominalizing suffix (glossed NMLZ) forms nouns out of verbal roots. Some of these are called **instrumental nominalizations**, because they designate the instrument used to accomplish the action expressed by the base verb.

*hai**ha***	*jecha**ha***
h-ai-ha	je-h-echa-ha
POSSM3-write-NMLZ	AGD-POSSM3-see-NMLZ
'(a) pencil'	'(a) monitor'

It is important to note here that this suffix is also used as a subordinator (like English 'that'; see **12.2.2**):

Ha'e ndoikomo'ãiha.
ha'e   nd-o-iko-mo'ã-i-ha
I.say NEG-3.ACT-be-NEG.FUT-NEG-NMLZ
'I say that there will not be (one).'

ha'e peẽme ahániriha
ha'e peẽme ahániri-ha
I.say to.you.PL no-NMLZ
'I tell you that no'

Locative nominalizations denote places or times where an event happens. They are obtained by adding the stressed suffix *-ha* (glossed NMLZ. LOC) to a base intransitive predicate (that is, a predicate that takes a subject but no object) that expresses the event.

*jeroky**ha***	*ke**ha***	*guapy**ha***	*hecha**ha***
jeroky-ha	ke-ha	guapy-ha	h-echa-ha
dance-NMLZ.LOC	sleep-NMLZ.LOC	sit-NMLZ.LOC	POSSM3-see-NMLZ.LOC
'the dance party'	'bedroom'	'seat'	'lookout, vantage point'

There are nominalizations that designate the agent or instrument of an action indicated by the base transitive predicate (that is, a predicate that takes both a subject and an object). These are called **agentive nominalizations**, and use the stressed suffix *-ha* or *-hára* (both glossed as NMLZ. AG). *-Hára* usually denotes professions, and *-ha* instruments or tools, but there are exceptions.

*ñotỹ**hára***	*pohãno**hára***
ñotỹ-hára	pohãno-hára
plant.seed-NMLZ.AG	cure-NMLZ.AG
'farmer'	'healer, doctor'

*jo'o**ha***	*nupã**ha***	*monda**ha***
jo'o-ha	nupã-ha	monda-ha
dig-NMLZ.AG	hit-NMLZ.AG	steal-NMLZ.AG
'shovel'	'whip; riding crop'	'thief'

The combination of *-ha* with the suffix *-re* (an infrequently used mark of past tense for nouns; see **3.7**) gives a past agentive nominalizer *-hare*. The combination of *-ha* with the suffix *-rã*, which marks the future tense for nouns (see **3.7**), yields a future agentive nominalizer *-harã*.

*hecha**hare***
h-echa-ha-re
POSSM3-see-NMLZ.AG-POST
'witness' (literally, '(the) one who saw')

*ñande Apo**hare***
ñande-apo-ha-re
1PL.INCL.INACT-make-NMLZ.AG-POST
'our Maker' (literally, '(the) one who made us')

*óga apo**harã***
óga   apo-ha-rã
house   make-NMLZ.AG-DEST
'future house builder' / '(the) one who will make a/the house'

*hetaite xénte hecha**harã** ohova'ekue*
h-eta-ite   xénte   h-echa-ha-rã   o-ho-va'ekue
POSSM3-numerous-very people POSSM3-see-NMLZ.AG-DEST 3.ACT-go-PAST
'a great number of people went to see (it)' (literally, 'very many people that would be viewers went')

3.2.1.1.2 Passive *-py*

Other nominalizations derived from transitive predicates designate the patient of an event (the participant that receives an action). These are called **passive nominalizations**, and use the stressed suffixes *-py/-pýra* (glossed as NMLZ.PASS), with the nasal forms *-mby/mbýra* used after nasal bases. The past passive nominalizer *-pyre* and the future passive nominalizer *-pyrã* are formed like their agentive counterparts above.

*hecha**py***
h-echa-py
POSSM3-see-NMLZ.PASS
'visible'

*kañ**mby***
kañy-mby
hide-NMLZ.PASS
'hidden'

*guerovia**py** / jerovia**py***
guerovia-py / jerovia-py
believe-NMLZ.PASS / believe-NMLZ.PASS
'belief' (literally, '(that which is) believed')

These nominalizations can have noun or adjective uses:

*Ehai **haipyre** pytyvõrãva*
e-h-ai   h-ai-py-re   pytyvõ-rã-va
IMP-POSSM3-write   POSSM3-write-NMLZ.PASS-POST   help-DEST-ADJZ
'Write help <u>articles</u>' (literally, 'Write <u>a written thing</u> that will be of help')

Kóva kuatia haipyre.
ko-va   kuatia   h-ai-py-re
PROX.SG-ADJZ text   POSSM3-write-NMLZ.PASS-POST
'This is a written text.'

*Guerovia**py** poravo**pyre**.*
guerovia-py   poravo-py-re
believe-NMLZ.PASS   choose-NMLZ.PASS-POST
'Selected beliefs.'

*Ñanereta rembiapo**pyrã***
ñane-r-etã   r-embi-apo-py-rã
1PL.INCL.INACT-POSSM-country   POSSM-NMLZ.REL-make-NMLZ.PASS-DEST
'Our government's <u>projects</u>' (literally, '<u>thing that will be the result of work</u>')

3.2.1.1.3 Adjectival *-va*

The basic role of the unstressed suffix *-va* is to create adjectives (it is an **adjectivizer**). By extension, since relative clauses are clauses that function as adjectives modifying a noun, this suffix can create relative clauses. These functions are discussed more fully in **3.3** and **12.2.1**. Here we show that *-va* can also function as a nominalizer to create the demonstrative pronouns *kó(v)a* 'this <u>thing</u>', *pé(v)a* 'that <u>thing</u> (around here)', *upé(v)a* 'that <u>thing</u> (over there)', and so on, obtained from the demonstrative determiners *ko* 'this', *pe* 'that (around here)' and *upe* 'that (over there)' (see **3.4.2**). This permeability between adjective uses and noun uses is very typical of Guarani, and is another indication that there is not as large a difference between these two word classes as in English.

*Umí**va** ojapo ko'ã**va**.*
umi-va   o-japo   ko'ã-va
NPROX.PL-ADJZ   3.ACT-make   PROX.PL-ADJZ
'Those (people) did these (things).'

Kóva, ko arriéro, Perurima oje'eha, ko'áğa he'íta peẽme añetetéva.
| kó-va | ko | arriéro | Perurima | o-je'e-ha | ko'áğa |
| PROX.SG-ADJZ | PROX.SG | peasant | Perurima | 3.ACT-is.said-NMLZ | now |

| he'i-ta | peẽme | añete-te-va |
| says-FUT | to.you.PL | truth-very-ADJZ |

'This one, this man that is called Perurima, he will now tell you (pl.) the very truth.'

Ani ejapo péva!
| ani | e-japo | pe-va |
| NEG.IMP | IMP-make | MED.SG-ADJZ |

'Don't do that!'

3.2.1.1.4 Abstract -*kue*

Other nominalizations based on adjectives (**deadjectival nominalizations**) or even on other nouns (**denominal nominalizations**) use the suffix -*kue* to designate abstract qualities (-*ngue* is used with nasal bases).

hepy 'expensive' > *hepykue* 'cost'
ky'a 'dirty' > *ky'akue* 'dirtiness'
kyra 'fat' > *kyrakue* '(the) fat, grease, lard; obesity'
mbarete 'strong' > *mbaretekue* 'strength'
puku 'long' > *pukukue* 'length'
porã 'beautiful' > *porãngue* 'beauty'
tuja 'old' > *tujakue* 'old age'
ty'ái 'sweat' > *ty'aikue* 'sacrifice'
vai 'ugly' > *vaikue* 'ugliness'

This stressed suffix -*kue* can also be used to nominalize whole predicates (that is, not just a verb, but a verb plus person markers):

okykue (from *oky* 'it rains')
o-ky-kue
3.ACT-rain-NMLZ.ABS
'rainfall'

iñarandukue (from *iñarandu* 's/he is educated')
iñ-arandu-kue
3.INACT-knowledge-NMLZ.ABS
'education'

*iñakãpohyi**kue*** (from *iñakãpohýi* 'their heavy head' / 'they have heavy heads')
iñ-akã+pohýi-kue
3.INACT-head+heavy-NMLZ.ABS
'the weight of their head'

The following examples serve as a summary of the different meanings of the nominalizing suffixes presented so far.

*su'u**ha***
su'u-ha
bite-NMLZ.AG
'something that bites'

*su'u**kue***
su'u-kue
bite-NMLZ.ABS
'(a/the) bite'

*su'u**py***
su'u-py
bite-NMLZ.PASS
'edible'

*su'u**pyrã***
su'u-py-rã
bite-NMLZ.PASS-DEST
'snack'

*su'u**pyre***
su'u-py-re
bite-NMLZ.PASS-POST
'bitten'

*su'ú**va***
su'u-va
bite-ADJZ
'that is/was bitten'

3.2.1.2 Nominalizing prefixes

3.2.1.2.1 Resultative/instrumental *t-embi-*

T-embi- is a nominalizing prefix that is used with transitive predicates. The resulting noun designates the object of the transitive predicate from which it is derived. The meaning is sometimes the result of the event (**resultative**), sometimes the instrument used to carry out an action (**instrumental**). Note that this prefix is relational/triform (hence glossed NMLZ.REL), composed of a first segment that can be *t-*, *r-* or *h-*, and of the nominalizing part *-embi-* (or *-emi-* for nasal bases).

tembi'u
t-embi-'u
NPOSSM-NMLZ.REL-ingest
'food' (literally, 'something that is ingest<u>ed</u>')

temimbo'e
t-emi-mbo'e
NPOSSM-NMLZ.REL-teach
'disciple' (literally, 'someone who is taught')

tembiporu
t-embi-poru
NPOSSM-NMLZ.REL-use
'utensil, tool' (literally, 'something that is use<u>d</u>')

tembiapo
t-embi-apo
NPOSSM-NMLZ.REL-make
'work' (literally, 'something that is ma<u>de</u>')

*Ahechaga'u ne**rembi'u**.*
a-h-echaga'u   ne-r-embi-'u
1SG.ACT-POSSM3-nostalgia   2SG.INACT-POSSM-NMLZ.REL-ingest
'I miss your <u>cooking</u>.' (Literally, 'I miss your <u>food</u>.')

*Ko'ã ta'angakuéra Quino **rembiapo**kue.*
ko'ã   t-a'anga=kuéra   Quino   r-embi-apo-kue
PROX.PL   NPOSSM-image=PL   Quino   POSSM-NMLZ.REL-make-POST
'These comics were made by Quino.' (Literally, 'These images are Quino's <u>work</u>.')

Notably, nouns derived by -*embi*- are generally already fixed in the language (**lexicalized**), and they sometimes have a meaning that is not directly derivable from the meaning of the parts (**non-compositional meaning**).

***tembi*reko**	ne***rembi*reko**	h***embi*reko**
t-embi-reko	ne-r-embi-reko	h-embi-reko
NPOSSM-NMLZ.REL-have	2SG.INACT-POSSM-NMLZ.REL-have	POSSM3-NMLZ.REL-have
'(a) wife'	'your wife'	'his wife'

Lexicalized words usually appear in the dictionary as independent words, without any reference to their component parts. When their meaning is compositional, I will identify their parts in the gloss for completeness.

The two passive nominalizers for transitive predicates, the prefix -*embi*- and the suffix -*py*, are very similar. However, -*embi*- is used to link the verb and its result or object to the agent of the action, whereas -*py* is used when the sole focus is on the object or patient. That is why many nominalizations with -*embi*- have a "tool" or "means" reading that is similar to an agentive meaning. This is also why -*embi*- is a relational prefix as well: it needs to relate the passive noun to the agent. This difference in whether the nominalization is **agent-oriented** or **patient-oriented** is clear in the following example. *Mombe'upy* 'legend' designates something told without reference to who did the telling; *rembihai* '(written) work, writings', on the other hand, designates the result of someone's action of writing (Shakespeare's, in this case).

Peteĩ **mombe'upy** *he'i Shakespeare* **rembihai** *osẽ'ỹva araresáre oñeñotỹhague hendive* . . .

peteĩ	mombe'u-py	he'i	Shakespeare	r-embi-h-ai
one	tell-NMLZ.PASS	says	Shakespeare	POSSM-NMLZ.REL-POSSM3-write

o-sẽ-'ỹ-va	ára-r-esa=re	o-ñe-ñotỹ-hague
3.ACT-go.out-PRIV-ADJZ	day-POSSM-eye=at	3.ACT-AGD-bury-NMLZ.PAST

hendive . . .
with.him/her

'A <u>legend</u> says that Shakespeare's unpublished <u>works</u> lie with him in his tomb . . . ' (more literally, 'A <u>legend</u> says that Shakespeare's <u>writings</u> that did not see the light of day were buried with him . . . ')

In other words, the use of *tembi*- or -*py* depends on the perspective adopted by the speaker with respect to what is designated by the nominalization: if the concept nominalized includes a role for the agent participant, then *-embi-* is appropriate. If no such role is conceptualized, then *-py* is appropriate. Such differences in conceptualization can perhaps be rendered in the translations as follows: ***tembi**hai* '(someone's) writing; written (by someone)' versus *hai**py*** '(something) writ<u>ten</u>'. Yet, although this difference may survive in current usage, as mentioned above many of these derived words are now lexicalized, and have developed specialized meanings.

Note that *-embi-* and *-py* can be combined in a single word:

*che**rembi**ayhu**py***
che-r-embi-ayhu-py
1SG.INACT-POSSM-NMLZ.REL-love-NMLZ.PASS
'my beloved' (literally, 'my love<u>d</u> <u>by someone</u>')

tembi**apouka**py
t-embi-apo-uka-py
NPOSSM-NMLZ.REL-make-MAKE2-NMLZ.PASS
'commandment' (literally, 'ma<u>de</u> to do <u>by someone</u>')

*h**emi**ñongatu**py***
h-emi-ñongatu-py
POSSM3-NMLZ.REL-put.away-NMLZ.PASS
'their hidden things' (literally, '<u>been put away</u> <u>by someone</u>')

3.2.1.2.2 Reflexive/passive/impersonal *je-*

Je-/ñe- is another nominalizing prefix used with both transitive and intransitive predicates to express a person or animal's doing or state expressed by the root's meaning. This prefix has many uses, including as a marker of passive voice or reflexives (see **6.3**).

***j**evy'a*
je-vy'a
AGD-rejoice
'happi<u>ness</u>'

***j**eka'u*
je-ka'u
AGD-get.drunk
'drunken<u>ness</u>'

*je*ke
je-ke
AGD-sleep
'(a/the) sleep'

*ñe*mopotĩ
ñe-mo-potĩ
AGD-MAKE1-clean
'(a) clea<u>n</u>ing'

Ogutaiterei ichupe la ñembyepoti.
o-guta-iterei　　　　ichupe　　la　　ñe-mby-epoti
3.ACT-please-very.much　to.him/her　DET.SG　AGD-MAKE1-excrement
'S/he loves <u>to clobber (people)</u>.'

. . . ohekávo je'upyrã hasývapeguarã
o-h-eka-vo　　　　　je-'u-py-rã　　　　　　　　h-asy-va=pe=guarã
3.ACT-POSSM3-seek-while　AGD-ingest-NMLZ.PASS-DEST　POSSM3-sickness-ADJZ=in=for

' . . . looking for <u>something to eat</u> for the sick' (literally, *je-'u-py-rã* '(something) destined to be eaten')

3.2.1.2.3 Reciprocal *jo-*

Jo-/ño-, on the other hand, marks reciprocal actions (like English 'each other' or 'one another'; see **6.4**). When used as a nominalizing prefix, it expresses a mutual action derived from the root's meaning. An alternate form of this prefix is often *ju-/ñu-*, when the root begins in a vowel.

*jo*poi
jo-poi
RECP-let.go
'separation'

*ño*pytyvõ
ño-pytyvõ
RECP-help
'mutual help'

*ju*asaha
ju-asa-ha
RECP-to.cross-NMLZ.LOC
'detour'

*Oĩ **jo**avy ha **ño**rairõ.* (also ***ju**avy*)
oĩ　　　　jo-avy　　ha　　ño-rairõ
there.is　RECP-err　and　RECP-attack
'There are disagreements and fights.'

3.2.1.2.4 Abstract *t-eko-*

A prefix with a more abstract meaning, *t-eko-* forms nouns designating qualities. As a noun, *-eko* is relational and means 'life, character, culture, essence'. Note in the translations the variety of suffixes that can fulfil a similar function in English.

***teko**irũ*
t-eko-irũ
NPOSSM-NMLZ.QUAL-friend
'comrade<u>ship</u>'

***teko**asy*
t-eko-asy
NPOSSM-NMLZ.QUAL-pain
'suffer<u>ing</u>'

***teko**'avy*
t-eko-'avy
NPOSSM-NMLZ.QUAL-err
'immoral<u>ity</u>'

***teko**guata*
t-eko-guata
NPOSSM-NMLZ.QUAL-walk
'wander<u>ing</u>; rest<u>less(ness)</u>'

***teko**guapy*
t-eko-guapy
NPOSSM-NMLZ.QUAL-sit
'tranquill<u>ity</u>'

***teko**ayhu*
t-eko-ayhu
NPOSSM-NMLZ.QUAL-love
'friend<u>ship</u>'

***teko*mbo'e**
t-eko-mbo'e
NPOSSM-NMLZ.QUAL-teach
'educa<u>tion</u>'

3.2.1.2.5 Abstract *mba'e-*

A final prefix, also used to form abstract nouns with a passive-like meaning, is *mba'e-*. Of note, *mba'e* is a noun that means 'thing', a meaning that is somewhat present in the uses of this item as a grammatical morpheme (see here, and also **3.5**, **4.10.3.3**, and **6.5**).

mba'embyasy
mba'e-mby-asy
NMLZ.ABS.P-MAKE1-pain
'sad<u>ness</u>'

Mba'e- often seems to refer to the abstract concept corresponding to the verbal root.

chemba'epota, chemba'epochy
che-mba'e-pota   che-mba'e-pochy
1SG.INACT-NMLZ.ABS.P-desire   1SG.INACT-NMLZ.ABS.P-anger
'my desire, my anger'

It is possible that *mba'e-* is specialized for the expression of abstract feelings or sensations. But note that the meaning 'sadness' can be conveyed by ***mba'embyasy***, but also by ***ñembyasy*** and ***temimbyasy***. Determining the exact differences in meaning and use of these different affixes requires further research on nominalizations.

3.2.1.3 Noun compounds

A **noun compound** is a word composed of two roots that functions as a noun. Usually, the first root is a noun, while the second root can be a noun, verb or modifier. Occasionally, it is the second root that is a noun. Composition is indicated in the glosses with a plus sign (+). This is a common way to form nouns in Guarani, which then become lexicalized. It is a strategy used to form academic neologisms as well. (See also **verb compounds** in **4.13**.)

Noun + noun compounds

angirũ
áng(a)+irũ
soul+friend
'friend'

ka'ay
ka'a+y
mate.leaf+water
'mate' (*Ilex Paraguaiensis* infusion)

pirapire
pira+pire
fish+leather
'money'

uvãkangue
uvã+kangue
thigh+bone
'femur'

hyakuãvu
hyakuã+vu
smell+ferment
'strong smell'

arayvoty
ára+yvoty
day+flower
'(the) spring' (literally, 'flower time')

avañe'ẽ
ava+ñe'ẽ
person+speech
'Guarani (language)'

pyao
py+ao
foot+clothes
'sock(s)'

NOMINALS

Noun + modifier

tovamokõi
t-ova+mokõi
NPOSSM-face+two
'hypocrisy'

mitãporã
mitã+porã
child+beautiful
'pretty child'

mitãrusu
mitã+rusu
child+grown
'adolescent'

tyeguasu
t-ye+guasu
NPOSSM-belly+big
'pregnancy'

py'amirĩ
py'a+mirĩ
chest+small
'coward'

avatimirĩ
avati+mirĩ
corn+small
'wheat'

Noun + verb

py'aguapy
py'a+guapy
chest+sit
'peace'

Verb + noun

guatapu
guata+pu
walk+noise
'sound of footsteps'

Keeping in mind that the difference between nouns and adjectives in Guarani is tenuous, there are also compounds that mostly function as adjectives (**adjective compounds**).

Noun + modifier

nambisakã
nambi+sakã
ear+transparent
'malnourished'

hekomirĩ
h-eko+mirĩ
POSSM3-essence+small
'modest'

3.2.2 Nominal/adjectival negation

This section concerns itself with lexical negation; that is, how to obtain a noun that is in some sense the negation of another word. The negation of nouns when they function as predicates is treated jointly with the negation of verbs and sentences in **4.9**.

Antonyms are pairs of terms that are opposites of one another in some sense. Many antonyms are **privatives** (expressing the absence of a property), obtained by adding the stressed suffix -'ỹ to a noun, adjective or verb.

kyhyje 'fear' > *kyhyje'ỹ* 'courage'
pore 'trace' > *pore'ỹ* 'absence'
vy'a 'joy' > *vy'a'ỹ* 'sadness'
hepy 'expensive' > *hepy'ỹ* 'cheap'
mendare 'married' > *mendare'ỹ* 'unmarried, bachelor'
poko 'to touch' > *poko'ỹha* 'the spiritual, the immaterial'
po'a 'luck' > *po'a'ỹ* 'bad luck'

3.2.3 Diminutives and attenuatives

Diminutives express a small size and are formed by the stressed suffixes *-mi* and *-'i*.

mitã 'child' > *mitã**mi*** / *mitã'i* 'small child'
óga 'house' > *oga**mi*** 'little house'
yvyra 'tree' > *yvyra'i* 'small tree'

As in many other languages, diminutives can be used to convey affection (think of English '-ie' in 'dogg-ie').

*Eju cherendápe, cherajy**mi***.
e-ju   che-r-enda=pe   che-r-ajy-mi
IMP-come   1SG.INACT-POSSM-place=in   1SG.INACT-POSSM-daughter.of.man-DIM
'Come by my side, my <u>dear</u> daughter.'

Attenuatives indicate that an action or property is less intense or less fully instantiated than in the prototypical case. In Guarani attenuatives are formed by the stressed suffixes *-vy* (for oral bases) or *-ngy* (for nasal bases).

puka 'laugh' > *puka**vy*** 'smile'
pohýi 'heavy' > *pohyi**vy*** 'somewhat heavy'
hope 'eyelid' > *hope**vy*** 'to doze'
hũ 'black' > *hũ**ngy*** 'blackish'
he 'tasty' > *he**vy*** 'somewhat tasty'
hovy 'blue' > *hovy**ngy*** 'bluish'
hasy 'it hurts' > *hasy**vy*** 'it hurts a little'
juru 'mouth; open' > *juru**vy*** 'half-open'
taku 'warmth' > *taku**vy*** 'lukewarm'

Note in the last example the use of the nasal *-ngy* allomorph in *hovyngy*, even though the base *hovy* is not nasal. This may be a case of **dissimilation**; that is, of trying to avoid identical or similar sounds close together. In this case, the object would have been to avoid the somewhat cacophonous **hovyvy*. However, the two variants *-vy* and *-ngy* seem to be in **free variation**; that is, speakers have a more or less free choice of which to use, regardless of the oral/nasal status of the base (see the next paragraph, where the root *-echa* is oral, and therefore so is *ahecha* 'I see', yet the word is *ahecha-ngy*, and an explanation in terms of dissimilation is impossible here).

Attenuatives are also used with predicates, as a kind of speaker evaluation to denote approximation or depreciation:

*ahecha**ngy***
a-h-echa-ngy
1SG.ACT-POSSM3-see-ATT
'I glimpse(d) (it)'

*nerasẽ**ngy***
ne-r-asẽ-ngy
2SG.INACT-POSSM-cry-ATT
'you are a crybaby'

3.3 Adjectival modifiers of the noun

Even though the examples with the nominalizing suffix *-kue* in **3.2.1.1.4** seem to single out an adjective category to which this suffix would apply, Guarani does not have a clear morphological class of adjectives. Most roots that can be used as adjectives do so without any specific marking that would distinguish them from verbs or nouns, and even suffixes like the adjectivizing series *-va* (unmarked for tense), *-va'ekue* (adjectivizing in the past) and *-va'erã* (adjectivizing in the future) yield both noun-like items as well as adjective-like items.

Hence, adjectival (or adjective-like) modifiers of the noun are identified by their semantics and the fact that they occur after the noun, but not by any specific endings or word make-up. This is clear in the examples below. On the left, each root that is exemplified is functioning as an adjective. This is contrasted to the uses on the right, where the same root functions as a verb/predicate, as a noun or even as an adverb.

*ao **potĩ***	*che**potĩ***
ao potĩ	che-potĩ
clothes clean	1SG.INACT-clean
'clean clothes'	'I am clean'

ovetã *jepe'a*	*ojepe'a*
ovetã je-pe'a	o-je-pe'a
window AGD-open	3.ACT-AGD-open
'open window'	'it opened'

NOMINALS 87

kuña **kane'õ**   *kane'õ chembojavy*   *che***kane'õ**
kuña   kane'õ   kane'õ che-mbo-javy   che-kane'õ
woman   tired   tired   1SG.INACT-MAKE1-err   1SG.INACT-tired
'(a) <u>tired</u> woman'   '<u>tiredness</u> makes me slip up'   'I <u>am tired</u>'

óga **porã**   *rejapo* **porã**
óga   porã   re-japo   porã
house   beautiful   2SG.ACT-make   well
'(a) <u>beautiful</u> house' 'you do/did (it) <u>well</u>'

tape **vai**   *remba'apo* **vai**
tape   vai   re-mba'apo   vai
road   ugly   2SG.ACT-work   bad
'(a) <u>bad</u> road'   'you work(ed) <u>badly</u>'

Often, when a relational root is used as an adjective, this is indicated by the appearance of the prefix *r-*:

tesa **rovy** (cf. *hovy* 'blue')
t-esa   r-ovy
NPOSSM-eye   POSSM-blue
'<u>blue</u> eye(s)'

korasõ **rasy**   (cf. *tasy* 'pain')
korasõ   r-asy
heart   POSSM-pain
'<u>aching</u> heart'

ijuru **renyhẽ** (cf. *tenyhẽ* 'fullness')
i-juru   r-enyhẽ
3.INACT-mouth   POSSM-full
'their mouths <u>full</u>'

The main Guarani **adjectivizer** is the unstressed suffix *-va*. (Although more frequently it is used as a suffix that forms relative clauses; see **12.2.1**.)

hykuéva
h-ykue-va
POSSM3-juice-ADJZ
'<u>juicy</u>'

hi'áva
hi'a-va
bear.fruit-ADJZ
'fruit<u>ful</u>; fertile'

hi'á'ỹva
hi'a-'ỹ-va
bear.fruit-PRIV-ADJZ
'fruit<u>less</u>'

It can also be used to single out one or more items in a group (**set partitive** uses):

omombe'u chupe peteĩva
o-mombe'u   chupe   peteĩ-va
3.ACT-tell   to.him/her   one-ADJZ
'one <u>of them</u> told her'

iñaranduka peteĩvape umi mbohapy apytégui hérava . . .
iñ-aranduka   peteĩ-va=pe   umi   mbohapy   apyte=gui   h-éra-va
3.INACT-book   one-ADJZ=pe   NPROX.PL   three   centre=from   POSSM3-name-ADJZ
'in one <u>of</u> his books from the trilogy called . . .'

Ha opyhy mokõi pyao ombojo'a mokõivéva.
ha   o-pyhy   mokõi   py+ao   o-mbo-jo'a   mokõi-ve-va
and   3.ACT-grab   two   foot+clothes   3.ACT-MAKE1-fold two-more-ADJZ
'And he took two socks and put the two <u>of them</u> together (i.e., rolled them into a ball).'

3.4 Determiners

Determiners are morphemes that express whether a noun is definite/indefinite, or the quantity of a noun, for example. They are similar to adjectives in that they also modify a noun, but there are two main differences. First, instead of generally attributing a quality to a noun, they indicate what members are being identified of the category the noun designates, if any. Second, in Guarani they come before the noun, unlike adjectives, which come after the noun (see **3.3**).

The most common types of determiners are definite/indefinite articles, quantifiers and demonstratives. It is important to bear in mind that the Guarani noun phrase does not require any determiners. Bare nouns are enough to form a grammatical noun phrase.

***Para ape** hovy sakã asy*
para	ape	h-ovy	sakã	asy
sea	surface	POSSM3-blue	clear	intense

'The sea was an intense light blue'

***taita** pire cha'ĩ*
taita	pire	cha'ĩ
grandfather	skin	wrinkle

'grandfather's wrinkles'

Bare nouns can have a **generic** interpretation; that is, they do not refer to specific individuals but rather to a kind or class of individuals. They are used often in sentences that refer to universal truths or make generalizations about a whole category of individuals.

***Kuña** ikatupyry.*
kuña	i-katupyry
woman	3.INACT-skilful

'Women are skilful.'
(Note: without a context to indicate what the interpretation should be, this can also mean 'the woman is skilful'.)

***Tejukuéra** ojepire'óvo, osẽ jevy ichupekuéra ipire pyahu.*
teju=kuéra	o-je-pire-'o-vo	o-sẽ	jevy
lizard=PL	3.ACT-AGD-skin-REMOVE-while	3.ACT-go.out	again
ichupe=kuéra	i-pire	pyahu	
to.him/her=PL	3.INACT-skin	new	

'Lizards, as they shed, grow new skins.'

When determiners appear, however, they do so before the noun they determine, as I will exemplify in the following sections.

3.4.1 Articles

Articles are determiners indicating whether the noun they accompany has a definite or indefinite **referent**, or a new versus an already-known referent in discourse. Before contact with Spanish, Guarani did not have any definite or indefinite articles. Strictly speaking, modern Guarani does not have any articles. However, speakers very often employ *la* as a kind of article, usually for singular noun phrases (from the Spanish feminine singular definite article *la*). Likewise, *lo* is used usually for (collective) plural noun phrases (from the Spanish masculine plural definite article *los*).

*Ou **la** arriéro ha ovy'apa **lo** kuña.*
o-u	la	arriéro	ha	o-vy'a-pa	lo	kuña
3.ACT-come	DET.SG	peasant	and	3.ACT-joy-all	DET.PL	woman

'<u>The</u> man came and <u>the</u> women were all happy.'

***la** hi'ýva ojagarra pya'e hağuáicha*
la	hi-'ýva	o-jagarra	pya'e	hağua-icha
DET.SG	3.INACT-handle	3.ACT-grab	fast	for-as

'he grabbed <u>its</u> handle (i.e., of a whip) to (use it) fast'

Jaha lo mitã.
ja-ha	lo	mitã
1PL.INCL.ACT-go	DET.PL	child

'<u>Let's</u> go boys!'

Even though *la* comes from a Spanish singular article, and is usually described as singular in Guarani grammars, it is often used with plural noun phrases as well.

*Peñatendévará lo kuñakaraikuéra, **la** penememby kuñáre*
pe-ñatendé-va'e-rã	lo	kuña+karai=kuéra
2PL.ACT-pay.attention-ADJZ-DEST	DET.PL	woman+gentleman=PL

la	pene-memby+kuña=re
DET.SG	2PL.INACT-child.of.woman+woman=at

'Ladies, you must pay attention to your daughters'

***la** chesosiokuéra, **la** cheirũnguéra*
la	che-sosio=kuéra	la	che-irũ=nguéra
DET.SG	1SG.INACT-mate=PL	DET.SG	1SG.INACT-friend=PL

'my mates, my friends'

It is common for *la* to be found at the beginning of a relative clause marked with the relativizer *-va* (and it may even be used in the absence of the relativizer). Again, here *la* may be used in a plural noun phrase.

*He **la** ja'úva.*
he la ja-'u-va
tasty DET.SG 1PL.INCL.ACT-ingest-ADJZ
'<u>What</u> I and you are eating is tasty.'

*pórke **la** ápe oúvako ndoureíri hína*
pórke la ápe o-u-va=ko
because DET.SG here 3.ACT-come-ADJZ=VERD
nd-o-u-rei-ri hína
NEG-3.ACT-come-in.vain-NEG PROG
'because <u>those</u> who come here do not come for no reason'

*¡Ndénteko **la** rembotuichaitereíva!*
nde-nte=ko la re-mbo-tuicha-ite-rei-va
you.SG-only=VERD DET.SG 2SG.ACT-MAKE1-big-very-in.vain-ADJZ
'You are just exaggerating!' (Literally, 'Just <u>things that</u> you alone make really big for no reason!')

*Ojapo **la** chupekuéra ogustávante.*
o-japo la chupe=kuéra o-gusta-va-nte
3.ACT-make DET.SG to.him/her=PL 3.ACT-please-ADJZ-only
'They do only <u>what</u> pleases them.'

*emombe'úta mba'e **la** rehecha*
e-mombe'u-ta mba'e la re-h-echa
IMP-tell-FUT thing DET.SG 2SG.ACT-POSSM3-see
'you will tell <u>what</u> you see'

Both *la* and *lo* are extremely common in speech, but their use is frowned upon in more academic or formal registers. Neither of them indicates gender, only number. Notably, they can co-occur with possessive prefixes (as in one of the examples above and also in **3.6**). Even though they come from Spanish definite articles, it is not clear that they are definite in Guarani, since they can occur with an indefinite, non-specific interpretation. In the example below, the speaker is not talking about a specific food or meal, but rather about anything, any small thing, to eat.

*ikatu haǧuáicha oguereko **la** imba'e ho'umiva'erã*
ikatu   haǧua-icha   o-guereko   la   i-mba'e
be.able   for-as   3.ACT-have   DET.SG   3.INACT-thing
ho-'u-mi-va'e-rã
3.ACT-ingest-DIM-ADJZ-DEST
'so that they would have a little <u>some</u>thing to eat'[13]

*Barbie oheka **la** forma oenamora haǧua Víctorpe.*
Barbie   o-h-eka   la   forma   o-enamora
Barbie   3.ACT-POSSM3-seek   DET.SG   form   3.ACT-make.fall.in.love
haǧua   Víctor=pe
for   Víctor=in
'Barbie looks for <u>a</u>/<u>the</u> way to make Victor fall in love.'

Indefinite noun phrases can appear with the numeral *peteĩ* 'one':

***peteĩ** porandu iporãva*
peteĩ   porandu   i-porã-va
one   question   3.INACT-beautiful-ADJZ
'<u>a</u> beautiful question'

*Itúva ha isy oguereko **peteĩ** jagua'i.*
i-túva   ha   i-sy   o-guereko   peteĩ   jagua'i
3.INACT-father   and   3.INACT-mother   3.ACT-have   one   dog-DIM
'His/her/their father and his/her/their mother have <u>a</u> little dog.'

*Ohójeko Perurima ohechamívo **peteĩ** iñamígope.*
o-ho-jeko   Perurima   o-h-echa-mi-vo   peteĩ
3.ACT-go-it.is.said   Perurima   3.ACT-POSSM3-see-used.to-while   one
iñ-amígo=pe
3.INACT-friend=in
'They say that Perurima used to go visit a friend.'

Another indefinite determiner is *ambue* '(an)other'. The noun determined by *ambue* may be singular or plural. A plural interpretation is possible even for nouns without plural marking.

***ambue** mba'e*
ambue   mba'e
other   thing
'<u>another</u> thing / <u>the other</u> thing / <u>other</u> things'

---

[13] Example from Gynan (2017, 101).

NOMINALS   93

*Panambi hovy ha **ambue** mombe'uranguéra*

panambi	h-ovy	ha	ambue	mombe'u-rã=nguéra
butterfly	POSSM3-blue	and	other	tell-DEST=PL

'The blue butterfly and <u>other</u> stories'

*ombotove narcopolítica . . . ha **ambue** jepokuaa vai*

o-mbo-tove	narcopolítica	ha	ambue	je-pokuaa	vai
3.ACT-MAKE1-not.be	narcopolitics	and	other	AGD-habit	bad

's/he repudiated narcopolitics . . . and <u>other</u> bad habits'

3.4.2 Demonstratives

Demonstratives are morphemes that help to identify a referent by locating it in space or time (this language function of ostension is more generally called **deixis**). The system of demonstratives in Guarani is much more extensive than that in English. English recognizes singular 'this' / plural 'these' (for things or events close to the speaker, or **proximal**) and singular 'that' / plural 'those' (for things or events not close to the speaker, or **distal**). Guarani, on the other hand, makes many more distinctions. For this reason, the glosses for demonstratives in the examples are very technical. Readers can return to the tables in this section until they become familiar with the system.

Guarani has two main sets of demonstratives. One set is used when the referent is present at the time of the utterance, for example because it is visible to speaker and addressee; another set is used when the referent is removed or absent.

Within the set used for present referents, Guarani further differentiates three different demonstratives according to distance: proximal to speaker, proximal to addressee (or **medial**) and distal to both speaker and addressee. This three-way distinction can be understood in English as 'this', 'that close to you'/'that here' and 'that (over) there'.

		Singular	Plural
Present in the communicative situation	Proximal to speaker	*ko*	*ã, ko'ã*
	Proximal to hearer (medial)	*pe, upe*	*umi*
	Distal to both	*amo*	*umi*

Some examples of these **co-present** demonstratives:

***ko** jagua*
ko	jagua
PROX.SG	dog

'<u>this</u> dog'

***pe** tape puku*
pe	t-ape	puku
MED.SG	NPOSSM-road	long

'<u>that</u> long road (here)'

***upe** panambi hovy*
upe	panambi	h-ovy
MED.SG	butterfly	POSSM3-blue

'<u>that</u> blue butterfly'

***amo** táva*
amo	táva
DIST.SG	town

'<u>that</u> town (<u>over there</u>)'

***ko'ã** ta'anga*
ko'ã	t-a'anga
PROX.PL	NPOSSM-image

'<u>these</u> pictures'

***umi** guyra*
umi	guyra
NPROX.PL	bird

'<u>those</u> birds'

Within the set used for referents removed from the communicative situation, or non-co-present, the paradigm again differentiates between three different demonstratives: a pair that refers to distant persons known to both speaker and addressee, a pair that refers to distant events known to both speaker and addressee, and a pair that refers to individuals or events that the speaker has no direct knowledge of.

NOMINALS

		Singular	Plural
Removed from the communicative situation	Implying speaker and hearer shared distant knowledge, mainly to refer to persons	*ku*	*umi*
	Implying speaker and hearer shared distant knowledge, specifically to refer to distant events	*ako*	*umi*
	Without speaker direct knowledge, may imply hearsay, can refer to something heard without being seen	*aipo*	*umi*

It is important to show removed or non-co-present demonstratives in their full context to help the reader grasp their usage:

*Che, **ako** Éfesope, añorairõ rire ramo tymba ñarõ ndive yvypóra rehehápente, mba'épa iporã vaerã mo'ã chéve?*
Che   ako   Éfeso=pe   a-ño-rairõ   rire   ramo
I   DIST.EV Ephesus=in   1SG.ACT-RECP-attack after   if
t-ymba   ñarõ=ndive   yvypóra=rehehápe=nte   mba'e=pa
NPOSSM-animal   wild=with   person=for.the.sake.of=only what=Q
i-porã-vae-rã-mo'ã   chéve
3.INACT-good-ADJZ-DEST-ALMOST   to.me
'Having fought with wild beasts in <u>that</u> Ephesus for the sake of humans, what of good will I gain?'

*Peteĩ kuña ndojaho'íri ramo iñakã, ojogua **ku** kuña oñemyakã perõvaekuépe.*
peteĩ   kuña   nd-o-jaho'i-ri   ramo   iñ-akã   o-jogua
one   woman   NEG-3.ACT-cover-NEG   when   3.INACT-head   3.ACT-resemble
ku   kuña   o-ñe-my-akã   perõ-vae-kué=pe
DIST.PER   woman   3.ACT-AGD-MAKE1-head   hairless-ADJZ-POST=in
'If a woman does not cover her head, it is the same as if <u>this</u> woman had made her head bald.'

*Akãrapu'ã ningo **umi** viajes espaciales kuéra, ndaha'éi nde ru almacen.*
akãrapu'ã=ningo   umi   viajes   espaciales=kuéra   nda-ha'e-i
progress=VERD   NPROX.PL   trips   spatial=PL   NEG-be-NEG
nde-r-u   almacen
2SG.INACT-POSSM-father   grocery.store
'Progress is (<u>those</u>) space trips, not your dad's grocery store.'

*Ndépa rerovia **aipo** Papá Noel.*
nde=pa	re-rovia	aipo	Papá Noel
you.SG=Q	2SG.ACT-believe	DIST.IND	Santa.Claus

'Do you believe in that guy Santa Claus?'

*Indivíduoko umi ohekáva **aipo** "certificado médico" ani haḡua oho odefende tetã.*
indivíduo=ko	umi	o-h-eka-va	aipo	certificado
individual=VERD	NPROX.PL	3.ACT-POSSM3-seek-ADJZ	DIST.IND	certificate
médico	ani=haḡua	o-ho	o-defende	t-etã
medical	NEG.IMP=for	3.ACT-go	3.ACT-defend	NPOSSM-country

'"Individuals" are those who look for a "medical certificate" so as not to go defend the country.'

Aipo is often associated with something heard but not seen:

*(Upe jave oñehendu peteĩ mbokapu mombyrymi.) -Jesu . . . **aipo** mbokapu . . .*
upe	jave	o-ñe-h-endu	peteĩ	mbo-kapu	mombyry-mi
MED.SG	during	3.ACT-AGD-POSSM3-hear	one	MAKE1-shot	far-DIM
Jesu	aipo	mbo-kapu			
Jesus	DIST.IND	MAKE1-shot			

'(At that moment, a shot is heard not very far.) -Jesus . . . that shot … '

As shown in the tables above, singular demonstratives show the finest-grained distinctions. In the plural, only *umi* is used, except when the referent is both present and proximal to the speaker (like English 'these'), in which case *ã* or *ko'ã* are used.

The demonstratives *upe* and *umi* are mostly used to convey the meanings 'in this way', 'in that way' or 'thus' (**notional deixis**, also called **modal deixis**). *Upe* and *umi* are also very common in storytelling, because the referents of most nouns in narration are in an imagined universe of discourse. However, *pe* is attested as well in this sort of non-co-present use:

*ou mboyvekuri la españolkuéra ojapo **pe** cacerío la karaikuéra*
o-u	mboyve=kuri	la	español=kuéra	o-japo	pe
3.ACT-come	before=DIR.PAST	DEM.SG	Spaniard=PL	3.ACT-make	MED.SG
cacerío	la	karai=kuéra			
hunt	DEM.SG	gentleman=PL			

'before the Spaniards came men hunted'[14]

---
[14] Example from Gynan (2017, 101).

Of these demonstratives, *pe*, *upe* and *umi* in particular are often used as if they were definite articles. In fact, demonstratives often appear in contexts where English would have simply a definite article. One can find examples like the following in narrations:

*Adrián ha Karolina oñani pya'e oñeha'ãvo ani **upe** yvyku'i yrembe'ypegua oipy hapypa ichupekuéra.*

Adrián	ha	Karolina	o-ñani	pya'e	o-ñe-h-a'ã-vo
Adrián	and	Carolina	3.ACT-run	fast	3.ACT-AGD-POSSM3-attempt-while

ani	upe	yvyku'i	y+r-embe'y=pegua
NEG.IMP	MED.SG	sand	water+POSSM-edge=from

oi-py+h-apy-pa	ichupe=kuéra
3.ACT-foot+POSSM3-hot-all	to.him/her=PL

'Adrián and Carolina ran fast trying to prevent the sand from the riverbank from burning their feet.'

***Umi** yvyra hoguekúiva'ekue* . . .

umi	yvyra	h-ogue+kúi-va'e-kue
NPROX.PL	tree	POSSM3-leaf+get.detached-ADJZ-POST

'The trees that have lost their leaves . . .'

Ku is used for a non-present referent, when not only the speaker but also the hearer both have direct knowledge of the referent. That is, when the referent is in the **common ground**.

*Chemandu'a nemichĩramo, pyhare ahendúramo **ku** pombéro opiã.*

che-mandu'a	ne-michĩ=ramo	pyhare	a-h-endu=ramo
1SG.INACT-remember	2SG.INACT-little=when	night	1SG.ACT-POSSM3-hear=when

ku	pombéro	o-piã
DIST.PER	pombero	3.ACT-cheep

'I remember when you were little, when I would hear that pombero cheep at night'. (The pombero is a mythical figure, also called "Lord of the night".)

Ako is used under the same conditions. It seems to refer primarily to events, but it can also refer to individuals in a way similar to *ku*.

*Ojejukáguive **ako** karai Arce, ahendúvo mbokapu aimo'ãjevýma oime ojejukáva.*

o-je-juka=guive	ako	karai	Arce	a-h-endu-vo
3.ACT-AGD-kill=since	DIST.EV	gentleman	Arce	1SG.ACT-POSSM3-hear-while

mbo-kapu	a-imo'ã-jevy-ma	o-ime
MAKE1-burst	1SG.ACT-think-again-already	3.ACT-be.located

o-je-juka-va
3.ACT-AGD-kill-ADJZ

'Since that Mr Arce was killed, whenever I hear shots, I already think again there is someone being killed.'

If the hearer has no previous knowledge of the referent, *pe* or *upe* can be used.

***Pe** doctorpe aju adenuncia*

pe	doctor=pe	a-ju	a-denuncia
MED.SG	doctor=in	1SG.ACT-come	1SG.ACT-report

'I went to that doctor to file a complaint.'

Finally, in contrast to standard English, demonstratives can co-occur with possessive prefixes.

*ehupi **pe ndea**o*

e-hupi	pe	nde-ao
IMP-lift	MED.SG	2SG.INACT-clothes

'pick up your clothes (there).'

***Ko** che irũ niko oike ka'aguy marã'ỹme . . .*

ko	che-irũ	niko	o-ike	ka'aguy	marã'ỹ=me . . .
PROX.SG	1SG.INACT-friend	VERD	3.ACT-enter	forest	spotless=in

'This friend of mine is indeed entering into the virgin forest . . .'
(literally, 'this my friend is indeed entering into the virgin forest. . .')

3.4.3 Numerals and quantifiers

Before contact with Spanish, Guarani had four **cardinal numerals**: *peteĩ* '1', *mokõi* '2', *mbohapy* '3' and *irundy* '4'. In the twentieth century, several complementary academic systems were created to extend the numeral set. The one I present briefly here is usually attributed to Professor Reinaldo Decoud Larrosa.

The first extension is the use of *po* 'hand' for the number 5, and *pa* for '10'. This latter is derived by the deletion of the first vowel (**apheresis**) of *opa* 'end, totality, complete', because 10 is the end number of the modern decimal system.

The rest of the numbers are obtained by deleting the first syllable of a number and combining it with *po* and *pa*. For example, *poteĩ* (*po+teĩ*, the latter being the shortened form of *peteĩ* '1') is '6', and *pokõi* (*po+kõi*, the latter being the shortened form of *mokõi* '2') is '7'. *Sa*, short form of *rasa* 'very', is '100', and *su*, short form of *guasu* 'big', is '1,000'.

0	*mba'eve* ('nothing')
1	*peteĩ*
2	*mokõi*
3	*mbohapy*
4	*irundy*
5	*po*
6	*poteĩ*
7	*pokõi*
8	*poapy*
9	*porundy*
10	*pa*
11	*pateĩ*
12	*pakõi*
13	*pa'apy*
14	*parundy*
15	*papo*
16	*papoteĩ*
17	*papokõi*
w	*papoapy*
19	*paporundy*
20	*mokõipa*
21	*mokõipa peteĩ*
30	*mbohapypa*
40	*irundypa*
100	*sa*
200	*mokõisa*
1,000	*su*
1,000,000	*sua*
10,000,000	*pasua*
100,000,000	*sasua*

As of today, this system is purely of academic use. In the colloquial language, Spanish numerals are in common use beyond *irundy* '4'.

*Hepykue oñeimo'ã ohupyty amo 14.200 **sua** dólar.*
h-epy-kue	o-ñe-imo'ã	o-h-upyty	amo
POSSM3-expensive-NMLZ.ABS	3.ACT-AGD-think	3.ACT-POSSM3-achievement	DIST.SG

14.200 sua	dólar
14.200 million	dollar

'The cost is estimated to have reached 14,200 <u>million</u> dollars.'

To talk about age, English uses the verb 'to be'. Guarani, on the other hand, uses *(gue)reko* 'to have', with the word *ary* 'year':

*-Mbovy **ary** reguereko? -Aguereko irundy **ary**.*
mbovy	ary	re-guereko	a-guereko	irundy	ary
how.many	year	2SG.ACT-have	1SG.ACT-have	four	year

'-How <u>old</u> <u>are</u> you? -I <u>am</u> four <u>years</u> old.'

In a more colloquial register, the Spanish borrowing *año* 'year' is generally used (in the example below, accompanied with some phonetic simplifications such as the omission of /v/ in *mbovy* 'how many' or the simplification of the second-person singular person prefix from *re-* to *e-*):

*Mboy **año** ereko?*
mboy	año	e-reko
how.many	year	2SG.ACT-have

'How <u>old</u> <u>are</u> you?'

As mentioned in **3.1.1**, there is no plural number agreement with cardinal determiners.

mbohapy ovecha
mbohapy	ovecha
three	sheep

'three sheep'

*jopara katu **mokõi ñe'ẽ** onáva ojuehe*
jopara	katu	mokõi	ñe'ẽ	o-na-va	ojuehe
Jopara	just	two	language	3.ACT-stick-ADJZ	at.each.other

'Jopara, on the other hand, is <u>two languages</u> mixed between themselves'

Cardinal numbers figure in the neologisms used for the names of the days of the week and months of the year (see **15.7**). Occasionally, the times of the day can be given using these academic numerals.

*ara**pokõi** ha arate**ĩ** jave **poteĩ** aravo guive **poapy** aravo peve*
ára+pokõi ha   ara+teĩ   jave   poteĩ aravo guive   poapy aravo peve
day+seven and day+one   during six   hour   since   eight hour   until
'during Saturdays and Sundays from six to eight'

Ordinal numbers are formed with the ordinal stressed suffix *-ha* and are placed after the head noun. (Do not confuse with the nominalizer *-ha* in **3.2.1.1.1**.)

*káso **peteĩha***
káso   peteĩ-ha
short.story one-TH
'the first short story'

*Pe Tupã remimbou **mokõiha** ombopu ituru.*
pe   Tupã r-emi-mbo-u   mokõi-ha o-mbo-pu
MED.SG God   POSSM-NMLZ.REL-MAKE1-come two-TH   3.ACT-MAKE1-sound
i-turu
3.INACT-trumpet
'The second messenger of God (=angel) sounded his trumpet.'

*Pe ovecha ra'y ojokávo séllo **mbohapyha**, ahendu pe oikovéva **mbohapyha** he'i ramo: "Eju!".*
pe   ovecha r-a'y   o-joka-vo   sello mbohapy-ha
MED.SG   sheep   POSSM-son   3.ACT-break-while seal   three-TH
a-h-endu   pe   o-iko-ve-va   mbohapyha he'i
1SG.ACT-POSSM3-hear MED.SG 3.ACT-be-more-ADJZ   three   says
ramo   e-ju
recently IMP-come
'As the Lamb broke the third seal, I immediately heard the third that was living say: "Come!".'

Distributives (that is, 'X *number* each') can be formed by **reduplication** (doubling) of the cardinal number (marked with the tilde ~ in the gloss). Of note, the sentence below is ambiguous between a meaning where each of three persons drank one glass and a meaning where each person drank three glasses. Perhaps for this reason, it is common to use

Spanish distributives in the spoken language (for example, *uno a uno* 'one by one').

*Ha'ekuéra ho'u mbohapy kagua **peteĩteĩ**.*
ha'e=kuéra	ho-'u	mbohapy	kagua	peteĩ~teĩ
s/he=PL	3.ACT-ingest	three	drinking-glass	one~one

'They drank three glasses <u>each</u>.'/'They drank <u>each one of</u> three glasses.'

***mokõimokõi** tapicha oikékuri pýpe*
mokõi~mokõi	t-apicha	o-ike-kuri	pýpe
two~two	NPOSSM-fellow.man	3.ACT-enter-DIR.PAST	inside

'People entered inside <u>in twos</u> / <u>two by two</u>.'

Quantifiers more generally indicate some non-exact quantity (or zero) of the noun they accompany, when they function as noun determiners (but see **9** for a more general overview of quantification).

*upe **opa** jaguarehe jahecháva*
upe	opa	jagua=rehe	ja-h-echa-va
MED.SG	all	dog=at	1PL.INCL.ACT-POSSM3-see-AJDZ

'that which we (and you) can see in <u>all</u> dogs'

***opavave** mitã'i ha mitãkuña'íicha*
opavave	mitã-'i	ha	mitã+kuña-'i-icha
all	child-DIM	and	child+woman-DIM-as

'like <u>all</u> little boys and little girls'

*¡**Nda'opavavéi** itítuloko oho tetã ambuépe!*
nda-'opavave-i	i-título=ko	o-ho	t-etã	ambue=pe
NEG-all-NEG	3.INACT-diploma=VERD	3.ACT-go	NPOSSM-country	other=in

'<u>Not everyone</u> who has a (college) diploma goes to another country!'

***atýra** so'okangue*
atýra	so'o+kangue
heap	meat+bone

'<u>a lot of</u> bones'

***mayma** yvypóra*
mayma	yvypóra
every	person

'<u>every</u> human being'

maymáva hasývapeguarã
maymáva h-asy-va=pe=guarã
every   POSSM3-sickness-ADJZ=in=for
'for each patient / for all patients'

*Ko'ã ñembohasa ojejapo ñe'ẽjoapy **ñavo** rupírehe.*
ko'ã   ñe-mbo-h-asa   o-je-japo   ñe'ẽ+joapy   ñavo−rupi=rehe
PROX.PL AGD-MAKE1-POSSM3-pass 3.ACT-AGD-make speech+union   each=through=at
'These translations are made for each sentence.'

*oĩ **heta** tape'i*
oĩ   h-eta   t-ape-'i
there.is POSSM3-numerous   NPOSSM-road-DIM
'there are many passages'

***opaichagua** pira*
opa-icha=gua   pira
all-as=from   fish
'all sorts of fish'

***mbovy** guyra*
mbovy   guyra
few   bird
'few birds'

*oñorairõ hikuái **oimeraẽ** mba'erehe*
o-ño-rairõ   hikuái oimeraẽ   mba'e=rehe
3.ACT-RECP-attack   they   any   thing=because
'they fought for any reason'

***mba'evéichagua** jeporavo'ỹre*
mba'eve-icha=gua   je-poravo='ỹre
nothing-as=from   AGD-choose=without
'without any (form of) discrimination'

Note that *heta* is a relational root. It can be used in a compound word with another root. It can also have predicative uses with the meaning 'to be numerous'. In both these cases, the *r-* prefix is used.

*ava**reta***
ava+r-eta
person+POSSM-numerous
'a multitude of people'

*ñande**reta***
ñande-r-eta
1PL.INCL.INACT-POSSM-numerous
'we (and you) are numerous / there are many of us'

Plural agreement is possible, but optional, with many of these quantifiers.

*mayma **yvypóra***
mayma   yvypóra
every   person
'every human being'

*maymáva tapicha**kuéra***
maymáva   t-apicha=kuéra
every   NPOSSM-fellow.man=PL
'all the people / every fellow man'

3.5 Pronouns

3.5.1 Personal pronouns

Having an explicit subject in a sentence is not obligatory in Guarani, since the prefixes that accompany a verb are enough to identify it in many cases. Free-standing personal pronoun forms (that is, not prefixed to the verb) do exist, but are used only when a contrast with other participants in the event or insistence on the subject is needed.

*Ndefelínte **che** aipota.*
nde-feli-nte   che   ai-pota
2SG.INACT-happy-only   I   1SG.ACT-want
'I, I only want you (to be) happy.'

*Ha'e oikuaa **che** ko imba'eva.*
ha'e   oi-kuaa   che=ko   i-mba'e-va
s/he   3.ACT-know   I=VERD   3.INACT-thing-ADJZ
'She knows I am (truly) hers.'

Áğa jasypahápe, **nde** *reñomongetáta hendive.*

áğa	jasy+pa-ha=pe	nde	re-ño-mongeta-ta	hendive
now	moon+end-NMLZ=in	you.SG	2SG.ACT-RECP-converse-FUT	with.him

'But at the end of the month, you (not me) will discuss it with him.'

The free-standing personal pronoun forms are given in the table below. Different forms are used for different grammatical functions in the sentence: subject, indirect object, direct object (marked only for humans and sometimes animals), separative (also known as **ablative**) and **oblique** object (an object marked with a special postposition). The reason the table below has no free-standing direct object pronouns for first and second person will be explained in **4.2**.

Person/Number	Subject	Indirect object	(Animate) direct object	Separative ('from')	Oblique object (with =*rehe*)
1SG	che	chéve	–	chehegui	cherehe
2SG	nde	ndéve	–	ndehegui	nderehe
3	ha'e	(i)chupe	(i)chupe	(i)chugui	hese
1PL inclusive	ñande	ñandéve	–	ñandehegui	ñanderehe
1PL exclusive	ore	oréve	–	orehegui	orerehe
2PL	peẽ	peẽme	–	pendehegui	penderehe
3PL	ha'e(kuéra)	(i)chupe (kuéra)	(i)chupe (kuéra)	(i)chugui (kuéra)	hese(kuéra)

Points to note:

- The third person pronouns are very commonly found as *chupe*, *chupekuéra*, *chugui*, *chuguikuéra*, without the initial *i*.

Egueru **chéve** ...

e-gueru	chéve
IMP-bring	to.me

'Bring (to) me ...'

Eremína **ichupe nde**.

ere-mi-na	ichupe	nde
2SG.say-PLEAD-REQ	to.him/her	you.SG

'You tell him/her.'

*Atĩma **pendehegui** ambaʼejerure haguã.*
a-tĩ-ma   pendehegui   a-mbaʼe-jerure   haguã
1SG.ACT-feel.shame-already from.you.PL   1SG.ACT-THING-petition   for
'It already makes me ashamed to be asking things <u>from you</u>.'

*chemanduʼáta **hese***
che-manduʼa-ta   hese
1SG.INACT-remembrance-FUT   at.him/her
'I will remember <u>him/her</u>.'

*María Pytyvõhára, eñemboʼe **orerehe**.*
María Pytyvõ-hára   e-ñemboʼe   ore=rehe
María help-NMLZ.AG   IMP-prayer   we.not.you=at
'Mary, Help of Christians, pray <u>for us</u>.'

It is important to realize that Guarani has two forms for first-person plural pronouns (and verbal prefixes as well). In English, if I say to someone (to the **addressees** of my speech), 'we need to go', those people may not know whether by 'we' I mean myself and them or myself and some other people but not them. In Guarani this is always unambiguously clear. There is an **inclusive** form (*ñande*) that is used to refer to the speaker and other people including whoever is being addressed, and an **exclusive** form (*ore*) that is used to refer to the speaker and other people in the speaker's group, but excluding whoever is being addressed. (This language property is called **clusivity**.) For example, the first sentence below would be used by a student addressing other students, whereas the second sentence would be used by a student addressing, say, teachers:

***Ñande ja**estudia porã.*
ñande   ja-estudia   porã
we&you   1PL.INCL.ACT-study   well
'<u>We (and you)</u> studied well.'

***Ore ro**estudia porã.*
ore   ro-estudia   porã
we.not.you   1PL.EXCL.ACT-study   well
'<u>We (excluding you)</u> studied well.'

Another example is given by the following sentence, from a blog post by a Paraguayan, writing for Paraguayans:

*Mba'erã **jay'u** terere **ñande** Paraguaigua?*
mba'e-rã   ja-y+'u   terere   ñande   Paraguai=gua
what-DEST   1PL.INCL.ACT-water+ingest   terere   we&you   Paraguay=from
'Why do we Paraguayans drink terere?' (Terere is a chilled infusion made with mate (*Ilex Paraguayensis*) leaves.)

If the writer of the blog had been addressing non-Paraguayans, the question would have been:

*Mba'erã **roy'u** terere **ore** Paraguaigua?*
mba'e-rã   ro-y+'u   terere   ore   Paraguai=gua
what-DEST   1PL.EXCL.ACT-water+ingest   terere   we.not.you Paraguay=from
'Why do we Paraguayans drink terere?'

The following example can also clarify this point. Clearly, Mary Help of Christians is going to pray for a group that includes the speaker, but not for herself. Therefore, when addressing Mary, the speaker uses *orerehe* to exclude Mary from the group being prayed for.

*María Pytyvõhára, eñembo'e **orerehe**.*
María   Pytyvõ-hára   e-ñembo'e   ore=rehe
María   help-NMLZ.AG   IMP-prayer   we.not.you=at
'Mary, Help of Christians, pray for us.'

The third-person forms *(i)chupe* and *(i)chupekuéra* are used for both direct objects and indirect objects. The first- and second-person indirect object forms cannot be used for direct objects, since some special marking is required when the direct object is first- or second-person, as shown in the examples below (see **4.2**).

***Ro**hayhu.*
ro-h-ayhu
1.ACT>2SG-POSSM3-love
'I/We love you (sg.).'

***Po**hayhu.*
po-h-ayhu
1.ACT>2PL-POSSM3-love
'I/We love you (pl.).'

Even though the postposition =*gui* 'from' is unstressed when used with nouns or phrases, the separative personal pronouns are stressed on this last syllable *gui*.

*He'i avei cherecomendataha iñirũnguérape ojogua hağuã **cheheguí**nte la chipa.*
he'i avei che-recomenda-ta-ha   iñ-irũ=nguéra=pe
says also 1SG.INACT-recommend-FUT-NMLZ   3.INACT-friend=PL=in
o-jogua=hağuã   chehegui-nte   la   chipa
3.ACT-buy=for   from.me-only   DET.SG   chipa
'He also said that he would recommend me to his friends so that they would buy chipa only from me.'

*Animo'ãkena avave ohekýi **ndehegui** neñe'ẽ.*
ani-mo'ã-ke-na   avave   o-h-ekýi   ndehegui
NEG-NEG.FUT-FORCE-REQ   nobody   3.ACT-POSSM3-take.away from.you.SG
ne-ñe'ẽ
2SG.INACT-language
'That/Let nobody ever take your language from you.'

Because they are independent words, these personal pronouns are never subject to pronunciation changes based on nasal harmony, unlike person prefixes (for the nasal variants of person-marking prefixes see **3.6** and **4.1.2**).

Further, these pronouns have **reflexive** forms; that is, object pronouns used prototypically when a subject performs an action unto itself (cf. the English pronouns ending in '-self', '-selves').

Person/ Number	Subject	Indirect/ direct object	Separative ('from')	Oblique object (with =*rehe*)
1SG	chete	chejupe	chejehegui	chejehe
2SG	ndete	ndejupe	ndejehegui	ndejehe
3	ha'ete	ijupe	ijehegui/ ojehegui	ijehe
1PL inclusive	ñandete	ñandejupe	ñandejehegui	ñandejehe
1PL exclusive	orete	orejupe	orejehegui	orejehe
2PL	pendete	pendejupe	pendejehegui	pendejehe
3PL	ha'ekuéraite	ijupe(kuéra)	ijehegui(kuéra)	ijehe(kuéra)

*ha'e avei **chejupe** . . .*
ha'e   avei   chejupe
I.say   also   to.myself
'I also said to myself . . .'

*Ojeguereko hetaiterei gente omba'apóva **ijehegui**.*
o-je-guereko   h-eta-iterei   gente   o-mba'apo-va
3.ACT-AGD-have   POSSM3-numerous-very.much   people   3.ACT-work-ADJZ
ijehegui
from.him/herself
'A great number of people are found that work by themselves (i.e., without a commercial licence).'

*Peñatendéke **pendejehe** ha entéro ovecha atýre.*
pe-ñatende-ke   pendejehe   ha   entéro   ovecha   aty=re
2PL.ACT-pay.attention-FORCE   at.yourselves   and   whole   sheep   group=at
'Look out for yourselves and for the entire flock.'

The forms *chete*, *ndete*, and so on, being subject forms, are not truly reflexive. They have an emphatic use similar to the English forms in '-self'.

***chete** ajapova'ekue*
chete   a-japo-va'e-kue
I.myself   1SG.ACT-make-ADJZ-POST
'I myself did it'

*Jehova ningo oheja **ñandete** jadesidi.*
Jehova=ningo   o-h-eja   ñandete   ja-desidi
Jehovah=VERD   3.ACT-POSSM3-leave   we.ourselves   1PL.INCL.ACT-decide
'But Jehovah lets us decide ourselves.'

This emphatic import is most often reinforced by the emphatic particle *voi*. The particle *voi* can sometimes carry by itself the emphatic meaning.

***Orete voi** rohendu va'ekue pe yvágagui oñe'ẽva.*
orete=voi   ro-h-endu-va'e-kue   pe   yvága=gui
we.ourselves=EMPH   1PL.EXCL.ACT-POSSM3-hear-ADJZ-POST   MED.SG   sky=from
o-ñe'ẽ-va
3.ACT-speak-ADJZ
'We ourselves heard who spoke from the heavens.'

Ore voi rohecha va'ekue ore resa tee rupi Jesucristo pokatu.
ore=voi ro-h-echa-va'e-kue
we.not.you=EMPH 1PL.EXCL.ACT-POSSM3-see-ADJZ-POST
ore-r-esa-tee=rupi Jesucristo pokatu
1PL.EXCL.INACT-POSSM3-eye-one's.own=through Jesus.Christ might
'<u>We ourselves</u> saw with our own eyes the might of Jesus Christ.'

3.5.2 Interrogative pronouns

Interrogative pronouns are used to ask a question whose answer is not simply 'yes' or 'no'; for example, in English, 'what' (non-human subject or object), 'who' (human subject or object), 'whom' (human object) or 'whose' (possessive). For ease of exposition, I present them in this section together with other **interrogative words** that are not pronouns but can be determiners or pro-adverbials (a kind of "pronoun for adverbs").

mba'e	'what'
máva / ava	'who'
mba'éicha	'how'
mamo / moõ	'where'
araka'e	'when'
mba'erã / ma'erã /mba'upe	'what for'
mba'ére / mba'égui	'why'
mbovy / mboy	'how much' / 'how many'
araka'epeve	'until when'
araka'eguive	'since when'
avamba'e	'whose'

Points to note:

- Most of these interrogative words are composed of two morphemes (however, for reasons of clarity, I will gloss them as one single interrogative word):
  - *Mba'éicha* 'how' is composed of *mba'e* 'thing' and *-icha* 'as' (literally, 'like what?').
  - *Mba'erã* 'what for' is *mba'e* 'thing' plus nominal destinative aspect *-rã* (literally, 'for what?').
  - *Mba'ére* 'why' is *mba'e* 'thing' plus =*re* 'at' (literally, 'because of what?').
  - *Mba'égui* 'why' is *mba'e* 'thing' plus =*gui* 'from' (literally, 'from what?').
  - *Araka'epeve* 'until when' is *araka'e* 'when' plus =*peve* 'until'.

NOMINALS 111

- *Araka'eguive* 'since when' is *araka'e* 'when' plus *=guive* 'since'.
- *Avamba'e* 'whose' is *ava* 'person' plus *mba'e* 'thing', replicating the structure of possessive pronouns (see **3.5.5**).
• These interrogative words occur most often (but not obligatorily) with one of the interrogative enclitics *=pa* or *=piko*: *mba'épa* 'what', *moõpiko* 'where'.

Mba'éichapa reiko.
mba'é-icha=pa   re-iko
what-as=Q   2SG.ACT-be
'<u>How</u> are you?'

Mba'épa iporã vaerã mo'ã chéve.
mba'e=pa   i-porã-vae-rã-mo'ã   chéve
what=Q   3.INACT-good-ADJZ-DEST-ALMOST   to.me
'<u>What</u> of good will I gain?'

Mba'e ere?
mba'e   ere
what   2SG.ACT.say
'<u>What</u> did you say?'

Mba'e carrérata piko upéva.
mba'e   carréra-ta=piko   upe-va
what   career-FUT=Q   MED.SG-ADJZ
'What career would that be?'

Moõpa reime.
moõ=pa   re-ime
where=Q   2SG.ACT-be.located
'<u>Where</u> are you?'

¿Ha **moõ** rupi ñambopila?
ha   moõ=rupi   ña-mbo-pila
and   where=through   1PL.INCL.ACT-MAKE1-battery
'And <u>where</u> does one put the batteries?'

moõguipa jaju, **máva**pa ñande ha **moõ**gotopa jaha
moõ=gui=pa   ja-ju   máva=pa   ñande   ha
where=from=Q   1PL.INCL.ACT-come   who=Q   we&you   and
moõ=goto=pa   ja-ha
where=toward=Q 1PL.INCL.ACT-go
'<u>Where</u> do we come <u>from</u>, <u>who</u> are we, and <u>where</u> do we go?'

*Nde piko **moõ**gua.*
nde=piko moõ=gua
you.SG=Q where=from
'Where are you from?'

*Nde piko **moõ**gui reju.*
nde=piko moõ=gui re-ju
you.SG=Q where=from 2SG.ACT-come
'Where are you coming from?'

***Araka'é**pa oğuahẽ Marta.*
araka'e=pa o-ğuahẽ Marta
when=Q 3.ACT-arrive Marta
'When did Marta arrive?'

***Mba'e**rã jay'u terere ñande Paraguaigua?*
mba'e-rã ja-y+'u terere ñande Paraguai=gua
what-DEST 1PL.INCL.ACT-water+ingest terere we&you Paraguay=from
'Why do we Paraguayans drink terere?'

***mba'égui**pa remaña péicha ndesýre*
mba'e=gui=pa re-maña pe-icha nde-sy=re
what=from=Q 2SG.ACT-look.at MED.SG-as 2SG.INACT-mother=at
'why are you looking at your mother like that?'

***Mboy** peime?*
mboy pe-ime
how.many 2PL.ACT-be.located
'How many are you?'

3.5.3 Indefinite and negative pronouns

Indefinite pronouns refer to non-specific objects, people, events or places. **Negative pronouns** are indefinite pronouns that include negation. Most negative pronouns carry the ending *-ve* (except *ni peteĩ*, calqued from the Spanish *ni uno* 'not even one'). As with many of the interrogatives in **3.5.2**, several of these can function as pronouns or as determiners of a noun.

mba'eve	'nothing'
(m)avave	'nobody'
ni peteĩ	'no one, none'

mamove / moõve	'nowhere'
maymáva	'everyone, everything'
mokõive	'both'
ambuéva	'other one'
oimeraẽva	'anyone'
peteĩ mba'e	'something'

*Ndaipotái **mba'eve**.*
nd-ai-pota-i　　　　mba'eve
NEG-1SG.ACT-want-NEG　nothing
'I don't want <u>anything</u>.' (Literally, 'I don't want <u>nothing</u>'; for double negation, see **4.9**.)

***Avave** ndoikuaái cheréra.*
avave　　nd-oi-kuaa-i　　　che-r-éra
nobody　NEG-3.ACT-know-NEG　1SG.INACT-POSSM-name
'<u>Nobody</u> knows my name.' (Literally, '<u>Nobody</u> doesn't know my name.')

*Ndahaséi **mamove** nendie.*
nd-a-ha-se-i　　　　　mamove　　ne=ndie
NEG-1SG.ACT-go-want-NEG　nowhere　　2SG.INACT=with
'I don't want to go <u>anywhere</u> with you.' (Literally, 'I don't want to go <u>nowhere</u> with you.')

***Mokõive** tajýra opyta hye guasu itúvagui.*
mokõive　t-ajýra　　　　　　o-pyta　　h-ye+guasu
both　　NPOSSM-daughter.of.man　3.ACT-stay　POSSM3-belly+big
i-t-úva=gui
3.INACT-NPOSSM-father=from
'<u>Both</u> daughters got pregnant by their father.'

*jeroviapy, jepokuaa, ñe'ẽ ha **ambuéva***
jerovia-py　　je-pokuaa　ñe'ẽ　　　ha　　ambuéva
believe-NMLZ.PASS　AGD-habit　language　and　other
'beliefs, customs, language, and <u>other things</u>'

*Aporanduse ndéve **peteĩ mba'e**.*
a-porandu-se　　　　　　ndéve　　peteĩ　mba'e
1SG.ACT-question-want　to.you　one　　thing
'I want to ask you <u>something</u>.'

There are also adverbial proforms (pronouns replace nouns; proforms replace other word classes; adverbial proforms replace time, space and manner adverbials):

araka'eve	'never'
máramo	'never'
mba'evéicharõ / mba'evéicharamo	'in no way'
mba'eveichavéramo	'in absolutely no way'
mamove	'nowhere'

***Araka'eve** ndaikatúi ake nderógape.*
araka'eve   nda-ikatu-i   a-ke   nde-r-óga=pe
never   NEG-be.able-NEG   1SG.ACT-sleep   2SG.INACT-POSSM-house=in
'I can <u>never</u> sleep in your house.'

***máramo** soja nome'ẽi "kamby"... **mba'eveichavéramo** nome'ẽi kamby*
máramo   soja   n-o-me'ẽ-i   kamby   mba'eveichavéramo
never   soy   NEG-3.ACT-give-NEG milk   in.absolutely.no.way
n-o-me'ẽ-i   kamby
NEG-3.ACT-give-NEG   milk
'<u>Never</u> does soy give (=produce) "milk"... <u>in absolutely no way</u> does it give milk'

***Mba'evéicharamo** ndahamo'ãi!*
mba'evéicharamo   nd-a-ha-mo'ã-i
in.no.way   NEG-1SG.ACT-go-FUT.NEG-NEG
'I will not go, <u>absolutely not</u>!'

3.5.4 Demonstrative pronouns

Demonstrative pronouns identify what the speaker is referring to directly by giving information about the location of this referent in space or time (deictic information), without the help of a noun. These pronouns are formed straightforwardly by adding the unstressed suffix *-va* (which creates adjectives or nouns) to the demonstrative determiners.

***Kóva** peteĩ hu'y.*
ko-va   peteĩ   hu'y
PROX.SG-ADJZ   one   arrow
'<u>This</u> is an arrow.'

*Ojehecha **péva** ndaikatumo'ãiha.*
o-je-h-echa　　　　　pe-va　　　　nda-ikatu-mo'ã-i-ha
3.ACT-AGD-POSSM3-see　MED.SG-ADJZ　NEG-be.able-FUT.NEG-NEG-NMLZ
'One can see that <u>that</u> is not possible.'

*Ndorojapói **upéva**.*
ndo-ro-japo-i　　　　　　upe-va
NEG-1PL.EXCL.ACT-make-NEG　MED.SG-ADJZ
'We didn't do <u>that</u>.'

*Ava rógapa **amóva**.*
ava　　　r-óga=pa　　　　amo-va
person　POSSM-house=Q　DIST.SG-ADJZ
'Whose house is <u>that (over there)</u>?'

***Umíva** ndereka.*
umi-va　　　　　nde-r-eka
NPROX.PL-ADJZ　2SG.INACT-POSSM-seek
'<u>Those ones</u> are looking for you (sg.).'

In colloquial speech, the /v/ of this suffix is very often elided yielding the forms *kóa, péa, umía,* and so on.

*Auto tujango **kóa**!*
auto　tuja=ngo　　ko-va
car　　old=VERD　PROX.SG-ADJZ
'But <u>this</u> is an old car!'

***Péa** niko ñande rekove.*
pe-va=niko　　　　　ñande-r-ekove
MED.SG-ADJZ=VERD　1PL.INCL.INACT-POSSM-life
'<u>This</u> is our life.'

*Upéicha **umía** rojuga.*
upe-icha　　　umi-va　　　　　ro-juga
MED.SG-as　NPROX.PL-ADJZ　1PL.EXCL.ACT-play
'We played <u>those sorts of things</u>.'

3.5.5 Possessive pronouns

Possessive pronouns replace a noun and identify its referent by who its owner or possessor is. They are equivalent to the English pronouns 'mine', 'yours', 'ours', and so on. The morphological structure of these possessive pronouns takes advantage of the syntax of possession by juxtaposition (see **3.6**). They are composed of a person prefix from the inactive series (see **4.1.2**) plus *mba'e* 'thing'; literally, they mean 'my thing', 'your thing', and so on.

Person/Number	
1SG	*chemba'e*
2SG	*nemba'e*
3	*imba'e*
1PL inclusive	*ñanemba'e*
1PL exclusive	*oremba'e*
2PL	*penemba'e*
3PL	*imba'e(kuéra)*

*ko ñe'ẽ **ñanemba'e***
ko ñe'ẽ ñane-mba'e
PROX.SG language 1PL.INCL.INACT-thing
'this language is <u>ours</u>'

*Hi'ã chéve **chemba'e** péva.*
hi'ã chéve che-mba'e pe-va
seems to.me 1SG.INACT-thing MED.SG-ADJZ
'It seems to me that that is <u>mine</u>.'

*Jeporavo **penemba'é**nte ha ndaha'éi **avavemba'e**.*
je-poravo pene-mba'e-nte ha nda-ha'e-i avave-mba'e
AGD-choice 2PL.INACT-thing-only and NEG-be-NEG nobody-thing
'The choice is <u>yours (pl.)</u> and <u>nobody else's</u>.'

***Avamba'é**pa pe ao ky'a.*
ava-mba'e=pa pe ao ky'a
person-thing=Q MED.SG clothes dirty
'<u>Whose</u> are those dirty clothes?'

3.6 Possessive noun phrases

Possessive noun phrases indicate a relation of possession between nouns. The order is generally **possessor-possessum**. The possessive relation is indicated by simple juxtaposition with no extra marking in the case of a possessor that is a full noun phrase (see the examples with kinship terms below), or by a possessive prefix in the case of a pronominal possessor. If the possessum is a relational root (see **3.1.3**), then it is additionally marked with the corresponding prefix.

Maria ajaka
María   ajaka
María   basket
'Maria's basket'

***che*ajaka**
che-ajaka
1SG.INACT-basket
'my basket'

***nde*resa**
nde-r-esa
1SG.INACT-POSSM-eye
'your eye(s)'

hóga
h-óga
POSSM3-house
'his/her/their house'

membykuña ména
memby+kuña   ména
child.of.woman+woman   husband
'a woman's son-in-law' (literally, 'husband of female child')

membykuimba'e ra'y
memby+kuimba'e   r-a'y
child.of.woman+man   POSSM-son.of.father
'a man's grandson'

Kili kamisa jyva votõ kuára
kili   kamisa   jyva   votõ   kuára
Aquilino   shirt   sleeve   button   hole
'the buttonhole of Aquilino's shirt sleeve'

The inverted order **possessum-possessor** is found when the so-called "possessor" actually expresses what something is made of or where it comes from:

kuairũ mbokaja
kua+irũ   mbokaja
finger+friend   coconut.palm
'coconut ring' (i.e., a ring made of coconut)

chipa so'o
chipa   so'o
chipa   meat
'meat chipa' (i.e., a chipa filled with meat)

pohã ka'aguy
pohã   ka'aguy
medicine forest
'medicine of the forest'[15]

Possessive prefixes are used when the possessor can be referenced and identified simply by person and number. In reality, these are not exclusively used to mark possession. Rather, they are the inactive person prefixes that are used more generally to refer to the subject of some intransitive verbs, a function that will be explained in **4.1.2**. Note that, as a result of nasal harmony (see **2.2.3**), these prefixes have variants for non-nasal and for nasal bases.

Person/Number	Non-nasal bases	Nasal bases
1SG	*che-*	*che-*
2SG	*nde-*	*ne-*
3	*i-, ij-, hi'-*	*iñ-*
1PL.INCL	*ñande-*	*ñane-*
1PL.EXCL	*ore-*	*ore-*
2PL	*pende-*	*pene-*

Points to note:

- For non-nasal bases and third-person possessors, *i-* is used with consonant-initial bases, *ij-* with bases beginning with an unstressed vowel and *hi'-* with those beginning with a stressed vowel:

  ipo
  i-po
  POSSM3-hand
  'his/her/their hand(s)'

---

[15] Example from Palacios Alcaine (1999, 41).

*ij*ao
ij-ao
POSSM3-clothes
'his/her/their clothes'

hi'áva
hi-'áva
POSSM3-hair
'his/her/their hair'

- For nasal bases, *iñ-* is used unless the base begins with a nasal or nasal-oral consonant:

*iñ*akã
iñ-akã
POSSM3-head
'his/her/their head(s)'

*i*nambi
i-nambi
POSSM3-ear
'his/her/their ear(s)'

*i*mbarakaja
i-mbarakaja
POSSM3-cat
'his/her/their cat(s)'

- The borrowed determiners *la* and *lo* often coexist with possessive prefixes (see **3.4.1**):

la ndepo
la   nde-po
DET.SG 2SG.INACT-hand
'your (sg.) hand(s)'

lo ñanemba'e teete
lo   ñane-mba'e   tee-te
DET.PL 1PL.INCL.INACT-thing one's.own-very
'our very own things'

- The stressed postposition =*gua* 'from' encodes a generic relation of belonging to, provenance from a place or time, or sometimes the material something is made of:

Che niko paraguaigua, paraguaygua.
che=niko   paraguái=gua   paraguay=gua
I=VERD   Paraguay=from   Asunción=from
'I am <u>from</u> Paraguay, <u>from</u> Asunción.'

jagua ogagua
jagua   óga=gua
dog   house=from
'dog <u>of</u> the house'

- Exclusive possession (as in English 'my own') is expressed with the stressed suffix *-tee*:

Che ahai cheñe'ẽteeme.
che   a-h-ai   che-ñe'ẽ-tee=me
I   1SG.ACT-POSSM3-write 1SG.INACT-language-one's.own=in
'I write in my <u>own</u> language.'

Chemba'etee.
che-mba'e-tee
1SG.INACT-thing-one's.own
'It is my <u>own</u> thing. / It is <u>truly</u> my thing.'

3.7 Nominal temporal-aspectual markers

As we will see in **4.10.1**, the marking of **tense** on verbs allows a speaker to place an event within a timeline. Marking **aspect**, on the other hand, allows a speaker to give information about how an event unfolds (see **4.10.2**). In Guarani, however, it is not only verbs that can have tense or aspect information. In fact, Guarani often marks nouns and noun phrases with this temporal-aspectual information. For example, when you say in English 'I will build a house', the house does not exist and cannot be technically called such until it is built in the future (this is called an **effected object**, an object that comes into existence as a result of the action described by the verb). In Guarani, in this case the noun phrase must bear a suffix that indicates this future tense or what we can call **prospective aspect** (expressing that an event occurs subsequent to another one). Likewise, when you say in English 'look, that was my car', the relation of possession indicated by 'my car' is not true in the present, but in the past. In this case, in Guarani the noun phrase must bear a suffix indicating past tense or

post-stative aspect (expressing that an event has ceased to occur at the time of another event).

These two tense/aspect suffixes for noun phrases are the stressed nominal suffix *-kue* (post-stative, POST) and the stressed nominal suffix *-rã* (destinative, DEST). *-Kue* (*-ngue* with nasal bases) indicates that the noun phrase expresses a property that was true at a prior time but has ceased to be true at the time of speech. (Do not confuse this tense/aspect suffix with the homophonous abstract nominalizer *-kue*; see **3.2.1.1.4**.)

*cheroga**kue***
che-r-óga-kue
1SG.INACT-POSSM-house-POST
'my former house'

*akã**ngue***
akã-ngue
head-POST
'a decapitated head of a dead person or animal' (Literally, 'something that used to be a head')

*vaka akã**ngue** yvyguy*
vaka   akã-ngue   yvy=guy
cow   head-POST   earth=under
'buried cow head' (a way of cooking a cow's head for food)

Ko'ã ta'angakuéra Quino rembiapokue.
ko'ã   t-a'anga=kuéra   Quino   r-embi-apo-kue
these NPOSSM-image=PL   Quino   POSSM-NMLZ.REL-make-POST
'These comics were made by Quino.' (Literally, 'These images are Quino's work.')

There is a rare stressed suffix *-re* that is used instead of *-kue* to indicate this post-stative aspect/past tense for nouns and adjectives. It is much more frequently used in combination with *-ha* to yield a past agentive nominalizer (see **3.2.1.1.1**) or with *-py* to yield a past passive nominalizer (see **3.2.1.1.2**).

*mena**re***
ména-re
husband-POST
'ex-husband'

mendare
menda-re
marry-POST
'married'

Chakore
cháko-re
Chaco.region-POST
'veteran of the Chaco War'

mokõi Lópe ra'yre
mokõi   Lópe   r-a'y-re
two   López   POSSM-son.of.man-POST
'two of López's <u>former</u> boys (i.e., former soldiers)'

On the other hand, *-rã* indicates that the noun phrase denotes a property that will be true in some future time. Most often, it is not necessary to indicate this in the English equivalent sentences, but it is obligatory in Guarani. In particular, as stated above, *-rã* is required for objects that come into being as a result of the event described by the verb (**effected objects**), and also in prospective contexts with non-specific objects (with verbs like 'make', 'build', 'look for', 'find' or 'buy', for example).

cherogarã
che-r-óga-rã
1SG.INACT-POSSM-house-DEST
'my <u>future</u> house'

ajapo orerembi'urã
a-japo   ore-r-embi-'u-rã
1SG.ACT-make   1PL.EXCL.INACT-POSSM-NMLZ.REL-ingest-DEST
'I am making our food' (i.e., the food does not exist before the end of its making)

Ikatu pejogua chuguikuéra y ha penerembi'urã
ikatu   pe-jogua   chugui=kuéra   y   ha
be.able   2PL.ACT-buy from.him/her=PL   water   and
pene-r-embi-'u-rã
2PL.INACT-POSSM-NMLZ.REL-ingest-DEST
'You can buy from them water and your food' (i.e., what will be your food after you buy it from them)

NOMINALS   123

. . . ojapo Ñanderu Tenonde ava ayvurã.

o-japo	ñande-r-u	t-enonde	ava	ayvu-rã
3.ACT-make	1PL.INCL.INACT-POSSM-father	NPOSSM-front	person	word-DEST

'. . . Our Father the First made the foundation of the human language.' (Literally, *ava ayvurã* 'that which was <u>destined to be</u> the human word'.)

Tomasa oipota ojuhu peteĩ iñirũrã neporãva

Tomasa	oi-pota	o-juhu	peteĩ	iñ-irũ-rã	ne-porã-va
Tomasa	3.ACT-want	3.ACT-find	one	3.INACT-friend-DEST	SUP-beautiful-SUP

'Tomasa wanted him to find a very beautiful partner' (i.e., a non-specific someone who <u>will be</u> a very beautiful partner)

Mitãnguéra ningo hína ñaneretã raperã.

mitã=nguéra	ningo	hína	ñane-r-etã	r-ape-rã
child=PL	VERD	PROG	1PL.INCL.INACT-POSSM-country	POSSM-road-DEST

'Children are the road<u>-to-be</u> (i.e., the future) of our country.'

These markers are used when the individual designated by the noun does not exist in the present time, or the property designated is not true at the present time, for any reason. For example, *cheroga**kue*** 'my former house' can be used either because I do not own the house anymore, or because I do not live there anymore, or because the thing denoted is physically not a house anymore. Likewise, *cherogarã* 'my future house' is appropriate when referring to an existing house that I will live in (but do not live in currently), or even in reference to materials that will be used in the construction of a house for me.

Note that the semantic contribution of the destinative *-rã* is often similar to the opposition of specific referents/non-specific referents in English:

ojuhuse peteĩ iñirũ neporãva

o-juhu-se	peteĩ	iñ-irũ	ne-porã-va
3.ACT-find-want	one	3.INACT-friend	SUP-beautiful-SUP

's/he wants to find a (specific) friend (of his/hers) who is beautiful'

ojuhuse peteĩ iñirũrã neporãva

o-juhu-se	peteĩ	iñ-irũ-rã	ne-porã-va
3.ACT-find-want	one	3.INACT-friend-DEST	SUP-beautiful-SUP

's/he wants to find a friend who <u>will be</u> beautiful' (i.e., (a non-specific) beautiful somebody who <u>will be</u> his/her friend)

The combination of the destinative *-rã* followed by the post-stative *-kue* has a **frustrative** interpretation.

*cheroga**rãngue***
che-r-óga-rã-ngue
1SG.INACT-POSSM-house-DEST-POST
'my former future house' (i.e., something that, in the past, was going to be my future house)

*Ñande jajapóne hutisiakuéra rembiapo**rãngue***.
ñande   ja-japo-ne   hutisia=kuéra   r-embi-apo-rã-ngue
we&you   1PL.INCL.ACT-make-DUB   justice=PL   POSSM-NMLZ.REL-make-DEST-POST
'We will do the work that justice will not do.' (Literally, 'the work that was for justice to do'.)

Although it is a logical possibility, these two suffixes can never be combined in the reverse order (for example, the form **cherogakuerã* to mean something like 'my future former house' does not exist).

4
Verbs

I noted in **1.5** and **3** that most Guarani roots have very flexible behaviour: many can behave like nouns or verbs depending on the sentence context. For this reason, it is difficult to define "verb" as something that expresses an action, and one has to resort to specific morphological properties. Thus, in Guarani, verbs are defined as a class of roots that can:

1. require the presence of a number of **arguments** (subjects, objects, and so on), broadly corresponding to a number of participants in an event. **Intransitive** verbs take a single argument, its subject; **transitive** verbs take a subject and an object. Other verbs, called **ditransitive**, take a subject, a direct object and an indirect object.
2. appear with one of the prefixes from the set of **active personal markers**: *a-, re-, o-, ja-/ña-, ro-, pe-* (*a**karu*** 'I eat/ate'; *re**guata*** 'you (sg.) walk(ed)').
3. appear with the unstressed **future tense/prospective aspect** suffix *-ta* (*oúta* 's/he/it will come').
4. appear with the **optative** prefix *t-* (to express permission, wishes or hopes: *tou* 'let him/her/it come').
5. appear with the following voice affixes: **antipassive, sociative causative** and **causative of transitive verbs** (see **6** for explanation of these voices and examples). (The causative of intransitive verbs and the agent-demoting voice prefix can also appear with non-verbal roots and therefore do not define the verb class uniquely.)
6. be turned into a noun or an adjective with a **deverbal nominalizing** affix (*hechapy* 'visible'; *tembiporu* 'tool'; see **3.2.1.1** and **3.2.1.2**.).

Verbs can be divided according to the number and kinds of arguments they take mainly into **intransitive** (taking only a subject) and **transitive**

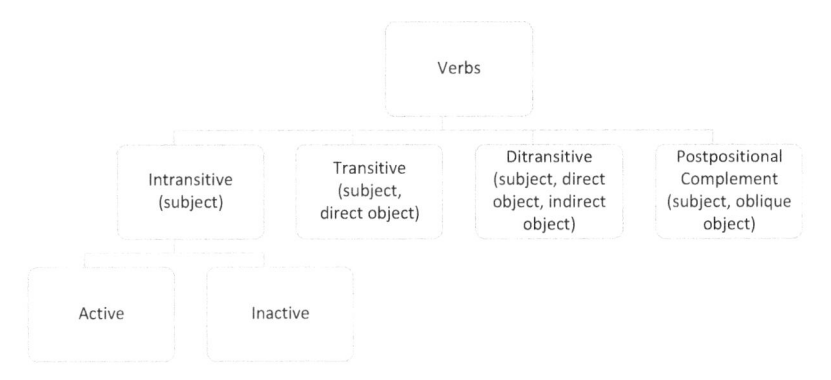

Figure 4.1 Main classes of verbs. *Source*: Author.

(taking a subject and a direct object). A few verbs are **ditransitive** (taking a subject, a direct object and an indirect object). Others also take two arguments like transitives, one a subject and the other an oblique object marked with a postposition (**postpositional complement verbs**). Within the intransitive class, some verbs are **active** and others **inactive**, depending on the shape of the person prefixes that accompany them.

4.1 Intransitive verbs

Intransitive predicates take only a subject and do not take any objects. In Guarani they belong to either an **active** class (prototypically, events under the control of an active, agent-like instigator) or an **inactive** class (prototypically, events that are not under the control of the single participant, who instead receives or experiences somewhat passively the action). The subject of active predicates is expressed with an active prefix from the *a-* set below, whereas the subject of inactive predicates is expressed with an inactive prefix from the *che-* set below. (I will explain the special 1>2SG and 1>2PL active prefixes in **4.2**.)

Guarani active subject prefixes

Person/Number	Non-nasal bases	Nasal bases
1SG	*a-*	*a-*
2SG	*re-*	*re-*
3	*o-*	*o-*
1PL inclusive	*ja-*	*ña-*
1PL exclusive	*ro-*	*ro-*

Person/Number	Non-nasal bases	Nasal bases
2PL	pe-	pe-
1>2SG	ro-	ro-
1>2PL	po(ro)-	po(ro)-

Guarani inactive prefixes

Person/Number	Non-nasal bases	Nasal bases
1SG	che-	che-
2SG	nde-	ne-
3	i-, ij-, hi'-	iñ-
1PL inclusive	ñande-	ñane-
1PL exclusive	ore-	ore-
2PL	pende-	pene-

Points to note:

- As said in **3.6**, the inactive prefixes are not specifically for subjects, but also refer to possessors.

4.1.1 Active verbs

As was mentioned in **4.1**, **active** verbs are prototypically actions under the control of a volitional, animate agent, but this is by no means a necessary condition. Verb roots like *ke* 'sleep' or *g̃uahẽ* 'arrive' are grammatically active even though they are not semantically active (at least not clearly). (Readers should be aware that this class is not called *active* but *areal* in traditional grammars, because the first-person singular prefix is *a-*. Some transitive verbs in this class are referred to as *aireal* verbs, because the first-person singular prefix is *ai-*. See **4.2**.)

The examples below show one verb with each of the person prefixes. Notably, the base form of verbs in Guarani can have present or past meanings, depending on context.

aguata
a-guata
1SG.ACT-walk
'I walk(ed)'

*re**mba'apo***
re-mba'apo
2SG.ACT-work
'you (sg.) work(ed)'

*o**ke***
o-ke
3.ACT-sleep
's/he/it/they sleep(s)/slept'

*ja**puka***
ja-puka
1PL.INCL.ACT-laugh
'we (and you) laugh(ed)'

*ro**sapukái***
ro-sapukái
1PL.EXCL.ACT-yell
'we (excluding you) yell(ed)'

*pe**purahéi***
pe-purahéi
2PL.ACT-sing
'you (pl.) sing/sang'

*o**ğuahẽ** (hikuái)*
o-ğuahẽ   (hikuái)
3.ACT-arrive (they)
'they arrive(d)'

There are several differences between this conjugation system and what we know from English. First, remember that Guarani has two first-person plural prefixes, one **inclusive** if the prefix includes the speaker(s) and the addressee(s), and one **exclusive** if the addresse(s) are not included in the prefix. The same is true, as we saw in **3.5.1**, for personal pronouns, and generally, anywhere else Guarani uses a first-person plural pronoun.

Second, all prefixes become nasalized with nasal bases, but this only causes a change in spelling for prefixes containing the consonants /ɟ/ <j> and /ⁿd/ <nd>, which alternate with /ɲ/ <ñ> and /n/ <n>. So for active verbs that means the only orthographic alternation is *ja-/ña-* for the first-person plural inclusive:

VERBS   129

*ja*puka	but	*ña*g̃uahẽ
ja-puka		ña-g̃uahẽ
1PL.INCL.ACT-laugh		1PL.INCL.ACT-arrive
'we (and you) laugh(ed)'		'we (and you) arrive(d)'
*ja*karu	but	*ña*kehe'ẽ
ja-karu		ña-ke+he'ẽ
1PL.INCL.ACT-eat(intransitive)		1PL.INCL.ACT-sleep+sweet/salty
'we (and you) eat/ate'		'we (and you) sleep/slept deeply'

Third, the form *o-* is not marked for number: there are no distinct third-person singular and third-person plural person prefixes. Rather, when it needs to be indicated unambiguously that a third-person subject is plural, a special subject pronoun, *hikuái* 'they', is used. Note that the use of *hikuái* is not obligatory to indicate a third-person plural, but it is used specially to avoid ambiguity. Also, pay attention to its uncommon placement: it is always postverbal; that is, it must always come after the verb, never before.

oikuaa **hikuái**
oi-kuaa   hikuái
3.ACT-know   they
'they know/knew'

Mba'éretepa imombyry **hikuái** *kuaatykuéragui.*
mba'ére-te=pa i-mombyry hikuái kuaa-ty=kuéra=gui
why-very=Q   3.INACT-far they   know-collective=PL=from
'Why are/were they cut off from the sciences?'

4.1.2 Inactive verbs

Inactive (or **stative**) verbs represent, prototypically, events that are not actions but rather states, or events that happen to a participant that has no control or volition. Strictly speaking, these "verbs" are in reality noun/adjective roots that function as predicates in a sentence when they are prefixed with inactive person markers (see **1.5**). (Remember also from **1.5** that the fact that Guarani has two different types of intransitive predicates is known as **split intransitivity**, or as **active/stative** split.)

*che****mandu'a***
che-mandu'a
1SG.INACT-remembrance
'I remember(ed)'

*che****vare'a***
che-vare'a
1SG.INACT-hunger
'I am/was hungry'

*nde****resarái***
nde-r-esarái
2SG.INACT-POSSM-oblivion
'you (sg.) forget/forgot'

*ne****mandu'a***
ne-mandu'a
SG.INACT-remembrance
'you (sg.) remember(ed)'

*i****porã***
i-porã
3.INACT-beautiful
's/he/it is/was pretty'

*ñande****katupyry***
ñande-katupyry
1PL.INCL.INACT-skilful
'we (and you) are/were smart'

*ñande****japu***
ñande-japu
1PL.INCL.INACT-falsehood
'we (and you) tell/told lies'

*ñane****rasẽ***
ñane-r-asẽ
1PL.INCL.INACT-POSSM-cry
'we (and you) cry/cried'

*ore**are***
ore-are
1PL.EXCL.INACT-lateness
'we (excluding you) are late'

*pende**yvate***
pende-yvate
2PL.INACT-high
'you (pl.) are tall'

*pene**memby***
pene-memby
2PL.INACT-child.of.woman
'you (pl.) have children' (said to a woman; *memby* is the term used for 'child of a woman')

We can see from the above examples that for inactive verbs there are more oral/nasal alternations: *nde-/ne-* for second-person singular, *ñande-/ñane* for first-person plural inclusive and *pende-/pene-* for second-person plural: that is, all prefixes containing the consonant /ⁿd/ <nd>, which alternates with /n/ <n>. Like *o-* for active verbs, the third-person inactive *i-* can be either singular or plural.

A last word of caution to readers: first, this class is not called *inactive* but *chendal* in traditional grammars, because the first-person singular prefix for this class is *che-*; second, whether an intransitive verb is active (areal) or inactive (chendal) is unpredictable from its meaning. Even though the subjects of most active intransitive verbs are semantically active (that is, they are agents that initiate and control the action), and most subjects of inactive intransitive verbs are not active (they usually suffer or experience an event), there are many common exceptions. Therefore, when each verb is learned, it must be memorized with its accompanying prefix set.

4.2 Transitive verbs

Transitive verbs take two arguments, a subject and a direct object. Prototypically, the subject is the **agent** in control of the action and the direct object is the **patient** that experiences the effects of the action. When the direct object is a noun phrase that refers to a human participant, it is marked with the postposition =pe 'in'. If the direct object refers to an animal or a thing, it has no special marking (but see **5.1** and **5.2** for more explanation and some exceptions).

*Mario o**hayhu** ijaryisýpe.*
Mario o-h-ayhu i-jarýi+sy=pe
Mario 3.ACT-POSSM3-love 3.INACT-grandmother+mother=in
'Mario <u>loves</u> his great-grandmother.'

*Ko'áğa re**mongarú**ta nerymba guéi.*
ko'áğa re-mo-ngaru-ta ne-r-ymba guéi
now 2SG.ACT-MAKE1-eat(intransitive)-FUT 2SG.INACT-POSSM-animal ox
'Now you (sg.) will <u>feed</u> your ox.'

*Che ha nde ja**joguá**ta juky.*
che ha nde ja-jogua-ta juky
I and you.SG 1PL.INCL.ACT-buy-FUT salt
'You and I will <u>buy</u> salt.'

The order need not be subject-verb-object as normally found in English (see chapter **8** for more on word order in sentences). The order verb-object-subject shown in the next two examples is particularly common as an alternative:

ojukapáta lo mitãme la fanatismo
o-juka-pa-ta lo mitã=me la fanatismo
3.ACT-kill-all-FUT DET.PL child=in DET.SG fanaticism
'fanaticism will destroy the boys'

opilla chupe la sakritan
o-pilla chupe la sakritan
3.ACT-nab to.him/her DET.SG sacristan
'the sacristan nabbed him'

For some transitive verbs, the active prefixes have an added *-i*, and for this reason, they are called *aireales* in the traditional terminology. The set of aireal prefixes is as follows:

Guarani active subject prefixes (aireal verbs)

Person/Number	Non-nasal bases	Nasal bases
1SG	*ai-*	*ai-*
2SG	*rei-*	*rei-*
3	*oi-*	*oi-*
1PL inclusive	*jai-*	*ñai-*
1PL exclusive	*roi-*	*roi-*
2PL	*pei-*	*pei-*

Some examples with verbs in this aireal class:

*Ai**pytyvõ** ichupe.*
ai-pytyvõ ichupe
1SG.ACT-help to.him/her
'I help(ed) him/her.'

*Ndépa rei**kuaa** cheréra.*
nde=pa rei-kuaa che-r-éra
you.SG=Q 2SG.ACT-know 1SG.INACT-POSSM-name
'Do you (sg.) know my name?'

*Kola akói oi**nupã** imbarakaja.*
Kola akói oi-nupã i-mbarakaja
Kola always 3.ACT-beat 3.INACT-cat
'Kola always punishes his cat.'

*Roi**kotevẽ** pirapire.*
roi-kotevẽ pira+pire
1PL.EXCL.ACT-need fish+skin
'We need money.'

This *-i* is part of the prefix and not part of the root because it (generally) disappears when other prefixes are added:

*a**poro**pytyvõ*
a-poro-pytyvõ
1SG.ACT-PEOPLE-help
'I help (people)'

ñepytyvõ
ñe-pytyvõ
AGD-help
'help (noun)'

ñopytyvõ
ño-pytyvõ
RECP-help
'mutual help'

Oresy orenupã.
ore-sy   ore-nupã
1PL.EXCL.INACT-mother   1PL.EXCL.INACT-beat
'Our mother beats us.'

ñenupã
ñe-nupã
AGD-beat
'(a/the) torture'

Importantly, several common verbs have a root that begins with *i* but they are not from the aireal class. These are *iko* 'to be, to live, to exist', *ime* 'to be located', *ikove* 'to live', *ike* 'to enter', *imo'ã* 'to think', *ity* 'to throw'.

Transitive verbs in Guarani present three complications from the viewpoint of a speaker of English. The first one is that it seems safe to assume that the person prefix represents the subject of the verb. Yet, this prefix sometimes obligatorily represents the direct object of the verb, instead of the subject. The second one is that there are special subject prefixes when the subject is first-person and the direct object is second-person. The third one is that relational verbs change their prefix to *h-* or *r-* depending on the person prefix used before them. I will explain each one of these unexpected properties in turn.

First, the choice of a verb prefix for transitive verbs always depends on the relative importance of subject and object, with the first person being more important than the second, and the second more important than the third (the so-called **person hierarchy**, often schematized as 1 > 2 > 3). Notably, when the direct object is higher in the person hierarchy than the subject, it is the object that must be marked on the verb, and this is done by an inactive person prefix. Another way of saying this is that the person prefix always refers to the participant that is higher in the person hierarchy, and does so with an active prefix if this highest participant is the agent (also when both participants are third-person), and with an inactive prefix if the highest participant is the patient. (Incidentally, this is the reason I am calling the prefixes **active** and **inactive**: active prefixes refer to the agent of transitive verbs, inactive prefixes to the patient.)

ainupã ichupe (**1SG subject** > 3 object: active prefix)
ai-nupã   ichupe
1SG.ACT-beat   to.him/her
'I beat him/her'

*che*nupã ha'e (**1SG object** > 3 subject: inactive prefix)
che-nupã   ha'e
1SG.INACT-beat s/he
's/he beat me'

*a*gueru pakova (**1SG subject** > 3 object: active prefix)
a-gueru   pakova
1SG.ACT-bring banana
'I bring bananas'

ha'e *che*gueru (**1SG object** > 3 subject: inactive prefix)
ha'e che-gueru
s/he 1SG.ACT-bring
's/he brings/brought me'

***Che**gueru reiete.* (**1SG object** > 3 subject: inactive prefix)
che-gueru   rei-ete
1SG.ACT-bring   in.vain-very
'They brought me for nothing.'

*Ehendu nderúpe, **nde**reru ypy va'ekue.* (**2SG object** > 3 subject: inactive prefix)
e-h-endu   nde-r-u=pe   nde-reru   ypy
IMP-POSSM3-hear   2SG.INACT-POSSM-father=in   2SG.INACT-bring   beginning
va'ekue
PAST
'Listen to your father that brought you at the beginning'

136   A GRAMMAR OF PARAGUAYAN GUARANI

*aagradeceterei peẽme **ore**visitahaguére ikatuhaguáicha peikuaami la situación* (**1PL object** > 2PL subject: inactive prefix)
a-agradece-terei peẽme ore-visita-hague=re
1SG.ACT-thank-very.much to.you.PL 1PL.EXCL.INACT-visit-NMLZ.PAST=at
ikatu=haǧua-icha pei-kuaa-mi la situación
be.able=for-as 2PL.ACT-know-DIM DET.SG situation
'I thank you very much for visiting us so that you will know the situation a little'

Therefore, whereas the active prefixes are indeed subject prefixes exclusively, the inactive prefixes can be subject prefixes (with intransitive inactive verbs), but are markers of a patient that is high in the person hierarchy with transitive verbs.

Interestingly, when the subject is second-person plural and the direct object is first-person singular, the active prefix *pe-* for the agent can apparently also be used together with the inactive prefix *che-* for the patient. In the first example below, *che-* marks the first-person singular direct object and *pe-* marks the second-person plural subject (see also the fourth example). In all the other cases, if the subject must be indicated, it is done with a free personal pronoun (see the second and third examples below).

*Ma'erãvoi piko **peche**gueru la sapy'aiterã.* (1SG object > 2PL subject)
ma'erã=voi=piko pe-che-gueru la sapy'a-ite-rã
what.for=EMPH=Q 2PL.ACT-1SG.INACT-bring DET.SG a.little.while-very-DEST
'What for then did you (pl.) bring me for such a short time?'

*Ma'erãvoi piko **nde che**gueru la sapy'aiterã.* (1SG object > 2SG subject)
ma'erã=voi=piko nde che-gueru la sapy'a-ite-rã
what.for=EMPH=Q you.SG 1SG.INACT-bring DET.SG a.little.while-very-DEST
'What for then did you (sg.) bring me for such a short time?'

*Ma'erãvoi piko **pende ore**gueru la sapy'aiterã.* (1PL object > 2PL subject)
ma'erã=voi=piko pende ore-gueru la sapy'a-ite-rã
what.for=EMPH=Q you.PL 1PL.EXCL.INACT-bring DET.SG a.little.while-very-DEST
'What for then did you (pl.) bring us for such a short time?'

*Aguyjetaite **peche**rendurehe.*
aguyje=ta-ite pe-che-r-endu=rehe
thanks=multitude-very 2SG.ACT-1SG.INACT-POSSM-listen=at
'Many thanks for (your) listening to me.'

The second complication occurs when a transitive verb has a first-person singular or plural subject and a second-person singular or plural direct object. In this case, a single prefix is used for both participants: the **portmanteau** prefix *ro-* encodes both a first-person (singular or plural) subject and a second-person singular object simultaneously; the portmanteau prefix *po-* encodes both a first-person (singular or plural) subject and a second-person plural object simultaneously.

*ro*hayhu (never *ahayhu ndéve)
ro-h-ayhu
1>2SG-POSSM3-love
'I/we love you (sg.)'

*po*hayhu (never *ahayhu pendéve)
po-h-ayhu
1>2PL-POSSM3-love
'I/we love you (pl.)'

¡***Ro**ha'arõhína cheru!*
ro-h-a'arõ=hína   che-r-u
1>2SG-POSSM3-wait=PROG 1SG.INACT-POSSM-father
'I was waiting for you (sg.), dad!'

***Ro**gueromandu'áta.*
ro-guero-mandu'a-ta
1>2SG-MAKE.SOC-remember-FUT
'I will remember you (sg.) (in the sense of 'commemorate' or 'memorialize').'

***Po**hendu hína Capiataguive.*
po-h-endu=hína   Capiata=guive
1>2PL-POSSM3-listen=PROG Capiata=since
'I am listening to you (pl.) from Capiata.'

*Ajegueraha **po**juhu haǧua.*
a-je-gueraha   po-juhu   haǧua
1SG.ACT-AGD-carry   1>2PL-find for
'I am/was brought to meet you (pl.).'

The reader must pay attention to the fact that the 1 > 2SG form *ro-* is homophonous with the prefix for the first-person plural exclusive *ro-*:

*ro*hayhu most frequently means '<u>I/we</u> love <u>you (sg.)</u>' but it could also mean '<u>we (excluding you)</u> love' in some contexts.

The third and last complication is that if the verbal root is relational, it takes the prefix *h-* with active, imperative and portmanteau person prefixes, and the prefix *r-* with inactive person prefixes (see **4.6** for more details).

*a**h**endu ichupe*
a-h-endu   ichupe
1SG.ACT-POSSM3-listen   to.him/her
'I listen to him/her'

rohendu
ro-h-endu
1>2SG-POSSM3-listen
'I listen to you'

nde cherendu
nde   che-r-endu
you.SG   1SG.INACT-POSSM-listen
'you listen to me'

ha'e nerendu
ha'e   ne-r-endu
s/he   2SG.INACT-POSSM-listen
's/he listens to you'

Putting all these observations together in a table, the person prefix marking on transitive verbs is as follows:

Object / Subject	1SG	1PL.INCL	1PL.EXCL	2SG	2PL	3
1SG				ro-	po-	a(i)-
1PL.INCL				ro-	po-	ja(i)-/ña(i)-
1PL.EXCL				ro-	po-	ro(i)-
2SG	che-	ñan(d)e-	ore-			re(i)- (e(i)-)
2PL	che-	ñan(d)e-	ore-			pe(i)-
3	che-	ñan(d)e-	ore-	n(d)e-	pe(n)de-	o(i)-

Points to note:

- The dark grey cells are combinations of persons that are not readily expressible. If prompted to say something like that, speakers can usually find a periphrastic formulation, for example:

  che amombe'úta ñandéve
  che   a-mombe'u-ta   ñandéve
  I   1SG.ACT-tell-FUT   to.us&you
  'I will tell us (something)'

- If the subject is the same as the direct object (light grey cells), the event is **reflexive** (the agent acts on him- or herself) and the **agent-demoting** prefix *je-/ñe-* is used (see **6.3**).
- If the subject and the direct object are both third-person, but they are different participants, then the verb is marked with the active third-person prefix *o-*.
- Note, therefore, that the full paradigm of active marking that is often presented as basic in grammars is in reality only found with third-person objects.
- The almost complete paradigm of inactive prefixes is found with third-person subjects, except for the third-person inactive *i-*.

4.3 Ditransitive verbs

When a verb requires a subject and two objects, one direct and one indirect, it is called **ditransitive**. These are usually verbs that refer to an event of transfer of something concrete or abstract. They are often verbs of communication or verbs of giving. The indirect object is often human or animal (that is, **animate**), because it is the recipient of the transfer. It is marked with *=pe/=me* 'in' if it is a noun phrase; otherwise it is a direct object pronoun. The direct object is the thing transferred (often **inanimate**), and it has no special marking.

Amombe'úta ndéve la ojehuva'ekue.
a-mombe'u-ta   ndéve   la   o-jehu-va'e-kue
1SG.ACT-tell-FUT   to.you.SG   DET.SG   3.ACT-happen-ADJZ-POST
'I will tell you what happened.'

Cheresarái nda'éi peẽme peteĩ mba'e.
che-r-esarái nd-a'e-i peẽme peteĩ mba'e
1SG.INACT-POSSM-oblivion NEG-say-NEG to.you.PL one thing
'I forgot to <u>tell</u> you something.'

*To**me'ẽ** ñanembo'ehárape iñaranduka.*
t-o-me'ẽ ñane-mbo'e-hára=pe iñ-aranduka
OPT-3.ACT-give 1PL.INCL.INACT-teach-NMLZ.AG=in 3.INACT-book
'Let him/her <u>give</u> his/her book to our teacher.'

If the direct object (the thing transferred) is human, although it would be usually also marked with =*pe*/=*me*, it remains unmarked in order to avoid ambiguity in deciding which is the person transferred and which is the recipient of the transfer.

*Ome'ẽ **ita'ýra** Ñandejárape.*
o-me'ẽ i-t-a'ýra ñande-jára=pe
3.ACT-give 3.INACT-NPOSSM-son.of.father 1PL.INCL.INACT-lord=in
'He gave <u>his son</u> to our Lord.'[16]

4.4 Postpositional complement verbs

Transitive verbs are not the only verbs that take two arguments. Some other verbs (in their vast majority active) require a subject and another complement which is a phrase headed by a **postposition** (see **5**). Each particular verb specifies and requires (that is, **governs**) a given postposition. The three postpositions that can be required are =*re(he)* 'at', =*ndi(ve)* 'with' and =*gui* 'from'. The portmanteau prefixes *ro-* and *po-* are never used with these verbs.

The majority of postpositional complement verbs require the unstressed postposition =*re(he)*:

*a**ikotevẽ** nde**rehe***
ai-kotevẽ nde=rehe
1SG.ACT-need 2SG.INACT=at
'I <u>need</u> you'

---

[16] Example from Melià *et al.* (1997, 48).

VERBS 141

*che**mandu'á**ta **he**se*
che-mandu'a-ta   hese
1SG.INACT-remembrance-FUT   at.him/her
'I will <u>remember</u> him/her'

*mba'éguipa re**maña** péicha nde**sý**re*
mba'e=gui=pa   re-maña   pe-icha   nde-sy=re
what=from=Q   2SG.ACT-look.at   MED.SG-as   2SG.INACT-mother=at
'why are you <u>looking at</u> your mother like that?'

*ha'e o**ma'ẽ** pe tapé**re***
ha'e   o-ma'ẽ   pe   t-ape=re
s/he   3.ACT-look.at   MED.SG   NPOSSM-road=at
's/he <u>looks at</u> that road'

*o**mbokapu** hikuái mitãmí**re***
o-mbo-kapu   hikuái   mitã-mi=re
3.ACT-MAKE1-shot   they   child-DIM=at
'they <u>shot</u> the little boy'

*a**menda**se nde**rehe***
a-menda-se   nde=rehe
1SG.ACT-marry-want   2SG.INACT=at
'I want to <u>marry</u> you'

*ani re**ndyvu** che**rehe***
ani   re-ndyvu   che=rehe
NEG.IMP   2SG.ACT-spit   1SG.INACT=at
'do not <u>spit at</u> me'

*Ñandejára o**ñangareko** maymá**re***
ñande-jára   o-ñangareko   mayma=re
1PL.INCL.INACT-lord   3.ACT-take.care.of   every=at
'Our Lord <u>takes care of</u> everyone'

*ha'e o**poko** che**rehe***
ha'e   o-poko   che=rehe
s/he   3.ACT-touch   1SG.INACT=at
's/he <u>touched</u> me'

hesaho sapy'a aguaráre
h-esaho   sapy'a   aguara=re
POSSM3-notice   suddenly   fox=at
's/he suddenly noticed a fox'

ajojái nderehe
a-jojái   nde=rehe
1SG.ACT-taunt   2SG.INACT=at
'I make fun of you'

oja hese
o-ja   hese
3.ACT-stick   at.him/her
's/he/it stuck to him/her/it'

ajopy ichupe chejehe
a-jopy   ichupe   chejehe
1SG.ACT-press   to.him/her   at.myself
'I pressed him/her against me/myself.'

ani rejahéi ndesýre
ani   re-jahéi   nde-sy=re
NEG.IMP   2SG.ACT-offend 2SG.INACT-mother=at
'do not scorn your mother'

Ani repena cherehe!
ani   re-pena   che=rehe
NEG.IMP   2SG.ACT-worry   1SG.INACT=at
'Don't worry about me!'

Cherehe nereñembohorymo'ãi.
che=rehe   ne-re-ñe-mbo-h-ory-mo'ã-i
1SG.INACT=at   NEG-2SG.ACT-AGD-MAKE1-POSSM3-joy-NEG.FUT-NEG
'You will not make fun of me.'

The word *aguyje* 'thanks' also requires =*rehe* to express the reason that thanks are being given and =*pe*/=*me* for whoever is being thanked:

Aguyje peẽme cherenduhaguére ha chepytyvõhaguére.
aguyje peẽme che-r-endu-hague=re ha
thanks to.you.PL 1SG.INACT-POSSM-listen-NMLZ.PAST=at and
che-pytyvõ-hague=re
1SG.INACT-help-NMLZ.PAST=at
'<u>Thanks</u> <u>to</u> you <u>for</u> listening to me and <u>for</u> helping me.'

A few verbs that require a complement headed by the unstressed postposition =*gui* 'from' are shown in the following examples.

*o**kañy** che**gui** chekyse*
o-kañy chehegui che-kyse
3.ACT-become.lost from.me 1SG.INACT-knife
'I <u>lost</u> my knife'

*E**poi** che**gui**, he'i oka'úva.*
e-poi chehegui he'i o-ka'u-va
IMP-set.free from.me says 3.ACT-get.drunk-ADJZ
'<u>Let go of</u> me, said the drunk person.'

*ani nde**resarái** ndeypykuéra**gui***
ani nde-r-esarái nde-ypy=kuéra=gui
NEG 2SG.INACT-POSSM-oblivion 2SG.INACT-origin=PL=from
'do not <u>forget</u> your ancestors'

*a**ñepyrú**ta chekorapý**gui***
a-ñepyru-ta che-korapy=gui
1SG.ACT-begin-FUT 1SG.INACT-yard=from
'I will <u>begin with</u> my yard'

Other roots with a more adjectival/adverbial meaning also require =*gui*:

*ko kagua **henyhẽ** ý**gui***
ko kagua h-enyhẽ y=gui
PROX.SG drinking.glass POSSM3-full water=from
'this glass is <u>full of</u> water'

*Umi mba'eporã i**mombyry** chu**gui**kuéra.*
umi mba'e+porã i-mombyry chugui=kuéra
NPROX.PL thing+beautiful 3.INACT-far from.him/her=PL
'Such beautiful things are <u>far from</u> them.'

*ore**kuerái** neme**mbýgui***
ore-kuerái ne-memby=gui
1PL.EXCL.INACT-annoyance 2SG.INACT-child.of.woman=from
'we are <u>fed up with</u> your child'

*Che**kuerái** che maĩna po'a'ỹ ha mboriahú**gui**, ha a**tĩ**ma pende**hegui** amba'ejerure haguã.*
che-kuerái   che-maĩna   po'a-'ỹ   ha   mboriahu=gui ha
1SG.INACT-annoyance 1SG.INACT-godmother   luck-PRIV   and   poverty=from   and
a-tĩ-ma   pendehegui   a-mba'e-jerure   haguã
1SG.ACT-feel.shame-already   from.you.PL   1SG.ACT-THING-petition for
'Godmother, I am <u>fed up with</u> the bad luck and the poverty, and I already feel shame coming to you to ask for things.'

Reciprocal or **symmetric verbs** are those verbs where the same action that applies to the object applies to the subject in the reverse direction. Think about English verbs used with 'one another' or 'each other'. In Guarani these verbs require the unstressed enclitic =*ndi(ve)* 'with'. Several of these verbs are a combination of the reciprocal prefix *jo-/ño-* (*ju-/ñu-* before a vowel) and a verbal root. The pronoun *oñondive* means 'with each other'.

*Ai**koporã** he**ndive**. Roi**koporã** oño**ndive**.*
a-iko+porã   hendive   ro-iko+porã   oñondive
1SG.ACT-be+good   with.him/her   1PL.EXCL.ACT-be+good with.each.other
'I <u>get along with</u> him/her. We <u>get along</u>.'

*Ai**kovai** ne**ndive**. Jai**kovai** oño**ndive**.*
a-iko+vai   ne=ndive   ja-iko+vai   oñondive
1SG.ACT-be+bad 2SG.INACT=with 1PL.INCL.ACT-be+bad   with.each.other
'I <u>do not get along with</u> you. We (and you) <u>do not get along</u>.'

*Re**juasápa** nderú**ndive**. Pe**juasápa** oño**ndive**.*
re-juasa=pa   nde-r-u=ndive   pe-juasa=pa
2SG.ACT-run.into=Q 2SG.INACT-POSSM-father=with   2PL.ACT-run.into=Q
oñondive
with.each.other
'Did you <u>run into</u> your father? Did you <u>run into</u> each other?'

*Oñorairõ hembirekó**ndive**. Oñorairõ oño**ndive**.*
o-ño-rairõ   h-embireko=ndive   o-ño-rairõ   oñondive
3.ACT-RECP-attack   POSSM3-wife=with   3.ACT-RECP-attack   with.each.other
'He <u>fights with</u> his wife. They <u>fight with</u> one another.'

There are other predicates that require =*ndi(ve)* but are not symmetric:

*Reñemyrõ pa'í**ndive**.*
re-ñemyrõ   pa'i=ndive
2SG.ACT-take.offence   priest=with
'You <u>feel resentful towards</u> the priest.' (But this does not entail that the priest feels resentful towards you.)

*Cherajy i**pochy** isý**ndi**.*
che-r-ajy   i-pochy   i-sy=ndi
1SG.INACT-POSSM-daughter.of.man   3.INACT-anger   3.INACT-mother=with
'My daughter <u>is angry at</u> her mom.' (But this does not entail that the mother is angry at my daughter.)

Only one verb requires the postposition =*pe*/=*me*: the very common verb *ñe'ẽ* 'to speak' when it means 'to speak (in) a language'. It requires =*rehe* with the meaning 'to speak about someone'.

*Re**ñe'ẽ**piko guaraní**me** tẽra karaiñe'ẽ**me**.*
re-ñe'ẽ=piko   guarani=me   tẽra   karai+ñe'ẽ=me
2SG.ACT-speak=Q   Guarani=in   or   gentleman+language=in
'Do you <u>speak (in)</u> Guarani or <u>(in)</u> Spanish?'

*Oñe'ẽ che**rehe**.*
o-ñe'ẽ   che=rehe
3.ACT-speak   1SG.INACT=at
'S/he spoke about me.'

4.5 Irregular verbs

Irregular verbs are those that have different forms of the root and/or the person prefixes (that is, different **allomorphs** of the root or prefixes).

Three Guarani verbs have changes in the root: *ho* 'to go', *ju* 'to come' and *'e* 'to say' (in boldface, the deviations from the assumed basic shape of the root).

Person/Number	*ho* 'to go'	*ju* 'to come'	*'e* 'to say'
1SG	a*ha*	a*ju*	**ha***'e*
2SG	re*ho*	re*ju*	**ere**
3	o*ho*	o*u*	**he***'i*
1PL inclusive	ja*ha*	ja*ju*	ja*'e*
1PL exclusive	ro*ho*	ro*ju*	ro*'e*
2PL	pe*ho*	pe*ju*	pe*je*

Points to note:

- The root allomorphs for 'to go' are *ha* and *ho*; for 'to come', *ju* and *u*; for 'to say', *'e*, *re*, *'i* and *je*.
- *'e* 'to say' also has person prefix allomorphy in the first-person singular (*ha-* instead of *a-*) and in the third person (*he-* instead of *o-*).
- Two of the negative forms of *'e* 'to say' are also irregular (see **4.9** for the regular formation of predicate negation): *(che) nda'éi* 'I don't/didn't say' and *(ha'e) nde'íri* s/he doesn't/didn't say'. The form for the second-person singular, *(nde) nde'eréi*, is not really irregular, only that the appearance of the glottal stop before the root is to be remarked.

Other irregular verbs only show different forms of the person prefix in the first-person singular (*ha-* instead of *a-*) and in the third person (*ho-* instead of *o-*), just like *'e* 'to say'. I give all forms here and apply boldface to the irregular (or unexpected) allomorphs.

Person/Number	*'u* 'to eat/drink something (transitive), to ingest'	*y'u* 'to drink water'	*'yta* 'to swim'	*'a* 'to fall'
1SG	**ha***'u*	**hay***'u*	**ha***'yta*	**ha***'a*
2SG	re*'u*	re*y'u*	re*'yta*	re*'a*
3	**ho***'u*	**hoy***'u*	**ho***'yta*	**ho***'a*
1PL inclusive	ja*'u*	ja*y'u*	ja*'yta*	ja*'a*
1PL exclusive	ro*'u*	ro*y'u*	ro*'yta*	ro*'a*
2PL	pe*'u*	pe*y'u*	pe*'yta*	pe*'a*

Points to note:

- The second-person singular imperative forms are irregular because they add *h* at the beginning: **he***'u* 'eat (something)', **hey***'u* 'drink water', **he***'yta* 'swim', **he***'a* 'fall'.

- First-person singular and third-person negative forms are irregular in that they "revert" to the regular person prefixes: *nda'úi* 'I don't eat (transitive)', *ndo'úi* 's/he doesn't eat (transitive)', *nday'úi* 'I don't drink water', *ndoy'úi* 's/he doesn't drink water', *nda'ytái* 'I don't swim', *ndo'ytái* 's/he doesn't swim', *nda'ái* 'I don't fall', *ndo'ái* 's/he doesn't fall'. Verbal negation is described in **4.9**.
- This last point suggests that the first-person singular and third-person forms add an *h* to avoid a sequence of syllables with glottal stop onsets. (The addition of such a sound to regularize or facilitate pronunciation is called **epenthesis**.)

4.6 Relational (multiform) verbs

As was mentioned in **3.1.3**, some verbal roots require the use of relational prefixes. The prefix *h-* (for the third-person pronominal possessor) is the one used with active prefixes, portmanteau person prefixes and imperative prefixes. The prefix *r-* (for all other cases of possession) is used with inactive person prefixes. The non-possessed prefix *t-* yields a nominal interpretation. I exemplify with the root *-ayhu* 'to love'.

ahayhu ichupe
a-h-ayhu   ichupe
1SG.ACT-POSSM3-love   to.him/her
'I love him/her'

rohayhu
ro-h-ayhu
1>2SG-POSSM3-love
'I love you'

ehayhu
e-h-ayhu
IMP-POSSM3-love
'love (2sg imperative)'

nde cherayhu
nde   che-r-ayhu
you.SG   1SG.INACT-POSSM-love
'you love me'

*peteĩha **t**ayhu*
peteĩ-ha   t-ayhu
one-TH   NPOSSM-love
'first love'

Except for the change in their initial consonant prefix, these verbs behave in all other respects like any other verb. Some more examples:

*o**h**eka ho'úva'erã umi tapỹiha rupi*
o-h-eka   ho-'u-va'erã   umi   tapỹi-ha=rupi
3.ACT-POSSM3-seek 3.ACT-ingest-must   NPROX.PL   native.dwelling-NMLZ.LOC=around
's/he <u>looked for</u> something to eat around those huts'

*Mávapa che**r**eka hína.*
máva=pa   che-r-eka   hína
who=Q   1SG.INACT-POSSM-seek   PROG
'Who is <u>looking for</u> me?'

*Oĩ heta la gente pero che ro**hetũ**míta.*
oĩ   h-eta   la   gente   pero   che   ro-h-etũ-mi-ta
there.is   POSSM3-numerous DET.SG people   but   I   1>2SG-POSSM3-kiss-DIM-FUT
'There are a lot of people but I will <u>kiss</u> you a little.'

*Ahasénte nendive ha uperire che**retũ**.*
a-ha-se-nte   ne=ndive   ha   upe=rire   che-r-etũ
1SG.ACT-go-want-only   2SG.INACT=with   and   MED.SG=after   1SG.INACT-POSSM-kiss
'I want to go with you and then you <u>kiss</u> me.'

Some of these predicates are relational because they are compounds containing a relational root. I indicate the original relational root in the list below. (See **17.5** for a fuller list.)

Intransitive relational predicates

-ãimbiti 'teeth-clenching' (from *t-ãi* 'tooth')
-ãitarara 'teeth-chattering' (from *t-ãi* 'tooth')
-asẽ 'cry'
-atatĩ 'smoke' (from *t-ata* 'fire')
-endysyry 'drool' (from *t-endy* 'saliva')
-esarái 'to forget'

Transitive relational predicates

-*a'arõ* 'to wait'
-*apy* 'to burn'
-*asa* 'to pass'
-*ayhu* 'to love'
-*echa* 'to see'
-*echagi* 'to neglect' (from -*echa* 'to see')
-*echakuaa* 'to understand' (from -*echa* 'to see')
-*echambi* 'to suspect' (from -*echa* 'to see')
-*echaramo* 'to admire' (from -*echa* 'to see')
-*echavoi* 'to forebode' (from -*echa* 'to see')
-*eja* 'to leave'
-*eka* 'to seek'
-*enói* 'to call'
-*epyme'ẽ* 'to pay' (from -*epy* 'cost')
-*esy* 'to grill'
-*etũ* 'to smell; to kiss'
-*ovasa* 'to bless' (from -*ova* 'face')
-*upi* 'to lift'
-*upity* 'to reach'

4.7 Verbs with increments

Some transitive verbs have an increment immediately prefixed to the root that has no discernible meaning (this is called sometimes a linking element or an **interfix**). This increment is -*gue*- with all person prefixes that end in *o* (be it active, inactive or portmanteau prefixes), and -*re*- with inactive person prefixes that end in *e*. Below, I boldface the interfixes for the forms that have them.

Person prefix	*ru* 'to bring'	*nohẽ* 'to take out'
1SG.ACT	*aru* 'I bring'	*anohẽ* 'I take out'
1SG.INACT	*chereru* 'bring(s) me'	*cherenohẽ* 'take(s) me out'
1>2SG	*ro**gue**ru* 'I/we bring you (sg.)'	*ro**gue**nohẽ* 'I/we take you (sg.) out'
1>2PL	*po**gue**ru* 'I/we bring you (pl.)'	*po**gue**nohẽ* 'I/we take you (pl.) out'
2SG.ACT	*reru* 'you (sg.) bring'	*renohẽ* 'you (sg.) take out'

2SG.INACT	*nde**r**eru* 'bring(s) you (sg.)'	*ne**r**enohẽ* 'take(s) you (sg.) out'
3.ACT	*o**gue**ru* 's/he/it/they bring(s)'	*o**gue**nohẽ* 's/he/it/they take(s) out'
1PL.INCL.ACT	*jaru* 'we (and you) bring'	*ñanohẽ* 'we (and you) take out'
1PL.INCL.INACT	*ñande**r**eru* 'bring(s) us (and you)'	*ñane**r**enohẽ* 'take(s) us (and you) out'
1PL.EXCL.ACT	*ro**gue**ru* 'we (not you) bring'	*ro**gue**nohẽ* 'we (not you) take out'
1PL.EXCL.INACT	*ore**r**eru* 'bring(s) us (not you)'	*ore**r**enohẽ* 'take(s) us (not you) out'
2PL.ACT	*peru* 'you (pl.) bring'	*penohẽ* 'you (pl.) take out'
2PL.INACT	*pende**r**eru* 'bring(s) you (pl.)'	*pende**r**enohẽ* 'take(s) you (pl.) out'

Points to note:

- Other common verbs in this class are *raha* 'to carry', *reko* 'to have', *rovia* 'to believe'.

    *ro**gue**raha*
    ro-gueraha
    1PL.EXCL.ACT-carry
    'we carry/carried'

    *nde**r**eraha*
    nde-reraha
    2SG.INACT-carry
    's/he/it/they carry/carried you (sg.)'

- Speakers sometimes use the *-gue-* increment with prefixes not ending in *o*:

    *Ma'ẽrãvoi piko pe che**gue**ru la sapy'aiterã.*
    ma'ẽrã=voi=piko   pe-che-gueru   la
    what.for=EMPH=Q   2PL.ACT-1SG.INACT-bring   DET.SG
    sapy'a-ite-rã
    a.little.while-very-DEST
    'What for then did <u>you (pl.)</u> bring <u>me</u> for such a short time?'

VERBS   151

*A**gue**ru ndéve yva.*
a-gueru ndéve yva
1SG.ACT-bring to.you.SG fruit
'I bring you (sg.) fruit.'

In fact, the *-gue-* interfix is often used by speakers for the whole verbal paradigm: *a**gue**reko* 'I have', *re**gue**reko* 'you (sg.) have', *o**gue**reko* 's/he/it has', and so on.

- All verbs in this group begin with *r(o)-* or *n-*. All these verbs, either currently or at least historically, refer to events where the subject and object participants both accomplish the same action together, the subject being the instigator of the joint action (they are, or were, **comitative** (expressing accompaniment) or **sociative causative** verbs; see **6.6.2**).
- The *-re-* interfix used with inactive person prefixes that end in *e-* can sometimes be pronounced simply *-e-*:

*che**e**raha*
che-eraha
1SG.INACT-carry
'you take me (somewhere)'

- The interfix *-re-* is also required by the nominalizing prefix *-embi-*:

*tembi**re**ru*
t-embi-reru
NPOSSM-NMLZ.REL-bring
'(a) thing brought'

*tembi**re**raha*
t-embi-reraha
NPOSSM-NMLZ.REL-carry
'(a) thing sent'

4.8 Verbs with loss of initial consonant

Some verbal roots that begin with *j-* (when oral) or *ñ-* (when nasal) elide this first segment in the forms with personal inactive prefixes ending in *e* (the deletion of the beginning of a word is called **apheresis**). Some verbs in this class are *japi* 'to throw; to injure by shooting', *ja'o* 'to offend', *japo* 'to make', *javy* 'to err', *ñakã'o* 'to decapitate', *ñandu* 'to visit', *ñapĩ* 'to peel'.

*Ha'epa ne**andú**ta?* (cf. *ñandu* 'to visit')
ha'e=pa   ne-andu-ta
s/he=Q   2SG.INACT-visit-FUT
'Will s/he visit you?'

*Nde che**api**.* (cf. *japi* 'to throw')
nde   che-api
you.SG   1SG.INACT-throw
'You throw/threw me.'

This happens because the initial *j/ñ* was originally a third-person object prefix *i-* (the same one that survives as a vowel in aireal verbs; see **4.1.1**). Hence, when an inactive pronoun for the object was added, the object *i-* would have had to disappear. This pattern became fossilized in the modern language so that the reason for this loss of the initial segment is not recognized anymore by speakers. For this reason, sometimes the initial segment is conserved by speakers in forms that should lose it:

*Che aporandu ndéve ndépa che**ñandú**ta.*
che   a-porandu   ndéve   nde=pa   che-ñandu-ta
I   1SG.ACT-question to.you you.SG=Q 1SG.INACT-visit-FUT
'I am asking you if you will come to visit me.'[17]

Interestingly, some borrowed verbs from Spanish that begin with *a* add an initial *j/ñ* (another instance of **epenthesis**) possibly by analogy with this class of verbs and to avoid having two vowels in a sequence.

Ojagarra jey México-pe narcotráfico omomyakãva "El Chapo" Guzmán.
o-jagarra   jey   México=pe   narcotráfico   o-mo-myakã-va
3.ACT-grab   again   Mexico=in   drug.trafficking 3ACT-MAKE1-head.something-ADJZ
"El Chapo" Guzmán
El Chapo Guzmán
'They recaptured the drug trafficking head "El Chapo" Guzmán in Mexico.' (From Spanish *agarrar* 'to grab'.)

---

[17] Example from Gynan and López Almada (2014, 210).

Peñatendeporãke cherehe porque ni che voi naentendeporãi ko ha'étava peẽme.

pe-ñatende+porã-ke	che=rehe	porque	ni	che=voi
2PL.ACT-pay.attention+good-FORCE	1SG.INACT=at	because	not.even	I=EMPH
n-a-entende+porã-i	ko	ha'e-ta-va	peẽme	
NEG-1SG.ACT-understand+good-NEG	PROX.SG	I.say-FUT-ADJZ	to.you.PL	

'Pay attention to me well because I myself don't even understand what I will tell you.' (From Spanish *atender* 'to pay attention; to tend'.)

4.9 Verbal negation

The negation of all predicates, whether verbs or nouns, is accomplished by adding simultaneously the prefix *nd-* and the unstressed suffix *-i*. This has the effect of surrounding the predicate with the negation, and for that reason, the negation affix is called a **circumfix**. This circumfix has four main variants whose distribution is quite complex. The form of the prefix part depends mainly on whether the base being negated is oral or nasal. The form of the suffix part depends on whether the base ends in the front high vowels *i* or *ĩ*, or not. In the table below, I exemplify the main cases with the following active verbs:

- *jogua* 'to buy' (oral root not ending in a front high vowel)
- *maña* 'to look at' (nasal root not ending in a front high vowel)
- *jopi* 'to sting' (oral root ending in a front high vowel)
- *motĩ* 'to shame' (nasal root ending in a front high vowel)

	Oral, no *i* or *ĩ*	Nasal, no *i* or *ĩ*	Oral, *i*	Nasal, *ĩ*
1SG.ACT	**nd**ajoguái	**na**mañái	**nd**ajopíri	**na**motĩri
2SG.ACT	**nde**rejoguái	**ne**remañái	**nde**rejopíri	**ne**remotĩri
3.ACT	**nd**ojoguái	**no**mañái	**nd**ojopíri	**no**motĩri
1PL.INCL.ACT	**nd**ajajoguái	**na**ñamañái	**nd**ajajopíri	**na**ñamotĩri
1PL.EXCL.ACT	**nd**orojoguái	**no**romañái	**nd**orojopíri	**no**romotĩri
2PL.ACT	**nd**apejoguái	**na**pemañái	**nd**apejopíri	**na**pemotĩri

So, if the base is oral, the prefix part begins with the nasal-oral consonant *nd-*, whereas if the base is nasal, the prefix part begins with the nasal consonant *n-*. The suffix part is *-i*, unless the base ends in *-i* or *-ĩ*, in which case it is *-ri*. There are, however, two further constraints on the prefix part of the negation. For active person prefixes beginning in a vowel (the first-person singular active *a-* and the third-person active *o-*), the prefix part is *n(d)-*. When the active person prefix begins in a consonant, a **helping** (or **epenthetic) vowel** is added that is identical with the person prefix's vowel (**vowel harmony**), except arbitrarily for the second-person plural active prefix *pe-*, which adds *n(d)a-*, with the non-harmonic vowel *a*.

Nominal predicates are also negated with this same circumfix.

***nda**chepochýi*, ***nda**chevare'ái*
nda-che-pochy-i   nda-che-vare'a-i
NEG-1SG.INACT-anger-NEG NEG-1SG.INACT-hunger-NEG
'I am not angry, I am not hungry'

***nda**'itarovái hikuái*
nda-'i-tarova-i   hikuái
NEG-3.INACT-crazy-NEG   they
'they are not crazy'

***na**peneporãi*
na-pene-porã-i
NEG-2PL.INACT-beautiful-NEG
'you are not beautiful'

Note that in these cases, and any other cases when the person prefix is inactive, the prefix part of the negation is always *nda-* for oral bases and *na-* for nasal bases.

The negative circumfix always encloses the whole word or group of words that is being negated. So, in some cases the negation will surround a single verb, but in other cases it will surround a single word that is not a predicate (a pronoun, for example), or even a whole predicate with its complements.

***Nd**ajapói.*
nd-a-japo-i
NEG-1SG.ACT-make-NEG
'I didn't do it.'

***Nda**chéi la ajapóva.*
nda-che-i   la   a-japo-va
NEG-Í-NEG   DET.SG   1SG.ACT-make-ADJZ
'It wasn't me who did it.'

***Nda**cheplatahet**ái**.*
nda-che-pláta-h-eta-i
NEG-I-money-POSSM3-numerous-NEG
'I don't have a lot of money.' (The negation of *che* 'I' + *pláta* 'money' + *heta* 'much'.)

***Nd**aikuaasevéima mba'eve examengui.*
nd-ai-kuaa-se-ve-i-ma   mba'eve   examen=gui
NEG-1SG.ACT-know-want-more-NEG-already   nothing   exam=from
'I already don't want to know anything else about the exam.'
(The negation of *ai-kuaa-se-ve* 'I want to know more'.)

Guarani has **double negation** (also called **negative concord**); that is, a negated predicate requires any indefinite words to appear as negative:

*Ndaipotái **mba'eve**, ndajaposéi **mba'eve**.*
nd-ai-pota-i   mba'eve   nd-a-japo-se-i   mba'eve
NEG-1SG.ACT-want-NEG   nothing   NEG-1SG.ACT-make-want-NEG   nothing
'I don't want anything, I don't want to do anything.' (Literally, 'I don't want nothing, I don't want to do nothing.')

Ne'ĩra 'yet' is the only negative word that co-occurs with predicates in the affirmative; that is, non-negated predicates:

***ne'ĩra** reikuaa*
ne'ĩra   rei-kuaa
not.yet   2SG.ACT-know
'you don't know yet'

The negation of the future tense (see **4.10.1**) uses the suffix *-mo'ã* instead of *-ta*.

*namba'apo**mo'ã**i*
n-a-mba'apo-mo'ã-i
NEG-1SG.ACT-work-NEG.FUT-NEG
'I will not work'

*Ndaikatu**mo'ã**i gueteri reiko yvágape.*
nda-ikatu-mo'ã-i   gueteri   re-iko   yvága=pe
NEG-be.able-NEG.FUT-NEG   still   2SG.ACT-be   sky=in
'You will not be able to live in heaven yet.'

*Cherehe nereñembohory**mo'ãi**.*
che=rehe   ne-re-ñe-mbo-h-ory-mo'ã-i
1SG.INACT=at   NEG-2SG.ACT-AGD-MAKE1-POSSM3-joy-NEG.FUT-NEG
'You <u>will not</u> make fun of me.'

It is useful to end this section mentioning here the word *nahániri* (also *ahániri*) meaning 'no' (and its counterpart *heẽ* meaning 'yes').

Nahániri, ndaipotái.
nahániri   nd-ai-pota-i
no   NEG-1SG.ACT-want-NEG
'No, I don't want to/it.'

4.10 Expressing properties of events: tense, aspect, mood/modality, evidentiality

When languages express events, they usually convey information about when the event happened, how it happened and the speaker's own perspective of the event. These kinds of information are commonly known as **tense**, **aspect**, **mood** (or **modality**) and **evidentiality**. Here I introduce and define markers for each one of the first three of these categories in separate sections as it is customary (see **7** for more on evidentiality). However, the reader should be aware that it is seldom clear whether a given marker should be considered to express basically a tense, an aspect, a mood or an evidential, since these properties tend to cluster or be conveyed together. This is a research domain that is still the subject of much debate in the literature on Guarani.

4.10.1 Tense

Tense refers to the way in which a speaker situates the expressed event in time with respect to a reference point. As I pointed out in **4.1.1**, Guarani predicates in their bare form are non-future; that is, they can be interpreted as past or present depending on the context. This means that past is not obligatorily marked on Guarani predicates, but marking future is obligatory (contrary to English, where 'I am coming' can mean now in the present or sometime in the future). Generally, ensuring present or past interpretations of bare forms depends on the appearance of co-occurring past time expressions.

Reñe'ẽ heta.
re-ñe'ẽ   h-eta
2SG.ACT-talk POSSM3-numerous
'You talk(ed) a lot.'

*Ko'árape **ñamomaitei** ñandesykuérape.*
ko-'ára=pe   ña mo maitei   ñande-sy=kuéra=pe
PROX.SG-day=in   1PL.INCL.ACT-MAKE1-hello 1PL.INCL.INACT-mother=PL=in
'Today, let's greet our mothers.'

*Upe ára, **ou** peteĩ kuimba'e . . .*
upe   ára   o-u   peteĩ kuimba'e
MED.SG   day   3.ACT-come   one   man
'That day, a man came . . . '

The meaning of the verb is an important factor favouring a past or a present interpretation. If the event described by the verb has a natural endpoint (that is, the verb is said to be **telic**), it is naturally more compatible with past interpretations. In the first example below, the notion of -*'a* 'fall' includes implicitly that there is an endpoint to the fall. In the second example, the notion of -*upyty* 'achievement' includes implicitly an endpoint that is reached. Finally, in the third example, the notion of *mbokapu* 'to shoot' includes implicitly the endpoint when the shot hits the target. Therefore, use of these verbs in their bare form (with no explicit marking of tense) is naturally interpreted as conveying past tense.

*Ha'e oñe'ẽ aja chéve, **ho'a** cherehe pytũ ha **ha'a** yvýpe.*
ha'e   o-ñe'ẽ   aja   chéve   ho-'a   che=rehe   pytũ   ha
s/he   3.ACT-speak   while   to.me   3.ACT-fall 1SG.INACT=at dark   and
ha-'a   yvy=pe
1SG.ACT-fall   earth=in
'While s/he was talking to me, a darkness fell on me and I fell to the earth.'

*Hepykue oñeimo'ã **ohupyty** amo 14.200 sua dólar.*
h-epy-kue   o-ñe-imo'ã   o-h-upyty   amo
POSSM3-expensive-NMLZ.ABS   3.ACT-AGD-think   3.ACT-POSSM3-achievement DIST.SG
14.200 sua   dólar
14.200 million   dollar
'The cost is estimated to have reached 14,200 million dollars.'

He'i chéve la che irũ ¡*Embokapúna* hese!, ha
ambokapu mante.
he'i	chéve	la	che-irũ	e-mbo-kapu-na	hese	ha
says	to.me	DET.SG	1SG.INACT-friend	IMP-MAKE1-shot-REQ	at.him/her	and

a-mbo-kapu   mante
1SG.ACT-MAKE1-shot   only

'My friend <u>said</u> to me "shoot him!" And I just <u>shot</u> (him).'

On the other hand, predicates without a natural endpoint (that is, **atelic** predicates), such as activities or states, are naturally interpreted as present in the absence of other cues. This is especially true if the verbs describe events that are interpreted to last in time (**durative**).

*Chejegustaha **ojeroky** porãiterei.*
che-je-gusta-ha   o-jeroky   porã-iterei
1SG.INACT-AGD-please-NMLZ   3.ACT-dance   good-very.much
'My crush <u>dances</u> very well.'

*Jasy **opurahéi** chéve ha che **apurahéi** ndéve.*
jasy	o-purahéi	chéve	ha	che	a-purahéi	ndéve
moon	3.ACT-sing	to.me	and	I	1SG.ACT-sing	to.you.SG

'The moon <u>sings</u> to me and I <u>sing</u> to you.'

*Nd**ajeroviá**i voi hese.*
nd-a-jerovia-i=voi   hese
NEG-1SG.ACT-believe-NEG=EMPH   at.him/her
'I <u>do not believe</u> him/her.'

Basic future tense interpretations can be obtained by marking predicates with the unstressed suffix *-ta*. The negation of this future uses the stressed suffix *-mo'ã* (together with the circumfixal negation we saw in **4.9**).

*Ndejuká**ta**!*
nde-juka-ta
2SG.INACT-kill-FUT
'S/he/They <u>will</u> kill you!'

*Ko'ẽro amba'apó**ta**.*
ko'ẽro   a-mba'apo-ta
tomorrow   1SG.ACT-work-FUT
'I <u>will</u> work tomorrow.'

Ko'ẽro namba'apomo'ãi.
ko'ẽro   n-a-mba'apo-mo'ã-i
tomorrow NEG-1SG.ACT-work-NEG.FUT-NEG
'I will not work tomorrow.'

Ndajapomo'ãvéima péicha . . . añeñanduvai'ỹre ajapo jave hína.
nd-a-japo-mo'ã-ve-i-ma   pe-icha
NEG-1SG.ACT-make-NEG.FUT-more-NEG-already   MED.SG-as
a-ñe-ñandu-vai='ỹre   a-japo   jave   hína
1SG.ACT-AGD-feel-bad=without 1SG.ACT-make while   PROG
'I will not do it like that anymore . . . without feeling bad while I do it.'

The unstressed suffix *-ta* does not always indicate future. It can also be used as a marker of conjecture or lack of knowledge (this is called an **epistemic** reading; that is, an interpretation that indicates the knowledge state of the speaker):

Mba'e carrérata piko upéva.
mba'e   carréra-ta=piko   upe-va
what   career-FUT=Q   MED.SG-ADJZ
'What career would that be?'

The stressed suffix *-mo'ã* can sometimes have a frustrative reading of the type 'event X was going to happen (but it didn't)' (see **4.10.2**).

ohomo'ã
o-ho-mo'ã
3.ACT-go-ALMOST
's/he was about to go but didn't.'[18]

Jajotopárire javy'avévaerãmo'a.
ja-jo-topa=rire   ja-vy'a-ve-vae-rã-mo'a
1PL.INCL.ACT-RECP-meet-if   1PL.INCL.ACT-joy-more-ADJZ-DEST-ALMOST
'If we had met, we would have rejoiced more.'[19]

Uncertain or doubtful futures are marked with the **dubitative** future unstressed suffix *-ne*. The negation of this dubitative future is *chéne* 'perhaps not', which comes after the negative form of the verb.

---

[18] Example from Liuzzi (2006, 63).
[19] Example from Cadogan (1970, 38).

Ko'ẽro amba'apóne.
ko'ẽro   a-mba'apo-ne
tomorrow   1SG.ACT-work-DUB
'Tomorrow I will work <u>perhaps</u>.'

*Name'ẽi **chéne**.*
n-a-me'ẽ-i   chéne
NEG-1SG.ACT-give-NEG   perhaps.not
'I <u>may not</u> give (it to him/her).'

Note that this suffix more broadly indicates uncertainty or probability independently of any possible future tense interpretation. It is a means to indicate possibility or necessity, either of an action or state (**deontic modality**) or of an item of knowledge (**epistemic modality**).

*Péicha**ne**ko che avei raka'e . . .*
pe-icha-ne=ko   che   avei   raka'e
MED.SG-as-DUB=VERD   I   also   LONG.INF
'<u>Probably</u> I was like that too (back then) . . .'

*Amóva**ne** ndereka.*
amo-va-ne   nde-r-eka
DIST.SG-ADJZ-DUB   2SG.INACT-POSSM-seek
'<u>Surely</u> that is the one looking for you.'[20]

The meaning 'about to (do something)' (**immediate future** tense) is conveyed by the stressed suffix *-pota* (*-mbota* with nasal bases).

*jaha**pota***
ja-ha-pota
1PL.INCL.ACT-go-about.to
'we are <u>about to</u> go'

*Cheirũomano**mbota** hína.*
che-irũ   o-mano-mbota   hína
1SG.INACT-friend   3.ACT-die-about.to   PROG
'My friend is <u>about to</u> die.'

---

[20] Example from Liuzzi (2006, 83).

*Japytũmba**pota**itémavoi ha he'i chupe Perurima:* . . .
ja-pytũ-mba-pota-ité-ma=voi   ha   he'i   chupe
already-dark-completely-about.to-very-already=EMPH   and   says   to.him/her
Perurima
Perurima
'It is already <u>about to</u> become completely dark and Perurima says to him: . . .'

Finally, futures that include a meaning of obligation use the stressed suffix *-va'erã*. This suffix is often phonetically reduced: it can be pronounced as *-vaerã, -varã* or *-'arã*. The last example below shows that this suffix can be used to convey a "future in the past" or an obligation in the past.

*Reju**va'erã** cherógape.*
re-ju-va'erã   che-r-óga=pe
2SG.ACT-come-must   1SG.INACT-POSSM-house=in
'You <u>must</u> come to my house.'

*¡He'u**'arã**!*
he-'u-'arã
IMP-ingest-must
'You <u>have to</u> eat it!'

*Ojapo**va'erã** peteĩ purahéi.*
o-japo-va'erã   peteĩ   purahéi
3.ACT-make-must   one   song
'S/he <u>had to</u> compose a song.'

Even though marking past tense for Guarani verbs is not required, there are ways to do it explicitly. The particle *-va'ekue* and its phonological reduction *-(')akue* convey a past tense meaning (with perhaps a preference for remote past, not recent past, interpretations).

*Aha**va'ekue** la Chákope.*
a-ha-va'ekue   la   Cháko=pe
1SG.ACT-go-PAST DET.SG Chaco=in
'I <u>went</u> to the Chaco (at some point in the, perhaps distant, past).'

*Naimo'ãi**va'ekue** rejuhu otro cherekoviarã.*
n-a-imo'ã-i-va'ekue   re-juhu   otro
NEG-1SG.ACT-think-NEG-PAST   2SG.ACT-find   another
che-r-ekovia-rã
1SG.INACT-POSSM-replacement-DEST
'I <u>didn't</u> think you would find another to replace me.'

*Ha'eningo heñói'**akue** táva Caballerope.*
ha'e=ningo   h-eñói-'akue   táva   Caballero=pe
s/he=VERD   POSSM3-sprout-PAST   town   Caballero=in
'He was born in the town of Caballero.'

4.10.2 Aspect

Aspect is how language encodes the internal properties of events – whether they last or are instantaneous, whether they go to completion or not, and so on – independent of their location in time. Guarani has several aspect markers, which are sometimes difficult to differentiate from tenses. What is important for the reader is to understand how each marker differs from others and how they contribute to the meaning of a sentence.

Two markers serve to highlight the end or full development of an event (what is usually called **perfect** or **perfective aspect** in grammars). The unstressed suffix *-ma* (most often equivalent to the English word 'already') is a **completive aspect** marker. In the spoken language, it is sometimes used in conjunction with the prefix *ja-*, probably a borrowing of Spanish 'ya' meaning 'already', creating a circumfix that envelops the whole predicate. (Do not confuse this prefix *ja-* with the first-person plural inclusive active prefix *ja-*; see **4.1**.)

*oğuahẽ**ma***
o-ğuahẽ-ma
3.ACT-arrive-already
's/he has already arrived'

*ja*ohó*ma*
ja-o-ho-ma
already-3.ACT-go-already
's/he already went'

*ja*ndoikovéi*ma*
ja-nd-o-iko-ve-i-ma
already-NEG-3.ACT-be-more-NEG-already
'it doesn't function anymore'

*Ore **ja**rohóta**ma**, che patrón.*
ore   ja-ro-ho-ta-ma   che-patrón
we.not.you   already-1PL.EXCL.ACT-go-FUT-already   1SG.INACT-boss
'We will already be leaving, boss.'

Ko'ãga peikuaáma mba'érepa ndaguerekóiri peteĩ Mac!
ko'ãga   pei-kuaa-ma   mba'ére=pa   nd-a-guereko-iri   peteĩ   Mac
now   2PL.ACT-know-already   why=Q   NEG-1SG.ACT-have-NEG   one   Mac
'Now you (pl.) <u>already</u> know why I don't have a Mac!'

. . . enseguida peañamechũomoĩ chupe esposa, ha aeropuértope jaohóma.
enseguida   peañamechũ   o-moĩ   chupe   esposa   ha
immediately   good.grief   3.ACT-put   to.him/her   handcuff   and
aeropuérto=pe   ja-o-ho-ma
airport=in   already-3.ACT-go-already
' . . . immediately for God's sake they put handcuffs on him, and they went <u>already</u> to the airport.'

Another perfective aspect marker intimately related to the completive is the stressed suffix *-pa/-mba*, which emphasizes that the event applies to (and sometime exhausts) the whole object or subject (**totalitive aspect**). This is derived from the verbal root *pa* that means 'to finish' (for example, o**pa** 'it is <u>finish</u>ed').

*akaru**pa***
a-karu-pa
1SG.ACT-eat(intransitive)-all
'I am (<u>totally</u>) finished eating'; 'I ate <u>all</u>'

*Tahyikuéra omano**mba**.*
tahýi=kuéra   o-mano-mba
ant=PL   3.ACT-die-all
'The ants <u>all</u> died.'

Several other aspect markers are used when the speaker wants to highlight that an event is continuing or not fully completed, and when the endpoint is absent or not important (**imperfective aspect**). The most common is the particle *hína* which expresses the **continuous/progressive** aspect. It can often be translated by the English progressive in '-ing', but it sometimes has no equivalent in English, especially when one is talking about a habitual action or a lasting state. It can be attached to the predicate or have freer placement in the sentence.

*rehai **hína***
re-h-ai   hína
2SG.ACT-POSSM3-write   PROG
'you (sg.) <u>are</u> writ<u>ing</u>'

*peguata **hína***
pe-guata   hína
2PL.ACT-walk   PROG
'you (pl.) are walking'

*¡Roha'arõ**hína** cheru!*
ro-h-a'arõ=hína   che-r-u
1>2SG-POSSM3-wait=PROG   1SG.INACT-POSSM-father
'I was waiting for you, dad!'

*Pohendu **hína** Capiataguive.*
po-h-endu=hína   Capiata=guive
1>2PL-POSSM3-listen=PROG   Capiata=since
'I am listening to you (pl.) from Capiata.'

*Cheirũ omanombota **hína**.*
che-irũ   o-mano-mbota   hína
1SG.INACT-friend   3.ACT-die-about.to   PROG
'My friend is about to die.'

*pórke la ápe oúvako ndoureíri **hína***
pórke   la   ápe   o-u-va=ko   nd-o-u-rei-ri   hína
because   DET.SG   here   3.ACT-come-ADJZ=VERD   NEG-3.ACT-come.in.vain-NEG   PROG
'because those who come here do not come for no reason'

*Mitãnguéra ningo **hína** ñaneretã raperã.*
mitã=nguéra   ningo   hína   ñane-r-etã   r-ape-rã
child=PL   VERD   PROG   1PL.INCL.INACT-POSSM-country   POSSM-road-DEST
'Children are the road-to-be (i.e., the future) of our country.'

Hína can appear in the sentence at a variable distance from the predicate it modifies.

*Ha oiméne ndahetái ko'a gotyo **hína** hendarãkuéra.*
ha   o-ime-ne   nda-h-eta-i   ko'a   gotyo   hína   h-enda-rã=kuéra
and   3.ACT-be.located-DUB   NEG-POSSM3-numerous-NEG   here   towards   PROG   POSSM3-place-DEST=PL
'Well, it may be that around here they don't have a lot of room.'

Although in today's colloquial use it most frequently appears as the fixed form *hína*, in more traditional Guarani registers, *-ína* behaves like a verbal root and takes active person prefixes that agree with the subject of the predicate. It is sometimes written separate from the predicate, sometimes attached to it.

*rehai **reína***
re-h-ai　　　　　re-ína
2SG.ACT-POSSM3-write　2SG.ACT-PROG
'you (sg.) <u>are</u> writ<u>ing</u>'

*peguata **peína***
pe-guata　　　pe-ína
2PL.ACT-walk　2PL.ACT-PROG
'you (pl.) <u>are</u> walk<u>ing</u>'

*Ko jasypoapy jave ningo jagueromandu'a **ñaína** heta ára iñimportánteva.*
ko　　　jasy+poapy　　jave　　ningo　ja-guero-mandu'a
DEM.SG　moon+eight　　while　VERD　1PL.INCL.ACT-MAKE.SOC-remember
ña-ína　　　　　　　　h-eta　　　　　　ára　iñ-importánte-va
1PL.INCL-ACT-PROG　POSSM3-numerous　day　3.INACT-important-ADJZ
'During this August <u>we are</u> commemorat<u>ing</u> many important dates.'

*Vy'apavẽ ka'ay árare. Mamópa rekay'u **reína**.*
vy'a-pavẽ　　　ka'a+y　　　　　　ára=re　　mamó=pa
joy-supreme　mate.leaf+water　day=at　where=Q
re-ka+y+'u　　　　　　　　　　　　　　　re-ína
2SG.ACT-mate.leaf+water+ingest　2SG.ACT-PROG
'Happy mate day. Where are you drinking mate?' (Mate = *Ilex Paraguaiensis* infusion.)

*Anína reñembotavy**reína**.*
ani-na　　re-ñe-mbo-tavy-re-ína
NEG-REQ　2SG.ACT-AGD-MAKE1-stupid-2SG.ACT-PROG
'Please don't be playing dumb.'

It is important to note that *hína* has uses that do not seem to express the progressive aspect, but rather emphasis (see **7.1** for examples).

To express that an event recurs intermittently speakers use *hikóni* (**intermittent aspect**). This is often not directly translated in English.

*omba'apo **hikóni***
o-mba'apo　　hikóni
3.ACT-work　　INTERM
's/he is (<u>out and about</u>) working' (the assumption is that the person referenced is not working continuously)

*Aiko **hikóni** nderekávo.*
a-iko   hikóni   nde-r-eka-vo
1SG.ACT-be INTERM 2SG.INACT-POSSM-seek-while
'I am looking for you.' (In the sense that I have been repeatedly looking.)

*Ha'ekuéra omombe'u oréve mba'éichapa ohasa asy **hikóni** umi ermáno Alemaniaygua.*
ha'e=kuéra   o-mombe'u   oréve   mba'éicha=pa   o-h-asa
s/he=PL   3.ACT-tell   to.us.not.you   how=Q   3.ACT-POSSM3-pass
asy   hikóni   umi   ermáno   Alemania=ygua
pain   INTERM   NPROX.PL   brother   Germany=from
'They would tell us the troubles that were affecting our German brothers.' (From time to time, or on occasion.)

Habitual aspect is marked with the stressed suffix *-mi* for past habits, and with the unstressed suffix *-va* for non-past habits. (Do not confuse this latter with the adjectivizer *-va*; see **3.3**.)

*ajapo**mi***
a-japo-mi
1SG.ACT-make-used.to
'I used to make'

*ajapó**va***
a-japo-va
1SG.ACT-make-in.the.habit
'I am in the habit of making'

*Py'ỹi aha**mi** penderógape.*
py'ỹi   a-ha-mi   pende-r-óga=pe
often   1SG.ACT-go-used.to   2PL.INACT-POSSM-house=in
'I used to go to your house often.'

*Py'ỹi ahá**va** penderógape.*
py'ỹi   a-ha-va   pende-r-óga=pe
often   1SG.ACT-go-in.the.habit   2PL.INACT-POSSM-house=in
'I go to your house often.'

The particle *jepi* can also mark habitual present or past action.

*Apu'ã **jepi** voiete.*
a-pu'ã jepi voi-ete
1SG.ACT-get.up usually early-very
'I <u>usually</u> get up very early.'

*Ymavépa reho py'ỹi **jepi** tupa'ópe.*
yma-ve=pa re-ho py'ỹi jepi tupa'o=pe
before-more=Q 2SG.ACT-go often usually church=in
'Did you <u>use to</u> go frequently to church before?'

The **iterative aspect** (which conveys the repetition of an action) can be expressed with the stressed affix *-je(v)y*, which gives the idea of a single repetition. As an independent word, *jevy* means 'time' in the sense of 'occasion'. As a verb, it means 'to return'. It can also be used as an adverb with the meaning 'again'. As is common in many frequent words, the labiodental approximant /ʋ/ is most often elided.

*omoañete**jey***
o-mo-añete-jevy
3.ACT-MAKE1-true-again
's/he <u>reaffirms</u>'

*Ikatúpa rombojerokymi **jey**.*
ikatu=pa ro-mbo-jeroky-mi jevy
be.able=Q 1>2SG.MAKE1-dance-DIM again
'Can I get you to dance <u>again</u>?'

*Ipu **jey**ma.*
i-pu jevy-ma
3.INACT-sound again-already
'It (=the music) sounds <u>again</u> already.'

*nerendápe aju**jevy***
ne-r-enda=pe a-ju-jevy
2SG.INACT-POSSM-place=in 1SG.ACT-come-again
'I return by your side' (literally, 'I come <u>again</u> by your side')

To clearly express reiteration with more than a single repetition, speakers use the reduplication *-jevyvy*:

168   A GRAMMAR OF PARAGUAYAN GUARANI

romomarandujevyvy va'ekue
ro-mo-marandu-jevy~vy   va'ekue
1>2SG-MAKE1-warning-again~again   PAST
'I warned you <u>several times</u>'

This is a particular case of a more generic means of expressing iteration via reduplication of a predicate, which does not require the use of *jevy*. This kind of reduplication most frequently doubles the last syllable or the last two syllables of the predicate.

jajepohéipohéi
ja-je-po+héi~po+héi
1PL.INCL.ACT-AGD-hand+wash~hand+wash
'we wash our hands <u>over and over</u>'

oguatavérõ oguatave hikuái
o-guata-ve=rõ   o-guata-ve   hikuái
3.ACT-walk-more=when   3.ACT-walk-more   they
'when they <u>walked more and walked more</u>'

A kind of **quasi-eventive aspect** (sometimes called "incompletive", marking the fact that an event almost happened, but didn't) can be conveyed by the stressed suffix *-mo'ã*.

Ha'amo'ã.
ha-'a-mo'ã
1SG.ACT-fall-ALMOST
'I <u>almost</u> fell.'

Rohenoimo'ã ndekatu reju.
ro-h-enói-mo'ã   nde=katu   re-ju
1>2SG-POSSM3-call-ALMOST   you.SG=just   2SG.ACT-come
'I <u>was about to</u> call you but you (just) came.'

Other aspectual nuances can be conveyed by the use of **serial verb constructions**. These constructions contain a lexical verb followed by another lexical verb that has an auxiliary-like function and is the one responsible for conveying the aspectual meaning. Serial verb constructions are a special type of subordination by juxtaposition (see **12.2.2**) in which the predicates are understood to have the same subject and to denote a single event. The auxiliary-like verb is suffixed with the unstressed simultaneity marker *-vo* 'while'.

*ijapu **oikóvo***
i-japu o-iko-vo
3.INACT-falsehood 3.ACT-be-while

's/he <u>keeps on</u> lying' (**protractive aspect**) or 's/he <u>goes around</u> lying' (**frequentative aspect**)

*Cherecharõ aguahẽ **ahávo** umi cherapicha rógar upi . . .*
che-r-echa=rõ a-guahẽ a-ha-vo umi
1SG.INACT-POSSM-see=when 1SG.ACT-arrive 1SG.ACT-go-while NPROX.PL
che-r-apicha r-óga=rupi
1SG.INACT-POSSM-fellow.man POSSM-house=around

'When I am seen when I <u>am arriving</u> at people's houses . . . ' (a kind of **imminent prospective** reading)

4.10.3 Mood and modality

The expression of speaker intent or speaker attitudes, as well as the expression of the possibility, necessity, reality or desirability of an event, is called **modality**. **Mood** refers to the different linguistic means and the different categories a language uses for expressing modality.

4.10.3.1 Expressing commands

4.10.3.1.1 Basic imperative mood

The basic imperative in Guarani is used for second-person addressees, singular or plural. Forming the imperative is very simple, since it is almost always indicated by the same person prefixes used in the basic indicative mood (for first- and third-person imperatives, see **4.10.3.4.2**). The only difference between the imperative and the indicative mood is that for active and transitive verbs the imperative does have a dedicated second-person singular form: *e-*. The rest of the persons use the same active and inactive prefixes as the indicative to express the highest participant in the person hierarchy. Therefore, it is important to be aware that, except for the second-person singular imperative forms for active predicates, all other forms are ambiguous between an imperative and an indicative reading. The context in which they are used is sufficient to know which meaning is intended.

Active and transitive verbs

ekaru
e-karu
IMP-eat(intransitive)
'eat' (you.sg addressee)

pekaru
pe-karu
2PL.ACT-eat(intransitive)
'eat' (you.pl addressee)

eho
e-ho
IMP-go
'go' (you.sg addressee)

peho
pe-ho
2PL.ACT-go
'go' (you.pl addressee)

egueru
e-gueru
IMP-bring
'bring (it)' (you.sg addressee)

pegueru
pe-gueru
2PL.ACT-bring
'bring (it)' (you.pl addressee)

chegueru
che-gueru
1SG.INACT-bring
'bring me'

oregueru
ore-gueru
1PL.EXCL.INACT-bring
'bring us'

Inactive verbs

nemandu'a
ne-mandu'a
2SG.INACT-remembrance
'remember' (you.sg addressee)

penemandu'a
pene-mandu'a
2PL.INACT-remembrance
'remember' (you.pl addressee)

chemandu'a
che-mandu'a
1SG.INACT-remembrance
'remember me'

oremandu'a
ore-mandu'a
1PL.EXCL.INACT-remembrance
'remember us'

Verbs that are relational roots take the *h-* prefix with the second-person singular imperative *e-* prefix (as they do with any active person prefixes).

Ehendu!
e-h-endu
IMP-POSSM3-listen
'Listen!' (you.sg addressee)

Ehasa ko raya ha ehecha mba'e ajapo nderehe.
e-h-asa	ko	raya	ha	e-h-echa	mba'e	a-japo
IMP-POSSM3-pass	PROX.SG	line	and	IMP-POSSM3-see	what	1SG.ACT-make

nde=rehe
2SG.INACT=at
'Cross this line and see what I do to you.'

Upéicharamo ehenói Ñandejárape.
upe-icha=ramo	e-h-enói	ñande-jára=pe
MED.SG-as=if	IMP-POSSM3-call	1PL.INCL.INACT-lord-in

'Then, call our Lord.'

There are some cases where the imperative is not different from the indicative even in the second-person singular. First, the irregular verb meaning 'to say' (*ha'e, ere, he'i, ja'e, ro'e, peje*) has second-person imperative forms identical in both cases to the indicative forms:

ere	*peje*
ere	peje
IMP.2SG.ACT.say	IMP.2PL.ACT.say
'say' (you.sg addressee)	'say' (you.pl addressee)

Second, in the spoken colloquial language, *e-* is often used for the second singular active person prefix instead of *re-*. This makes the second singular imperative and indicative identical, therefore effectively making the indicative and imperative moods indistinguishable in all persons:

Apete. Ehechápa?
ape-te	e-h-echa=pa
here-very	2SG.ACT-POSSM3-see=Q

'Right here. See?'

Mboy año ereko?
mboy	año	e-reko
how.many	year	2SG.ACT-have

'How old are you?'

4.10.3.1.2 Imperative modalizers

It is common for the basic imperative to be combined with suffixes that express further nuances of force, coercion, mitigation or politeness (we can call these **imperative modalizers**):

- the forceful imperative *-ke* (unstressed suffix), used to convey a certain amount of force or coercion
- the requestative *-na* (unstressed suffix), to convey a polite, mitigated request (in traditional Guarani grammars this is often called "rogative", from the Spanish word for 'pray')
- the pleading imperative *-mi* (stressed suffix), which is mitigative with affectionate nuances
- and the urging imperative *-py* (unstressed suffix), which is used to incite somebody to action or when an order must be repeated.

These nuances are difficult to convey accurately in the English translations. The translations will attempt to convey a feel for the use of these suffixes, even though their meaning would not necessarily be expressed that way by an English speaker. Moreover, sometimes the usual descriptions of their meanings given here do not seem to coincide very well with the general thrust of the sentence. This makes learning the use of these suffixes particularly challenging for a non-native speaker.

*emba'apó**ke***
e-mba'apo-ke
IMP-work-FORCE
'work (I command you)'

*ehechá**na***
e-h-echa-na
IMP-POSSM3-see-REQ
'look, please'

*ehendu**mi***
e-h-endu-mi
IMP-POSSM3-listen-PLEAD
'please listen just a minute'

*eguatá**py***
e-guata-py
IMP-walk-URG
'walk then!'

*Peñatendé**ke** pendejehe ha entéro ovecha atýre.*
pe-ñatende-ke   pendejehe   ha   entéro   ovecha   aty=re
2PL.ACT-pay.attention-FORCE at.yourselves and   whole   sheep   group=at
'Do look out for yourselves and for the entire flock.'

VERBS   173

He'i chéve la che irũ: ¡Embokapúna hese!, ha ambokapu mante.
he'i   chéve   la   che-irũ   e-mbo-kapu-na   hese   ha
says   to.me   DET.SG   1SG.INACT-friend   IMP-MAKE1-shot-REQ   at.him/her   and
a-mbo-kapu   mante
1SG.ACT-MAKE1-shot   only
'My friend said to me "shoot him!" And I just shot (him).'

Eremi upe ñu'aũrenda ha toroñaka'ouka mandi voi.
ere-mi   upe   ñu'aũ   r-enda   ha
IMP.2SG.ACT.say-PLEAD   MED.SG   skin.mole   POSSM-place   and
to-ro-ñaka'o-uka   mandi   voi
OPT-1>2SG-decapitate-MAKE2   once.and.for.all   EMPH
'Now tell me <u>please</u> where this mole is so they may chop your head off once and for all.'

All these imperative modalizing suffixes can be stacked together, yielding nuances of meaning that are extremely difficult to render. In fact, even native speakers often cannot verbalize the differences between the diverse combinations.

*eju**mína***
e-ju-mi-na
IMP-come-PLEAD-REQ
'<u>will you</u> come <u>please</u>?'

*emombe'ú**kena***
e-mombe'ú-ke-na
IMP-tell-FORCE-REQ
'<u>come on</u>, tell us <u>please</u>'

*peguapy**míkena***
pe-guapy-mi-ke-na
2PL.ACT-sit-PLEAD-FORCE-REQ
'<u>please do sit</u>, you all'

*jahapá**kena***
ja-ha-pa-ke-na
1PL.INCL.ACT-go-all-FORCE-REQ
'<u>come on please</u>, let's all go!'

*Emombe'u**mína** chéve rejapova'erã ko'ẽro.*
e-mombe'u-mi-na   chéve   re-japo-va'e-rã   ko'ẽro
IMP-tell-PLEAD-REQ   to.me   2SG.ACT-make-ADJZ-DEST   tomorrow
'<u>Please</u> tell me what you will do tomorrow.'

*Pehkriví**kena** ñandéve peẽ mitã pyahu Paraguái membýva kuénto ha novéla guaraníme.*
p-ehkriví-ke-na   ñandéve   peẽ   mitã   pyahu   Paraguái
2PL.ACT-write-FORCE-REQ   to.us&you   you.PL   child   new   Paraguay
memby-va   kuénto   ha   novéla   guarani=me
child.of.woman-ADJZ   short.story   and   novel   Guarani=in
'You, new children of Paraguay, write us short stories and novels in Guarani.'

*Ndepaciencia**míkena** cherehe.*
nde-paciencia-mi-ke-na   che=rehe
2SG.INACT-patience-PLEAD-FORCE-REQ   1SG.INACT=at
'Be patient with me.'

All of these imperative modalizers can be attached to non-verbal predicates. In fact, they can be attached to many different word classes. This is evidence that imperative modalizers can have freer placement in the clause than one would expect from their use as verb suffixes. Their behaviour is sometimes more like that of a 'floating' particle, often coming in the second position in the sentence (after the first phrase).

*Ndepya'é**ke**!*
nde-pya'e-ke
2SG.INACT-fast-FORCE
'Be quick!'

*Animo'ã**kena** avave ohekýi ndehegui neñe'ẽ*
ani-mo'ã-ke-na   avave   o-h-ekýi   ndehegui
NEG-NEG.FUT-FORCE-REQ   nobody   3.ACT-POSSM3-take.away   from.you.SG
ne-ñe'ẽ
2SG.INACT-language
 'That/<u>Let</u> nobody ever take your language from you'

*ejedehá**na** nde la cántogui, mágiante**na** ejapo*
e-je-deha-na   nde   la   cánto=gui   magia-nte-na   e-japo
IMP-AGD-leave-REQ   you.SG   DEM.SG   singing=from   magic-only-REQ   IMP-make
'forget the singing, <u>please</u>, do only magic'

VERBS

*Amo kotýpe**na** pemoĩmi.*
amo	koty=pe-na	pe-moĩ-mi
DIST.SG	room=in-REQ	2PL.ACT-put-PLEAD
'Please, put it in that room.'

*Araka'evé**kena** ani jajavy ha ñaimo'ã Guarani ikatuha ombyai ñanecastellanope.*
araka'eve-ke-na	ani	ja-javy	ha	ña-imo'ã
never-FORCE-REQ	NEG.IMP	1PL.INCL.ACT-err	and	1PL.INCL.ACT-think
Guarani	ikatu-ha	o-mby-ai	ñane-castellano=pe
Guarani	be.able-NMLZ	3.ACT-MAKE1-bad	1PL.INCL.INACT-Spanish=in
'Let's never make the mistake of thinking that Guarani can ruin our Spanish.'

4.10.3.1.3 Prohibitive mood

Negated imperatives are also called **prohibitives**. They are different from both the non-negative imperative forms and the negative declarative forms. The word *ani* is placed in front of the predicate to be negated, while the predicate itself is marked with the unstressed suffix *-t(e)i*.

***Ani** rehó**tei**.*
ani	re-ho-tei
NEG.IMP	2SG.ACT-go-NEG.IMP
'Do not go.'

***Ani** eré**tei** . . . Ndarekopáiko hína!*
Ani	ere-tei	nd-a-reko-pa-i=ko
NEG.IMP	IMP.2SG.ACT-say-NEG.IMP	NEG-1SG.ACT-have-all-NEG=VERD
hína
PROG
'Don't say (that) . . . I don't have everything!'

***Ani** pejú**ti** peje chéve la ndaipóri kuña iporãva mba'e hína porque peikuaa porã la oĩha.*
ani	pe-ju-ti	peje	chéve	la
NEG.IMP	2PL.ACT-come-NEG.IMP	2PL.ACT-say	to.me	DET.SG
ndaipóri	kuña	i-porã-va	mba'e	hína	porque
there.is.not	woman	3.INACT-pretty-ADJZ	thing	PROG	because
pei-kuaa+porã	la	oĩ-ha
2PL.ACT-know+good	DET.SG	there.is-NMLZ
'Don't come and say to me that there are no women that are pretty and so on because you know well that there are.'

The suffix part -t(e)i is in fact optional. It is often left out.

***ani** reho*
ani   re-ho
NEG.IMP   2SG.ACT-go
'<u>do not</u> go'

***Ani** repoko cherehe ha'e niko ndéve.*
ani   re-poko   che=rehe   ha'e   niko   ndéve
NEG.IMP   2SG.ACT-touch   1SG.INACT=at   I.say   VERD   to.you.SG
'I did tell you <u>not to</u> touch me.'

***Ani** rejepy'apy chekarai.*
ani   re-je-py'a+py   che-karai
NEG.IMP   2SG.ACT-AGD-chest+press   1SG.INACT-gentleman
'Don't worry, mister.'

In line with what we saw above in terms of their free placement, imperative modalizers may attach to *ani* and not to the predicate.

*aní**na** upéicha**ti***
ani-na   upe-icha-ti
NEG.IMP-REQ   MED.SG-as-NEG.IMP
'<u>please</u> don't (do that)'

*Aní**kena** peimo'ã ko'ã mba'e ñanohẽta peteĩ syrýkype.*
ani-ke-na   pe-imo'ã   ko'ã   mba'e
NEG.IMP-FORCE-REQ   2PL.ACT-think   PROX.PL   thing
ña-nohẽ-ta   peteĩ   syrýky=pe
1PL.INCL.ACT-take.out-FUT   one   all.of.a.sudden=in
'<u>Do not</u> think that these things will be achieved all of a sudden.'

Another way, albeit less frequent, in which Guarani expresses the negation of imperatives (and optatives; see **4.10.3.4.2**) is via the privative stressed suffix -'ỹ. This suffix means, more generally, 'without' (see **3.2.2** for its use to create antonyms, **5.4** for its use as the postposition 'without' and **12.2.1** for its use to negate relative clauses).

*eju'**ỹ**na*
e-ju-'ỹ-na
IMP-come-PRIV-REQ
'please <u>don't</u> come'

VERBS   177

4.10.3.2 Expressing possibility and ability

Possibility is expressed by the morpheme *ikatu* which does not vary according to person or number (for this reason, I will gloss it 'be.able').

***ikatu** japurahéi*
ikatu   ja-purahéi
be.able   1PL.INCL.ACT-sing
'we (including you) can sing'

***ikatu** apurahéi*
ikatu   a-purahéi
be.able   1SG.ACT-sing
'I can sing'

***Ikatu** pejogua chuguikuéra y ha penerembi'urã.*
ikatu   pe-jogua   chugui=kuéra   y   ha
be.able   2PL.ACT-buy   from.him/her=PL   water   and
pene-r-embi-'u-rã
2PL.INACT-POSSM-NMLZ.REL-ingest-DEST
'You can buy from them water and your food.'

***Ikatú**pa rombojerokymi jey.*
ikatu=pa   ro-mbo-jeroky-mi   jevy
be.able=Q   1>2SG-MAKE1-dance-DIM   again
'Can I get you to dance again?'

The negation of this morpheme uses the regular predicate negation circumfix. The word that results, *ndaikatúi,* is often pronounced *ndikatúi* in the spoken colloquial language.

*nda**ikatú**i roho*
nda-ikatu-i   ro-ho
NEG-be.able-NEG   1PL.EXCL.ACT-go
'we (excluding you) cannot go'

*nda**ikatú**i jaha*
nda-ikatu-i   ja-ha
NEG-be.able-NEG   1PL.INCL.ACT-go
'we (including you) cannot go'

*Araka'eve **ndaikatúi** ake nderógape.*
araka'eve nda-ikatu-i   a-ke   nde-r-óga=pe
never   NEG-be.able-NEG   1SG.ACT-sleep   2SG.INACT-POSSM-house=in
'I <u>can never</u> sleep in your house.'

Even though *ikatu* is invariable, it sometimes appears with person markers in speech, and is thereby used as a main verb meaning 'to be able to', under conditions not well understood.

*ndo**roikatu**véima roguata*
ndo-ro-ikatu-ve-i-ma   ro-guata
NEG-1PL.EXCL.ACT-be.able-more-NEG-already   1PL.EXCL.ACT-walk
'<u>we</u> were already not able to walk anymore'

Physical or cognitive ability can be expressed by the (aireal) verb *kuaa* 'to know', which in this modal use behaves as a stressed predicate suffix.

*ojapi**kuaa** ha ojapiporã*
o-japi-kuaa   ha   o-japi+porã
3.ACT-injure.by.shooting-know   and   3.ACT-injure.by.shooting+good
's/he <u>can</u> shoot and s/he shoots well'

*añe'ẽ**kuaa** guaraníme*
a-ñe'ẽ-kuaa   guarani=me
1SG.ACT-speak-know   Guarani=in
'I <u>can</u> speak Guarani'

*Carlos omboguata**kuaa** kóche, traytor katu nomboguata**kuaá**i.*
Carlos   o-mbo-guata-kuaa   kóche   traytor   katu
Carlos   3.ACT-MAKE1-walk-know   car   tractor   just
n-o-mbo-guata-kuaa-i
NEG-3.ACT-MAKE1-walk-know-NEG
'Carlos <u>can</u> drive a car, but a tractor he <u>cannot</u> drive.'

*Ha'e ho'yta porã, iñamígo katu ndo'yta**kuaá**i.*
ha'e   ho-'yta   porã   iñ-amígo   katu   nd-o-'yta-kuaa-i
s/he   3.ACT-swim   good   3.INACT-friend   just   NEG-3.ACT-swim-know-NEG
'S/he swims well, but her/his friend cannot swim.'[21]

---

[21] Example from Ortiz et al. (1991, 118).

4.10.3.3 Expressing obligation and permission

Obligation is conveyed by the stressed suffix *-va'erã/-vaerã* (see **4.10.1**) or by the free morpheme *tekotevẽ* 'be necessary'. Like *ikatu* 'be able', this latter does not vary with person and number (and I will therefore gloss it 'be.necessary').

Roha'arõ**va'erã** anga.
ro-h-a'arõ-va'erã anga
1PL.EXCL.ACT-POSSM3-wait-must poor.thing
'Unfortunately, we must wait.'

*Añetépiko apu'ã**va'erã***.
añete=piko a-pu'ã-va'erã
true=Q 1SG.ACT-get.up-must
'Do I really have to get up?'

Tekotevẽ *aha ko'ãga*.
tekotevẽ a-ha ko'ãga
be.necessary 1SG.ACT-go now
'I have to go now.'

Tekotevẽ *rejujevy ko'ẽro*.
tekotevẽ re-ju-jevy ko'ẽro
be.necessary 2SG.ACT-come-again tomorrow
'You have to come back tomorrow.' (The word for 'tomorrow' is most often found as *ko'ẽrõ* in written texts; the spelling chosen here, *ko'ẽro*, is less common, but has the advantage of signalling clearly that stress falls on the penultimate vowel, not on the last vowel.)

The verb 'to need (something)' is the active verb *kotevẽ* (aireal). It is used with the postposition =*rehe* 'at' when the meaning is that of needing a person.

*ai**kotevẽ** nderehe*
ai-kotevẽ nde=rehe
1SG.ACT-need 2SG.INACT=at
'I need you'

*Pe mbarakaja oi**kotevẽ** tembi'u.*
pe mbarakaja oi-kotevẽ t-embi-'u
MED.SG cat 3.ACT-need NPOSSM-NMLZ.REL-ingest
'That cat needs food.'

*Ñande ikatu ñai**kotevẽ** avei ambue árape.*
ñande	ikatu	ñai-kotevẽ	avei	ambue	ára=pe
we&you	be.able	1PL.INCL.ACT-need	also	other	day=in

'We may <u>need</u> (them) too another day.'

The expression of permission is carried out with the unstressed suffix *-mba'e* (from the word *mba'e* 'thing') or with the second-position clitic *katu* 'just'.

*terehó**mba'e***
te-re-ho-mba'e
OPT-2SG.ACT-go-thing
'go, <u>then</u>'

*ehó**katu***
e-ho=katu
IMP-go=just
'<u>go ahead</u>, go' / '<u>just</u> go'

4.10.3.4 Expressing desire and volition

4.10.3.4.1 Volitive mood

The **volitive mood** expresses wants and desires. The stressed volitive suffix *-se* is used when the person that wants an event to happen is also the subject, agent or experiencer of that desired event. Sentences with *-se* are equivalent to English sentences with two clauses, one with the verb 'want', the other with the desired predicate as a to-infinitive, and identical subjects in both clauses. However, in Guarani there is only one clause in this construction, since the equivalent of the English verb 'want' is just a verb suffix.

*aha**se***
a-ha-se
1SG.ACT-go-want
'I <u>want to</u> go'

*Oikuaa**se** nderéra.*
oi-kuaa-se	nde-r-éra
3.ACT-know-want	2SG.INACT-POSSM-name

'S/he <u>wants to</u> know your name.'

Ha chendive piko reñorairõse avei.

ha	che=ndive=piko	re-ño-rairõ-se	avei
and	1SG.INACT=with =Q	2SG.ACT-RECP-attack-want	also

'And with me you want to fight too?'

Remomba'aposevépa ichupekuéra.

re-mo-mba'apo-se-ve=pa	ichupe=kuéra
2SG.ACT-MAKE1-work-want-more=Q	to.him/her=PL

'Do you want to make them work more?'

If the experiencer of the desire or want is different from the agent or experiencer of the event wanted, Guarani uses the (aireal) verb *pota* 'want', in a construction now more similar to the English one. In one clause there is the verb *pota* 'want' with the prefix corresponding to the participant experiencing the wanting, and in the other clause there is the verb expressing the event desired with its own person prefix. What is different is that, whereas in English the second verb (expressing the event desired) is in the to-infinitive form and its subject is actually the object of the first verb (for example, 'I want him to go', not *'I want he to go'), in Guarani the second verb is marked with a person prefix like any other verb. There is therefore no indication that the second verb is subordinated to the first.

*Ai**pota** oho.*

ai-pota	o-ho
1SG.ACT-want	3.ACT-go

'I want him/her to go.' (Literally, 'I want s/he goes.')

*Ai**pota** repromete chéve cherayhutaha.*

ai-pota	re-promete	chéve	che-r-ayhu-ta-ha
1SG.ACT-want	2SG.ACT-promise	to.me	1SG.INACT-POSSM-love-FUT-NMLZ

'I want you to promise me that you will love me.'

The difference between these two forms for expressing desires can be shown with the following contrasting pair. The use of *oipota* in the first example below makes it clear that Tomasa wanted somebody else to find a very beautiful partner; whereas the use of *-se* in the second example makes it clear that Tomasa herself wanted to find a beautiful partner.

*Tomasa oi**pota** ojuhu peteĩ iñirũrã neporãva.*

Tomasa	oi-pota	o-juhu	peteĩ	iñ-irũ-rã
Tomasa	3.ACT-want	3.ACT-find	one	3.INACT-friend-DEST

ne-porã-va
SUP-beautiful-SUP
'Tomasa <u>wanted</u> him to find a very beautiful partner.'

Tomasa ojuhuse peteĩ iñirũrã neporãva
Tomasa o-juhu-se   peteĩ iñ-irũ-rã   ne-porã-va
Tomasa 3.ACT-find-want   one   3.INACT-friend-DEST   SUP-beautiful-SUP
'Tomasa <u>wanted</u> to find a very beautiful partner'.

The verb *pota* is not only used to talk about wanting other events to occur, but also about wanting things.

*Roipota **orepláta**.*
roi-pota   ore-pláta
1PL.EXCL.ACT-want   1PL.EXCL.INACT-money
'We want <u>our money</u>.'

*Ha **mba'epiko** reipota, che áma!*
ha   mba'e=piko   rei-pota   che-áma
And   what=Q   2SG.ACT-want   1SG.INACT-lady
'And <u>what</u> do you want, my love?'

*Ndoipotaimi **la oñembojarúa** akue.*
nd-oi-pota-i-mi   la   o-ñe-mbo-jaru-va   akue
NEG-3.ACT-want-NEG-used.to   DET.SG   3.ACT-MAKE1-prank-ADJZ   PAST
'They didn't want <u>to be made fun of</u>.'

4.10.3.4.2 Hortative and optative mood

The first-person plural **hortative**, similar to English 'let's', is used to exhort a group including oneself to carry out an action. It is conveyed simply by using the first-person inclusive plural prefix.

***ja**ike*
ja-ike
1PL.INCL.ACT-enter
'<u>let's</u> go in'

***ña**ha'arõ*
ña-h-a'arõ
1PL.INCL.ACT-POSSM3-wait
'<u>let's</u> wait'

*Ja*ha lo mitã.
ja-ha	lo	mitã
1PL.INCL.ACT-go	DET.PL	child

'Let's go, boys!'

*Ja*pukami ha upekuévo, *ña*mbohory ñande rekove . . .
ja-puka-mi		ha	upe kue vo
1PL.INCL.ACT-laugh-DIM		and	MED.SG-POST-while

ña-mbo-h-ory	ñande-r-ekove …
1PL.INCL.ACT-MAKE1-POSSM3-joy	1PL.INCL.INACT-POSSM-life

'Let's laugh a little and while we're at it let's brighten up our life . . .'

The **optative mood** is used to indicate wishes and hopes and it is marked by the prefix *t-*, followed by person markers. It is often translated in English by the auxiliary verbs 'let' or 'may'. For inactive person prefixes, the helping vowel *-a-* is added to avoid a clash of two consonants. For active person prefixes, a helping vowel is inserted which is identical to the vowel in the person marker (**vowel harmony**), except in the second-person plural, which inserts *-a-* (we saw that exactly the same happens with the negation prefix; see **4.9**).

*t*amba'apo
t-a-mba'apo
OPT-1SG.ACT-work
'I have decided to work'

*to*rokaru
to-ro-karu
OPT-1PL.EXCL.ACT-eat(intransitive)
'let's eat' or 'that we eat' (but excluding the addressee)

*ta*peho
ta-pe-ho
OPT-2PL.ACT-go
'(I wish that/may) you (pl.) go'

*Te*reğuahẽ porãite! (also written *Te*reguahẽporãite!)
te-re-ğuahẽ	porã-ite
OPT-2SG.ACT-arrive	good-very

'Welcome!' (One addressee.)

*Tape****g̃****uahẽ porãite!* (also written *Tapeguahẽporãite!*)
ta-pe-g̃uahẽ   porã-ite
OPT-2PL.ACT-arrive   good-very
'Welcome!' (Multiple addressees)

*Ñandejára **ta**nderovasa.*
ñande-jára   ta-nde-r-ovasa
1PL.INCL.INACT-lord   OPT-2SG.INACT-POSSM-bless
'God bless you.' (One addressee.)

*Ñandejára **ta**penderovasa.*
ñande-jára   ta-pende-r-ovasa
1PL.INCL.INACT-lord   OPT-2PL.INACT-POSSM-bless
'God bless you.' (Multiple addressees.)

*t****a****oreañuamba nemborayhu*
ta-ore-añua-mba   ne-mbo-r-ayhu
OPT-1PL.EXCL.INACT-embrace-all 2SG.INACT-MAKE1-POSSM-love
'(that/may) your love embrace us all'

The optative mood is often found in the verb of a subordinate clause that is an order or mandate (see also **12.2.2**). In the first clause of the following example, the subordinate verb *tou* is marked with the optative because it is an order that will be verbally given for someone to come. In the second clause, the subordinate verb *tahechauka* is marked with the optative to convey a sense of purpose or goal.

*Peje chupe **t**ou, **t**ahechaukámandivoi peẽme.*
peje   chupe   t-o-u
2PL.ACT.say to.him/her   OPT-3.ACT-come
t-a-h-echa-uka=mandi=voi   peẽme
OPT-1SG.ACT-POSSM3-see-MAKE2=once.and.for.all=EMPH to.you.PL
'Tell him to come, so I can make you see once and for all.'

Both the hortative mood prefix and the optative mood prefix can co-occur with imperative modalizers.

*jahá**ke***
ja-ha-ke
1PL.INCL.ACT-go-FORCE
'come on, let's go!'

topuʼãkena ñaneánga
t-o-puʼã-ke-na ñane-ánga
OPT-3.ACT-get.up-FORCE-REQ 1PL.INCL.INACT-soul
'let/may our soul rise'

The optative can occur with non-verbal predicates.

taʼupéichakena!
ta-ʼupe-icha-ke-na
OPT-MED.SG-as-FORCE-REQ
'I <u>hope</u> so!' / '<u>Let/may it</u> be so!'

The negation of optative forms is accomplished via the stressed privative suffix -ʼỹ.

touʼỹ
t-o-u-ʼỹ
OPT-3.ACT-come-PRIV
'may he <u>not</u> come' / 'I <u>don't</u> want him to come'.

Voice markers (which will be presented in more detail below in **6**) can also co-occur with the optative.

toñembojeroviákena nderéra
t-o-ñe-mbo-jerovia-ke-na nde-r-éra
OPT-3.ACT-AGD-MAKE1-believe-FORCE-REQ 2SG.INACT-POSSM-name
'hallowed <u>be</u> thy name' (literally, '<u>be</u> your name <u>made</u> belief')

Finally, there is a **desiderative** affix *-ngaʼu* (unstressed), that can be translated as 'hopefully', 'I wish that' or 'if only'.

Rehechángaʼu.
re-h-echa-ngaʼu
2SG.ACT-POSSM3-see-DES
'<u>I wish</u> you saw (it).'

4.10.3.5 Expressing negative evaluations

Like many other Amazonian languages, Guarani can express a kind of **frustrative** modality with the stressed suffix *-rei* 'in vain', which conveys a negative evaluation of an action, or its fruitlessness. It is often found accompanied by the particle *mante*, meaning 'only'.

Mba'eichaitépa ñande mbopochy ñamba'aporeírõ.
mba'eicha-ite=pa ñande mbo-pochy ña-mba'apo-rei=rõ
how-very=Q we&you MAKE1-anger 1PL.INCL.ACT-work-in.vain=if
'How very frustrating it is if we work <u>in vain</u>!'

Upéi katu ohejarei mante hikuái . . .
upéi katu o-h-eja-rei mante hikuái
then just 3.ACT-POSSM3-leave-in.vain only they
'And then they just <u>abandoned</u> him . . .'

Gua'u is used for simulated, non-realized actions, or actions with a concealed or non-serious intent. In this use, it can convey the notion that an event is fake or in jest. Somewhat more broadly, it can also express the speaker's evaluation of an action. This particle does not necessarily attach to a predicate but has freer placement in the sentence.

*Mba'e la ojapo la idivertídovea péicha, ikatu, ofarrea, oho omongeta **gua'u** algun kuñápe?*
mba'e la o-japo la i-divertído-ve-va
what DET.SG 3.ACT-make DET.SG 3.INACT-fun-more-ADJZ
pe-icha ikatu o-farrea o-ho o-mongeta gua'u
MED.SG-as be.able 3.ACT-party 3.ACT-go 3.ACT-converse fake
algun kuña=pe
some woman=in
'What did they do that was more fun like, maybe, party, go talk <u>so to speak</u> with some woman?'

*La Prinsésa okémavoi ha pe arriéro nambisakã upéichante avei; Perurimákatu ikerambu **gua'u**.*
la prinsésa o-ke-ma=voi ha pe arriéro
DET.SG princess 3.ACT-sleep-already=EMPH and MED.SG peasant
nambi+sakã upe-icha-nte avei Perurima=katu i-kerambu
ear+transparent MED.SG-as-only also Perurima=just 3.INACT-snore
gua'u
fake
'The Princess already slept and so did the malnourished man; Perurimá just <u>faked</u> snoring.'

*. . . mokõi tahachi oñekytĩ**gua'u** ombotavypotávo huvichápe . . .*
mokõi   tahachi   o-ñe-kytĩ-gua'u   o-mbo-tavy-pota-vo
two   soldier   3.ACT-AGD-cut=fake   3.ACT-MAKE1-stupid-about.to-while
h-uvicha=pe
POSSM3-boss=in
' . . . two soldiers that <u>faked</u> being injured and were about to fool their superior . . . '

Anga expresses speaker commiseration for an event participant. This particle also has somewhat free placement in a sentence.

*Jairo heta **anga** osufri okakuaa aja.*
Jairo   h-eta   anga   o-sufri   o-kakuaa   aja
Jairo   POSSM3-numerous   poor.thing   3.ACT-suffer 3.ACT-grow.up while
'Jairo suffered a lot growing up, <u>poor thing</u>.'

*Ajevérõ niko, ko mitã poriahu rerekóva ápe mba'eve vera ivaíva **anga** ndojapói.*
ajevérõ   niko   ko   mitã   poriahu   re-reko-va   ápe
as.a.result   VERD   PROX.SG   child   poor   2SG.ACT-have-ADJZ   here
mba'eve   vera   i-vai-va   anga   nd-o-japo-i
nothing   completely   3.INACT-bad-ADJZ   poor.thing   NEG-3.ACT-make-NEG
'And so this indigent child you have here has done absolutely nothing bad, <u>poor soul</u>.'

4.11 Verbalizations

The process of turning roots of different classes into verbs is called **verbalization**. Guarani only has one dedicated verbalizer, the stressed suffix *-'o*, which turns a noun into a verb. The resulting meaning is often that of a 'removal' of the object denoted by the base noun.

*pire**'o***
pire-'o
skin-REMOVE
'<u>to</u> skin'

*nambi**'o***
nambi-'o
ear-REMOVE
'<u>to</u> cut (an animal's) ears'

*ñakã'**o***
ñakã-'o
head-REMOVE
'to decapitate' (The noun root for 'head' is *akã* – *ñaka* being the form the root takes as a verb with the loss of the initial consonant or apheresis; see **4.8**.)

*juru'**o***
juru-'o
mouth-REMOVE
'to open'

*hogue'**o***
h-ogue-'o
POSSM3-leaf-REMOVE
'to strip the leaves off, to defoliate'

ky'o
ky-'o
louse-REMOVE
'to delouse'

kyra'o
kyra-'o
grease-REMOVE
'to degrease'

*Kañõ rendyvu oñakã'**o** Florentín Oviedo kavaju.*
kañõ r-endyvu o-ñakã-'o Florentín Oviedo kavaju
cannon POSSM-spit 3.ACT-head-REMOVE Florentín Oviedo horse
'The cannon's spit de̲capitated Florentín Oviedo's horse.'

The prefix *mbo-* (and its allomorphs *mby-*, *mbu-*, *mo-*, *my-*, *mu-*) can also have verbalizing uses. (It is more generally a prefix that turns intransitive verbs into transitive verbs; see **6.6.1**.)

***mbo**katupyry*
mbo-katupyry
MAKE1-skillful
'to teach, to train' (literally, 'to ma̲ke skillful')

*mo*aguĩ
mo-aguĩ
MAKE1-close.by
'to bring closer' (literally, 'to make close')

*mu*angekói
mu-angekói
MAKE1-annoyance
'to annoy' (literally, 'to make annoyed')

*my*akỹ
my-akỹ
MAKE1-wet(adjective)
'to wet' (literally, 'to make wet')

*mby*aku
mby-aku
MAKE1-hot
'to heat up' (literally, 'to make hot')

Although the distribution of the different prefix forms is variable, *mbu-* and *mby-* tend to occur with relational roots and roots that begin with *a*. If an *a*-initial root is nasal the forms are *mu-* and *my-*.

Some verbs can be derived from other verbs to obtain a sort of opposite or reversed meaning. *Jeheko-* is composed of the passive *je-* (see **6.3**) plus the abstract nominalizer for qualities *t-eko-* (see **3.2.1.2.4**).

mbo'e 'to teach' ~ *jehekombo'e* 'to be trained; to learn'
jopy 'to press against' ~ *jehekojopy* 'to subjugate; to persecute; to exploit'
mosã 'to tie' ~ *mosãso* 'to untie' (with the help of the verbal root *so* 'to become detached')

4.12 Modifiers of the verb

Guarani **adverbs** are generally indicators of time or space, or are unmarked roots that can fulfil an adverbial function.

Eju ko'áğa!
e-ju   ko'áğa
IMP-come now
'Come now!'

*Eju **ko'ápe**!*
e-ju   ko'ápe
IMP-come   here
'Come here!'

*Eju **pya'e**!*
e-ju   pya'e
IMP-come   fast
'Come quickly!'

***tuicha** ñanepytyvõta*
tuicha   ñane-pytyvõ-ta
big   1PL.INCL.INACT-help-FUT
'it will help us greatly'

*noñe'ẽi **mbegue***
n-o-ñe'ẽ-i   mbegue
NEG-3.ACT-speak-NEG   slow
's/he doesn't speak slowly'

*Kuarahy overa **asy**.*
kuarahy   o-vera   asy
sun   3.ACT-shine   pain
'The sun shines intensely.'

Time adverbs or time expressions are often the only indication of whether a predicate should be interpreted as past or present.

*Aháma **kuehe** pe mbo'ehaópe.*
a-ha-ma   kuehe   pe   mbo'ehao=pe
1SG.ACT-go-already yesterday   MED.SG   school=in
'I already went to school yesterday.'

***Yma**vépa reho py'ỹi jepi tupa'ópe.*
yma-ve=pa   re-ho   py'ỹi   jepi   tupa'o=pe
before-more=Q   2SG.ACT-go   often   usually   church=in
'Did you use to go frequently to church before?'

*Mba'e **la ndekaria'y tiempo** ijuntopa ndehermanokuérandi pejuga.*
mba'e la nde-karia'y tiempo i-junto-pa
what DET.SG 2SG.INACT-young.man time 3.INACT-together-all
nde-hermano=kuéra=ndi pe-juga
2SG.INACT-sibling=PL=with 2PL.ACT-play
'What did you all play together, you and your siblings, <u>when you were a young man</u>?'

The roots *porã* 'good', *vai* 'bad' and *kuaa* 'to know' very often form a word unit with the predicate when used adverbially. This is not always consistently reflected by the spelling in texts, however.

*Neremba'apo**porã**i.*
ne-re-mba'apo+porã-i
NEG-2SG.ACT-work+good-NEG
'You don't work <u>well</u>.'

*¡Nemomarandu**vai**pa hína hikuái!*
ne-mo-marandu-vai-pa hína hikuái
2SG.INACT-MAKE1-warning-bad-all PROG they
'You are completely <u>ill</u>-informed!' (Literally, 'They are informing you all <u>wrong</u>!')

4.13 Verb compounds

A **verb compound** is a word composed of two roots that functions as a verb. One of the roots is a verb, the other a noun or adjective. (See also **noun compounds** in 3.2.1.3.)

Noun + verb

hepyme'ẽ
h-epy+me'ẽ
POSSM3-price+give
'to pay'

y'u
y+'u
water+ingest
'to drink'

py'apy
py'a+py
chest+press
'to worry'

pokyty
po+kyty
hand+rub
'to rub (with one's hands); to fondle'

Verb + adjective

kehe'ẽ
ke+he'ẽ
sleep+sweet/salty
'to sleep deeply'

karuhe
karu+he
eat(intransitive)+tasty
'to eat with pleasure'

guatapokã
guata+pokã
walk+scarce
'to walk with slow, long strides'

5
Postpositions

The marking of how noun phrases are related by their meaning and their function to a predicate is accomplished in Guarani by means of **postpositions**; that is, particles that occur at the end of the noun phrase they modify (unlike prepositions, which precede the noun phrase they modify). All Guarani postpositions are pronounced forming a unit with the noun phrase to their left and are therefore **enclitics**, not independent words (hence, I render them using an equals sign = in glosses and in the text). Some also show alternations in shape (primarily nasalization) due to the sounds in the preceding word they attach to, which is another indication that they are not independent words.

As mentioned before, the current orthographic recommendation by the Paraguayan Academy is to attach only monosyllabic postpositions to the preceding word. Postpositions with more than one syllable are written as independent words. In this work, I have generally chosen to attach all postpositions to the preceding word in keeping with their common enclitic status (unless the original orthography of the example departs from this and is maintained to facilitate recognition of other examples that use the same conventions).

5.1 Postpositions marking a predicate's complements

By far the most frequent ·postposition is =*pe* (and its nasal allomorph =*me*). Its basic meaning is **locative**, translated as 'in, on, at, to' (see **5.2**). A very important use of this postposition is to indicate that a human noun phrase that accompanies a verb is its direct object. Animals are sometimes marked with =*pe* in this case as well, especially if they are important to humans or personified in some way. Inanimate direct objects (that is, things, places, events) are unmarked.

Oha'arõ tapiaite imembykuérape.
o-h-a'arõ   tapia-ite   i-memby=kuéra=pe
3.ACT-POSSM3-wait   always-very   3.INACT-child.of.woman=PL=in
'She always waited <u>for</u> her children.'
(Note: 'wait' takes a direct object in Guarani, hence, marked with =*pe* when it is human.)

Cinco motivo rehayhu haǧua jaguakuérape.
cinco   motivo   re-h-ayhu=haǧua   jagua=kuéra=pe
five   reason   2SG.ACT-POSSM3-love=for   dog=PL=in
'Five reasons to love <u>dogs</u>.'

Cheru ojukapáta tahyikuéra.
che-r-u   o-juka-pa-ta   tahýi=kuéra
1SG.INACT-POSSM-father   3.ACT-kill-all-FUT   ant=PL
'My father will kill all <u>the ants</u>.'

The locative =*pe*/=*me* also marks indirect objects in ditransitive constructions (these indirect objects are **recipients** of verbs of transfer or communication, for example).

Ame'ẽta kóva chesýpe.
a-me'ẽ-ta   ko-va   che-sy=pe
1SG.ACT-give-FUT   PROX.SG-ADJZ   1SG.INACT-mother=in
'I will give this <u>to</u> my mother.'

Tome'ẽ ñanembo'ehárape iñaranduka.
t-o-me'ẽ   ñane-mbo'e-hára=pe   iñ-aranduka
OPT-3.ACT-give   1PL.INCL.INACT-teach-NMLZ.AG=in   3.INACT-book
'Let him/her give his/her book <u>to</u> our teacher.'

*Amombe'úta **ndéve** la ojehuva'ekue*
a-mombe'u-ta   ndéve   la   o-jehu-va'e-kue
1SG.ACT-tell-FUT   to.you.SG   DET.SG   3.ACT-happen-ADJZ-POST
'I will tell <u>(to) you</u> what happened'

In **4.4**, I showed some verbs that require their complements to bear specific postpositions; for example, =*rehe* 'at' or =*gui* 'from' (=*hegui* in construction with personal pronouns).

*Chemandu'áta nde**rehe**, nanderesaráiri che**hegui**.*

che-mandu'a-ta	nde=rehe	na-nde-r-esarái-ri
1SG.INACT-remembrance-FUT	2SG.INACT=at	NEG-2SG.INACT-POSSM-oblivion-NEG

chehegui
from.me

'I will remember you, do not forget me.'

*Natekotevẽi amomandu'a Jesús omano peteĩ korasõ destrozado **reheve**.*

na-tekotevẽ-i	a-mo-mandu'a	Jesús	o-mano
NEG-be.necessary-NEG	1SG.INACT-MAKE1-remembrance	Jesus	3.ACT-die

peteĩ korasõ	destrozado	reheve
one heart	destroyed	with

'I do not need to remind (you) that Jesus died <u>of</u> a broken heart.'

*Chekuerái che maĩna po'a'ỹ ha mboriahú**gui**, ha atĩma pende**hegui** amba'ejerure haguã.*

che-kuerái	che-maĩna	po'a-'ỹ	ha	mboriahu=gui
1SG.INACT-annoyance	1SG.INACT-godmother	luck-PRIV	and	poverty=from

ha	a-tĩ-ma	pendehegui	a-mba'e-jerure	haguã
and	1SG.ACT-feel.shame-already	from.you.PL	1SG.ACT-THING-petition	for

'Godmother, I am fed up <u>with</u> the bad luck and the poverty, and I already feel shame coming to you to ask for things.'

Arguments that express the **beneficiary** of an action are marked with =*pe* in combination with the postposition =*guarã* 'for'.

*Ajapo chesý**peguarã**.*

a-japo	che-sy=pe=guarã
1SG.ACT-make	1SG.INACT-mother=in=for

'I made (it) <u>for</u> my mother.'

*Ohaiva'erã hikuai mbo'ehára**peguarã***

o-h-ai-va'erã	hikuái	mbo'e-hára=pe=guarã
3.ACT-POSSM3-write-must	they	teach-NMLZ.AG=in=for

'They will have to write it <u>for</u> the teacher'

Recipient- and beneficiary-marking =*pe* becomes =*ve* in combination with personal pronouns: *chéve, ndéve*, and so on (see **3.5.**1.) These pronouns ending in =*ve* do not have the same distribution as the more general =*pe*-marked phrases: they are never locative, for example, hence 'in/inside you' is rendered by *ndepýpe*, never by *ndéve*.

*Ame'ẽ ko ryguasu **ndéve**.*
a-me'ẽ　　　　ko　　　　ryguasu　ndéve
1SG.ACT-give　PROX.SG　hen　　　to.you.SG
'I gave you this hen.'

*Ahai ko kuatia **ndéve**.*
a-h-ai　　　　　　　　　　ko　　　　kuatia　ndéve
1SG.ACT-POSSM3-write　PROX.SG　text　　to.you.SG
'I wrote you this letter.'

5.2 Postpositions of place

The following (non-exhaustive) table lists the most common spatial postpositions (and their variants if they have them).

Postposition	Allomorphs	Meaning
got(y)o	*ngot(y)o* with nasal bases	'towards'
gua	*ygua* with bases ending in non-high vowels	'from, of' (provenance)
gui	*hegui* with personal pronouns	'from'
guive		'from a starting point; since'
jerére		'around'
pe	*me* with nasal bases *ve* with personal pronouns	'in, on, at, to'
peve	*meve* with nasal bases	'to an endpoint; until'
rapykuéri (relational)		'behind'
rehe	*re* in free variation *hese* as third-person pronoun (third person + *rehe*)	'at, about'
rovake (relational)		'in front of, in the presence of'
rupi		'around; through'
'ári		'on top of'

Points to note:

- *Guive* and *peve* contain the =*ve* allomorph of =*pe* which is generally used with personal pronouns.
- *Jerére* 'around' can be decomposed in *jere* 'turn' and =*re* 'at'.
- More specific spatial relations are expressed by combining a lexical root with the general locative =*pe*:
    pýpe 'inside', from *py* 'foot'
    rendápe 'next to', from *-enda* 'place' (relational)
    renondépe 'facing', from *-enonde* 'front' (relational)

Amaña cherúrehe cállepe. Ko'áğa ohasahína orekorapýrupi. Oúkuri merkádogui ha oikéta orerógape.

a-maña	che-r-u=rehe	cálle=pe	ko'áğa
1SG.ACT-look.at	1SG.INACT-POSSM-father=at	street=in	now

o-h-asa=hína	ore-korapy=rupi	o-u-kuri
3.ACT-POSSM3-pass=PROG	1PL.EXCL.INACT-yard=through	3.ACT-come-DIR.PAST

merkádo=gui	ha	o-ike-ta	ore-r-óga=pe
market=from	and	3.ACT-enter-FUT	1PL.EXCL.INACT-POSSM-house=in

'I look at my father in the street. Now he is walking through our yard. He just came back from the market and will enter into our house.'

Jaháta ñandetávagotyo kavaju'ári.

ja-ha-ta	ñande-táva=gotyo	kavaju='ári
1PL.INCL.ACT-go-FUT	1PL.INCL.INACT-town=towards	horse=upon

'We will go towards our town on horses.'

ojuhu hikuái juky iñasãiva hóga jerére

o-juhu	hikuái	juky	iñ-asãi-va	h-óga	jerére
3.ACT-find	they	salt	3.INACT-extended-ADJZ	POSSM3-house	around

'they found salt that spread all around their houses'

5.3 Postpositions of time

Postposition	Allomorphs	Meaning
aja		'during'
guive		'since'
jave		'during'

(continue)

mboyve		'before'
peve	*meve* with nasal bases	'until'
ramo, rõ		'when'
rire		'after'
vove		'during'

*mayma oguerekóva 15 ary **guive** 40 **peve***
mayma   o-guereko-va   15   ary=guive   40=peve
every   3.ACT-have-ADJZ   15   year=since   40=until
'everybody from 15 to 40 years of age'

*nahesakãi **aja** ha'eha culpable*
na-h-esakã-i   aja   ha'e-ha   culpable
NEG-POSSM3-transparency-NEG   during   be-NMLZ   guilty
'while/as long as it isn't clear that s/he is guilty'

*Ka'aguýre apytávo ka'aruete ro'y **jave**.*
ka'aguy=re   a-pyta-vo   ka'aru-ete   r-o'y   jave
forest=at   1SG.ACT-stay-while   dusk-very   POSSM-cold   while
'Stopping by the woods on a cold evening.'

*Teñói **mboyve** ñeñangareko omoporã tyeguasu ñemohu'ã.*
t-eñói   mboyve   ñe-ñangareko   o-mo-porã   t-ye+guasu
NPOSSM-sprout   before   AGD-take.care.of   3.ACT-MAKE1-good   NPOSSM-belly+big
ñe-mo-h-u'ã
AGD-MAKE1-POSSM3-summit
'Before the birth, taking care of oneself improves pregnancy outcomes.'

*Mba'épa oikóta ndehegui rekakuaa**rire**.*
mba'e=pa   o-iko-ta   ndehegui   re-kakuaa=rire
what=Q   3.ACT-be-FUT   from.you.SG   2SG.ACT-grow.up=after
'What will you be after you grow up?'

*Ohendupa**rire** mburuvicha guasúpe, oho meme hapére.*
o-h-endu-pa=rire   mburuvicha   guasu=pe   o-ho   meme
3.ACT-POSSM3-listen-all=after   leader   big=in   3.ACT-go   all
h-ape=re
POSSM3-road=at
'After they all heard the king, they all went their way.'

*Michĩ **vove** ojehero "mitã".*
michĩ vove o-je-h-ero mitã
little during 3.ACT-AGD-POSSM3-dub child
'<u>When</u> (they are) little, they are called "child".'

5.4 Other postpositions

Postposition	Allomorphs	Meaning
gui		'because of'
icha		'as, like'
káusa		'because of (a negative cause)'
ndive	ndi, ndie (in free variation)	'with' (comitative)
pe	me with nasal bases	'with' (instrument)
pópe		'with' (manner)
ramo		'instead of'
ramo, rõ		'if'
rehe		'with' (instrument)
rupi		'because'
rupive		'by means of'
'ỹ, 'ỹre(he), rehe'ỹ		'without'

Points to note:

- *Káusa* is a borrowing of the Spanish noun *causa* 'cause'. Its meaning, however, is 'because of X's fault', and thus, *káusa* can only be used for causal relations that are judged negatively.
- Several of these postpositions are relational: *-ehe (hese), -enonde, -apykuéri, -endápe, -enondépe.*

*Ejumína che**ndie**.*
e-ju-mi-na che=ndive
IMP-come-PLEAD-REQ 1SG.INACT=with
'Please come <u>with</u> me.'

*Ndesy iporã yvoty**icha**.*
nde-sy i-porã yvoty-icha
2SG.INACT-mother 3.INACT-beautiful flower-as
'Your mother is beautiful <u>like</u> a flower.'

Cheru almacénpe chedeprovechovégui.
che-r-u almacén=pe che-deprovecho-ve=gui
1SG.INACT-POSSM-father grocery.store=in 1SG.INACT-profitable-more=because.of
'<u>Because</u> I am more useful in my father's grocery store.'

Peñeha'arõta torypópe.
pe-ñe-h-a'arõ-ta t-ory=pópe
2PL.ACT-AGD-POSSM3-wait-FUT NPOSSM-joy=with
'We await you with joy.' (Literally, 'You are awaited with joy'.)

Maino omongaru Ñanderu Tenondépe eirete marangatúrehe.
maino o-mo-ngaru ñande-r-u
hummingbird 3.ACT-MAKE1-eat(intransitive) 1PL.INCL.INACT-POSSM-father
t-enonde=pe eirete marangatu=rehe
NPOSSM-front=in honey wise=with
'Maino (the hummingbird) fed Our Father the First <u>with</u> the royal honey.'

upéva ojehúrõ
upe-va o-jehu=rõ
MED.SG-ADJZ 3.ACT-happen=if
'<u>if</u> that happens'

omomarandu chupe iñe'ẽ pyrusu guasúpe outaha
o-mo-marandu chupe i-ñe'ẽ pyrusu guasu=pe
3.ACT-MAKE1-warning to.him/her 3.INACT-speak large big=in
o-u-ta-ha
3.ACT-come-FUT-NMLZ
'he told him <u>with</u> his big commanding voice that he would return'

*Cheru **rupi** che aikove.*
che-r-u rupi che a-ikove
1SG.INACT-POSSM-father through I 1SG.ACT-live
'I live <u>because of</u> my father.'

*ndaha'éi la gérra **káusa** katuete*
nda-ha'e-i la gérra káusa katuete
NEG-be-NEG DET.SG war because.of surely
'it isn't necessarily <u>because of</u> the war' (i.e., 'the war isn't necessarily to blame')

*Mba'asy ñemonguera pohã ñana **rupive** . . .*
mba'+asy	ñe-mo-nguera	pohã	ñana	rupive
thing+pain	AGD-MAKE1-get.healthy	medicine	herb	by.means.of

'The cure of illnesses <u>by means of</u> medicinal plants . . .'

*nde**rehe'ỹ** ndavy'ái*
nde−rehe'ỹ	nd-a-vy'a-i
2SG.INACT=without	NEG-1SG.ACT-joy-NEG

'<u>without</u> you I am not happy'

*pemoĩ opa mba'e Ñandejára pópe peneñembo'é**pe***
pe-moĩ	opa	mba'e	ñande-jára	po=pe	pene-ñembo'e=pe
2PL.ACT-put	all	thing	1PL.INCL.INACT-lord	hand=in	2PL.INACT-prayer=in

'put all things in the hands of Our Lord <u>by means of</u> your prayers'

*Kururúicha, typychá**pe** oñemosẽ.*
kururu-icha	typycha=pe	o-ñe-mo-sẽ
frog-as	broom=in	3.ACT-AGD-MAKE1-go.out

'He was kicked out <u>with</u> a broom like a frog.'

*Mayma yvypóra ou ko yvy ári iñapytĩ**'ỹre** ha peteĩcha tekoruvicharenda; ha ikatu **rupi** oikuaa añetéva ha añete**'ỹ**va.*
mayma	yvypóra	o-u	ko	yvy=ári	iñ-apytĩ='ỹre
every	person	3.ACT-come	PROX.SG	earth=upon	3.INACT-link=without
ha	peteĩ-cha	t-eko-r-uvicha-r-enda		ha	ikatu
and	one-as	NPOSSM-NMLZ.QUAL-POSSM-boss-POSSM-place		and	be.able
rupi	oi-kuaa	añeté-va	ha	añete-'ỹ-va	
through	3.ACT-know	true-ADJZ	and	true-PRIV-ADJZ	

'All human beings come upon this Earth <u>without</u> ties (i.e., free) and in possession of equal dignity; and <u>because of that</u> they can know what is true and what is <u>un</u>true.'

6
Voice

The term **voice** is generally known to speakers of English to refer to the active voice (when the subject of a verb is the actual agent of an action) and the passive voice (when the subject of the verb is the patient that receives or is affected by an action). Guarani has more voices than English; therefore, I use the term here to refer to how Guarani:

- expresses the semantic participants of an event (agent or patient, generally) in the form of grammatical functions (subjects, objects or obliques), and in so doing,
- possibly decreases or increases the number of arguments a predicate takes.

Voices are mostly marked via prefixes in Guarani.

6.1 Active voice

The **active voice** is defined by the verb taking one of the person prefixes of the active set (see **4.1.1**). This can be for the only argument of an intransitive predicate (symbolized S) or for the agent argument of a transitive predicate (symbolized A).

Intransitive predicates: the active person prefix marks the S (subject) argument

aguata
a-guata
1SG.ACT-walk
'I walk(ed)'

*ja*puka
ja-puka
1PL.INCL.ACT-laugh
'we laugh(ed)'

*re*ñani
re-ñani
2SG.ACT-run
'you (sg.) run/ran'

Transitive predicates: the active person prefix marks the A (agent) argument

*pei*nupã ichupe
pei-nupã   ichupe
2PL.ACT-hit   to.him/her
'you (pl.) hit him/her'

*ja*hecha ichupekuéra
ja-h-echa   ichupe=kuéra
1PL.INCL.ACT-POSSM3-see   to.him/her=PL
'we see them'

We must note that, although the active voice is generally conceptualized as the basic or canonical voice assignment, in Guarani it can only be used if:

- the predicate is intransitive and active (that is, it belongs to the grammatical class that takes active prefixes),
- or, as we saw in **4.2**, if the patient participant (P) of a transitive predicate is third person.

6.2 Inactive voice

I will call the **inactive voice**:

- the expression of the only argument (S) of an intransitive predicate with one of the prefixes of the inactive set (see **4.1.2**)

- or the expression of the patient argument (symbolized P) of a transitive verb with one of the prefixes of the inactive set. In this case, the agent argument (A) can optionally be expressed with a subject pronoun.

Intransitive predicates: the inactive person prefix marks the S (subject) argument

***che*atĩa**
che-atĩa
1SG.INACT-sneeze
'I sneez(ed)'

***ne*porã**
ne-porã
2SG.INACT-beautiful
'you are beautiful'

Transitive predicates: the inactive person prefix marks the P (patient) argument

***ore*nupã**
ore-nupã
1PL.EXCL.INACT-hit
'we are hit' / 's/he/they/you hit us'

*upéva **che**pytyvõ*
upe-va   che-pytyvõ
MED.SG-ADJZ   1SG.INACT-help
'that helps/helped me'

The inactive voice with adjectives or nouns expresses a **predication**; that is, the attribution of a quality or state to the subject. This can be accomplished directly by prefixing the noun or adjective with an inactive person prefix, without the use of a copular verb (such as English 'to be') (see **8.2**).

***nde*tuja**
nde-tuja
2SG.INACT-old
'you are old'

VOICE   205

*i****pochy***
i-pochy
3.INACT-anger
's/he is angry'

An active intransitive verb that usually expresses an event that progresses in time can take instead an inactive prefix to express a continuing state.

a*karu* vs. ***che****karu*
a-karu   che-karu
1SG.ACT-eat(intransitive)   1SG.INACT-eat(intransitive)
'I eat' vs. 'I am a big eater'

nde*karuvai*
nde-karu-vai
2SG.INACT-eat(intransitive)-bad
'you have bad table manners' / 'you eat indiscriminately' (literally, 'you eat badly')
(Note: the expression *karuvai* should be used with care because it can also refer to somebody who has sex with a putatively sexually undesirable person.)

This malleability of Guarani roots and the importance of the speaker's choice of active versus inactive voice is particularly clear in the following example:

*Upéi katu aju che, yvypóraicha ajuva'ekue, **a**karu ha **ha**'úva vino, ha peje cherehe, **che**karu ha **che**ka'uha.*

Upéi	katu	a-ju		che	yvypóra-icha	a-ju-va'ekue
then	just	1SG.ACT-come		I	person-as	1SG.ACT-come-PAST
a-karu			ha	ha-'u-va		vino	ha	peje
1SG.ACT-eat(intransitive)		and	1SG.ACT-drink-ADJZ		wine	and	2PL.ACT.say
che=rehe		che-karu			ha	che-ka'u-ha
1SG.INACT=at	1SG.INACT-eat(intransitive)		and	1SG.INACT-get.drunk-NMLZ

'And then I came, I came like a person, eat<u>ing</u> and drin<u>k</u>ing wine, and you said to me that I <u>am a glutton</u> and <u>a drunk</u>.'

Remember from **4.2** that using inactive prefixes (that is, using the inactive voice) is obligatory when the patient participant (P) is higher in the 1 > 2 > 3 person hierarchy than the agent participant (A).

***Che**gueru reiete.* (1SG object > 3 subject)
che-gueru   rei-ete
1SG.ACT-bring   in.vain-very
'They brought me for nothing.'

*Ehendu nderúpe, **nde**reru ypy va'ekue.* (2SG object > 3 subject)
e-h-endu   nde-r-u=pe   nde-reru   ypy   va'ekue
IMP-POSSM3-hear   2SG.INACT-POSSM-father=in   2SG.INACT-bring   beginning   PAST
'Listen to your father that brought you at the beginning.'

Even though this voice looks like a traditional passive (and is often translated as such), the A (agent) argument can still appear as an independent subject pronoun, or the second-person plural, as an active person prefix. This is not usually true of passives, which is why I am calling this voice inactive.

*ndejukáta **hikuái***
nde-juka-ta   hikuái
2SG.INACT-kill-FUT   they
'they will kill you'

*Aguyjetaite **pe**cherendurehe.*
aguyje=ta-ite   pe-che-r-endu=rehe
thanks=multitude-very   2SG.ACT-1SG.INACT-POSSM-listen=at
'Many thanks for (your) listening to me.'

The active and inactive voices are expressed by the person prefixes in each respective class. The remaining voices we will see next have dedicated voice prefixes, with the exception of the causative for transitive verbs which uses a suffix. Of note, all verb forms with a voice marker take active prefixes in their conjugation.

6.3 Passive/reflexive/impersonal voice

Passive, reflexive and impersonal interpretations are expressed in Guarani with the same prefix *je-/ñe-*. This voice prefix is used in the following cases:

- with intransitive verbs to eliminate the subject and achieve an impersonal or a generic meaning

- with transitive verbs to indicate that an action is performed upon the subject by a non-specified agent (passive meaning) or by the subject itself (reflexive meaning).

It is difficult to give a single name to this voice given its many functions. Yet, since all these uses have in common that they demote the agent participant (A), either by eliminating or by turning it into a patient, I have been calling it the **agent-demoting voice** and glossing it AGD.

6.3.1 With intransitive verbs: generic and impersonal interpretations

When used with an intransitive verb (a verb that takes only a subject), the prefix *je-/ñe-* requires conjugation with the third-person singular active prefix *o-* and is interpreted as an event without an agent (impersonal) or with a unspecified agent (generic). In impersonal readings, the third-person singular verb prefix is just a dummy subject without meaning (much like English 'it rains'). Intended generic and impersonal meanings are often very similar.

Generic/impersonal meanings

oje̱jeroky
o-je-jeroky
3.ACT-AGD-dance
'there is dancing' (literally, 'it is danced'; impersonal meaning)

oje̱japo
o-je-japo
3.ACT-AGD-make
'one makes / it is made' (generic/impersonal reading)

Mba'éichapa oje̱japóne oje̱jeroky haǧua oje'a'ỹre
mba'éicha=pa   o-je-japo-ne   o-je-jeroky   haǧua   o-je-'a='ỹre
how=Q   3.ACT-AGD-make-DUB 3.ACT-AGD-dance   for   3.ACT-AGD-fall=without
'What does one have to do to dance without falling?' (generic reading)

Oje̱japóma he'íva léi 1328/98
o-je-japo-ma   he'í-va   léi   1328/98
3.ACT-AGD-make-already   says-ADJZ   law   1328/98
'What law 1328/98 says has already been done' (impersonal reading)

Mba'éichapa oje'e ko ñe'ẽ avañe'ẽme

mba'éicha=pa	o-je-'e	ko	ñe'ẽ	ava+ñe'ẽ=me
how=Q	3.ACT-AGD-say	PROX.SG	word	person+language=in

'How does <u>one</u> say this word in Guarani?' (generic reading)

This prefix also functions as a nominalizer (mostly with active intransitive verbs; see **3.2.1.2.2**):

*je**ka'u** (from active intransitive *ka'u* 'to get drunk')
je-ka'u
AGD-get.drunk
'drunkenness'

*ñe**mano** (from active intransitive *mano* 'to die')
ñe-mano
AGD-die
'death'

However, inactive intransitive verbs and transitive verbs can also be nominalized this way:

*ñe**mandu'a** (from inactive intransitive *mandu'a* 'to remember; memory')
ñe-mandu'a
AGD-remember
'remembrance'

*ñe**mondo** (from transitive *mondo* 'to send')
ñe-mondo
AGD-send
'shipment, commission'

6.3.2 With transitive verbs: passive and reflexive interpretations

When used with a transitive verb (a verb that takes both a subject and an object), the prefix *je-/ñe-* conveys one of two meanings:

- that the action is performed on the subject that is indicated by the active person prefix on the verb (passive meaning), or
- that the action is performed by the subject unto itself (reflexive meaning).

Passive/reflexive meanings

*re**je**japi*
re-je-japi
2SG.ACT-AGD-injure.by.shooting
'you were shot' / 'you shot yourself'

*o**ñe**kytĩ*
o-ñe-kytĩ
3.ACT-AGD-cut
's/he was cut' / 's/he cut him/herself'

Out of context, these forms are ambiguous between a passive and a reflexive reading. This ambiguity results in part from the fact that sentences with a *je-* marked transitive verb cannot express overtly the agent participant (A). A sentence like English 'You were shot by a soldier' where 'a soldier' is the agent of the shooting is not possible using this voice in Guarani. (One has to use an inactive prefix instead: *tahachi ndeapi* 'a soldier shot you'.) However, in context, it is usually clear which interpretation is intended. In the following example, it is clear that somebody else is waiting for the people addressed, not themselves. The interpretation must be passive.

*Pe**ñe**ha'arõta torypópe.*
pe-ñe-h-a'arõ-ta   t-ory=pópe
2PL.ACT-AGD-POSSM3-wait-FUT   NPOSSM-joy=with
'We await you with joy.' (Literally, 'you will be awaited with joy'.)

In the next example, little children do not call themselves "child", but other people call them that. Again, the interpretation must be passive.

*Michĩ vove o**je**hero "mitã".*
michĩ   vove   o-je-h-ero   mitã
little during 3.ACT-AGD-POSSM3-dub   child
'When (they are) little, they are called "child".'

Finally, in the following example, it is clear that the speakers are washing their own hands over and over (reflexive interpretation), not having their hands washed by somebody else (although that interpretation is certainly possible).

*ja**je**pohéipohéi*
ja-je-po+héi~po+héi
1PL.INCL.ACT-AGD-hand+wash~hand+wash
'we wash our hands over and over'

Aireal verbs normally lose the final *i* of the person prefix in the agent-demoting voice, but forms that conserve it are also heard in the modern language (there is variation in how speakers say these verb forms). However, *i* appears next to the root in this case, not with the active prefix, which indicates that speakers treat it now as part of the root. That is, you may hear either of the forms *ojepuru* or *ojeipuru* presented below, but never *oijepuru*.

*o**i**puru*
oi-puru
3.ACT-use
's/he uses (it)'

*o**je**puru/o**jei**puru*
o-je-(i)puru
3.ACT-AGD-use
'it is used'

Another example is given below with the aireal verb *pytyvõ* 'to help':

*Jajeprováta ha ñañetentáta, ha katu jarresivíta **ñeipytyvõ**.*
ja-je-prova-ta   ha   ña-ñe-tenta-ta   ha   katu
1PL.INCL.ACT-AGD-test-FUT and   1PL.INCL.ACT-AGD-tempt-FUT   and just
ja-rresivi-ta   ñe-ipytyvõ
1PL.INCL.ACT-receive-FUT   AGD-help
'We will be tested and we will be tempted, but we will (also) receive help.'

Finally, remember that the agent-demoting prefix is also present in the derivation of reflexive pronouns (see **3.5.1**) and as a nominalizer to convert predicates into nouns (see **3.2.1.2.2**).

6.4 Reciprocal voice

The **reciprocal voice** is used when a plural subject is composed of individuals that are agents of an action and simultaneously patients thereof (equivalent to English predicates with 'each other' or 'one another'). It employs the prefix *jo-/ño-*. A plural subject is obviously required in this voice.

Reciprocal meanings

*ja**jo**hayhu*
ja-jo-h-ayhu
1PL.INCL.ACT-RECP-POSSM3-love
'you and I love each other' / 'we love one another'

*ro**ño**nupã*
ro-ño-nupã
1PL.EXCL.ACT-RECP-beat.up
's/he and I beat each other up' / 'we beat one another up'

*Ja**jo**topárire javy'avévaerãmo'a.*
ja-jo-topa=rire   ja-vy'a-ve-vae-rã-mo'a
1PL.INCL.ACT-RECP-meet-if   1PL.INCL.ACT-joy-more-ADJZ-DEST-ALMOST
'If we had met (one another), we would have rejoiced more.'

*Ápe ñandekuéra ja**jo**su'upareíta.*
ápe   ñande=kuéra   ja-jo-su'u-pa-rei-ta
here   we&you=PL   1PL.INCL.ACT-RECP-bite-all-in.vain-FUT
'Here we and you will bite each other to no avail.'

*Mokõi kuña ikatu o**ño**hetũ.*
mokõi   kuña   ikatu   o-ño-h-etũ
two   woman   be.able   3.ACT-RECP-POSSM3-kiss
'Two women can kiss (one another).'

The reciprocal voice can involve more than two individuals, in which case it is interpreted as indicating that each individual acts upon all other individuals, and is acted upon by the other individuals.

*Opavave o**ño**añuava'erã hermanokuéraicha.*
opavave   o-ño-añua-va'erã   hermano=kuéra-icha
all   3.ACT-RECP-embrace-must brother=PL-as
'Everyone should embrace one another as brothers.'

The reciprocal prefix can also function to convert predicates into nouns with a reciprocal meaning. See **3.2.1.2.3**.

6.5 Antipassive voice

Just as the passive voice leaves out the agent subject of a transitive verb (and expresses the patient as subject), the **antipassive voice** leaves out the direct object of a transitive verb (hence the name **antipassive**). When this voice is used, the direct object that is left out is understood as a generic or unspecified object. The antipassive voice uses the prefix *poro-* (glossed PEOPLE) when the direct object is to be understood as human and *mba'e-* (glossed THING) when the direct object is to be understood as non-human (referring to either animals or things). Some speakers may use the prefix *po-* instead of *poro-*. Importantly, this voice cannot be used with verbs that take an object marked with a postposition (**4.4**). It is only used with transitive verbs that take a direct object.

Antipassive meanings

ro***poro***mbo'e
ro-poro-mbo'e
1PL.EXCL.ACT-PEOPLE-teach
'we teach/taught (people)'

pe***mba'e***jogua
pe-mba'e-jogua
2PL.ACT-THING-buy
'you buy/bought (things)' / 'you are/were shopping'

Ñañeha'ãke ja***poro***hayhu.
ña-ñe-h-a'ã-ke   ja-poro-h-ayhu
1PL.INCL.ACT-AGD-POSSM3-attempt-FORCE   1PL.INCL.ACT-PEOPLE-POSSM3-love
'Let's strive to love people.'

Aju a***poro***mbo'évo.
a-ju   a-poro-mbo'e-vo
1SG.ACT-come 1SG.ACT-PEOPLE-teach-while
'I came to teach (everyone / the people).'[22]

A***mba'e***porandusemi ndéve.
a-mba'e-porandu-se-mi   ndéve
1SG.ACT-THING-question-want-DIM to.you
'I would like to ask you something.'

---
[22] Example from Melià *et al.* (1997, 123).

*Péicha o**mba'e**mombe'úmi ta'ýrape Mbatovigua ypykue.*
pe-icha   o-mba'e-mombe'u-mi   t-a'ýra=pe   Mbatovi=gua
MED.SG-as   3.ACT-THING-tell-used.to   NPOSSM-son.of.father=in   Mbatovi=from
ypy-kue
origin-POST
'Those were the stories the elders from Mbatovi used to tell their sons.'
(Literally, 'Thus used to recount (things) the elders from Mbatovi to their sons.')

*Guaranikuéra o**mba'**ejuka ha oipirakutu.*
guarani=kuéra   o-mba'e-juka   ha   oi-pira+kutu
guarani=PL   3.ACT-THING-kill   and   3.ACT-fish-pierce
'The Guarani hunted (animals) and fished.'

*Mbokapĩ ha'e peteĩ mboka ojeipuruha o**poro**ñongatu téra o**poro**juka hağua.*
mbokapĩ   ha'e   peteĩ   mboka   o-jei-puru-ha   o-poro-ñongatu
rifle   be   one   firearm   3.ACT-AGD-use-NMLZ.AG   3.ACT-PEOPLE-protect
téra   o-poro-juka   hağua
or   3.ACT-PEOPLE-kill   for
'A rifle is a firearm that is used to protect (people) or to kill (people).'

*Peñepyrũ pe**mba'e**mombe'u.*
pe-ñepyrũ   pe-mba'e-mombe'u
2PL.ACT-begin   2PL.ACT-THING-tell
'Begin to write stories.' (Literally, 'Begin to tell (things)'.)

*Atĩma pendehegui a**mba'e**jerure hağuã.*
a-tĩ-ma   pendehegui   a-mba'e-jerure   hağuã
1SG.ACT-feel.shame-already   from.you.PL   1SG.ACT-THING-petition   for
'It already makes me ashamed to be asking things from you.'

A subordinate verb inflected with the antipassive voice prefix may not need a person prefix.

*Upe ñe'ẽmbohasa oñeme'ẽ **poro**pytyvõ hağuáichante avañe'ẽ jekuaápe.*
upe   ñe'ẽ+mbo-h-asa   o-ñe-me'ẽ   poro-pytyvõ=hağua-icha-nte
MED.SG   language+MAKE1-POSSM3-pass   3.ACT-AGD-give   PEOPLE-help=for-as-only

ava+ñe'ẽ   je-kuaa=pe
person+language   AGD-know=in

'The translations are given only <u>to aid</u> (people, readers) in the understanding of Guarani.'

6.6 Causative voice

The **causative voices** are the only voices in Guarani that can add an argument to a verb. Causative constructions are derived from base events by creating a more complex event. In this more complex event a new participant, the **causer**, makes the former subject of the base event (the **causee**) perform the action indicated by the base event. Such causatives are often equivalent to English expressions such as 'make someone do something', 'get someone to do something' or 'have someone do something'. For example, taking the base event expressed by 'she runs' a causative construction could be 'I make her run.'

In Guarani there are three causatives. The **intransitive causative** and the **sociative causative** apply to intransitive verbs and yield a transitive verb with two participants. The **transitive causative** applies to a transitive verb and yields an event with three participants: in addition to the causer that instigates the causee's action, there is also an **affectee** that receives or is affected by the causee's action.

Since causative events involve several different participants, I will give some schematic representations here to facilitate the reader's understanding of each participant's involvement and how they are represented in causative sentences. In the schemas, C designates the causer, the causee will be A or S (since they are made to perform actions) and the affectee will be P (since they are affected by or receive an action).

6.6.1 Causative voice for intransitive verbs

Intransitive verbs take the prefix *mbo-/mo-* (glossed MAKE1) to form a transitive causative verb, in which the subject participant (the **causer**) makes the object participant (the **causee**, animate or inanimate) do something, undergo a process or enter a state. This causative can be used indistinctly whether the base event is expressed by an active or an inactive root. The causer is marked with an active person prefix, while the causee is marked as a direct object. This is the most frequently used causative in Guarani.

The schemas below show how the participant marked by a person prefix for an intransitive verb becomes a cause marked as a direct object in the causativized transitive verb.

Source intransitive verb

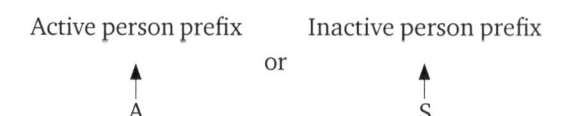

Active person prefix   Inactive person prefix
         ↑   or   ↑
         A   S

Derived causative verb

Active person prefix   Direct object marking
         ↑   ↑
         C   ─────────────▶   A/S

ambopuka ichupe (from *a-puka* 'I laugh')
a-mbo-puka   ichupe
1SG.ACT-MAKE1-laugh   to.him/her
'I make him/her laugh'

amomba'apo pohãnoharakuérape (from *a-mba'apo* 'I work')
a-mo-mba'apo   pohãno-hara=kuéra=pe
1SG.ACT-MAKE1-work   cure-NMLZ.AG=PL=in
'I make the doctors work'

ambojapu cherajýpe (from *che-japu* 'I lie (=tell lies)')
a-mbo-japu   che-r-ajy=pe
1SG.ACT-MAKE1-falsehood   1SG.INACT-POSSM-daughter.of.man=in
'I make my daughter tell lies'

amokane'õ maymávape (from *che-kane'õ* 'I am tired')
a-mo-kane'õ   maymáva=pe
1SG.ACT-MAKE1-tired   every=in
'I make everybody tired'

Pembojere peneánga tesapegotyo (from *a-jere* 'I turn (intransitive)')
pe-mbo-jere   pene-ánga   t-esape=gotyo
2PL.ACT-MAKE1-turn(intransitive)   2PL.INACT-soul   NPOSSM-light=towards
'Turn your soul to the light.' (Literally, 'Make your soul turn to the light'.)

A GRAMMAR OF PARAGUAYAN GUARANI

Ñamboguata ñandejagua. (from *a-guata* 'I walk')
ña-mbo-guata ñande-jagua
1PL.INCL.ACT-MAKE1-walk 1PL.INCL.INACT-dog
'We make our dog walk.'

Remomba'aposevépa ichupekuéra. (from *a-mba'apo* 'I work')
re-mo-mba'apo-se-ve=pa ichupe=kuéra
2SG.ACT-MAKE1-work-want-more=Q to.him/her=PL
'Do you want to make them work more?'

This causative is extremely frequent, since it can be used with virtually any predicate. As we can see from the examples, both active and inactive roots can be made into a causative this way. The causative versions of inactive roots often have the general meaning of 'causing someone to be in a particular state'.

ombotavy maymávape (from *che-tavy* 'I am stupid')
o-mbo-tavy maymáva=pe
3.ACT-MAKE1-stupid every=in
's/he/they fool(s) everybody' (literally, 's/he/they make(s) everybody a fool')

Since *mbo-* prefixed verbs are transitive, they take inactive prefixes if the causee is higher in the person hierarchy than the causer:

Chembovy'a ahecha ko orden del díape.
che-mbo-vy'a a-h-echa ko orden del día=pe
1SG.INACT-MAKE1-joy 1SG.ACT-POSSM3-see PROX.SG order of.the day=in
'It made me happy to see this order of the day.'

Kane'õ ñandembojavy.
kane'õ ñande-mbo-javy
tiredness 1PL.INCL.INACT-MAKE1-err
'Tiredness makes us make mistakes.'

As stated in **4.11**, the prefix variants *m(b)u-* and *m(b)y-* tend to occur with relational roots and roots that begin in *a*. However, with some relational roots *mbo-/mo-* and the *h-* variant are used.

mbohéra (from *t-éra* '(a) name')
mbo-h-éra
MAKE1-POSSM3-name
'to name (someone something)'

*moh*enda (from *t-enda* '(a) place')
mo-h-enda
MAKE1-POSSM3-place
'to place (something somewhere)'

A small complication in the use of this causative is that several oral roots beginning with a voiceless stop /p/, /t/ or /k/ form it in an irregular way. Even though the roots are oral, they take the nasal variant of the causative prefix (*mo-*) and at the same time change their own initial stop consonant into the corresponding nasal-oral consonant with an identical place of articulation. It is not possible to predict which roots show this behaviour: they must be learned by heart. (See a fuller list of these roots in **17.4.2**.)

*k*aru 'to eat (intransitive)' > *mong*aru 'to make (someone) eat' (not **mbokaru*)
*k*akuaa 'to grow (intransitive)' > *mong*akuaa 'to raise' (not **mbokakuaa*)
*k*yra 'fat, grease' > *mong*yra 'to fatten' (not **mbokyra*)
*p*e 'flat' > *momb*e 'to lay flat' (not **mbope*)
*p*áy 'to wake up (intransitive)' > *momb*áy 'to wake someone up' (not **mbopáy*)
*t*yky '(a) drop' > *mond*yky 'to make drip; to distil' (not **mbotyky*)

6.6.2 Sociative causative

When the causer not only instigates an action but also performs the action together with the causee, the sociative causative prefix *ro-* or *guero-* is used (glossed MAKE.SOC). (For the conditions governing the use of the variants *ro-* or *guero-* see **4.7**.) Contrast the following examples:

*ña**mbo**guata ñandejagua*
ña-mbo-guata   ñande-jagua
1PL.INCL.ACT-MAKE1-walk   1PL.INCL.INACT-dog
'we make our dog walk' (but we ourselves do not walk)

*ja**guero**guata ñandejagua*
ja-guero-guata   ñande-jagua
1PL.INCL.ACT-MAKE.SOC-walk   1PL.INCL.INACT-dog
'we walk our dog' (and we ourselves walk together with it)

However, unlike the intransitive causative, this voice is not really productive: it cannot be used with all intransitive verbs or nominal roots, and often it does not have a sociative causative meaning, but rather a different conventionalized meaning. Many of these verbs that have lexicalized meanings are psychological verbs of emotion or feelings (**psych-verbs**). In the example below, the speaker is afraid but she is not making her child afraid, neither is her child necessarily independently afraid.

*Che ro**guero**kyhyje chememby.* (From *akyhyje* 'I am afraid')
che   ro-guero-kyhyje   che-memby
I   1>2SG-MAKE.SOC-fear   1SG.INACT-child.of.woman
'I am afraid for you, my child.'[23]

Likewise, in the first example below, the person whose feelings are reported is ashamed of their mother but they are not making their mother ashamed, neither is their mother necessarily independently ashamed. This is even clearer in the second example below, since a language cannot be made to feel shame: only the people speaking it can feel shame.

*Ha'e o**(gue)ro**tĩ isýpe.* (From *atĩ* 'I am ashamed'.)
ha'e   o-(gue)ro-tĩ   i-sy=pe
s/he   3.ACT-MAKE.SOC-feel.shame 3.INACT-mother=in
'S/he is ashamed of his/her mother.'

*tapicha iñe'ẽ guaraníva o**guero**tĩ iñe'ẽ*
t-apicha   i-ñe'ẽ   guarani-va   o-guero-tĩ
NPOSSM-fellow.man   3.INACT-language   Guarani-ADJZ 3.ACT-MAKE.SOC-feel.shame
i-ñe'ẽ
3.INACT-language
'the people whose language is Guarani are ashamed of their language'

Finally, in the example below, no participant is necessarily screaming, even though that is the meaning of the root *sapukái* 'to scream'. *Guerosapukái* in this sentence does not have a meaning composed of the sociative causative meaning + 'scream'. Rather, it has the conventionalized, non-compositional meaning 'to repudiate'.

*O**guero**sapukái aty ñomongeta ojapóva Abdo-Ortiz.*
o-guerosapukái   aty   ño-mongeta   o-japo-va   Abdo-Ortiz
3.ACT-repudiate   group   RECP-converse   3.ACT-make-ADJZ   Abdo-Ortiz
'They repudiate the meeting between Abdo and Ortiz.'

---

[23] Example from Ortiz *et al.* (1995, 72).

Guerokyhyje can also have the meaning 'to warn'.

*Salud o**guerokyhyje** impacto ojapóva karu vai.*
salud	o-guero-kyhyje	impacto	o-japo-va	karu	vai
health	3.ACT-MAKE.SOC-fear	impact	3.ACT-make-ADJZ	eat(intransitive)	bad

'(The Ministry of) Health warns of the impact that bad eating has.'

Guerohory means 'to congratulate' or 'to celebrate'.

Ro**guerohory** *guarani jeporu umi ndoikekatuirihápe.*
ro-guero-h-ory   guarani   je-poru   umi
1PL.EXCL.ACT-MAKE.SOC-POSSM3-joy   Guarani   AGD-use   NPROX.PL
nd-o-ike-katu-iri-há=pe
NEG-3.ACT-enter-be.able-NEG-NMLZ.LOC=in

'We celebrate the use of Guarani in places where it is not (commonly) used.'

Note that relational roots appear with the *h-* prefix in the sociative causative voice.

t-ory 'happiness' > *(gue)rohory* 'to congratulate'

6.6.3 Causative voice for transitive verbs

The third and last causative is the stressed causative suffix *–uka* (glossed MAKE2), used with transitive verbs. Of all the voice markers, this is the only one that is a suffix, not a prefix. When added to a transitive verb it yields a ditransitive verb with three arguments: in addition to the **causer** (the initiator of the causation event) and the **causee** (the participant who is instigated or made to act), since the base event already contains an affected participant, the derived verb expresses an **affectee** (the participant affected by the causee's action). The causer is marked as an active subject, the affectee as a direct object and the causee as an indirect object (when it appears in the sentence; it is often omitted). Note that the active prefix marks the initiator of the causation event; it is, as it were, the agent of *-uka*, not the agent of the actual verb or predicate.

Source transitive verb

Active person prefix   Direct object marking
         ↑   ↑
         A   P
         ————————————→

Derived ditransitive verb

Active person prefix   Direct object marking   (Indirect object marking)
         ↑   ↑   ↑
         C   A   P
         ————————————→————————————→

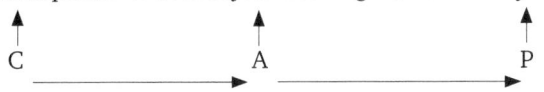

pehechauka (from *-echa* 'to see')
pe-h-echa-uka
2PL.ACT-POSSM3-see-MAKE2
'you show' (literally, 'you <u>make</u> someone see something')

Ajapouka cheaorã
a-japo-uka   che-ao-rã
1SG.ACT-make-MAKE2   1SG.INACT-clothes-DEST
'I am having clothes <u>made</u> for me' (by someone not mentioned)

Acosta ha'e pe ojukaukava'ekue periodista-pe
Acosta   ha'e pe   o-juka-uka-va'ekue   periodista-pe
Acosta   be   MED.SG   3.ACT-kill-MAKE2-PAST   journalist=in
'It was Acosta who <u>had</u> the journalist killed' (by someone not mentioned)

Reiporukána chéve viru
rei-poru-ka-na   chéve   viru
2SG.ACT-use-MAKE2-REQ   to.me   money
'Please lend me money' (literally, 'Please <u>let/make</u> me use money')

Forms like *reiporuka* 'you lend' (from *poru* 'to use') above show that this causative can also be lexicalized with a specific conventionalized meaning, not derivable from the meaning of the parts (that is, a non-compositional meaning).

     This suffix has the variants *-ka* (when the verb it attaches to ends in *u* as *poru* above) and *-yka* (when the verb ends in a different vowel).

oipysoyka ipepo
oi-pyso-yka   i-pepo
3.ACT-extend-MAKE2   3.INACT-wing
's/he <u>makes</u> it extend its wings'

The intransitive prefix and the stressed transitive suffix can be stacked, turning a base intransitive verb into a ditransitive verb. Thus, from *karu* 'to eat (intransitive)':

*ndesy o**mo**ngar**uka** chemitãme*
nde-sy　　　　　o-mo-ngaru-ka　　　　　　　　　　che-mitã=me
2SG.INACT-mother　3.ACT-MAKE1-eat(intransitive)-MAKE2　1SG.INACT-child=in
'your mother <u>has</u> my child <u>fed</u>' (literally, 'your mother <u>has</u> my child <u>made</u> to eat')

Lastly, the reader must bear in mind that this voice is often not the preferred means to express this kind of causation. For instance, if it is understood that the causer gave a verbal direction or command to the causee, then the verb *he'i* 's/he said' is often used. By way of example, compare the use of this *uka* causative in the translation of the Gospel of Luke in the Tupi-Guarani language Kaiwá (very closely related to Paraguayan Guarani) with the Paraguayan Guarani version that uses *he'i*.

Kaiwá

*Augusto ohai **uka** kwatia.*
Augusto　o-h-ai　　　　　　uka　　kwatia
Augusto　3.ACT-POSSM3-write　MAKE2　text
'Augusto <u>had</u> a text written' (referring to a census)

Paraguayan Guarani

*Augusto **he'i** oñemoĩ haguã kuatiáre opavave réra.*
Augusto　he'i　o-ñe-moĩ　　　haguã　kuatia=re　opavave　r-éra
Augusto　says　3.ACT-AGD-put　for　　text=at　　all　　　POSSM-name
'Augusto <u>said</u> to prepare a writing with everyone's name'

7
Evidentiality

In Guarani it is important for speakers to indicate the origin and strength of the evidence they possess to back the content of their statements. This is done by means of **evidential** markers. Given that English does not have a category of evidentials, these markers and their contributions to the meaning of the sentence in which they appear are difficult to translate. In fact, in most cases English speakers would simply not use anything equivalent. Guarani sentences without evidential markers are usually grammatical, but they may sound odd or incomplete to a native speaker. Even though I present evidential markers in a common section here, they actually do not belong to a unified paradigm, and sometimes can even co-occur rather freely, as the examples below show.

7.1 Emphatic and veridical markers

When speakers wish to convey an emphatic assertion they can use the stressed verbal particle *voi* (often found as a second-position enclitic; that is, coming at the end of the first phrase in a sentence).

*Iporã **voi**.*
i-porã   voi
3.INACT-beautiful EMPH
'It is (certainly) beautiful.'

*Oguereko **voi** peteĩ topadora'i neporãva.*
o-guereko   voi   peteĩ topadora-'i   ne-porã-va
3.ACT-have EMPH one   bulldozer-DIM SUP-good-SUP
'He (certainly) had a very good little bulldozer.'

Peje chupe tou, tahechaukámandivoi peẽme.
peje chupe t-o-u
2PL.ACT.say to.him/her OPT-3.ACT-come
t-a-h-echa-uka=mandi=voi peẽme
OPT-1SG.ACT-POSSM3-see-MAKE2-once.and.for.all=EMPH to.you.PL
'Tell him to come, so I can show you once and for all.'

Japytũmbapotaitémavoi.
ja-pytũ-mba-pota-ité-ma=voi
already-dark-all-about.to-very-already=EMPH
'It is (certainly) already about to become completely dark.'

Another common emphatic marker is the second-position clitic =*niko* (often pronounced *nio*), which conveys both emphasis and speaker knowledge of the truth of the assertion (glossed VERD for **veridical emphatic**). Given its basic emphatic and veridical value, this marker can furthermore be used to signal a contrast to some belief held by the hearer, or an intent to convince the hearer of the truth of the assertion. This marker has three other variants that the speaker is free to choose (they are in free variation): =*ko*, =*ngo* and =*ningo*. Being a second-position clitic, it attaches to the first word or whole phrase in the sentence.

*Ani repoko cherehe ha'e **niko** ndéve.*
ani re-poko che=rehe ha'e niko ndéve
NEG.IMP 2SG.ACT-touch 1SG.INACT=at I.say VERD to.you.SG
'I did tell you not to touch me.'

¡Ndénteko la rembotuichaitereíva!
nde-nte=ko la re-mbo-tuicha-ite-rei-va
you.SG-only=VERD DET.SG 2SG.ACT-MAKE1-big-very-in.vain-ADJZ
'You are just exaggerating!' (Literally, 'Just things that you alone make really big for no reason!')

Auto tujango kóa!
auto tuja=ngo ko-va
car old=VERD PROX.SG-ADJZ
'But this is an old car!'

*Jehova **ningo** oheja ñandete jadesidi.*
Jehova=ningo o-heja ñandete ja-desidi
Jehovah=VERD 3.ACT-leave we.ourselves 1PL.INCL.ACT-decide
'Jehovah indeed lets us decide ourselves.'

*Ha upéicharõ **ningo** jaiko ovakávo!*
ha	upe-icha=rõ=ningo	ja-iko	ovakávo
and	MED.SG-as=if=VERD	1PL.INCL.ACT-be	upside.down

'But then, we live upside down!'

Although this function is not well studied, the aspect marker *hína* (see **4.10.2**) seems to have an emphatic function similar to those of *voi* or *niko*:

*Ndaikatumo'ãi aha ka'api porque aháta **hína** apractica partidorã.*
nda-ikatu-mo'ã-i	a-ha	ka'api	porque	a-ha-ta	hína
NEG-be.able-NEG.FUT-NEG	1SG.ACT-go	mow	because	1SG.ACT-go-FUT	PROG

a-practica	partido-rã
1SG.ACT-practise	match-DEST

'I will not be able to go mow because I will go practise for the game.'

7.2 Markers of hearsay

Hearsay is a very important cross-linguistic category of evidentials, marking that the speaker's evidence for the assertion is from a third-party report, not first-hand evidence. These evidentials often correspond to English expressions such as 'they say', 'it is said', and so on. Guarani has several hearsay markers: *ndaje, ñandeko, jeko* and *-je*. *Ndaje* and *jeko*, and to some extent *ñandeko*, are generally second-position clitics, but they can all appear occasionally in other positions in the clause. The remaining one, *-je*, is an unstressed verb suffix.

*Jaipuru jevýta **ndaje** umi céntimo ha níkel 1 guarani.*
jai-puru-jevy-ta=ndaje	umi	céntimo	ha	níkel	1	guarani
1PL.INCL.ACT-use-again-FUT=it.is.said	NPROX.PL	cent	and	nickel	1	guarani

'We will use again the cents and the nickel worth 1 guarani.' (Literally, 'It is said that we will use again . . .')

*Oĩmbaréma oĩva'erã yvy apére **ñandeko** oiko kóa ko mba'e.*
oĩ-mba=rire-ma	oĩ-va'erã	yvy	ape=re	ñandeko	o-iko
there.is-all=after-already	there.is-must	earth	surface=at	it.is.said	3.ACT-be

ko-va	ko	mba'e
PROX.SG-ADJZ	PROX.SG	thing

'They say that after everything that had to be was already on the face of the Earth this thing happened.'

*Peteĩ jey **jeko** Perurima ojavykymi peteĩ Ermána de Karida . . .*

peteĩ	jey	jeko	Perurima	o-javyky-mi	peteĩ	ermána	de	karida
one	time	it.is.said	Perurima	3.ACT-grope-used.to	one	sister	of	charity

'One time, Perurimá had an affair with a Sister of Charity . . .' (literally, 'They say that one time . . .')

*Ohó**jeko** Perurima ohechamívo peteĩ iñamígope.*

o-ho-jeko	Perurima	o-h-echa-mi-vo	peteĩ	iñ-amígo=pe
3.ACT-go-it.is.said	Perurima	3.ACT-POSSM3-see-used.to-while	one	3.INACT-friend=in

'They say that Perurima used to go visit a friend.'

*Ohenoiuká**je** Perurima peteĩ pyharépe Añáme osena haguã hendive . . .*

o-h-enói-uka-je	Perurima	peteĩ	pyhare=pe	Aña=me
3.ACT-POSSM3-call-MAKE2-it.is.said	Perurima	one	night=in	devil=in

o-sena	haguã	hendive
3.ACT-dinner	for	with.him/her

'One night, Perurimá had the devil called to have dinner with him . . .' (literally, 'They say that one night . . .')

As we can see from the examples above, these markers are very common in narrations, legends, and so on, especially at the beginning when providing the setting for the story.

7.3 Markers of direct evidence

I use the term **direct evidence** for those cases where the speaker's basis for an assertion is having directly witnessed the relevant event, first-hand. The clearest marker of this kind is the unstressed particle *kuri*. Like *ndaje* and the other hearsay markers identified in **7.2**, *kuri* has a rather free distribution in the clause, although it often appears after the predicate. It is frequently used and interpreted as a recent past tense marker, but only when the speaker has direct evidence of the event asserted.

*Upe ka'aru nomýiri, te'onguetýicha **kuri**.*

upe	ka'aru	n-o-mýi-ri	t-e'ongue-ty-icha	kuri
MED.SG	afternoon	NEG-3.ACT-move-NEG	NPOSSM-corpse-collective-as	DIR.PAST

'The afternoon was still like a cemetery.'

*. . . Vera he'i voi **kuri** oikótaha.*
Vera he'i voi kuri o-iko-ta-ha
Vera says EMPH DIR.PAST 3.ACT-be-FUT-NMLZ
'. . . Vera <u>did</u> say there will be (gas).' (Journalist report in the context of gas shortages)

*Che ha'éma **kuri** mokoĩ orehermano ouhague do año ante.*
che ha'é-ma   kuri   mokoĩ ore-hermano   o-u-hague
I   I.say-already   DIR.PAST two   1PL.EXCL.INACT-brother   3.ACT-come-NMLZ.PAST
do   año   ante
two year   before
'I already sai<u>d</u> that two of our brothers came two years before.'

In **7.4** we will see that *kuri* occurs in contrast to another evidential, *ra'e*, in question-answer pairs.

7.4 Markers of reasoned evidence

I use the term **reasoned evidence** for those cases where the speaker's basis for an assertion is the result of an internal reasoning process. These markers have freer placement in the clause than the hearsay markers.

Ra'e indicates a recent realization through inference, often with an indication of surprise or counterexpectation (this is called **mirative**).

*EBY oipytyvõ radio maúpe **ra'e**.*
EBY oi-pytyvõ   radio mau=pe   ra'e
EBY 3.ACT-help   radio fake=in   RECENT.INF
'(<u>It turned out that</u>) The EBY helped illegal radio stations.' (EBY stands for *Entidad Binacional Yacyretá* 'Binational entity for the management of the dam Yacyretá'.)

*Ndevaléngo **ra'e**.*
nde-vale=ngo   ra'e
2SG.INACT-be.worth=VERD   RECENT.INF
'<u>It turned out that</u> you were good (i.e., you were worth it), <u>in the end</u>.'

*Ikatu te'onguety voi **ra'e**.*
ikatu   t-e'ongue-ty   voi   ra'e
be.able   NPOSSM-corpse-collective   EMPH   RECENT.INF
'It was, <u>perhaps</u>, a cemetery.'

EVIDENTIALITY   227

*Ohechakuaa ramo hikuái ho'aha mitãkuña'i aña poguýpe **ra'e**.*

o-h-echa+kuaa		ramo	hikuái	ho-'a-ha	mitã+kuña-'i
3.ACT-POSSM3-see+know		when	they	3.ACT-fall-NMLZ	child+woman-DIM

aña	po=guy=pe	ra'e
devil	hand=under=in	RECENT.INF

'Only then did they realize that they had fallen into the hands of a bad girl.'

¿Cherupiko ndohejaira'e hetã pytaguáre?

che-r-u=piko	nd-o-h-eja-i=ra'e
1SG.INACT-POSSM-father=Q	NEG-3.ACT-POSSM3-leave-NEG=RECENT.INF

h-etã	pytagua=re
POSSM3-country	abroad=at

'Didn't my father leave his country to go abroad?'

*Froilán jerure **ndaje** oguahẽ tárdema **ra'e**.*

Froilán	jerure	ndaje	o-guahẽ	tárde-ma	ra'e
Froilán	petition	it.is.said	3.ACT-arrive	late-already	RECENT.INF

'<u>They say</u> that Froilán's petition was already late.'

Ra'e often co-occurs with the marker of uncertainty or wonderment *mbo* in the complex marker *mbora'e*, which reinforces its surprise value. It can also be combined with the form *nipo* of the uncertainty marker in *nipo ra'e*, to reinforce an implied counterexpectation.

*Hãã, ava kuimba'e **mbora'e**!*

hãã	ava+kuimba'e	mbo=ra'e
ah	person+man	UNCERTAIN=RECENT.INF

'Ah, a man!'

*omano **nipo ra'e***

o-mano	nipo	ra'e
3.ACT-die	UNCERTAIN	RECENT.INF

'<u>It turned out that (contrary to what I thought/even though I doubted it</u>) s/he died.'

*Peẽ **nipo ra'e** penderesarái Ñande Ru Tenondégui.*

peẽ	nipo	ra'e	pende-r-esarái
you.PL	UNCERTAIN	RECENT.INF	2PL.INACT-POSSM-oblivion

ñande-r-u	t-enonde=gui
1PL.INCL.INACT-POSSM-father	NPOSSM-front=from

'It so happens that you have forgotten Our Father the First.'

Raka'e, on the other hand, signals a longer chain of reasoning, often with a distant past value.

*Ko ógape ndaje oiko **raka'e** che taitachu*.
ko óga=pe ndaje o-iko raka'e che-taitachu
PROX.SG house=in it.is.said 3.ACT-be LONG.INF 1SG.INACT-great.grandfather
'They say that my great-grandfather lived in this house.'

*Ñorairõguasúpe omano **raka'e** heta kuimba'e ñaneretãme*.
ño-rairõ+guasu=pe o-mano raka'e h-eta
RECP-attack+big=in 3.ACT-die LONG.INF POSSM3-numerous
kuimba'e ñane-r-etã=me
man 1PL.INCL.INACT-POSSM-country=in
'In the Great War there died many men in our country.'

(Context: a man finds his son-in-law killed in the forest, having disobeyed his advice not to go back there)
*Mba'érepiko nerehendúi**raka'e** cheñe'ẽ*.
mba'ére=piko ne-re-h-endu-i=raka'e che-ñe'ẽ
why=Q NEG-2SG.ACT-POSSM3-listen-NEG=LONG.INF 1SG.INACT-word
'Why did you not listen to my words?' (The man realizes at that moment that the son-in-law must not have listened to his warnings.)

These two markers of reasoned evidence can be used in interrogative sentences as well as in declarative sentences. In question-answer pairs, *ra'e* often signals the questioner's lack of evidence, while *kuri* signals direct evidence for the respondent's answer.

*-Mba'epa ere **ra'e**. -Che ha'e **kuri** "nahániri"*.
mba'e=pa ere ra'e che ha'e kuri nahániri
what=Q 2SG.ACT.say RECENT.INF I I.say DIR.PAST no
'-What did you say? -I said "no".'

As several of the examples in this section show, the emphatic, hearsay and reasoning markers can be combined:

*Ñorairõ Guasu rapekue**voi niko raka'e***.
ño-rairõ guasu r-ape-kue=voi niko raka'e
RECP-attack big POSSM-road-POST=EMPH VERD LONG.INF
'Because it had been once the Great War's road.'

8
Basic clauses

8.1 Word order in simple clauses

A **clause** is a group of words including a predicate (either a verb, or a noun/adjective/adverb with an inactive person prefix) with its arguments and adverbial modifiers. A clause can be understood as a simple sentence, with no sentences subordinated to it or coordinated with it. The most basic clause in Guarani is composed of a single predicate, with no noun phrases to accompany it. This is because both **subject drop** and **object drop** (that is, not expressing the subject and/or object by means of an independent, overt noun phrase) are allowed and very common.

Ahechá ma. (Object drop; subject expressed only by a prefix, object not expressed.)
a-h-echa-ma
1SG.ACT-POSSM3-see-already
'I saw (him/her/it) already.'

Cherecháma. (Subject drop; object expressed only by a prefix, subject not expressed.)
che-r-echa-ma
1SG.INACT-POSSM-see-already
'They/You saw me already.' / 'I have already been seen.'

It is more common to leave out subject noun phrases than it is to leave out object noun phrases. When an object referring to a human participant is present as a noun phrase, it most frequently appears after the verb (VO order).

*Ahecháma **ichupe**.*
a-h-echa-ma   ichupe
1SG.ACT-POSSM3-see-already   to.him/her
'I already saw him/her.'

The position of subject noun phrases, when they appear in the sentence, is variable. They can appear before or after the verb so both SV and VS orders are commonly attested.

***Chavuku** ou jey yvýpe.* (SV)
Chavuku   o-u   jevy   yvy=pe
Chavuku   3.ACT-come again   earth=in
'Chavuku returned to Earth.'

*Opuka ha oñembohorýnte **ha'e**.* (VS)
o-puka   ha   o-ñe-mbo-h-ory-nte   ha'e
3.ACT-laugh and   3.ACT-AGD-MAKE1-POSSM3-joy-only s/he
'S/he laughed and just enjoyed himself/herself.'

In the sections that follow I present some basic clause types.

8.2 Predicative and equative clauses

Equative clauses establish that two noun phrases refer to the same person, object, place or event. **Predicative clauses** assign some property to a referent. In English, both of these usually require a form of the verb 'to be'. In Guarani juxtaposition alone suffices to establish these relationships.

Oreretã mburuvicha Mario Abdo Benítez (equative clause)
ore-r-etã   mburuvicha   Mario Abdo Benítez
1PL.EXCL.INACT-POSSM-country   leader   Mario Abdo Benítez
'The president of our country is Mario Abdo Benítez'

Ndesy orembo'ehára (equative clause)
nde-sy   ore-mbo'e-hára
2SG.INACT-mother   1PL.EXCL.INACT-teach-NMLZ.AG
'Your mother is our teacher'

Ndesy mbo'ehára (predicative clause)
nde-sy mbo'e-hára
2SG.INACT-mother teach-NMLZ.AG
'Your mother is a teacher'

Che chekane'õ (predicative clause)
che che-kane'õ
I 1SG.INACT-tiredness
'I am tired'

Pe karia'y hekomirĩ.
pe karia'y h-eko+mirĩ
MED.SG young.man POSSM3-essence+small
'This young man is modest.'

Since these sentences have no verb, they have the same structure as possessive phrases (see **3.6**). Although written examples out of context may seem unclear, in speech, prosody can be used to disambiguate the intended meaning. For example, if the structure is equative or predicative (not possessive), the speaker can introduce a prosodic boundary (a slight pause or an intonation change) between subject and predicate, thus signalling that they are two independent intonational phrases. Equative and predicative sentences can have emphatic or evidential markers, which also clarifies their predicational structure, because these markers often set the subject apart from the predicate.

*Ndesý**ngo** mbo'ehára.*
nde-sy=ngo mbo'e-hára
2SG.INACT-mother=VERD teach-NMLZ.AG
'But your mother is a teacher!'

*Ndetía **ndaje** iporã.*
nde-tía ndaje i-porã
2SG.INACT-aunt it.is.said 3.INACT-beautiful
'Your aunt is pretty (they say).'

8.3 Location and existence clauses

Guarani uses a specific copular verb to express the location of a person or thing: *-ime* 'to be located'. *Oĩ* can also be used with this location meaning in the third person.

Aime ko'ápe.
a-ime ko'ápe
1SG.ACT-be.located here
'I am here.'

Moõpa reime.
moõ=pa re-ime
where=Q 2SG.ACT-be.located
'Where are you?'

¿Moõ ñaime ñande?
moõ ña-ime ñande
where 1PL.INCL.ACT-be.located we&you
'Where are we?'

Oĩpa nderajy.
oĩ=pa nde-r-ajy
there.is=Q 2SG.INACT-POSSM-daughter.of.man
'Is your daughter here?' (Said to a man.)

The third-person forms *oime* or *oĩ* can both be used in impersonal sentences with the meanings 'there is' or 'there are':

Oĩ pa pakova.
oĩ=pa pakova
there.is=Q banana
'Are there bananas?'

Hetave mba'asy oĩ añete.
h-eta-ve mba'+asy oĩ añete
POSSM3-numerous-more thing+pain there.is true
'There are in truth many more illnesses.'

Ojejukáguive ako karai Arce, ahendúvo mbokapu aimo'ãjevýma oime ojejukáva.
o-je-juka=guive ako karai Arce
3.ACT-AGD-kill=since DIST.EV gentleman Arce
a-h-endu-vo mbo-kapu a-imo'ã-jevy-ma
1SG.ACT-POSSM3-hear-while MAKE1-burst 1SG.ACT-think-again-already
o-ime o-je-juka-va
3.ACT-be.located 3.ACT-AGD-kill-ADJZ
'Since that Mr Arce was killed, whenever I hear shots, I already think again there is someone being killed.'

The root *-iko* is used for the general meaning of 'existing, being alive' or for 'to be (in a certain physical or psychological state)', or very often, for 'to live (in a place)'.

*Edelio **oiko**ve gueteri.*
Edelio o-iko-ve gueteri
Edelio 3.ACT-be-more still
'Edelio is still alive.'

*-Mba'éichapa **reiko**. -**Aiko** porã.*
mba'éicha=pa re-iko a-iko porã
how=Q 2SG.ACT-be 1SG.ACT-be good
'-How are you? -I am well.'

***Peiko** kokuépe.*
pe-iko kokue=pe
2PL.ACT-be countryside=in
'You live in the countryside.'

*Che nd**aikó**i gueteri Paraguáipe.*
che nd-a-iko-i gueteri Paraguái=pe
I NEG-1SG.ACT-be-NEG still Paraguay=in
'I don't live in Paraguay yet.'

Finally, the word *ha'e* can also be used as a copula. Note that it does not vary by person (which is the same as *ikatu* or *tekoteve̋*, for example). Pay attention to not confuse this use of *ha'e* with other uses where it means 's/he says', 's/he' or 'and' (this latter is uncommon in the modern language: *ha* is almost exclusively used today to mean 'and').

*Che **ha'e** nderecháva.*
che ha'e nde-r-echa-va
I be 2SG.INACT-POSSM-see-ADJZ
'I am the one who saw you.'

*Ñande **ha'e** pe jajapóva ñamoambue haguã pe ñande **ha'e**va.*
ñande ha'e pe ja-japo-va
we&you be MED.SG 1PL.INCL.ACT-make-ADJZ
ña-mo-ambue=haguã pe ñande ha'e-va
1PL.INCL.ACT-MAKE1-other=for MED.SG we&you be-ADJZ
'We are what we do to change what we are.'

Ndaha'ei ne rãi ahecháva, yvága voi ahecha nde rehe ama'ẽrõ.
nda-ha'e-i   ne-r-ãi   a-h-echa-va   yvága
NEG-be-NEG   2SG.INACT-POSSM-tooth   1SG.ACT-POSSM3-see-ADJZ   sky
voi   a-h-echa   nde=rehe   a-ma'ẽ=rõ
EMPH   1SG.ACT-POSSM3-see   2SG.INACT=at   1SG.ACT-look.at=when
'What I see <u>isn't</u> your teeth, it is the sky that I see when I look at you.'

8.4 Sentences expressing possession

8.4.1 Non-verbal possessive sentences

Guarani does not need a possessive verb (like English 'to have') or any other verb to express possession in many cases. Verbless sentences are most common when talking about possession of a body part, kinship terms or others where possession is viewed as obligatory or non-contingent (these cases are called **inalienable possession**). In those cases, the possessor is expressed by an inactive person prefix attached to the possessum. The whole complex functions as a predicate which accepts the attachment of further affixes or clitics to modify it.

Ipepo. (Inalienable possession of body part.)
i-pepo
3.INACT-wing
'It <u>has</u> wings.'

*Panambi **ipepo***. (Inalienable possession of body part.)
panambi   i-pepo
butterfly 3.INACT-wing
'Butterflies <u>have</u> wings. / The butterfly <u>has</u> wings.'

*Che **chemembyse***. (Inalienable possession: kinship.)
che   che-memby-se
I   1SG.INACT-child.of.woman-want
'I want to <u>have</u> a child.' (Said by a woman; *memby* is the term used for 'child of a woman'.)[24]

Nañandevirumo'ãi. (Alienable possession.)
na-ñande-viru-mo'ã-i
NEG-1PL.INCL.INACT-money-NEG.FUT-NEG
'We will not <u>have</u> any money.'

---

[24] Example from Velázquez-Castillo (1996, 66).

Although no verb is present, these sentences are usually not ambiguous between a predicative and a possessive reading: *Che **chememby*** can only mean 'I <u>have</u> a child' because 'I am my child' does not (usually) make sense; likewise *nde **chememby*** usually means 'you <u>are</u> my child' because 'you have my child' would normally be an instance of alienable possession and it would require a possessive verb (see **8.4.2**).

In verbless sentences, numerals are used outside the predicate, before or after:

*-Mbovýpa ndejyva. -Chejyva **mokõi**.*
mbovy=pa   nde-jyva   che-jyva   mokõi
how.many=Q 2SG.INACT-arm 1SG.INACT-arm two
'-How many arms do you have? -I have <u>two</u> arms.'

*Che ningo viúda, areko 28 áño ha **mokõi** chememby.*
che ningo viúda a-reko   28 áño ha   mokõi
I   VERD   widow 1SG.ACT-have 28 year and two
che-memby
1SG.INACT-child.of.woman
'I am a widow, I am 28 years old and I have <u>two</u> children.'

*Che chememby **peteĩ** mitãkuimba'e, ha dos día rire ha'e avei imemby **peteĩ** mitãkuimba'e.*
che che-memby   peteĩ mitã+kuimba'e ha   dos día rire
I   1SG.INACT-child.of.woman one child+man   and two day after
ha'e avei i-memby   peteĩ mitã+kuimba'e
s/he also 3.INACT-child.of.woman one child+man
'I had <u>a</u> son, and two days later she had <u>a</u> son too.'

8.4.2 Verbal possessive sentences

Generally mostly used for transient or contingent possession (**alienable possession**), in these constructions the possessor is animate, it is the clausal subject, and the possessum is the object of the verb *reko* ('to have'; verb with increments *-gue-* and *-re-*).

*Cheru **oguereko** mbohapy kavaju.*
che-r-u   o-guereko mbohapy kavaju
1SG.INACT-POSSM-father 3.ACT-have three   horse
'My father <u>has</u> three horses.'

Vy'apavẽ ñame'ẽva'ekue añónte jareko.
vy'a-pavẽ	ña-me'ẽ-va'ekue	año-nte	ja-reko
joy-supreme	1PL.INCL.ACT-give-PAST	alone-only	1PL.INCL.ACT-have

'We only <u>have</u> the happiness we have given (others).'

Cherereko porã
che-rereko	porã
1SG.INACT-have	good

'She took good care of me' (literally, '<u>had</u> me well')

Ndererekovéima pe mborayhu rerekova'ekue iñepyrũrã. (The original example has the non-standard spelling *vaekue*, reflecting the common pronunciation.)
nde-re-reko-ve-i-ma		pe	mbo-r-ayhu
NEG-2SG.ACT-have-more-NEG-already		MED.SG	MAKE1-POSSM-love
re-reko-va'ekue	i-ñepyrũ-rã		
2SG.ACT-have-PAST	3.INACT-begin-DEST		

'You do not <u>have</u> anymore that love that you <u>had</u> to begin.'

As mentioned in **3.4.3**, the age of someone is expressed with the verb *reko*. Contrast in the next example the use of *reko* and verbless possession.

Che ningo viúda, areko 28 áño ha mokõi chememby.
che	ningo	viúda	a-reko	28	áño	ha	mokõi
I	VERD	widow	1SG.ACT-have	28	year	and	two

che-memby
1SG.INACT-child.of.woman

'I am a widow, I <u>am</u> 28 years old and I have two children.'

8.5 Questions

A **yes/no question** is an interrogative sentence that expects a "yes" or "no" answer. (As mentioned above in **4.9**, *heẽ* is 'yes' and *(n)ahániri* is 'no'.) Unlike in English, in Guarani these interrogatives do not have special question intonation or different word order. Instead, we know that something is a question from the appearance of *=pa* and *=piko* (often pronounced *=pio*, sometimes *=iko*) in second position in the sentence. These clitics attach to the first phrase in the sentence, which is usually the element that is the focus of the question. The difference between *=pa* and *=piko* is not clear from the extant literature. Traditional grammars mention other interrogative particles such as *pipo* or *tiko*, but the only two in very general use in the modern language are =*pa* and =*piko*.

Although written usage varies, many sources recommend not writing question marks where interrogatives are identified by the use of a particle.

*Ndé**pa** Pablo.*
nde=pa   Pablo
you.SG=Q   Pablo
'Are you Pablo?'

*Chepy'a**piko** oporohayhu.*
che-py'a=piko   o-poro-h-ayhu
1SG.INACT-heart=Q   3.ACT-PEOPLE-POSSM3-love
'Does my heart love (others)?'

*Añeté**piko** apu'ãva'erã.*
añete=piko   a-puã-va'erã
true=Q   1SG.ACT-get.up-must
'Do I really have to get up?'

Questions in subordinate clauses (sometimes called **indirect questions**) are formed exactly the same way as main clause questions. There is no difference in interrogative clitics, verb forms or word order.

*Eporandu chupe oĩ**pa** itúva.*
e-porandu   chupe   oĩ=pa   i-túva
IMP-question to.him/her there.is=Q   3.INACT-father
'Ask him/her if his/her father is there.'

*Ndaikuaái oimé**pa** ambue tembiapopyre ohechauka porãvéva.*
nd-ai-kuaa-i   o-ime=pa   ambue
NEG-1SG.ACT-know-NEG   3.ACT-be.located=Q   other
t-embi-apo-py-re   o-h-echa-uka
NPOSSM-NMLZ.REL-make-NMLZ.PASS-POST   3.ACT-POSSM3-see-MAKE2
porã-ve-va
good-more-ADJZ
'I don't know whether there is another work that shows (it) better.'

An **open question** is a question that cannot be answered by "yes" or "no". It contains an interrogative word or phrase that must be answered with a content phrase. One of the interrogative clitics usually appears with the interrogative word, but they are often left out.

Mba'épiko jajapóta.
mba'é=piko ja-japo-ta
what=Q 1PL.INCL.ACT-make-FUT
'What are we going to do?'

Moõpa rehose.
moõ=pa re-ho-se
where=Q 2SG.ACT-go-want
'Where do you want to go?'

Mávandipa repytáta.
máva=ndi=pa re-pyta-ta
who=with=Q 2SG.ACT-stay-FUT
'With whom are you going to stay?

Ndaikuaái araka'épa oğuahẽta.
nd-ai-kuaa-i araka'e=pa o-ğuahẽ-ta
NEG-1SG.ACT-know-NEG when=Q 3.ACT-arrive-FUT
'I don't know when s/he will arrive.'

If an interrogative particle is absent, at least closing question marks should be used. Actual usage varies here, since closing question marks are sometimes used even when an interrogative particle appears. Some writers also use opening question marks as in Spanish.

¿Moõ ñaime ñande?
moõ ña-ime ñande
where 1PL.INCL.ACT-be.located we&you
'Where are we?'

¿Cherupiko ndohejaira'e hetã pytaguáre?
che-r-u=piko nd-o-h-eja-i=ra'e
1SG.INACT-POSSM-father=Q NEG-3.ACT-POSSM3-leave-NEG=RECENT.INF
h-etã pytagua=re
POSSM3-country abroad=at
'Didn't my father leave his country to go abroad?'

The interrogative dubitative particle =(ni)mbo/=(ni)po conveys a general sense of wonderment, doubtfulness or internal uncertainty.

*Mba'éicha**mbo** ha'éta ndéve . . .*
mba'éicha=mbo ha'e-ta ndéve
how=UNCERTAIN I.say-FUT to.you.SG
'How do I say this to you . . . ?'

*Mba'é**mbo** ojehu chéve ko árape . . .*
mba'e=mbo o-jehu chéve ko ára=pe
what=UNCERTAIN 3.ACT-happen to.me PROX.SG day=in
'I wonder what is happening to me today . . . ?'

These interrogative particles can also have exclamative uses. *Piko* can appear by itself to show surprise.

*Atopaseté**pa** ko Remígiarehe aína*
a-topa-se-te=pa=ko Remígia=rehe a-ína
1SG.ACT-meet-want-very=Q=VERD Remígia=at 1SG.ACT-PROG
'I am so desiring meeting Remígia!'[25]

*Rejujeyvoí**piko**!*
re-ju-jevy=voi=piko
2SG.ACT-come-again=EMPH=Q
'You came back??!!'

*-Ajujeyvoi. -**Piko**.*
a-ju-jevy=voi piko
1SG.ACT-come-again=EMPH Q
'-I came back. -Really??!!'

Finally, I said above that yes/no questions do not have special question intonation in Guarani, but that they have the same intonation of declaratives. While this seems to be largely true (specific studies of question intonation do not exist), special prosody can sometimes be discerned impressionistically at the interrogative particle (lengthening of the vowel, rise in pitch), but this seems to be a more general feature of prosodic phrasing in both interrogatives and declaratives (see **2.2.4**).

---

[25] Example from Melià *et al*. (1997, 131).

9
Quantification

In **3.4.3**, I presented examples of quantifiers that are placed before a noun and function as its determiner. But more generally, quantification can be expressed in other positions in the sentence. For example, *mbyte(re)* 'centre; half (of); average' always comes after the noun:

*umi mymba ruguy **mbyte***
umi   mymba   r-uguy   mbyte
NPROX.PL   domesticated.animal   POSSM-blood   half
'half of those animals' blood'

*okykue **mbyte***
o-ky-kue   mbyte
3.ACT-rain-NMLZ.ABS   half
'average rainfall'

*Ko'ãva rapykuéri oho Hosaías ha Judagua myakãhárakuéra **mbyte**re.*
ko'ã-va   r-apykuéri   o-ho   Hosaías   ha   Juda=gua
PROX.PL-ADJZ   POSSM-behind   3.ACT-go   Hoshaiah   and   Judah=from
my-akã-hára=kuéra   mbytere
MAKE1-head-NMLZ.AG=PL   half
'And after them there went Hoshaiah and half of the leaders of Judah.'

A quantifier can head its own noun phrase without the presence of a noun to modify (that is, it can behave like a pronoun).

*Maitei **opavavé**pe.*
maitei   opavave=pe
greetings   all=in
'Greetings to all.'

Quantification can also be expressed outside of the noun phrase, in other positions in the sentence.

*iñakãrague **mbovy***
iñ-akã-r-ague   mbovy
3.INACT-head-POSSM-hair   few
's/he has few hairs' (literally, 'his/her hairs are few')

*ñanderapicha okaraguakuéra **heta** oĩ ovendepáma ijyvy*
ñande-r-apicha   okára=gua=kuéra   h-eta
1PL.INCL.INACT-POSSM-fellow.man   countryside=from=PL   POSSM3-numerous
oĩ   o-vende-pa-ma   ij-yvy
there.is   3.ACT-sell-all-already   3.INACT-earth
'many of our small farmers have already sold all their land'[26]

The meaning of 'all' (**universal quantification**) can be applied to the subject by adding the stressed suffix *-pa* (see **4.10.2**) or the stressed suffix *-joa* to the predicate, or by using the stressed particle *meme*. (The reader must take care not to confuse this stressed suffix *-pa* with the unstressed interrogative clitic *=pa*; see **3.5.2** and **8.5**.)

*oho**pa** hikuái*
o-ho-pa   hikuái
3.ACT-go-all   they
'they all went'

*okaru**joa** hikuái*
o-karu-joa   hikuái
3.ACT-eat(intransitive)-all   they
'they are all eating / they all ate'

*umi hénte okorre**joa** upérupi oikuaa'ỹre omanotaha*
umi   hénte   o-korre-joa   upe=rupi
NPROX.PL   people   3.ACT-run-all   MED.SG=around
oi-kuaa='ỹre   o-mano-ta-ha
3.ACT-know=without   3.ACT-die-FUT-NMLZ
'those people all running around not knowing that they would die'

---

[26] Example from Gynan (2017, 94).

*Susana membykuéra ikyra **meme***
Susana   memby=kuéra   i-kyra   meme
Susana   child.of.woman=PL   3.INACT-fat   continuously
'Susana's children are <u>all</u> fat'

*Áğa katu ndaha'éi péichagua **meme** umi jaikóva yvy ape ári.*
áğa   katu   nda-ha'é-i   pe-icha=gua   meme   umi
now   just   NEG-be-NEG   MED.SG-as=from continuously   NPROX.PL
ja-iko-va   yvy   ape   ári
1PL.INCL.ACT-be-ADJZ earth surface upon
'But not <u>all</u> of those who live upon this Earth are like that.'

*Ohendu**pa** rire mburuvicha guasúpe, oho **meme** hapére.*
o-h-endu-pa   rire   mburuvicha   guasu=pe   o-ho
3.ACT-POSSM3-listen-all after   leader   big=in   3.ACT-go
meme   h-ape=re
continuously   3.INACT-road=at
'After they <u>all</u> heard the king, they <u>all</u> went their way.'

The suffix *-pa* is not only for subjects, but can also apply the meaning 'all' to the verb's object, whether it is expressed with an object noun phrase or an inactive person prefix:

*ha'u**pá**ta ko tembi'u*
ha-'u-pa-ta   ko   t-embi-'u
1SG.ACT-ingest-all-FUT PROX.SG NPOSSM-NMLZ.REL-ingest
'I will eat <u>all</u> this food'

*Karai ma'ẽrã ojogua**pa** ko'ã yvy.*
karai   ma'ẽrã   o-jogua-pa   ko'ã   yvy
gentleman whatshisname 3.ACT-buy-all PROX.PL earth
'Some guy bought <u>all</u> these lands.'

*Ñandejuka**pa** pe ñati'ũ.*
ñande-juka-pa   pe   ñati'ũ
1PL.INCL.INACT-kill-all MED.SG mosquito
'That mosquito will kill us <u>all</u>.'

Note that the particle *meme* is more generally an adverb meaning 'continuously', 'frequently' or 'always'.

ogueru **meme**
o-gueru meme
3.ACT-bring frequently
's/he brings (it) <u>often</u>'

Sapy'arãicha **meme** *jeko oúvante ou.*
sapy'a-rã-icha meme jeko o-u-va-nte u-u
a.little.while-DEST-as continuously it.is.said 3.ACT-come-ADJZ-only 3.ACT-come
'They say that <u>all</u> who came, came as if for a little while.'

Mba'érepa jajepy'apy ha ñañangareko **meme** *va'erã ñandejehe?*
mba'ére=pa ja-je-py'a+py ha ña-ñangareko
why=Q 1PL.INCL.ACT-AGD-chest+press and 1PL.INCL.ACT-take.care.of
meme va'erã ñandejehe
continuously must ourselves
'Why do we always have to worry about and take care of ourselves?'

A different morphological process can express several types of quantification: **reduplication**. It is often the predicate that is reduplicated but not exclusively (see **3.4.3** and **4.10.2** for other uses of reduplication).

Indefinite quantification ('some', 'a few')

*ohecha iñ***apysẽpysẽ** *óga*
o-h-echa iñ-apysẽ~pysẽ óga
3.ACT-POSSM3-see 3.INACT-stick.out~stick.out house
's/he saw <u>a few</u> houses poking up'

Universal quantification ('all')

*Chupekuéra ndoipy'apýi mba'eve, i***kyrakyra** *ha hesãijoa.*
chupe=kuéra nd-oi-py'a+py-i mba'eve i-kyra~kyra
to.him/her=PL NEG-3.ACT-chest+press-NEG nothing 3.INACT-fat~fat
ha h-esãi-joa
and POSSM3-health-all
'Nothing worries them, they are all fat and all healthy.'

*ojehete***pysopyso**
o-je-h-ete+pyso~pyso
3.ACT-AGD-POSSM3-body+extend~extend
's/he stretches <u>all</u> his/her body'

Distributivity over a predicate argument

*ha'ekuéra hoy'u mbohapy kagua peteĩ**teĩ***

ha'e=kuéra	ho-y+'u	mbohapy	kagua	peteĩ~teĩ
s/he=PL	3.ACT-water+ingest	three	glass	one~one

'They drank three glasses <u>each one</u>.'
(Note that this sentence is ambiguous between two possible readings of the reduplicated quantifier *peteĩteĩ*: one in which each person drank one glass, so three people drank three glasses total, and a second in which each person drank three glasses.)

The Spanish words *algúno* 'some', *entéro* 'all', *la majoría/la mayoría* 'most', *unos kuánto/unoh kuánto* 'several' and *la mita(d)* 'half' are all attested quantifier borrowings in Guarani. Although common in the spoken language, these uses tend to be avoided in formal/academic styles or in writing.

10
Degree expressions

Degree expressions establish the degree to which a quality or property is present, either absolutely or by comparison between different people, things or events.

10.1 Comparatives

In comparisons of equality, most commonly, Guarani marks the "yardstick" or **standard of comparison** with the unstressed enclitic =*icha* (=*cha* after a morpheme ending in *i*) 'like, as'. Neither the thing compared nor the graded property on which to base the comparison bears any special marking.

upéicha
upe-icha
MED.SG-as
'this way, that way' (literally, 'like that')

ndéicha
nde-icha
2SG.INACT-as
'like you'

Amo yvyra yvate cherógaicha.
amo yvyra yvate che-r-óga-icha
DIST.SG tree tall 1SG.INACT-POSSM-house-as
'That tree over there is as tall as my house.' (Literally, 'That tree is tall as my house.')

Oñe'ẽ voi isýicha.
o-ñe'ẽ voi i-sy-icha
3.ACT-speak EMPH 3.INACT-mother-as
'S/he talks like his/her mother.'

Ndaipóri va'ekue mba'evéichagua ñu. (The original example has the non-standard spelling *vaekue*, reflecting the common pronunciation)
ndaipóri va'ekue mba'eve-icha=gua ñu
there.is.not PAST nothing-as=from field
'There weren't any kind of fields.' (Literally, 'there weren't fields of like anything'.)

Yvágaicha iporã yvy marae'ỹ.
yvága-icha i-porã yvy marae'ỹ
sky-as 3.INACT-beautiful earth spotless
'The land without evil was beautiful like the sky.'
(Note: *yvy marae'ỹ* 'the land without evil' is an important religious concept for Guarani peoples, a place of perfection to which they aspire by their deeds, somewhat similar to the notion of 'paradise'.)

When the standard of comparison is a not a noun phrase, but an adverb, or a phrase or clause that functions like an adverb, =*guáicha* is used (=*guaréicha* for standards of comparison located in the past, and =*guarãicha* for those located in the future).

tapiaguáicha
tapia=gua=icha
always=from=as
'as always'

kueheguaréicha
kuehe=guare=icha
yesterday=from.PAST=as
'like yesterday'

okéramoguáicha hína
o-ke=ramo=gua=icha hína
3.ACT-sleep=if=from=as PROG
'as if he was asleep'

Reikova'erã remanorõ **guarãicha**, *ha remba'apova'erã remano'ỹrõ* **guarãicha**.

re-iko-va'erã	re-mano=rõ	guarã=icha	ha	re-mba'apo-va'erã
2SG.ACT-be-must	2SG.ACT-die=if	from.FUT=as	and	2SG.ACT-work-must

re-mano-'ỹ=rõ	guarã=icha
2SG.ACT-die-PRIV=if	from.FUT=as

'You must live as if you are going to die, and you must work as if you are not going to die.'

Guarani also has dedicated comparative words of equality such as *ñemo'ã/ñaimo'ã* (literally, 'it is believed that/we believe that'), *ha'ete* 'it is the same as' (literally, 'be-very') and *ojoja* 'they are equal' (literally, 'they are close to one another'; note that *ojoja* requires the postposition =*ndive*). These all come before the standard of comparison noun phrase.

. . . *omaña hağua opa mba'e* **ñemo'ã** *umi tigre ivare'áva.*

o-maña=hağua	opa	mba'e	ñemo'ã	umi	tigre
3.ACT-look.at=for	all	thing	we.believe.that	NPROX.PL	tiger

i-vare'a-va
3.INACT-hunger-ADJZ

'. . . to look at all things like those hungry tigers.'

Reñe'ẽ **ha'eténte** *ndesy.*

re-ñe'ẽ	ha'e-te-nte	nde-sy
2SG.ACT-speak	be-very-only	2SG.INACT-mother

'You talk exactly like your mother.'

Umi karai **ojoja** *oñondive.*

umi	karai	o-jo-ja	oñondive
NPROX.PL	gentleman	3.ACT-RECP-get.closer	with.each.other

'Those gentlemen are like one another.'[27]

Ñaimo'ã*vaicha kuarahy ha ndaha'éi kuarahy.*

ñaimo'ã-va-icha	kuarahy	ha	nda-ha'e-i	kuarahy
we.believe.that-ADJZ-as	sun	and	NEG-be-NEG	sun

'He seemed like a sun, but he wasn't the sun.'

Comparisons of similarity use the word *ojogua* 'it resembles' (it requires the postposition =*pe*).

---

[27] Example from Melià *et al.* (1997, 145)

*Ñandeyvy ára ha ára **ojogua** peteĩ kure chikéro**pe**.*
ñande-yvy　　　ára　ha　ára　o-jogua　　　peteĩ　kure　chikéro=pe
1PL.INCL.INACT-earth　day　and　day　3.ACT-resemble　one　pig　pigsty=in
'Our Earth day after day <u>resembles</u> a pigsty.'

In comparisons of superiority, the degree word takes the stressed suffix -*ve* 'more', both for absolute comparisons (that is, those with no standard of comparison) and for relative comparisons (that is, those with a standard of comparison). In relative comparisons, the standard of comparison noun phrase is marked with the postposition =*gui* ('from').

*Húpiter ituicha**ve** jasy ha'e Ganímedes.*
Húpiter　i-tuicha-ve　　　jasy　ha'e　Ganímedes
Jupiter　3.INACT-big-more　moon　be　　Ganimedes
'Jupiter's <u>largest</u> moon is Ganymede.'

*Che amba'apo**ve** ndehe**gui**.*
che　a-mba'apo-ve　　　ndehegui
I　　1SG.ACT-work-more　from.you
'I work <u>more</u> <u>than</u> you.'

Comparisons of inferiority can be expressed using the stressed suffix -*'ive*. This is in fact not a single morpheme, but rather the diminutive suffix -*'i* followed by the stressed suffix -*ve* 'more', thus deriving the inferiority meaning by composition.

*omba'apo**'ive** ñande hígado ha pitikiri'i kuéra*
o-mba'apo-'i-ve　　　　　　ñande-hígado　　　ha　pitikiri'i=kuéra
3.ACT-work-DIM-more　　1PL.INCL.ACT-liver　and　kidney=PL
'our liver and kidneys work <u>less</u>'

However, very often, comparisons of inferiority are obtained by simply substituting a degree adjective with its opposite and using a comparison of superiority.

10.2 Superlatives

Guarani has many ways of indicating a very high degree or the highest degree of a property. Most commonly, absolute superlatives (that is, those with no standard of comparison) are marked with the stressed suffix *-ite* 'very' (with variants *-te*, especially when the base ends in a mid front vowel, or *-ete*, when the base ends in a high vowel).

*iva**ete***
i-vai-ete
3.INACT-ugly-very
's/he/it is very ugly'

*Ndaikuaai**ete**.*
nd-ai-kuaa-i-ete
NEG-1SG.ACT-know-NEG-very
'I <u>really</u> don't know.'

*. . . ndoui**ete**voi iñakãme mba'eve iporãmíva.*
nd-o-u-i-ete=voi   iñ-akã=me   mba'eve
NEG-3.ACT-come-NEG-very=EMPH 3.INACT-head=in nothing
i-porã-mi-va
3.INACT-beautiful-DIM-ADJZ
'. . . and he couldn't <u>really</u> think of anything (that was) beautiful.'
(Literally, 'and nothing came <u>at all</u> into his head that is beautiful.')

*Oiko peteĩ mba'e ñaha'arõ'ỹ **et**é**va**.*
o-iko   peteĩ   mba'e   ña-h-a'arõ-'ỹ-ete-va
3.ACT-be one   thing   1PL.INCL.ACT-POSSM3-wait-PRIV-very-ADJZ
'Something happened that we didn't expect <u>at all</u>.'[28]

*Haime**te** añehundi, haime**te** añemotĩ*
opavave renondépe.
háime-te   a-ñe-hundi   háime-te   a-ñe-mo-tĩ
almost-very 1SG.ACT-AGD-sink   almost-very 1SG.ACT-AGD-MAKE1-feel.shame
opavave r-enonde=pe
all   POSSM-front=in
'I am <u>just</u> on the brink of sinking, I am <u>just</u> on the brink of being ashamed in front of everybody.'

*ko'ãga ha tapia**ite** guarã*
ko'ãga   ha   tapia-ite=guarã
now   and   always-very=for
'now and forever <u>and ever</u>'

---

[28] Example from de Canese and Acosta Alcaraz (2007, 144).

This suffix is often used with the meaning 'real, true'.

*guarani**ete***
guarani-ete
Guarani-very
'true Guarani' (that is, Guarani as free as Spanish influence as possible)

*Che kuimba'e**te** voi.*
che   kuimba'e-te=voi
I   man-very=EMPH
'I am a real man.'

*Cheko paraguayo**ite**.*
che=ko   paraguayo-ite
1SG.INACT=VERD   Paraguayan-very
'I am a real Paraguayan.'

As we can see above, this extremely frequent suffix can modify all kinds of different lexical roots. In the example below, we can see that it can also modify grammatical morphemes, in this case, an affix.

*amba'apopota**ite***
a-mba'apo-pota-ite
1SG.ACT-work-about.to-very
'I am just about to work' (note that *-ite* modifies the immediate future *-pota*)

Relative superlatives combine the absolute superlative suffix *-ite/-te/-ete* with the comparative suffix *-ve*.

*Péro iporã**iteve** ningo ko Manu ohaiva'ekue.*
péro   i-porã-ite-ve   ningo ko   Manu   o-h-ai-va'ekue
but   3.INACT-good-very-more   VERD PROX.SG   Manu   3.ACT-POSSM3-write-PAST
'But in reality what Manú wrote is much better.'

Another possible superlative is the unstressed circumfix *nde- . . . -va*, which surrounds the adjective.

*MCNOC ombosako'i Paraguaýpe movilización **nde**kakuaá**va**.*
MCNOC   o-mbo-sako'i   Paraguay=pe   movilización   nde-kakuaa-va
MCNOC   3.ACT-MAKE1-prepare   Asunción=in   demonstration   SUP-grow.up-SUP
'The MCNOC (the National Board of Coordination of Rural Organizations) prepares a very big demonstration in Asunción.'

*Tomasa oipota ojuhu peteĩ iñirũrã **ne**porãva.*
Tomasa	oi-pota	o-juhu	peteĩ iñ-irũ-rã	ne-porã-va
Tomasa	3.ACT-want	3.ACT-find	one 3.INACT-friend-DEST	SUP-beautiful-SUP

'Tomasa wanted him to find a very beautiful partner.'

Elative superlatives indicate a very large degree of a quality. Guarani uses for the expression of elatives the stressed suffix *-iterei* (with variants *-terei*, especially when the base ends in a mid front vowel, or *-eterei*, when the base ends in a high vowel). *-Rasa* is often considered a superior grade of elative, and there are (presumably) greater, elevated degrees such as *-pavẽ*, *-vete* or *-vusu*, but these are not really productive in the modern language.

*chekane'õ**iterei***
che-kane'õ-iterei
1SG.INACT-tiredness-very.much
'I am super tired'

*aagradece**terei** peẽme orevisitahaguére ikatuhaguáicha peikuaami la situación*
a-agradece-terei   peẽme   ore-visita-hague=re
1SG.ACT-thank-very.much   to.you.PL   1PL.EXCL.INACT-visit-NMLZ.PAST=at
ikatu=hagua-icha   pei-kuaa-mi   la   situación
be.able=for-as   2PL.ACT-know-DIM   DET.SG   situation

'I thank you very much for visiting us so that you will know the situation a little'

*Hasy**eterei** piko ndéve che karai.*
h-asy-eterei=piko   ndéve   che-karai
POSSM3-pain-very.much=Q   to.you.SG   1SG.INACT-gentleman

'Does it hurt you very much, my dear?'

*okyhyje**rasa***
o-kyhyje-rasa
3.ACT-fear-extremely
's/he was extremely frightened'

*hesaho mba'evai**rasa**rehe*
h-esaho   mba'e-vai-rasa=rehe
POSSM3-notice   thing-ugly-extremely=at

'the sudden sight of a monster' (literally, *mba'evairasa* 'an extremely ugly thing')

*vy'a**pavẽ***
vy'a-pavẽ
joy-supreme
'happiness, bliss'

*vy'a**pavẽ** nearambotýre*
vy'a-pavẽ ne-ára-mboty=re
joy-supreme 2SG.INACT-day-conclude=at
'happy birthday' (literally, 'happiness on your birthday'; *aramboty* is the neologism coined for 'birthday')

*mburuvicha**vete***
mburuvicha-vete
leader-supreme
'<u>supreme</u> leader' (i.e., 'president', 'king', etc.)

*aguyje**vete***
aguyje-vete
thanks-supreme
'gratitude' (literally, '<u>supreme</u> state of grace')

*Ñanderu**vusu***
ñande-r-u-vusu
1PL.INCL.INACT-POSSM-father-great
'Our <u>Great</u> Father' (a foundational figure in many Guarani creation stories)

The roots *asy* (cf. *t-asy* 'pain') and *tuicha* 'big' have been grammaticalized as elative markers, although there seem to be lexical constraints on their use. For example, *tuicha* can co-occur with negative/undesirable degree properties, while *asy* has a positive connotation, and it seems to be used with colours, as well as with properties expressing fragility, purity and so on. When used with an active predicate, *asy* conveys a notion of effort and difficulty, and also a positive valuation of this effort by the speaker.

*ao hovy **asý**va*
ao h-ovy asy-va
clothes POSSM3-blue pain-ADJZ
'(a piece of) <u>intense</u> blue clothing'

*Ivevúi **asy** pe kambuchi.*
i-vevúi　　　　　　asy　pe　　　kambuchi
3.INACT-lightweight　pain　MED.SG　clay.jug
'This jug is delicate/fragile.'

*omba'apo **asy** productor rural ha mba'apohára urbano*
ohasáva actividad económica
o-mba'apo　asy　productor　rural　ha　mba'apo-hára　urbano
3.ACT-work　pain　producer　rural　and　work-NMLZ.AG　urban
o-h-asa-va　　　　　　　actividad　económica
3.ACT-POSSM3-pass-ADJZ　activity　economic
'the <u>difficulty</u> with which rural producers and urban workers sustain their economic activity'

*Kóva **tuicha** ombojorea Mbatovípe.*
ko-va　　　　　　tuicha　o-mbo-jorea　　　Mbatovi=pe
PROX.SG-ADJZ　big　　　3.ACT-MAKE1-ruin　Mbatovi=in
'This <u>greatly</u> ruined Mbatovi.'

Finally, reduplication can also serve a superlative, intensifying function.

*mymba i**porãporã**va*
mymba　　　　　　　　i-porã~porã-va
domesticated.animal　3.INACT-beautiful~beautiful-ADJZ
'<u>very</u> beautiful animals'

11
Noun incorporation into the verb

Noun incorporation refers to the addition of a noun argument to a verbal root to form a single morphological word. This word still functions as a verb: it can, for example, take further verb prefixes and suffixes, it has further noun arguments like a subject, and so on. English uses this resource in a very limited way: think for example of 'house-hunting' (where 'house' is the object of 'hunt').

Guarani noun incorporation works as in English by attaching the verb's object (without any determiners or modifiers) to the left of the verb itself (as if it was a prefix). Most incorporated nouns are body parts (inalienable possessums), but non-body parts can also be incorporated. Noun incorporation serves to background the incorporated object (making it less important) and to foreground the event itself that involves the object.

Moreover, the incorporated object most often does not designate an actual participant in the event. For example, whereas *omboty ijuru* simply means 's/he closed his/her mouth', *ojurumboty* below with noun incorporation means 's/he kept someone quiet'. Body-part incorporation is used to highlight emotional states, habitual behaviour or permanent characteristics of discourse participants. Non-body-part incorporation, on the other hand, highlights that an activity is of social importance, or is institutionalized in some way. In many cases, the incorporated structures have specific conventionalized non-compositional meanings.

hay'u
ha-y+'u
1SG.ACT-water+ingest
'I drink water' (from *y* 'water' and *'u* 'to eat something, to ingest')

*Nde katu reajuna jave emona aséite neakãre ha ej**ovahéi**.*
nde   katu   re-ajuna   jave   e-mona   aséite   ne-akã=re
you.SG   just   2SG.ACT-fast   while   IMP-smear   oil   2SG.INACT-head=at
ha   e-j-ova+héi
and   IMP-AGD-face+wash

'But you, when you fast, smear oil on your head and <u>wash your face</u>.' (From relational *-ova* 'face' and *(jo)héi* 'to wash'.)

*Ko'ã mba'e hína la omongy'áva yvyporakuérape, ndaha'éi okaruhaguére oje**pohei'ỹ**re.*
ko'ã   mba'e   hína   la   o-mo-ngy'a-va
PROX.PL   thing   PROG   DET.SG   3.ACT-MAKE1-dirty-ADJZ
yvypóra=kuéra=pe   nda-ha'e-i   o-karu-hague=re
person=PL=in   NEG-be-NEG   3.ACT-eat(intransitive)-NMLZ.PAST=at
o-je-po+héi='ỹre
3.ACT-AGD-hand+wash=without

'These are the things that befoul people, not eating without <u>washing hands</u>.' (From *po* 'hand' and *(jo)héi* 'to wash'.)

*upémarõ ai**popete** chupe*
upémarõ   ai-po+pete   chupe
finally   1SG.ACT-hand+slap   to.him/her

'finally I <u>slapped his/her hand</u>' (from *po* 'hand' and *pete* 'to slap')

*o**hovapete** chupe*
o-h-ova+pete   chupe
3.ACT-POSSM3-face+slap to.him/her

'they <u>slapped</u> him/her <u>in the face</u>' (from relational *-ova* 'face' and *pete* 'slap')

*che**py'ahesaho***
che-py'a+h-esa+ho
1SG.INACT-chest+POSSM3-eye+go

'the <u>eyes</u> of my <u>soul go away</u> from me' (from *py'a* 'chest; soul', relational *-esa* 'eye' and *ho* 'to go')

*h**etevevui**hápeve*
h-ete+vevúi-ha=peve
POSSM3-body-lightweight-NMLZ=until

'until their <u>bodies</u> became <u>lighter</u>' (from *-ete* 'body' and *vevúi* 'lightweight')

ojepy'amongeta
o-je-py'a+mongeta
3.ACT-AGD-chest+converse
's/he <u>thought to him/herself</u>' / 's/he reflected' (from *py'a* 'chest; heart' and *mongeta* 'to converse')

*Omongakuaa kure, o**mandi'okyty** ha o**aramirõapo**.*
o-mo-ngakuaa   kure   o-mandi'o+kyty   ha   o-aramirõ+apo
3.ACT-MAKE1-grow.up   pig   3.ACT-manioc+grind   and   3.ACT-starch+make
'She raises the pigs, <u>grates (the) manioc</u>, and <u>makes (the) starch</u>.' (From *mandi'o* 'manioc' and *kyty* 'to grate', and from *aramirõ* 'starch' and *-apo* 'to make'.)

*Umi yvyra **hoguekúi**va'ekue . . .*
umi   yvyra   h-ogue+kúi-va'ekue
NPROX.PL   tree   POSSM3-leaf+get.detached-PAST
'The trees that have lost their leaves . . . ' (from *-ogue* 'leaf' and *kúi* 'to become detached')

A few examples below show that the predicate with an incorporated object often still takes another direct object like any transitive verb. This means that the incorporated object is not a "real" object (think about how in English one can say 'house-hunting for a mansion').

*o**jurumboty** haguã heta periodista*
o-juru+mboty=haguã   h-eta   periodista
3.ACT-mouth+close=for   POSSM3-numerous   journalist
'to <u>silence</u> many journalists (i.e., their questions)' (from *juru* 'mouth' and *mboty* 'to close')

*avakuéra o**pirakutu** opaichagua pira*
ava=kuéra   o-pira+kutu   opa-icha=gua   pira
person=PL   3.ACT-fish+pierce   all-as=from   fish
'people <u>fish</u> all sorts of fish' (from *pira* '(a) fish' and *kutu* 'to pierce')

*Paraguái oje**hetepyso** turismo*
Paraguái   o-je-h-ete+pyso   turismo
Paraguay   3.ACT-AGD-POSSM3-body+extend   tourism
'Paraguay <u>expands</u> tourism' (from *-ete* 'body' and *pyso* 'to extend, to stretch')

Of note, noun incorporation has lost much of its original productivity: it survives mostly in lexicalized cases or with specific verbs and verb-object combinations. The verbs *johéi* 'to wash' (with apheresis to *-héi*), *juka* 'to kill', *kutu* 'to pierce' and *pete* 'to slap' are those most frequently occurring with incorporated objects.

12
Complex sentences

A **complex sentence** is a sentence with more than one predicate (and its associated arguments). Each predicate-argument structure is a clause. Some sentences are complex because they coordinate two clauses that are of equal hierarchy, whereas others are complex because they have a **main clause** and a **subordinate clause** that depends on the main clause.

12.1 Coordinated clauses

Coordinated clauses are clauses that are put together in a complex sentence and that are of equal hierarchy.

By juxtaposition without a coordinator (asyndetic coordination)
This happens often with verbs of movement.

Ehóna eñeno mba'e.
e-ho-na   e-ñeno   mba'e
IMP-go-REQ   IMP-lie.down   thing
'Please go (<u>and</u>) lie down to sleep or something.' (This is a common expression meaning that the addressee is saying or doing something stupid or unimportant.)

oimérõ la dueño tou togueraha
o-ime=rõ   la   dueño   t-o-u   t-o-gueraha
3.ACT-be.located=if   DET.SG   owner   OPT-3.ACT-come   OPT-3.ACT-carry
'if (if be that) the owner comes <u>and</u> takes (it)'

With a coordinating copulative conjunction

The most common conjunction is the **copulative conjunction** *ha* 'and'. The historical form *ha'e* 'and' is sometimes used in writing instead of *ha*, but it is much less frequent. *Tẽra* is a simple **disjunctive conjunction**. The copulative *ha* 'and' and the disjunctive *tẽra* 'or' (also spelled *térã*) are also used for nominal conjunction: *che* **ha** *nde* 'myself and you', *che* **tẽra** *nde* 'myself or you'.

*Ojapova'erã peteĩ purahéi **ha** ndouetevoi iñakãme mba'eve iporãmíva.*
o-japo-va'erã   peteĩ   purahéi   ha   nd-o-u-i-ete=voi
3.ACT-make-must one   song   and   NEG-3.ACT-come-NEG-very=EMPH
iñ-akã=me   mba'eve   i-porã-mi-va
3.INACT-head=in nothing   3.INACT-beautiful-DIM-ADJZ
'He had to make a song and nothing beautiful came into his head.'

*Luisa **tẽra** José ohóta ñemuhame.*
Luisa   tẽra   José   o-ho-ta   ñemu-ha=me
Luisa   or   Jose   3.ACT-go-FUT   trade-NMLZ.LOC=in
'Luisa or José will go to the store.'

Yrõ is presumably the combination of privative *-'ỹ* with conditional *=rõ*, which is consistent with its interpretation as 'or if not' or 'otherwise'.

*Oúta María **yrõ** oúta Isabel.*
o-u-ta   María   yrõ   o-u-ta   Isabel
3.ACT-come-FUT   María   otherwise   3.ACT-come-FUT   Isabel
'María will come or if not Isabel will come.'

With an adversative conjunction

Adversative conjunctions are often composed of *katu* (roughly meaning 'but' or 'just') preceded by another morpheme that conveys nuances of meaning; for example, *ha* 'and', *tẽra* 'or' (also spelled *térã*), *ãga* 'now' (variously spelled *ágã*, *ağa* or *áğa*). (Remember that *katu* is more generally a clitic particle that comes in second position in the sentence because it needs a word on its left to "lean on" for pronunciation.)

*Jajepropváta ha ñañetentáta, **ha katu** jarresivíta ñeipytyvõ.*
ja-je-prova-ta   ha   ña-ñe-tenta-ta   ha   katu
1PL.INCL.ACT-AGD-test-FUT   and   1PL.INCL.ACT-AGD-tempt-FUT   and   just
ja-rresivi-ta   ñe-ipytyvõ
1PL.INCL.ACT-receive-FUT   AGD-help
'We will be tested and we will be tempted, but/and yet we will (also) receive help.'

*Oĩporãningo ko'ã mba'e pyahu jaiporu **hakatu** ore mbo'eharakuéra romopyendava'erã hekombo'ehápe.*
oĩ-porã=ningo   ko'ã   mba'e pyahu jai-poru   ha=katu
there.is-good=VERD PROX.PL thing new   1PL.INCL.ACT-use and=just
ore   mbo'e-hára=kuéra   ro-mo-py+enda-va'erã
we.not.you   teach-NMLZ.AG=PL   1PL.EXCL.ACT-MAKE1-foot+place-must
h-eko-mbo'e-ha=pe
POSSM3-NMLZ.QUAL-teach-NMLZ.LOC=in
'It is good that we use these new things <u>but</u> we the teachers must apply them properly in the classrooms.'

*Chéveguarã tekoteṽe ñañembokatupyry pya'e porã ko'ã tecnología jepurúpe **tẽra katu** japytáta tapykuépe.*
chéve=guarã   tekoteṽe   ña-ñe-mbo-katupyry   pya'e   porã
to.me=for   be.necessary   1PL.INCL.ACT-AGD-MAKE1-skillful   fast   good
ko'ã   tecnología   je-puru=pe   tẽra katu   ja-pyta-ta
PROX.PL   technology   AGD-use=in   or just   1PL.INCL.ACT-stay-FUT
t-apykue=pe
NPOSSM-behind=in
'In my opinion, we must train ourselves quickly in the use of these technologies <u>otherwise</u> we will remain behind.'

*Araka'evékena ani jajavy ha ñaimo'ã Guarani ikatuha ombyai ñanecastellanope, **tẽra katu** castellano upe ñaneguaraníme.*
araka'eve-ke-na   ani   ja-javy   ha   ña-imo'ã   Guarani
never-FORCE-REQ   NEG.IMP   1PL.INCL.ACT-err   and   1PL.INCL.ACT-think   Guarani
ikatu-ha   o-mby-ai   ñane-castellano=pe   tẽra katu
be.able-NMLZ   3.ACT-MAKE1-bad   1PL.INCL.INACT-Spanish=in or   just
castellano   upe   ñane-guarani=me
Spanish   MED.SG   1PL.INCL.INACT-Guarani=in
'Let's never make a mistake and think that Guarani can ruin our Spanish, <u>or vice versa</u>, Spanish (ruin) our Guarani.'

*Oikomo'ãva **ha upéi** ndoikói.*
o-iko-mo'ã-va   ha   upéi   nd-o-iko-i
3.ACT-be-ALMOST-ADJZ   and   then   NEG-3.ACT-be-NEG
'Something that was going to be <u>but</u> isn't.'

These adversative conjunctions are often used to introduce an adversative follow-up sentence (therefore, they are not strictly for coordination of clauses inside a complex sentence).

COMPLEX SENTENCES

Ñande Paraguaigua ñañemoarandu'ỹ rehe ñañe'ẽvoi guaraníme.
***Ága katu** ñañe'ẽ, ñamoñe'ẽ ha jahaiporãséramo ko ñe'ẽme ñañemoarandumanteva'erã.*

ñande	Paraguái=gua	ña-ñe-mo-arandu='ỹrehe
we&you	Paraguay=from	1PL.INCL.ACT-AGD-MAKE1-knowledge=without

ña-ñe'ẽ=voi	guarani=me	ága	katu	ña-ñe'ẽ
1PL.INCL.ACT-language–EMPH	Guarani=in	now	just	1PL.INCL.ACT-language

ña-mo-ñe'ẽ	ha	ja-h-ai+porã-se=ramo
1PL.INCL.ACT-MAKE1-language	and	1PL.INCL.POSS3-write+good-want=if

ko	ñe'ẽ=me	ña-ñe-mo-arandu-mante-va'erã
PROX.SG	language=in	1PL.INCL.ACT-AGD-MAKE1-knowledge-only-must

'We Paraguayans speak Guarani without having studied it. <u>However</u>, if we want to speak, read and write it well we simply must study it.'

Uvei has the meaning 'rather' or 'instead'.

*Ani pejepy'apy mba'evére, pemoĩ **uvei** opa mba'e Ñandejára pópe pene ñembo'épe.*

ani	pe-je-py'a+py	mba'eve=re	pe-moĩ	uvei	opa
NEG.IMP	2PL.ACT-AGD-chest+press	nothing=at	2PL.ACT-put	rather	all

mba'e	ñande-jára	po=pe	pene-ñembo'e=pe
thing	2PL.INCL.INACT-lord	hand=in	2PL.INACT-prayer=in

'Do not worry about anything, <u>rather</u> put all things in the hands of Our Lord in your prayers.'

Adversative clauses where a subsequent clause contradicts a previous negative clause have no special marking (cf. Spanish *sino* 'but (rather)'). Speakers may use the suffix *-nte* 'only'.

*Ndaiñate'ỹiri, itavý**nte**ko.*

nda-iñ-ate'ỹ-iri	i-tavy-nte=ko
NEG-3.INACT-laziness-NEG	3.INACT-stupid-only=VERD

'S/he isn't lazy, s/he is <u>just</u> stupid.'

Sometimes the coordinator *ha* 'and' is used and the adversative meaning is understood from the meaning of the sentence:

*Ñaimo'ãvaicha kuarahy **ha** ndaha'éi kuarahy.*

ñaimo'ã-vaicha	kuarahy	ha	nda-ha'e-i	kuarahy
we.believe.that-seems	sun	and	NEG-be-NEG	sun

'He seemed like a sun, <u>but</u> he wasn't the sun.'

Note that the Spanish borrowings *péro* 'but' or *aunque/áunke* 'even though' are very commonly used as adversative conjunctions. The Spanish correlative conjunction *ni . . . ni* 'neither . . . nor' also occurs in Guarani. All of these are avoided in more formal or academic styles.

12.2 Subordinate clauses

Complex sentences with more than one clause (that is, more than one predicate with its arguments) can also be the result of subordination of clauses. **Subordinate clauses** are all the clauses whose morphological and/or syntactic form depends in some way on another clause, which we call the **main clause**. Subordinate clauses fulfil a function with respect to the main clause and this function serves to classify them. There are three types of subordinate clauses: **relative clauses** (also **adjective clauses**), **complement clauses** (also **noun clauses**) and **adverbial clauses**. In Guarani the first two can be considered to be sentences converted into nouns by the addition of a suffix (**sentential nominalizations**). Subordination of a clause is marked in Guarani on the subordinate clause's own predicate, via a specific suffix or postposed particle. There is no other difference between main and subordinate predicates (that is, there is no specific verb form, no specific word order and so on). In some restricted cases, there is no overt marking of subordination (see **12.2.2**).

12.2.1 Relative clauses

Relative clauses are clauses that function like adjectives (that is, they describe or modify a noun or pronoun in the main clause) or sometimes like nouns themselves (functioning as the subject or an object of the main clause). In both cases the subordinate predicate is marked with the unstressed suffix *-va*, or in rarer cases *-va'e*, which is the historical form (cf. *ha* and *ha'e* in **12.1**). Because *-va* serves to form adjective clauses, but also to turn words of other classes into adjectives, I have been consistently glossing it as ADJZ, **adjectivizer** (see **3.2.1.1.3**).

To the historical form *-va'e*, one adds *-kue* to mark past tense in the subordinate (*-va'ekue*), or *-rã* to mark future tense (*-va'erã*). Both *va'ekue* and *va'erã* have phonetically reduced forms without the glottal stop, *vaekue* and *vaerã*, that are very common in speech. The forms *akue* and *arã*, further reduced, are also used, but mostly as markers of past tense or future tense.

Relative clauses that function as adjectives

*Pe kuimba'e **iporãva** che ména.* (Modifies *kuimba'e* 'man'.)

pe	kuimba'e	i-porã-va	che-ména
MED.SG	man	3.INACT-beautiful-ADJZ	1SG.INACT-husband

'That beautiful man is my husband.' (Literally, 'That man who is beautiful is my husband.')

*¡Ehupi pe ndeao **remombova'ekue** yvýpe!* (Modifies *ao* 'clothes'.)

e-hupi	pe	nde-ao	re-mombo-va'e-kue	yvy=pe
IMP-lift	MED.SG	2SG.INACT-clothes	2SG.ACT-toss-ADJZ-POST	earth=in

'Pick up your clothes that you tossed on the floor!'

When the noun modified by a relative clause is interpreted as the subject of the relative clause, this is called a **subject relative**. If the noun modified by the relative clause is the object of the relative clause, this is called an **object relative**. For this, English uses word order and some optional marking on the relative pronoun: think about the English 'the woman who saw the man' (subject relative) versus 'the woman who(m) the man saw' (object relative). In Guarani the difference between these two interpretations is not explicitly indicated, but it can sometimes be inferred by the meaning of the clause.

*Aheka peteĩ aranduka **ome'ẽva'ekue** che ru.* (Modifies *aranduka* 'book', the object of 'gave'.)

a-h-eka	peteĩ	aranduka	o-me'ẽ-va'e-kue	che-r-u
1SG.ACT-POSSM3-seek	one	book	3.ACT-give-ADJZ-POST	1SG.INACT-POSSM-father

'I am looking for a book that my dad gave me.'

*Aheka peteĩ kuña **ome'ẽva'ekue ko** aranduka.* (Modifies *kuña* 'woman', the subject of 'gave'.)

a-h-eka	peteĩ	kuña	o-me'ẽ-va'e-kue	ko	aranduka
1SG.ACT-POSSM3-seek	one	woman	3.ACT-give-ADJZ-POST	PROX.SG	book

'I am looking for a woman that gave me this book.'

Often the appearance of active or inactive person prefixes on the subordinate verb indicates which interpretation is intended.

*peteĩ kuña **nderechava'ekue***

peteĩ	kuña	nde-r-echa-va'e-kue
one	woman	2SG.INACT-POSSM-see-ADJZ-POST

'a woman who saw you' (subject relative)

*peteĩ kuña **rehechava'ekue***
peteĩ	kuña	re-h-echa-va'e-kue
one	woman	2SG.ACT-POSSM3-see-ADJZ-POST

'a woman <u>who(m) you saw</u>' (object relative)

The marking of a human direct object with =*pe* can also clarify the interpretation intended.

*peteĩ kuña **ohechava'ekue peteĩ arriérope***
peteĩ	kuña	o-h-echa-va'e-kue	peteĩ	arriéro=pe
one	woman	3.ACT-POSSM3-see-ADJZ-POST	one	peasant=in

'a woman <u>who saw a man</u>' (subject relative)

When such marking is not used, however, word order can make the subject of the relative clause clear. Noun phrases that come before the subordinate verb tend to be interpreted as subjects (especially if there is a pause at the beginning of the relative clause), those that come after, as objects. In fact, prosody is very important in clarifying the intended interpretation in speech, but it cannot be rendered very accurately in writing.

*peteĩ kuña **ohechava'ekue peteĩ arriéro***.
peteĩ	kuña	o-h-echa-va'e-kue	peteĩ	arriéro
one	woman	3.ACT-POSSM3-see-ADJZ-POST	one	peasant

'a woman <u>who saw a man</u>.' (subject relative)

*peteĩ kuña **peteĩ arriéro ohechava'ekue***.
peteĩ	kuña	peteĩ	arriéro	o-h-echa-va'e-kue
one	woman	one	peasant	3.ACT-POSSM3-see-ADJZ-POST

'a woman <u>who(m) a man saw</u>.' (object relative)

Relative clauses that function as nouns

Instead of modifying a noun or pronoun, it is common for relative clauses to function directly as noun phrases themselves.

*Ojejukáguive ako karai Arce, ahendúvo mbokapu aimo'ãjevýma oime **ojejukáva***.
o-je-juka=guive	ako	karai	Arce	a-h-endu-vo
3.ACT-AGD-kill=since	DIST.EV	lord	Arce	1SG.ACT-POSSM3-hear-while
mbo-kapu	a-imo'ã-jevy-ma		o-ime	o-je-juka-va
MAKE1-burst	1SG.ACT-think-again-already		3.ACT-be.located	3.ACT-AGD-kill-ADJZ

'Since that Mr Arce was killed, whenever I hear shots, I already think again there is <u>someone being killed</u>.'

*Re'u **re'uséva**.*
re-'u   re-'u-se-va
2SG.ACT-ingest   2SG.ACT-ingest-want-ADJZ
'You eat <u>what(ever) you want to eat</u>.'

*Emombe'umína chéve **rejapova'erã ko'ẽro**.*
e-mombe'u-mi-na   chéve   re-japo-va'e-rã   ko'ẽro
IMP-tell-PLEAD-REQ   to.me   2SG.ACT-make-ADJZ-DEST   tomorrow
'Please tell me <u>what you will do tomorrow</u>.'

*Ndaipóri **ouséva** plázape.*
ndaipóri   o-u-se-va   pláza=pe
there.is.not   3.ACT-come-want-ADJZ   square=in
'There is no one <u>who wants to come to the square</u>.' (Literally, 'there is not <u>who wants to come to the square</u>.')

Especially in colloquial speech, Guarani relative clauses are very frequently headed by the borrowed determiner *la*:

*He **la ja'úva**.*
he   la   ja-'ú-va
tasty DET.SG   1PL.INCL.ACT-ingest-ADJZ
'<u>What we are eating</u> is delicious.'

*Emombe'umína **la rehecháva**.*
e-mombe'u-mi-na   la   re-h-echa-va
IMP-tell-PLEAD-REQ   DET.SG   2SG.ACT-POSSM3-see-ADJZ
'Please tell me <u>what you see</u>.'

Negated relative clauses use the regular negation circumfix *n(d)-....-(r)i* or the stressed privative suffix *-'ỹ*, both occurring before the relativizer *-va*.

*Jukysy **ndo'úiva** araka'eve ndokakuaái.*
jukysy   nd-o-'u-i-va   araka'eve   nd-o-kakuaa-i
soup   NEG-3.ACT-ingest-NEG-ADJZ   never   NEG-3.ACT-grow.up-NEG
'<u>Those who don't</u> eat soup never grow.'

*vy'a **ijojaha'ỹva***
vy'a   i-joja-ha-'ỹ-va
joy   3.INACT-equal-NMLZ-PRIV-ADJZ
'an unparalleled happiness' (literally, 'a happiness <u>that does not</u> have equal')

Era espacialpe ndaipóri ojehu'ỹva.
era   espacial=pe   ndaipóri   o-jehu-'ỹ-va
era   spatial=in   there.is.not 3.ACT-happen-PRIV-ADJZ
'In the Space Age nothing is impossible.' (Literally, 'In the Space Age there isn't something <u>that doesn't</u> happen.')

Pévako aipota'ỹva.
pe-va=ko   ai-pota-'ỹ-va
MED.SG-ADJZ=VERD   1SG.ACT-want-PRIV-ADJZ
'That is what I <u>don't</u> want.'[29]

Lastly, when the subordinate predicate is not a verb, but is instead a noun, adjective or adverb of the phrase with a postposition, the stressed enclitic =*gua* is used instead of -*va*. This occurs commonly when the subordinate clause is a type of clause that does not require a verb in Guarani (these usually require the copula 'to be' in English).

*Egueru chéve pe kyse **mesa'árigua**.*
e-gueru   chéve   pe   kyse   mesa='ári=gua
IMP-bring   to.me   MED.SG   knife   table=upon=from
'Go bring me the knife <u>that is on the table</u>.'

*ñaneirũ **ñanderapykuepegua** oñekaramava'erã ñandepytarehe*
ñane-irũ   ñande-r-apykue=pe=gua
1PL.INCL.INACT-friend   1PL.INCL.INACT-POSSM-behind=in=from
o-ñe-karama-va'erã   ñande-pyta=rehe
3.ACT-AGD-grab-must   1PL.INCL.INACT-heel=at
'our classmate <u>who is behind us</u> must hold onto our heel'

***Francisco de Asís rekoviagua** oúta Paraguáipe.*
Francisco de Asís   r-ekovia=gua   o-u-ta   Paraguái=pe
Francis of Assisi   POSSM-replacement=from   3.ACT-come-FUT Paraguay=in
'<u>The successor of Francis of Assisi</u> will come to Paraguay.' (Literally, '<u>S/he who is Francis of Assisi's replacement</u> will come to Paraguay.')

12.2.2 Complement clauses

A **complement clause** fulfils the functions of a noun phrase, functioning as the subject, object or other complement of the main verb. The predicate of a subordinate complement clause is most commonly marked with the stressed suffix -*ha* (which is a more general nominalizer; see **3.2.1.1.1**),

---
[29] Example from Melià *et al.* (1997, 112).

with the variant -*hague* if the subordinate predicate has a past interpretation. Juxtaposition without an explicit subordinator is used in some specific cases. Interrogative and exclamative subordinate clauses are simply marked with the main clause interrogative/exclamative enclitics and therefore can be considered a case of subordination by juxtaposition.

With the subordinator -*ha*/-*hague*

The most frequent kind of complement clause occurs with the stressed nominalizing suffix -*ha* (equivalent to the English complementizer 'that') attached to the subordinate predicate. As we saw in **3.2.1.1.1**, this suffix is more generally used to form nouns from non-noun words. In reality, complement clauses in Guarani are simply clauses that have been made to function like nouns via the addition of -*ha* to their predicate.

*Ha'e ndoikomo'ãi**ha***.
ha'e nd-o-iko-mo'ã-i-ha
I.say NEG-3.ACT-be-NEG.FUT-NEG-NMLZ
'I say that there will not be (one).'

*Aikuaa cherayhu**ha***.
ai-kuaa   che-r-ayhu-ha
1SG.ACT-know 1SG.INACT-POSSM-love-NMLZ
'I know that you/s/he/they love(s) me.'

*Peimo'ãpiko che aju**hague** aru haguã py'aguapy ko yvyári? Ha'e peẽme ahaniri**ha**, jejoavy uvei.*
pe-imo'ã=piko che a-ju-hague   a-ru   haguã
2PL.ACT-think=Q I   1SG.ACT-come-NMLZ.PAST 1SG.ACT-bring for
py'a+guapy   ko   yvy=ári   ha'e peẽme   ahániri-ha
chest+sit   PROX.SG earth=upon   I.say to.you.PL no-NMLZ
je-jo-avy   uvei
AGD-RECP-err   rather
'Do you think that I came to bring peace upon this Earth? I tell you that no, but rather division.'

*aagradeceterei peẽme orevisita**hagué**re ikatuhaguáicha peikuaami la situación*
a-agradece-terei   peẽme   ore-visita-hague=re
1SG.ACT-thank-very.much to.you.PL   1PL.EXCL.INACT-visit-NMLZ.PAST=at
ikatu=haguã-icha   pei-kuaa-mi   la   situación
be.able=for-as   2PL.ACT-know-DIM   DET.SG   situation
'I thank you very much for visiting us so that you will know the situation a little'

268 A GRAMMAR OF PARAGUAYAN GUARANI

With the subordinator -*ha*, when the subordinate predicate has a future interpretation, this is marked directly on the predicate. This is in contrast with past interpretations that require the subordinator -*hague*.

*Aikuaa cheanduta**ha**.*
ai-kuaa　　　　che-andu-ta-ha
1SG.ACT-know　1SG.INACT-visit-FUT-NMLZ
'I know that you/s/he/they will visit me.'

Aipota repromete chéve cherayhutaha.
ai-pota　　　　re-promete　　chéve　　che-r-ayhu-ta-ha
1SG.ACT-want　2SG.ACT-promise　to.me　1SG.INACT-POSSM-love-FUT-NMLZ
'I want you to promise me that you will love me.'

By juxtaposition

This option occurs when the main subordinating predicate is a verb of command, perception, volition or permission, or in **serial verb** type constructions when the main subordinating predicate is a verb of movement.

*E**momarandu** ichupe t**ou**.*
e-mo-marandu　　　　ichupe　　　　t-o-u
IMP-MAKE1-warning　to.him/her　OPT-3.ACT-come
'Let him/her know to come.'

*Ai**pota** re**ikuaa** porã kóva . . .*
ai-pota　　　　rei-kuaa　　　porã　ko-va
1SG.ACT-want　2SG.ACT-know　good　PROX.SG-ADJZ
'I want you to know this well . . .'

*Panambi oñe**ha'ã** oñe**momombyry**.*
panambi　　o-ñe-h-a'ã　　　　　　　　　o-ñe-mo-mombyry
butterfly　　3.ACT-AGD-POSSM3-attempt　3.ACT-AGD-MAKE1-far
'The butterfly tried to move away.'

*Ha nderu piko nder**eja** reh**echa** la tele.*
ha　　nde-r-u=piko　　　　　　　　nde-r-eja　　　　　　　　　re-h-echa
and　2SG.INACT-POSSM-father=Q　2SG.INACT-POSSM-leave　2SG.ACT-POSSM3-see
la　　　　tele
DET.SG　TV
'And does your dad let you watch TV?'

Cherejántena tahami.
che-r-eja-nte-na   t-a-ha-mi
1SG.INACT-POSSM-leave-only-REQ OPT-1SG.ACT-go-PLEAD
'Please just <u>let</u> me <u>go</u>.'

Eho egueru chéve peteĩ apyka.
e-ho   e-gueru   chéve   peteĩ   apyka
IMP-go IMP-bring to.me   one   chair
'<u>Go</u> <u>bring</u> me a chair.'

Often, however, verbs of saying take a subordinate clause marked by =*haguã* 'for':

*ojerure ojapo **haguã** condonación*
o-jerure   o-japo=haguã   condonación
3.ACT-petition 3.ACT-make=for   pardon
'they beg for a pardon' (literally, 'they beg <u>for that</u> they make a pardon')

*Tupã he'i Abrahámpe ojeapi'o **haguã**.*
Tupã he'i   Abrahám=pe   o-je-api-'o=haguã
God   says   Abraham=in   3.ACT-AGD-skin-REMOVE=for
'God said to Abraham to circumcise.' (Literally, 'God said to Abraham <u>for</u> the skin to be removed.')

Interrogative/exclamative

These complement clauses express a question or an exclamation. The question/exclamation markers =*pa* and =*piko* replace the subordinator -*ha*. (Note that the same is true in the English translations.)

*Nde reikuaápa **mba'épa** oikóta ndehegui rekakuaa rire.*
nde   rei-kuaa=pa   mba'e=pa   o-iko-ta   ndehegui
you.SG   2SG.ACT-know=Q   what=Q   3.ACT-be-FUT   from.you.SG
re-kakuaa   rire
2SG.ACT-grow.up   after
'Do you already know <u>what</u> you will be after you grow up?'

*Oporandu oký**pa**.*
o-porandu   o-ky=pa
3.ACT-question   3.ACT-rain=Q
'S/he asks <u>whether</u> it is raining.'

12.2.3 Adverbial clauses

As their name makes clear, **adverbial clauses** are subordinate clauses that function as an adverb modifying the predicate in the main clause. I will give here a classification in terms of the adverbial meaning they contribute to the verb in the main clause.

12.2.3.1 Purposive

A **purposive clause** expresses the purpose or reason for the event in the main clause. The predicate of a purposive clause is marked with the stressed complementizer *haguã* 'for', positioned after the verb.

*. . . oguerekova'erã mayma garantía oikotevẽva oñedefende **haguã**.*
o-guereko-va'erã   mayma   garantía   oi-kotevẽ-va   o-ñe-defende=haguã
3.ACT-have-must   every   guarantee   3.ACT-need-ADJZ   3.ACT-AGD-defend=for
'. . . they shall have every guarantee necessary (in order) to defend themselves.'

*Peimo'ãpiko che ajuhague aru **haguã** py'aguapy ko yvyári?*
pe-imo'ã=piko   che   a-ju-hague   a-ru   haguã
2PL.ACT-think=Q   I   1SG.ACT-come-NMLZ.PAST   1SG.ACT-bring   for
py'a+guapy   ko   yvy=ári
chest+sit   PROX.SG   earth=upon
'Do you think that I came (in order) to bring peace upon this Earth?'

If the subordinate clause is negative, *ani haguã* 'so as not to' can be used, but preceding the verb. (Another option is to use the privative marker *-'ỹ*, suffixed to the subordinate predicate.) *Ani* and *haguã* do not form a single unit and can be separated by other markers.

*Oñeha'ãningo **ani haguã** ahecha.*
o-ñe-h-a'ã=ningo   ani   haguã   a-h-echa
3.ACT-AGD-POSSM3-attempt=VERD   NEG.IMP   for   1SG.ACT-POSSM3-see
'He tries not to let me watch (it).' (Literally, 'S/he does make an effort so that I will not see (it).')

*Panambi oñeha'ã oñemomombyry **ani haguã** oñeñandu vai.*
panambi   o-ñe-h-a'ã   o-ñe-mo-mombyry   ani   haguã
butterfly   3.ACT-AGD-POSSM3-attempt   3.ACT-AGD-MAKE1-far   NEG.IMP   for
o-ñe-ñandu   vai
3.ACT-AGD-feel   bad
'The butterfly tried to move away so as not to feel bad.'

anivéma haguã nerasẽ
ani-ve-ma haguã ne-r-asẽ
NEG.IMP-more-already for 2SG.INACT-POSSM-cry
'so that you don't cry anymore already'

Other possible purposive subordinators are the complex postposition *ikatu haguãicha* 'in order to be able to', and *-vo* 'as, while' (generally a marker of simultaneous events), used when the main verb encodes movement.

*. . . avei avave oikuaa'ỹre mávarepa revota, **ikatu hag̃uaicha** avave nandejopýi upe jeporavo apópe.*
avei avave oi-kuaa='ỹre máva=re=pa re-vota ikatu
also nobody 3.ACT-know=without who=at=Q 2SG.ACT-vote be.able
hag̃ua-icha avave na-nde-jopy-i upe je-poravo apo=pe
for-as nobody NEG-2SG.INACT-press-NEG MED.SG AGD-choose make=in
' … and also that nobody knows who you vote for, so that nobody pressures you in the making of that choice.'

*ovevejoa hembi'u reká**vo***
o-veve-joa h-embi-'u r-eka-vo
3.ACT-fly-all POSSM3-NMLZ.REL-ingest POSSM-seek-while
'they all flew together to look for their food' (literally, 'they all flew together while searching for their food')

*Aju aporombo'é**vo**.*
a-ju a-poro-mbo'e-vo
1SG.ACT-come 1SG.ACT-PEOPLE-teach-while
'I came to teach (everyone / the people).'[30]

The technical legal expression 'to have the right to' can be rendered by *reko derécho*, which is a calque from Spanish that contains the Spanish loanword *derécho* 'right'. The purpose complement in this expression is marked by *-vo*.

*mayma yvypóra oguereko derecho hesãi**vo***
mayma yvypóra o-guereko derecho h-esãi-vo
every person 3.ACT-have right POSSM3-health-while
'every person has the right to be healthy'.

12.2.3.2 Concessive

A **concessive clause** expresses a proposition in opposition to the one expressed by the main clause, but one that does not prevent the

---
[30] Example from Melià *et al.* (1997, 123).

proposition in the main clause being true. The main concessive subordinator is *(ramo) jepe* '(even) though', used when the subordinate clause is viewed as an impediment or hindrance to the main clause.

*Ndachekatupyrýi **ramo jepe** cheñe'ẽme, ndaupéichai hína chemba'ekuaápe.*
nda-che-katupyry-i   ramo   jepe   che-ñe'ẽ=me
NEG-1SG.INACT-skillful-NEG   if   though   1SG.INACT-language=in
nda-upe-icha-i   hína   che-mba'e+kuaa=pe
NEG-MED.SG-as-NEG   PROG   1SG.INACT-thing+know=in
'<u>Even though</u> I am not skilled in my speech, it is not so for my knowledge.'

*Ñandereta **ramo jepe**, peteĩnte Crístondive.*
ñande-r-eta   ramo   jepe   peteĩ-nte   Cristo=ndive
1PL.INCL.INACT-POSSM-numerous   if   though   one-only   Christ=with
'<u>Even though</u> we are many, we are one with Christ.'

When the concessive clause expresses a proposition that is not real, but potential, its predicate appears in the optative.

*Mayma yvypóra oguereko derecho osẽvo oimeraẽva tetãgui, taha'e **jepe** hetãtee.*
mayma   yvypóra   o-guereko   derecho   o-sẽ-vo   oimeraẽva
every   person   3.ACT-have   right   3.ACT-exit-while   anyone
t-etã=gui   ta-ha'e   jepe   h-etã-tee
NPOSSM-country=from   OPT-be   though   POSSM3-country-one's.own
'Every person has the right to exit from any country, <u>even if</u> it be his/her own country.'

The particle *rãngue* means 'instead of'.

ahárãngue, aju
a-ha-rãngue   a-ju
1SG.ACT-go-instead.of   1SG.ACT-come
'instead of going, I come'

12.2.3.3 Causal

A **causal clause** expresses content that is the cause of the proposition expressed by the main clause. The postpositions *=gui*, *=rehe* and *=rupi*, which are locative noun postpositions in their basic use, can all express this causal relation when attached to a predicate.

*Oĩ **gui** Ysyry guasu Paraguái rembe'ýre avakuéra opirakutu opaichagua pira oĩva ko ysyrýpe.*

oĩ=gui	ysyry	guasu	Paraguái	r-embe'ý=re	ava=kuéra
there.is=from	river	big	Paraguay	POSSM-edge=at	person=PL

o-pira+kutu	opa-icha=gua	pira	oĩ-va	ko	ysyry=pe
3.ACT-fish+pierce	all-as=from	fish	there.is-ADJZ	PROX.SG	river=in

'Because it is on the banks of the Paraguay River, people fish all sorts of fish that are in that river.' (Literally, 'From being on the banks . . . ')

*Fiscalía oimputa ichupe ha ita'ýrape enriquecimiento ilícito, lavado de dinero ha ijapu**rehe** declaración jave.*

fiscalía	o-imputa	ichupe	ha
district.attorney's.office	3.ACT-bring.charges	to.him/her	and

i-ta'ýra=pe	enriquecimiento	ilícito	lavado	de dinero	ha
3.INACT-son.of.father=in	enrichment	illicit	laundering	of money	and

i-japu=rehe	declaración	jave
3.INACT-falsehood=at	statement	while

'The District Attorney's Office brought charges against him and his son for illegal enrichment, money laundering, and for having lied in a statement.' (Literally, 'at having lied . . . ')

*ha'e imarangatu ha imba'ekuaaiterei **rupi***

ha'e	i-marangatu	ha	i-mba'e+kuaa-iterei	rupi
s/he	3.INACT-wise	and	3.INACT-thing+know-very.much	through

'because he was so very divine and wise' (literally, 'through being so very divine and wise')

The Spanish borrowing *porque/pórke* 'because' is often used, especially in the spoken language:

*Cheru ndacherejai, **porque** che ajapo tapiaite opa mba'e ha'e oipotáva.*

che-r-u	nda-che-r-eja-i	porque
1SG.INACT-POSSM-father	NEG-1SG.INACT-POSSM-leave-NEG	because

che	a-japo	tapia-ite	opa	mba'e	ha'e	oi-pota-va
I	1SG.ACT-make	always-very	all	thing	s/he	3.ACT-want-ADJZ

'My father hasn't abandoned me, because I always do all the things that he wants.'

12.2.3.4 Conditional

Conditional clauses express some sort of condition for the main clause to become true. The main marker for **hypothetical** conditional clauses (those that talk about hypothetical situations for the main clause to be true) is the unstressed postposition =*rõ*/=*ramo* (both variants mean the same and can be used interchangeably; that is, they are in free variation). Note that these postpositions, when stressed, have the temporal meaning 'when' (see **12.2.3.6**). Like negative relative clauses, negative conditional clauses use the regular negation circumfix or the stressed privative suffix -'ỹ.

*Cherendú**ramo** ejúke!*
che-r-endu=ramo e-ju-ke
1SG.INACT-POSSM-listen=if IMP-come-FORCE
'<u>If</u> you heard me, come!'

*Oñorairõ peteĩ delfín ohasá**rõ**, tẽra peteĩ lobo marino opukavý **rõ** ichupekuéra, tẽra y ho'ysãitereivé**ramo**.*
o-ño-rairõ peteĩ delfín o-h-asa=rõ tẽra peteĩ
3.ACT-RECP-attack one dolphin 3.ACT-POSSM3-pass=if or one
lobo marino o-puka-vy=rõ ichupe=kuéra tẽra y
sea.lion 3.ACT-laugh-ATT=if to.him/her=PL or water
h-o'ysã-iterei-ve=ramo
POSSM3-cool-very.much-more=if
'They fought <u>if</u> a dolphin passed, or <u>if</u> a sea lion smiled at them, or <u>if</u> the water was colder.'

*. . . nacherendúi**rõ** ko'ápe, cherendútantevoi rádiore . . .*
na-che-r-endu-i=rõ ko'ápe che-r-endu-ta-nte=voi
NEG-1SG.INACT-POSSM-listen-NEG=if here 1SG.INACT-POSSM-listen-FUT-only=EMPH
rádio=re
radio=at
'. . . <u>if</u> you don't listen to me here, you will certainly hear me on the radio . . .'

Counterfactual conditionals (expressing what would have occurred if something that did not happen had happened) take the unstressed postposition =*rire* 'if' to mark the predicate in the subordinate clause (the contrary-to-fact content). Note that stressed *rire* has the basic temporal meaning 'after' (see **12.2.3.6**). Additionally, both the suffixes -*va'erã* 'must' (deontic modality) and -*mo'ã* 'almost' (quasi-eventive aspect) must be used to mark the predicate in the main clause.

*Aikuaá**rire**, ahava'erãmo'ã.*
ai-kuaa=rire a-ha-va'erã-mo'ã
1SG.ACT-know=if 1SG.ACT-go-must-ALMOST
'<u>If</u> I <u>had</u> known it, I <u>would have</u> gone.'

Ndokýirire, ahava'erãmo'ã.
nd-o-ky-i=rire   a-ha-va'erã-mo'ã
NEG-3.ACT-rain-NEG=if   1SG.ACT-go-must-ALMOST
'If it had not rained, I would have gone.'

*Ikatuete porã **va'erãmo'ã** ndahkrivíri ko novéla nachemokyre'ỹi **rire ramo** Juan Bautista Rivarola Matto.*
ikatu-ete   porã   va'erã-mo'ã   nd-a-hkrivi-ri   ko   novéla
be.able-very good   must-ALMOST   NEG-1SG.ACT-write-NEG   PROX.SG   novel
na-che-mo-kyre'ỹ-i   rire   ramo   Juan Bautista Rivarola Matto
NEG-1SG.INACT-MAKE1-up.to.it-NEG   after   if   Juan Bautista Rivarola Matto
'It is very likely that I would not have written this novel, if I hadn't been encouraged by Juan Bautista Rivarola Matto.'

12.2.3.5 Manner

Manner clauses express the way in which the event in the main clause unfolds. The predicate in the subordinate clause is marked with the stressed nominalizing suffix *-ha* (*-hague* for expressing the past tense in the subordinate clause), followed by *-icha* 'as'.

*ejapo katu reipota**háicha***
e-japo   katu   rei-pota-ha-icha
IMP-make   just   2SG.ACT-want-NMLZ-as
'do (it) as you want / do whatever you want'

*Tojapo ere**haguéicha**.*
t-o-japo   ere-hague-icha
OPT-3.ACT-make   2SG.ACT.say-NMLZ.PAST-as
'Let him/her do it as you said.'

Manner clauses marked with *-'ỹre(he)* 'without' express a kind of conditional result (resultative/conditional meaning).

*Ndajapomo'ãvéima péicha . . . añeñanduvai'**ỹre** ajapo jave hína.*
nd-a-japo-mo'ã-ve-i-ma   pe-icha
NEG-1SG.ACT-make-NEG.FUT-more-NEG-already   MED.SG-as
a-ñe-ñandu-vai-'ỹre   a-japo   jave   hína
1SG.ACT-AGD-feel-bad-without   1SG.ACT-make   while   PROG
'I will not do it like that anymore . . . without feeling bad while I do it.'

12.2.3.6 Temporal

Temporal clauses express the relative timing of the events indicated in the main and subordinate clauses. The sequential order of events is important in choosing a subordinating temporal particle.

Simultaneity of main and subordinate event

*Ahá**ramo** aguerabáta ndeao.*
a-ha=ramo   a-gueraha-ta   nde-ao
1SG.ACT-go=when   1SG.ACT-carry-FUT   2SG.INACT-clothes
'<u>When</u> I go, I will bring your clothes.'

*Oma'ẽ hesekuéra, ohechakuaá**vo** oikuaaporãitereiha.*
o-ma'ẽ   hese=kuéra   o-h-echa+kuaa-vo
3.ACT-look.at at.him/her=PL   3.ACT-POSSM3-see+good-while
oi-kuaa+porã-iterei-ha
3.ACT-know+good-very.much-NMLZ
'S/he looked at them, realiz<u>ing</u> that they knew (it) very well.'

*Oikó**vo** peteĩ yvyrarehe, ojejuhu peteĩ ysóndive.*
o-iko-vo   peteĩ   yvyra=rehe   o-je-juhu   peteĩ   yso=ndive
3.ACT-be-while   one   tree=at   3.ACT-AGD-find one   caterpillar=with
'<u>As</u> it was pacing around a tree, it ran into a caterpillar.'

*Rokaru **aja** oğuahẽ oreru.*
ro-karu   aja   o-ğuahẽ   ore-r-u
1PL.EXCL.ACT-eat(intransitive)   during   3.ACT-arrive 1PL.EXCL.INACT-POSSM-father
'<u>While</u> we ate, our father arrived.'

*Peteĩ mitãñepyrũ ha'e pe memby okakuaáva 8 arapokõindy peteĩha **jave**.*
peteĩ   mitã+ñepyrũ   ha'e   pe   memby   o-kakuaa-va
one   child+begin   be   MED.SG   child.of.woman   3.ACT-grow.up-ADJZ
8   ara-po+kõi-ndy   peteĩ-ha   jave
8   day-five+two-collective   one-TH   during
'An embryo is the child that grows <u>during</u> the first 8 weeks.'

Marking that one event precedes another

*Pohãnohára he'i jakaru **mboyve** jajepohéiporãva'erãha.*
pohãno-hára   he'i   ja-karu   mboyve
cure-NMLZ.AG   says   1PL.INCL.ACT-eat(intransitive)   before
ja-je-po+héi+porã-va'erã-ha
1PL.INCL.ACT-AGD-hand+wash+good-must-NMLZ
'Doctors say that we should wash our hands well <u>before</u> we eat.'

*Napeñangarekóiramo pendejehe, jepe pende rekove opa **peve**, pemanova'erã.*
na-pe-ñangareko-i=ramo   pendejehe   jepe   pende-r-ekove
NEG-2PL.ACT-take.care.of-NEG=if at.yourselves though 2PL.INACT-POSSM-life
o-pa=peve   pe-mano-va'erã
3.ACT-end=until   2PL.ACT-die-must
'If you do not take care of yourselves, even until your life ends, you will perish.'

Marking that one event follows another

*Mitãkuéraniko, okakuaapa **vove**, ovevepa.*
mitã=kuéra=niko   o-kakuaa-pa   vove   o-veve-pa
child=PL=VERD   3.ACT-grow.up-all   during 3.ACT-fly-all
'As soon as they are all grown up, children all fly.'[31]

*Nde reikuaápa mba'épa oikóta ndehegui rekakuaa **rire**.*
nde   rei-kuaa=pa   mba'e=pa   o-iko-ta   ndehegui
you.SG   2SG.ACT-know=Q what=Q   3.ACT-be-FUT   from.you.SG
re-kakuaa   rire
2SG.ACT-grow.up   after
'Do you already know what you will be after you grow up?'

*Mba'éichapa rembo'évaerã mitã onace **guive** 7 años peve.*
mba'éicha=pa   re-mbo'e-vaerã   mitã   o-nace   guive   7 años   peve
how=Q   2SG.ACT-teach-must child   3.ACT-be.born   since   7 years until
'How you must teach a child from when s/he is born until 7 years (of age).'

12.2.3.7 Locative

Locative clauses give information about the place where the events expressed by the subordinate and main predicates occur. They use the locative nominalizer *-ha*, followed by a postposition of place that indicates the exact relation between the location and the predicate.

*Kuña guápa oĩ**hápe**, mba'ekue jepe overajey.*
kuña   guápa   oĩ-ha=pe   mba'e-kue   jepe   o-vera-jevy
woman   industrious there.is-NMLZ=in   thing-POST   though 3.ACT-shine-again
'Where there is an industrious woman, even old things shine again.'
(This is a common Paraguayan saying.)

---

[31] Example from Melià *et al.* (1997, 196).

*Roguerohory guarani jeporu umi ndoikekatuiri**hápe**.*
ro-guero-h-ory   guarani   je-poru   umi
1PL.EXCL.ACT-MAKE.SOC-POSSM3-joy   Guarani   AGD-use   NPROX.PL
nd-o-ike-katu-iri-ha=pe
NEG-3.ACT-enter-be.able-NEG-NMLZ=in
'We celebrate the use of Guarani <u>in places where</u> it is not (commonly) used.'

*Pe mitã oju isy oju**hágui**.*
pe   mitã   o-ju   i-sy   o-ju-ha=gui
MED.SG   child   3.ACT-come   3.INACT-mother   3.ACT-come-NMLZ=from
'That child comes <u>from where</u> his/her mother comes.'[32]

This marker *-ha* can also be used for states of being (note also the appearance of *=guare* to indicate a past state and the fact that it is a relative clause functioning as a noun, not an adverbial clause in this case).

*Ka'u**hape**guare ndoikéi.*
ka'u-ha=pe=guare   nd-o-ike-i
get.drunk-NMLZ=in=from.PAST   NEG-3.ACT-enter-NEG
'What happened <u>in a state of</u> drunkenness does not count.'

---

[32] Example from Palacios Alcaine (1999, 87). I have kept the forms *oju* and *ojuhágui* as they appear in the original source, even though the verb 'to come' is irregular in Guarani and has the third person form *ou*, not *oju*.

13
Information structure

Sentences are organized with respect not only to their syntax; that is, what the verb, subject, object and other arguments or modifiers are. The way a sentence is built also needs to make clear what information is most relevant to the hearer, as well as what in the sentence constitutes background to situate this important information. This is called **information structure**. The group of words that represent the most relevant information conveyed by a sentence are its **focus** (plural **foci**), whereas the group of words that serve as background to this information are its **topic**.

In Guarani the marking of topics and foci is carried out by a combination of different means: prosodic (intonation, pauses), morphological (affixes, clitics, particles in general) and syntactic (word order). Prosodic marking is often the only cue to the information structure of an utterance, and sometimes no cue is present other than the discourse context and/or general extralinguistic knowledge. This makes it hard to illustrate information structure properties with written decontextualized examples. Where possible, I will give a prior utterance to help contextualize the examples.

I will briefly show here some of the various morphosyntactic resources Guarani speakers have at their disposal for this kind of sentence structuring. In what follows, note that the initial position in a sentence is of paramount importance. It is usually the position of privileged elements from an information structure viewpoint, whether foci or topics.

13.1 Focus

The **focus** of a sentence carries the information that is most relevant and of primary importance in the current discourse/dialogue context. It is the only part of a sentence that must appear obligatorily so the utterance makes sense in context.

Prosodic marking of focus in Guarani relies on making the stressed syllable of the focused item (word or phrase) longer and on placing the primary intonation peak of the sentence on this very same item. (The syllable on which the primary intonation peak falls is marked in the examples in this section in SMALL CAPS). Where the focused item appears in first position in the sentence, it is often followed by a second-position clitic.

PÉvako aipota'ỹva.
pe-va=ko ai-pota-'ỹ-va
MED.SG-ADJZ=VERD 1SG.ACT-want-PRIV-ADJZ
'That is what I don't want.'[33]

KÓva ahechaukamanteva'ekue peẽme opa cherembiapópe.
ko-va a-h-echa-uka-mante-va'ekue
PROX.SG-ADJZ 1SG.ACT-POSSM3-see-MAKE2-only-PAST
peẽme opa che-r-embi-apo=pe
to.you.PL all 1SG.INACT-POSSM-NMLZ.REL-make=in
'This I have made you see (=have shown to you) in all my work.'

AñeTÉpiko apu'ãva'erã.
añete=piko a-pu'ã-va'erã
true=Q 1SG.ACT-get.up-must
'Do I really have to get up?'

The unstressed clitic =*nte* often co-occurs with items in focus.

Nandévei rohenói, JUANpente
na-ndéve-i ro-h-enói Juan=pe-nte
NEG-to.you.SG-NEG 1>2SG-POSSM3-call Juan=in-only
'It wasn't you who I was calling, but Juan.'[34]

CHÉnte ajapo chepohãrã.
che-nte a-japo che-pohã-rã
I-only 1SG.ACT-make 1SG.INACT-medicine-DEST
'I myself/I alone make my remedies.'

Contrastive focus is a special type of focus that contradicts previous or expected information. It can be signalled by various means, but most importantly, it is always accompanied by a strong intonation peak and stress.

---

[33] Example from Melià *et al.* (1997, 112).
[34] Example from Cadogán (1987, 129).

Overt subject pronoun

Remember that subjects are often omitted from a sentence in Guarani, when it is apparent in the context who is realizing an action (subject drop). Therefore, when a subject noun phrase or an independent subject pronoun appear overtly, this often signals that they are the focus of the sentence, especially in cases of contrastive focus.

Eremína ichupe NDE.
ere-mi-na   ichupe   nde
2SG.say-PLEAD-REQ   to.him/her   you.SG
'You tell her.' (Not somebody else.)

Áğa jasypahápe, NDE reñomongetáta hendive.
áğa   jasy+pa-ha=pe   nde   re-ño-mongeta-ta   hendive
now   moon+end-NMLZ=in   you.SG   2SG.ACT-RECP-converse-FUT   with.him/her
'But at the end of the month, you (not me) will discuss it with him.'

Second-position particle

Because the first item in a sentence occupies this privileged position, the appearance of any second-position particle serves to delimit a possible focus of the sentence. For example, a focused phrase may be marked by the attachment of an evidential particle, since some evidentials may prefer to attach to the focused phrase to clarify what the evidential is referring to.

*-Pintura ohechauka ñandéve mba'éichapa mitã reko. - ¡Chéverõ ğuarã, oñoMI **katu** ichupe!*
pintura   o-h-echa-uka   ñandéve   mba'éicha=pa   mitã
painting   3.ACT-POSSM3-see-MAKE2   to.us&you   how=Q   child
r-eko   chéve=rõ   ğuarã   o-ñomi   katu   ichupe
POSSM-essence   to.me=if   for   3.ACT-hide   just   to.him/her
- 'Painting shows us kids' personality.' - 'In my opinion, it COVERS it!'

*Ko'ã mba'E **hína** la omongy'áva yvyporakuérape, ndaha'éi okaruhaguére ojepohei'ỹre.*
ko'ã   mba'e   hína   la   o-mo-ngy'a-va   yvypóra=kuéra=pe
PROX.PL   thing   PROG   DET.SG   3.ACT-MAKE1-dirty-ADJZ   person=PL=in
nda-ha'e-i   o-karu-hague=re   o-je-po+héi='ỹre
NEG-be-NEG   3.ACT-eat(intransitive)-NMLZ.PAST=at   3.ACT-AGD-hand+wash=without
'THESE THINGS are the ones that befoul people, (it is) not eating without washing one's hands.'

*Ndaha'ei ne rãi ahecháva, yvÁga **voi** ahecha nde rehe ama'ẽrõ.*

nda-ha'e-i	ne-r-ãi		a-h-echa-va		yvága	voi
NEG-be-NEG	2SG.INACT-POSSM-tooth		1SG.ACT-POSSM3-see-ADJZ		sky	EMPH

a-h-echa	nde=rehe	a-ma'ẽ=rõ		
1SG.ACT-POSSM3-see	2SG.INACT=at	1SG.ACT-look.at=when		

'It isn't your teeth that I see, <u>it is</u> the sky <u>that</u> I see when I look at you.'

13.2 Topic

The **topic** is the group of words that, intuitively, provides a background for the focus. That is, it tells us what the focus refers to, or what it says something about. Contrary to the focus, the topic can and indeed often is absent from an utterance, because it is understood or recoverable from the discourse or dialogue context. When the topic appears, however, it can be in first position, followed by a second-position clitic, and it often contains a secondary intonation peak (not marked in the examples).

*¡Akãrapu'ã! **Akãrapu'ã** ningo umi viajes espaciales kuéra, ndaha'éi nde ru almacen*

akãrapu'ã	akãrapu'ã=ningo	umi	viajes	espaciales=kuéra	nda-ha'e-i
progress	progress=VERD	NPROX.PL	trips	spatial=PL	NEG-be-NEG

nde-r-u	almacen
2SG.INACT-POSSM-father	grocery.store

'Progress?! <u>Progress</u> is those space trips, not your dad's grocery store.'

Similar to a contrastive focus, a **contrastive topic** marks a contrast with previous or subsequent topics. This is very similar to using the English expressions 'and as for . . .' or 'and what about . . . '. In the examples that follow, note how something important is going to be said about a new topic each time.

No morphological or syntactic marking

*Ha **nemembykuña'i** moõ?*

ha	ne-memby+kuña-'i		moõ
and	2SG.INACT-child.of.woman+woman-DIM		where

'And <u>(as for) your little daughter</u>, where (do we put her)?'

Second-position particle

As was mentioned above for focus, note that none of these are dedicated topic markers. Rather, they are more general markers with different functions that prefer to follow the first word or phrase in the sentence.

*Carlos omboguatakuaa kóche, traytor **katu** nomboguatakuaái.*
Carlos	o-mbo-guata-kuaa	kóche	traytor	katu
Carlos	3.ACT-MAKE1-walk-know	car	tractor	just

n-o-mbo-guata-kuaa-i
NEG-3.ACT-MAKE1-walk-know-NEG

'Carlos can drive a car, but <u>a tractor</u>, he cannot drive.'

*Tomasa oipota ojuhu peteĩ iñirũrã neporãva. Toma **katu** oipota oiko ichugui ballenakuéra mburuvicha.*
Tomasa	oi-pota	o-juhu	peteĩ	iñ-irũ-rã
Tomasa	3.ACT-want	3.ACT-find	one	3.INACT-friend-DEST

ne-porã-va	Toma	katu	oi-pota	o-iko	ichugui
SUP-beautiful-SUP	Toma	just	3.ACT-want	3.ACT-be	from.him

ballena=kuéra	mburuvicha
whale=PL	leader

'Tomasa wanted him to find a very beautiful partner, whereas <u>Tomás</u> wanted him to be the leader of the whales.'

*Ndaipóri tembiapo ivaíva. Pe ivaíva **ningo** ñamba'apo va'ẽraha.*
ndaipóri	t-embi-apo	i-vai-va	pe
there.is.not	NPOSSM-NMLZ.REL-make	3.INACT-bad-ADJZ	MED.SG

i-vai-va=ningo	ña-mba'apo-va'ẽra-ha
3.INACT-bad-ADJZ=VERD	1PL.INCL.ACT-work-must-NMLZ

'There is no work that is bad. <u>What is bad</u> is that we have to work.'

14
Order of affixes, clitics and other particles in the predicate

Recall that we said in **1.5** that Guarani is an agglutinative language. This means that the meanings that would be expressed in English by separate words are instead expressed by successively adding affixes, clitics or other particles to a root. Because of this, it if very important to know which order these morphemes must follow when added. Although this is a complex issue which can only be cursorily discussed here, some general guidelines can be given. First, we must note that the portion to the left of a predicate (where prefixes go) is smaller and better defined (morphosyntactically and prosodically) than that to the right.

In the left portion, if the optative prefix *t-* or any of its variants is present, it precedes all other prefixes. Active and inactive person/number markers (including the second-person singular imperative *e-*) are always prefixed, and follow the optative (the only person marker that is not prefixed is the third-person subject pronoun *hikuái*, which comes after the verb and is placed outside the predicate proper).

*To*purahéi.
t-o-purahéi
OPT-3.ACT-sing
'May s/he/they sing.'

Tereğuahẽ porãite.
te-re-ğuahẽ   porã-ite
OPT-2SG.ACT-arrive   well-very
'Welcome.' (To one person.)

Person markers are themselves followed by voice markers, if any. The antipassive prefixes *poro-* and *mba'ẽ-* always come before all other voice prefixes. The relative position of any remaining voice prefixes is determined by the order in which they have to be put together to derive the intended meaning (except for the causative for transitive verbs *-uka*, which comes after the verb). The following pairs of examples illustrate this point:

*a**ñemo**mano*
a-ñe-mo-mano
1SG.ACT-AGD-MAKE1-die
'I feign being dead' (literally, 'I make myself dead')

*aporo**mbo**jeharu*
a-poro-mbo-je-haru
1SG.ACT-PEOPLE-MAKE1-AGD-spoil
'I make people frustrated'

*ro**ñombo**vy'a*
ro-ño-mbo-vy'a
1PL.EXCL.ACT-RECP-MAKE1-joy
'we make each other happy'

*aporo**moño**rairõ*
a-poro-mo-ño-rairõ
1SG.ACT-PEOPLE-MAKE1-RECP-attack
'I make people fight (one another)'

*aporo**mbojo**juhu*
a-poro-mbo-jo-juhu
1SG.ACT-PEOPLE-MAKE1-RECP-find
'I make people meet one another.'[35]

Any nominalizers that may be necessary to turn a verb into a noun or an adjective come next, if the predicate is non-verbal. And last and closest to the root, since they serve to form a complex root, come any incorporated nouns (see 11). This exhausts all the possibilities for morphemes that precede a verb. The reader must bear in mind, however, that of all these possible logical combinations, only some make sense once the meaning of each added morpheme is taken into consideration.

---

[35] Examples from de Canese and Acosta Alcaraz (2007, 115).

toñembojeroviákena nderéra
t-o-ñe-mbo-jerovia-ke-na nde-r-éra
OPT-3.ACT-AGD-MAKE1-believe-FORCE-REQ 2SG.INACT-POSSM-name
'hallowed be thy name' (literally, '<u>be</u> your name <u>made</u> belief')

toñombojovahéi
t-o-ño-mbo-j-ova-héi
OPT-3.ACT-RECP-MAKE1-AGD-face+wash
'that they/let them make each other wash their faces'

The remaining morphemes follow the predicate root (the suffixes and enclitics, and any other postverbal particles). The portion to the right of the predicate presents many more options. Often, the right edge of an agglutinating predicate may be indicated by the presence of second-position clitics such as interrogative markers (see **8.5**) or evidential markers (see **7**). In the example below, the interrogative enclitic =*piko* signals the right edge of the predicate complex *rehekajevýma*:

Rehekajevýmapiko chera'y re'uva'erã.
re-h-eka-jevy-ma=piko che-r-a'y
2SG.ACT-POSSM3-seek-again-already=Q 1SG.INACT-POSSM-son.of.man
re-'u-va'erã
2SG.ACT-ingest-must
'You are already looking again for something to eat, my son?'

The negation circumfixes can also mark the left and right edges of the predicate complex (see **4.9**).

ndoroguatasevéi
ndo-ro-guata-se-ve-i
NEG-1PL.EXCL.ACT-walk-want-NEG
'we do not want to walk more'

However, many particles can appear outside of these positions, depending on how much of the predicate they modify. Inside the predicate's right portion, any derivational suffixes, such as the verbalizer -*'o*, come first. The transitive causative -*uka* follows. The roots *porã* 'good, well', *vai* 'bad(ly)' and *kuaa* 'to know' can also follow this (possibly derived) root to indicate (in)ability. The totalitive -*pa/-mba* can appear here (followed by imperative modalizers if the sentence is in an imperative or optative mood). The stressed volitional -*se* comes next, and degree and comparative markers (except the intensifier *-(e/i)te*) follow. Future tense markers can come next.

*-¡Po'akã'**oukapáta**! -oñarõ karai Rréi.*
po-'akã-'o-uka-pa-ta   o-ñarõ karai rréi
1>2PL-head-REMOVE-MAKE2-all-FUT 3.ACT-attack gentleman king
'"I will have all your heads chopped off!", yelled the King.'

The remainder of the right portion is not as strictly ordered. At this point, the suffixal negations *-(r)i* or *-'ỹ* may be added, followed by the intensifier *-(e/i)te*, the nominalizers/complementizers *-va* and *-ha*, and then the various indicators of tense, aspect, mood, modality and evidentiality. Other subordinators follow at the end.

 Note, however, that these regular orders are only approximations, and can be subverted under ill-understood conditions. For example, many morphemes that have been presented here (and in traditional Guarani grammars as well) as suffixes that attach to the end of a predicate can appear detached from the predicate, and even in front of it. Compare the following two equally acceptable examples:

*Ikane'õ**etereímavaicha**.*
i-kane'õ-eterei-ma-váicha
3.INACT-tiredness-very.much-already-seems
'S/he seems already very tired.'

***Etereímavaicha** ikane'õ.*
eterei-ma-váicha i-kane'õ
very.much-already-seems 3.INACT-tiredness
'S/he seems already very tired.'

This is particularly clear with the variable placement of imperative modalizers (see **4.10.3.1.2**):

*Amo kotýpe**na** pemoĩmi.*
amo koty=pe-na pe-moĩ-mi
DIST.SG room=in-REQ 2PL.ACT-put-PLEAD
'<u>Please</u>, put it in that room.'

Amo kotýpe pemoĩmína.
amo   koty=pe   pe-moĩ-mi-na
DIST.SG   room=in   2PL.ACT-put-PLEAD-REQ
'Please, put it in that room.'

The reader is well advised to take the ordering and placement rules given here as guidelines, and to remember that exposure to as many texts and dialogues in Guarani as possible is the best way to familiarize oneself with the language.

15
Common vocabulary

15.1 Food

aratiku	'chirimoya'
avakachi	'pineapple'
avati	'corn'
avatimirĩ	'wheat'
chipa	'small starch and cheese bread rolls'
chipa guasu	'a kind or corn souffle with cheese' (very different from *chipa*)
hi'apy	'food, foodstuff'
jety	'sweet potato'
jopara	'corn and bean stew'
karatĩ	'potato'
kumanda	'beans'
kure ro'o	'pork'
mamóne	'papaya'
mandi'o	'manioc'
manduvi	'peanut'
mbeju	'a starch and cheese flatbread'
mbokaja	'coconut palm'
mbokaja'a	'coconut' (fruit)
mbujape	'bread'
merõ	'melon'
narã	'orange'
pakova	'banana'
pira	'fish'
ryguasu ro'o	'chicken'
sevói	'onion'
sevoiry	'garlic'

sópa paraguái	'a kind of corn bread' (note: despite the Spanish word 'sopa' in the name, this is not a soup)
takuare'ẽ	'sugar cane'
tembi'u, rembi'u, hembi'u	'food, meal'
týra	'breads or sides to accompany a meal'
vaka ro'o	'beef'
vori	'a thick soup with cheese and cornmeal balls'
yva he'ẽ	'watermelon'
yva	'fruit; apple'
yvapytã	'strawberry'

15.2 Body parts

ahy'o	'throat'
ajúra	'neck'
akã	'head'
ape	'back'
apysa	'(inner) ear'
atĩ	'temple'
ati'y	'shoulder'
atúa	'nape of the neck'
aty	'temple'
áva	'hair'
juru	'mouth'
jyva	'arm'
jyvanga	'elbow'
káma	'breast; nipple'
kangue	'bone'
korasõ	'heart'
kũ	'tongue'
ku'a	'waist'
kuã	'finger'
kupy	'shin'
nambi	'(outer) ear'
ñe'ã	'heart'
po	'hand'
puru'ã	'navel'

py	'foot'
py'a	'stomach; heart'
pyapy	'wrist'
pysã	'toe'
pyta	'heel'
pytasã	'Achilles tendon'
pytasãngue	'ankle'
pyti'a	'chest'
syva	'forehead'
tague/rague/hague	'hair'
tãi/rãi/hãi	'tooth'
tãimbíra/rãimbíra/hãimbíra	'gingiva, gum'
tako/rako/hako	'vagina'
takuãi/rakuãi/hakuãi	'penis'
tañykã/rañykã/hañykã	'jaw, chin'
tapi'a/rapi'a/hapi'a	'testicle; penis'
tapypa'ũ/rapypa'ũ/hapypa'ũ	'lap (front part of lower trunk and thighs when seated)'
tatu	'vulva'
tatypy/ratypy/hatypy	'cheek'
ta'ỹi/ra'ỹi/ha'ỹi	'testicle'
tembe/rembe/hembe	'lip'
tembo/rembo/hembo	'penis'
tendyva/rendyva/hendyva	'beard'
tenymy'a/renymy'a/henymy'a	'knee'
tenypy'ã/renypy'ã/henypy'ã	'knee'
tesa/resa/hesa	'eye'
tete/rete/hete	'body'
tetyma/retyma/hetyma	'leg'
tevi/revi/hevi	'anus'
teviro'o/reviro'o/heviro'o	'buttocks'
titi	'nipple; breast'
tĩ	'nose'
topea/ropea/hopea	'eyelash'
tope(pi)/rope(pi)/hope(pi)	'eyelid'
tova/rova/hova	'face'
továi/rovái/hovái	'forehead'
tuguy/ruguy/huguy	'blood'
tumby/rumby/humby	'hip'

tumbyro'o/rumbyro'o/humbyro'o	'buttocks'
tye/rye/hye	'abdomen, belly'
tyvyta	'eyebrow'
uvã	'thigh'
uvãkangue	'femur'

15.3 Senses

apysa	'hearing'
he'andupáva	'taste'
hetũha	'smell'
pokoandu	'touch'
techapy	'sight'

15.4 Numbers

Note: only the numbers from 1 to 4 are from pre-contact Guarani and are the only ones in common use. In general, speakers use Spanish numbers above 4 or 5.

peteĩ	1
mokõi	2
mbohapy	3
irundy	4
po	5
pa	10
sa	100
su	1,000
sua	1,000,000

15.5 Kinship terms

Note: pre-contact Guarani had an extensive kinship system. Today, except for the most common terms in this list, speakers generally use Spanish kinship words.

jarýi	'grandmother'
jaryisy	'great-grandmother'
kypy'y	'a woman's younger sister'
kyvy	'a woman's brother'
kyvyraty	'a woman's brother's wife'
machu	'grandmother'
memby	'a woman's child'
ména	'husband'
menarã	'boyfriend, fiancé'
ñembokiha	'girlfriend'
óga(y)gua	'relative; family'
sy	'mother'
ta'ýra/ra'y/ita'ýra	'a man's son'
taita	'father'
taitachu	'great-grandfather'
taita guasu	'grandfather'
tajýra/rajý/itajýra	'a man's daughter'
tamói/ramói/hamói	'grandfather; ancestor'
teindy(ra)/reindy/heindy	'a man's sister'
tembireko/rembireko/hembireko	'wife'
tembirekorã/rembirekorã/hembirekorã	'fiancée'
temiarirõ/remiarirõ/hemiarirõ	'grandchild'
tovaja/rovaja/hovaja	'brother-in-law'
túva/ru/itúva	'father'
tyke'y(ra)/ryke'y/hyke'y	'a man's older brother'
tyke(ra)/ryke/hyke	'a woman's older sister'
tyvýra/ryvy/ityvýra	'a man's younger brother'
tyvyraty/ryvyraty/ityvyraty	'a younger brother's wife'
uke'i	'sister-in-law'

15.6 Animals

aguara	'fox'
guasu(tĩ), guasuvira	'deer'
jagua	'dog'
jaguarete	'tiger'
jatyta	'snail'
karãu	'ibis'
karumbe	'tortoise'
kavaju	'horse'

kavara	'goat'
kure	'pig'
kururu	'frog; toad'
kyju	'cricket'
leõ	'lion'
mainumby	'hummingbird'
mbarakaja	'cat'
mberu	'fly'
mbói	'snake'
mborevi	'tapir'
mburika	'donkey'
mbyju'i	'swallow'
muã	'firefly'
mykurẽ	'weasel'
ñakyrã	'cicada'
ñati'ũ	'mosquito'
ovecha	'sheep'
panambi	'butterfly'
pira	'fish'
pykasu	'pigeon'
ryguasu	'chicken'
sañarõ	'a kind of blue-green bee'
sevo'i	'earthworm'
tahýi	'ant'
tarave	'cockroach'
tarekaja	'turtle'
tatu	'armadillo'
teju	'lizard'
tuku	'grasshopper'
vaka	'cow'
ynambu	'tinamou'
yso	'caterpillar'

15.7 Time

General

angepyhare	'last night'
ára	'day'
arakue	'during the day'
arapokõindy	'week'

aravo	'hora'
aravo'i	'minute'
asaje	'early afternoon'
asajekue	'during the early afternoon'
asajepyte	'noon'
jasy	'month' (literally, 'moon')
ka'aru	'mid-afternoon'
ka'aruete	'late afternoon'
ka'arukue	'during mid-afternoon'
ka'arupytũ	'dusk'
ka'arupytũvo	'at dusk'
ko'áğa / ko'ãga	'now'
ko'ára	'today'
ko'ẽambuéro	'the day after tomorrow'
ko'ẽju	'dawn'
ko'ẽmbota	'on the verge of dawn'
ko'ẽro	'tomorrow'
ko'etĩ	'dawn'
kuehe ambue pyhare	'the night before last night'
kuehe ambue	'the day before yesterday'
kuehe	'yesterday'
pyhare	'night'
pyharekue	'at night'
pyharepyte	'midnight'
pyhareve	'morning'
pyhareveasaje	'from 10 a.m. to noon'
pyharevete	'early morning'

Neologisms for the days of the week

These are composed of the word *ára* 'day' plus a cardinal number from one to seven. Note that these forms sometimes delete the first syllable of the number (apheresis).

aratẽi	'Sunday' (literally, 'day one')
arakõi	'Monday' (literally, 'day two')
araapy	'Tuesday' (literally, 'day three')
ararundy	'Wednesday' (literally, 'day four')
arapo	'Thursday' (literally, 'day five')
arapotẽi	'Friday' (literally, 'day six')
arapokõi	'Saturday' (literally, 'day seven')

Neologisms for the months of the year

These are composed of the word *jasy* 'moon' plus a cardinal number from one to twelve. Note that these forms sometimes delete the first syllable of the number (apheresis).

jasyteĩ	'January' (literally, 'moon one')
jasykõi	'February' (literally, 'moon two')
jasyapy	'March' (literally, 'moon three')
jasyrundy	'April' (literally, 'moon four')
jasypo	'May' (literally, 'moon five')
jasypoteĩ	'June' (literally, 'moon six')
jasypokõi	'July' (literally, 'moon seven')
jasypoapy	'August' (literally, 'moon eight')
jasyporundy	'September' (literally, 'moon nine')
jasypa	'October' (literally, 'moon ten')
jasypateĩ	'November' (literally, 'moon eleven')
jasypakõi	'December' (literally, 'moon twelve')

15.8 Dwelling

apyka	'chair'
guapyha	'chair'
inimbe	'cot'
japepo	'(mud) pot'
kagua	'drinking-glass'
korapy	'yard'
kosina	'kitchen'
koty	'room'
kuimbe	'spoon'
kutuha	'fork'
kypa	'fork'
kyse	'knife'
mesa	'table'
ña'ẽmbe	'plate'
óga/róga/hóga	'house'
okẽ	'door'
ovetã	'window'
tapỹi	'native dwelling, hut'
tatakua	'stove'
tatarupa	'kitchen'

teko'a	'hamlet'
tekoha	'habitat of a Guarani group'
tenimbe/renimbe/henimbe	'cot'
tupa/rupa/hupa	'bed'

15.9 Colours

aky	'green'
hũ	'black'
hũngy	'grey'
ka'irague	'brown; chestnut'
morotĩ	'white'
pytã	'red'
pytã('y)ju	'orange'
pytãngy	'pink'
pytãrovy	'lilac; purple'
pytaũ	'purple'
pytũ	'dark'
sa'yju	'yellow'
tovy/hovy/rovy	'blue; green'
tovyju/hovyju/rovyju	'yellowish green'
tovy(ka)ngy/rovy(ka)ngy/hovy(ka)ngy	'light blue'
tovyũ/rovyũ/hovyũ	'(dark) green'

16
Text samples

This chapter presents five samples from a wide variety of Guarani-language sources. We begin with a transcription of an interview conducted with a Guarani speaker. Subsequent sections present extracts from published sources: a novel, a poem, a play and a newspaper article. In these samples, Spanish loanwords and Spanish words and expressions mixed in the Guarani sentences are boldfaced, regardless of their level of integration in the language.

16.1 Interview

The following is a transcript of an interview conducted with a Paraguayan Guarani speaker in Buenos Aires, Argentina, in 2013. The research assistant interviewer (a native speaker) is represented here by A and the interviewee, who shall remain anonymous, by B. The interview was recorded and subsequently transcribed by another native research assistant and translated into English by me. Sounds not clearly heard in the recording but that may have been spoken are enclosed in parentheses in the Guarani. Parentheses are used in the English translation for clarification/explanation. Words and phrases in Spanish are boldfaced.

A: *Ajapóta nde(ve)* **unas cuantas pregunta**'*i.* 'I will ask you a few small questions.'
B: **Sí**. 'Yes.'
A: *Mba'éicha nderéra hína nde*. 'What is your name?'
B: *Carlos Vera.*[36]
A: *Carlos Vera, mboy* **año** *ereko Carlos*. 'Carlos Vera ... What age are you, Carlos?'

---

[36] Pseudonym.

B: ***Cuarenta y cuatro año***. 'Forty-four.'
A: *Ndéiko nemenda … Ne**acompañá*** … 'Are you married … or with a partner … ?'
B: *Che amenda akue, ha upéi aje**separá**jey che. Amendá **cuando tenía veintiún año** arekope amenda akue ha upéi* … 'I got married. And then, we separated. I got married when I was 21 and then …'
A: *Ko'ápe*. 'Here?'
B: *No, Paraguáipe. Ha aje**separá**je(v)y akue **doce** … **despué de doce año***. 'No, in Paraguay, and we separated after … after 12 years.'
A: *Ha ndereko ndera'y*. 'And do you have kids?'
B: *Areko*. 'I do.'
A: *Mboy ereko*. 'How many do you have?'
B: ***Primer**, **la** che **la matrimonio** amendárõ guare areko (la) peteĩ mitã kuimba'e o**nace** ha upéa omano, **ma o meno**, **en el día del parto**, **ya** omano, **el mismo día** ha upéirire o**nace** akue peteĩ mitãkuña jey ha upéi, upéa Paraguaype. Upéi ore roju ko'ápe **la** mitãkuñaíndi ha roguereko akue **la** ore róga, la Paraguáipe ha ro**paga**pa haguã péa roju ko'ápe **la** … ko'ápe ha oho porã ko'ápe ha o**nacé** jey ko'ápe mokõi mitã*. 'When I first got married, I had a boy. He was born but he died more or less on the day of delivery. He died the same day he was born, and after that, a girl was born and then … that was all in Paraguay. Then we came here with the little girl but kept our house back in Paraguay. To pay for it completely we came here, and we did well here, and two more kids were born here.'
A: *Péako ipyahú(v)a **nomá***. 'But this was with the new one (i.e., new partner).'
B: ***No**, **no**, **la** cherembireko* … 'No, no, my wife …'
A: *Reko hendie*. 'You had them with her.'
B: *Ha roju ko'ápe **la** ore rógarã **Laferrére**pe ha pe **época de** iporãve **tiempo**pe, **ma o meno**, **aunque sea** ikatu **tiempo**pe jaju ápe **uno a uno** i**tiempo**. **Entonce** rojogua ha ndoroño**entende**véi **la** che rembirekóndi **entonce**, **ma o meno**, jo … je**separá**. Che ha … ehhh … **en el dos mil uno**, **cuando** ápe ivaive **la tiempo** pe **época** ivaípe ápe **la Buenos Aires**pe, che aha pe **tiempo la** Paraguáipe. Ha uperõguare aha **dos mil uno**ma ha **hasta el dos mil sei** aiko. Ha upépe ajuhu jey upépe **la** che **acompañá**rã jey ha **desde hoy en día**, **ma o meno**, aime hendie*. 'And we came here to buy a house in Laferrere and in that happier time, more or less, at least in that time we were able to come one by one, each at different times. Then we bought the house and I didn't see eye to eye anymore with my wife so we more or less separated. And in 2001, when it was the worse time, the worst we had here in

Buenos Aires, during that time I went back to Paraguay. I was there from 2001 to 2006. And there I found my partner and up until today, more or less, I have been with her.'

A: *Mboy ndera'y,* **completo**. 'How many children do you have in total?'

B: *Ha upéandi areko pe* **primero** *guarándi, areko* **cuatro***, peteĩ* **la muerto** *ha* **tre vivo**. *Ha koánga oguereko mbohapy mitãkuña péa ko ipyahúa.* 'Well, with that partner, the first one, I had four children; the one who died and the three that are alive. And since then, I have had three more girls.'

A: *Ha ereko* ... **nieto** *perekóma?* 'And do you ... do you all have grandchildren already?'

B: **No**, *ndaguerekói*. 'No, I don't.'

A: **Ni** *peteĩ*, **ni** *pe tuichavéa oĩa ápe*. 'Not one, nor the oldest one who is here.'

B: **No**, *mba'evénte*. 'No, just nothing.'

A: *Ndépio ereko nde***hermano**. 'Do you have siblings?'

B: *Aguereko che***hermano**. 'I have siblings.'

A: **Entre** *mboy peime?* 'How many of you are there?'

B: *Ore ko* **nueve hermano** *roime*. 'We are nine siblings.'

A: **Nueve hermano**. *Ha ápe, mboy oĩ?* 'Nine siblings. And how many are here?'

B: **Ni** *peteĩ ndaipóri ko'ápe*. 'Not even one is here.'

A: *Oĩmbaite amoite*. 'They are all over there.'

B: *Oĩmbapaite amo*. 'They are all over there.'

A: *Mba'e* **la** *yma* **la** *ndekaria'y* **tiempo** *yma pe i***tiempo** *i***junto***pa péicha nde***hermano***kuérandi pejuga, mba'e* **la broma** *ipohýivéa ejapo akue nde***hermano***kuéra(pe)?* 'What did you play when you were young, back then, all together with your siblings, what bad pranks did you do to your siblings?'

B: **La** ... **mucha vece***ko* **la** *yma ore***época** *ndoikatúivoi rojapo* **la broma la** *oresy, oretúa,* **ma o meno***, siempre he'ía ore* **la** *ndoipotaimi* **la** *oñembojarúa akue*. 'Most times back then in our time we couldn't make pranks, our mom, our dad, like, they always said they didn't want to be made fun of.'

A: *Ndépio* **mayor o** *mba'e mbytere péicha*. 'Are you the oldest or are you, like, in the middle?'

B: **No**, **ma o meno**, *che aime* **de lo nueve**, **ma o meno**, **creo que el tercer hijo**, *che*. 'No, like, of the nine I am, like, I think the third child.'

A: *Nde, ha mba'e* **la** *péicha kachi'íhápe,* **de repente**, **fiesta de San Juan**-*hápe* ... 'And so, what pranks did you play during San Juan festival for example ...'

B: *Upéicha umía rojuga.* 'We played those sorts of things.'
A: *... péicha **escuela** rapére, ndape**jugá**iri oimeraẽa **broma**?* '... so on the school road, did you prank about anything?'
B: *Ro**juga**, **sí**, **porque aparte la** ore róga oiko **siempre** o**juga**, roñembojaru, rojúmia péicha **escuela** ha mba'e, ha che che mandu'a la ... ore ... che**tía** róga peteĩ oĩ **la escuela** rapére la hóga ha roikemía ro'u chugui i**pomelo** ha mba'e.* 'We played, yes, because also in our house we were always playing, making pranks, we would come from school and ... and I, I remember our ... one of my aunt's houses was on the way from school, her house, and we would go in and eat her grapefruits and such.'
A: *Hmm.* 'Hmm.'
B: *Ha upéi, peteĩ **día**pe **la** ore **compañero**kuérandi la, ro ..., yma la petỹ jejapo **cigarro** poguasu.* 'And then, one day with my friends we ... back then tobacco was made into huge cigars.'
A: *Hmm.* 'Hmm.'
B: *Ha ore upéandi pe **cigarro** poguasurã rogueraha **la** ore **compañero** jogua ogueraha **la** isýpe ojapo haguã **cigarro de hoja**.* 'So we took the tobacco that was supposed to make the huge cigars that our classmate bought to bring home to his mother so that she could make into cigars.'
A: *Hmm.* 'Hmm.'
B: *Ha ro ..., ro'e upe **la** ore **compañero**kuérandi, ñahamína onakeakuaavéa ro'e, ha **entonce** roñemoĩ ha roisu'u **la** petỹ ha romokõ **la** hykuere.* 'So we ... we told to our classmates, let's see who is the best at chewing tobacco, and then we started chewing the tobacco and we drank its juice.'
A: *Hmm.* 'Hmm.'
B: *Ha oiméne pe **do cuadra** roju, ndoroikatuvéima roguata, **porque** roka'upaite.* 'And after walking like two blocks, we could not walk anymore because we all felt very dizzy.'

16.2 Narrative

This is a fragment of the second edition of *Kalaíto Pombéro*, the first novel written entirely in Guarani, by the Paraguayan author and scholar Tadeo Zarratea.[37] The English translation is mine. The orthography is as found in the original.

---

[37] Available at https://mbatovi.blogspot.com/2011/11/kalaito-pombero-novela-en-guarani.html.

Mboja'ore I
Chapter I

Ñasaindy iporãvéva pévagui nda'iporichéne. Aipo Jasyretã mba'e ndapeichaichéne voi. Mbatovípe ñaime ramo aguĩve voínte ñaime jasýgui. Tekoha ha'eñomi okañýva Paraguái korapy yképe, pyhare mimbi porãme oguapýva opukavy, ojesareko ára ru'ãre, ha mbyja ijaguaravéva ojeitýva oñani yvagapýre oñandúvo ima'ẽ.

'There is probably no prettier moonlight than this. Not even in Jasyretã, "the country of the moon". When in Mbatovi, we are just closer to the moon. This is a solitary hamlet, lost in a corner of Paraguay, that by beautiful clear nights sits down to observe, smiling, the zenith of the heavens, while the most prideful star runs in the sky feeling its gaze.'

Yvate ko oĩhína Mbatovi, yvy kandu rusu ru'ãitépe, ajevérõ niko ndareíri pe mbyja ka'arupy hi'yvỹiete avei upépe. Remañaha gotyo upégui rehecha yvy ojehykuavo ha iñasãimane katu ñu hovy porã. Mombyry ku ojekuaa yupa guasu mbytépe ramo guáicha ka'aguy avoamimi, ha sevo'i rapéicha ysyry ñuãha, takuarembo ha yvyrahũndy. Yvy pytã porã ojehecha pe tape tujáre, péva jeko aipo Lópe rapekue, ajevérõ ikatuete porãnte oime oreko hemiñongatupy, opa ohechase'ỹva ohecháva voi hendýrõ.

'Mbatovi sits high upon a big hill, and because of that it is not strange that the evening star is also close. Looking down from there, you can see the Earth spilling out, and immediately after the beautiful green fields spreading all over. In the distance, one can see tangled woods as if sitting in the middle of a lake, and like a trail of earthworms that bundle up the creeks, willows and guaranina groves. An intense red clay makes up the old roads that are said to have been Marshal López's roads, and that is why it may just well be that they have something hidden, since their gleam can be seen by even those who do not want to see.'

Mokõi Lópe ra'yre ndaje ouraka'e yvate guio oheka jeývo ivy'aha, opyta upépe opytu'umi ha ipahápe ndohasasevéi. Oiporavóje hikuái hembirekorã Mbya-Ka'yguã iporãvéva mokõi ha oñepyrũ oñemoña.

'They say that two of López's former boys (i.e., soldiers) descended from there, looking to regain their old homeland, but they stopped for a bit and never finished crossing. It is said that they chose two of the most beautiful Mbya-Ka'yguã women to marry and began to have children.'

Areterei peve ndaje avave ndoikuaáiraka'e Mbatovi, ha mbatoviguakuéra ndoikuaái mba'evéichagua táva ambue.

'They say that for a long time nobody got to know Mbatovi, and neither did the locals know anything about other towns.'

16.3 Poem

This is a fragment of the poem *Tataypýpe*, "By the fire", by the famed Paraguayan poet Susy Delgado.[38] The English translation is mine. The orthography is as found in the original.

Tataypýpe	**By the Fire**
I	I
Peju, peguapy,	Come you all, sit down,
peja tataypýpe.	get close to the fire.
Hu'umbaraíma	The manioc and sweet potatoes
mandi'o, jety,	are almost soft now;
ka'ay hakúma,	The mate is already hot,
ko'ẽmbotaite.	it is just about to be dawn.
Che sy, tataypýpe,	Mother is busying herself
oñetrahina.	by the fire.
Che ru rupa'úme,	Father receives the hungry children
mitã vare'a.	in his lap.
Peju, peguapy	Come you all, sit down
pepaypa haguã.	to wake up.
Tataypýpe oĩma	By the fire, there is already
ja'umi va'erã,	a bit to eat
ñanemoko'ẽ	that will make us
porã va'erã . . .	wake up pleasantly . . .

---

[38] Available at http://www.portalguarani.com/394_susy_delgado/16439_tataypype_2011__junto_al_fuego__poesias_de_susy_delgado.html.

II	II
Peju, peguapy,	Come you all, sit down,
peja pejtaypýpe	get close to the fire
pejera haguã.	and you will come out of your sleep.
Peju, peguapy,	Come you all, sit down
pekiririˉmba,	and be all quiet
pejapysaka.	and listen.
Tataypýpe oúma	There has already come by the fire
oñemboapyka	and sat
yma guareita,	something to be told
mombe'upyrã.	from a long time ago.
Tataypýpe oúva	The thing that came by the fire
oñehenduka,	to make itself heard
ñanemopiriˉ,	makes us shiver,
ñanembovy'a.	makes us happy.

16.4 Theatre

This is a fragment of the first scene of *Techaga'u rei opáma*, "The longing is over", by the Paraguayan author and scholar Félix de Guarania.[39] The English translation is mine. The orthography is as found in the original. Spanish words and phrases are boldfaced.

Techaga'u rei opáma

JOSE MARIA: *Ha! Apena roheja . . . ! ha néike ne rasẽ sa'i! Pero mba'é piko ojehu ndéve . . . Oimé piko rembyasýva . . . Tẽra piko nde rasy!* 'Ha! As soon as you stay alone, you cry and cry. But what is happening to you . . . something is bothering you . . . Or are you sick?'

SERAFINA: *Mba'evéko,* **el viejo** *. . . Ani repena cherehe!* 'It's nothing, love . . . Don't worry about me.'

JOSE MARIA: *Mba'éicha ani repená piko . . .! Mba'ére piko napena mo'ãi . . . Rejere jerénte niko, ha ne ahõ mbuku ha ne rasẽ . . . Ñaimo'ã katu oiméva ne* **gente** *manó mba'e.* 'What do you mean "don't worry"? How am I not going

---

[39] Available at http://www.portalguarani.com/391_felix_de_guarania/12340__techagau_rei_opama_acto_unico__teatro_en_guarani_de_felix_de_guarania.html.

	to worry? You are just moping around, sighing and crying. As if one of yours had died . . . '
SERAFINA:	*Ha'éma niko ndéve ndaha'eiha mba'eve!* 'I've told you already it is nothing!'
JOSE MARIA:	*Mba'é tiko añete ojehu ndéve . . . Nderevy'ái piko,* **Serafina***!* 'Really, what is happening to you? Are you not happy, Serafina?'
SERAFINA:	*Ha mba'é piko reipota che mbovy'a!* 'And what do you think should make me happy?'
JOSE MARIA:	*E'a! Ha mba'e piko oime rereko'ỹva . . . Nde róga porã, re'u re'uséva, reñemonde yma ñane retãme araka'eve reñemonde'ỹ haguéicha, reñepohano nde rasýramo, ne memby kuéra hesãimba.* 'Jeez! And what is there that you don't have? You have a nice house, you eat what you want, you wear clothes that you did not wear in our country, you get better when you are sick and your children are all healthy.'
SERAFINA:	*Ani erétei . . . Ndarekopáiko hína!* 'Don't say that, I don't have everything.'
JOSE MARIA:	*Upéva katu reiete eréta chéve! Jaju guié ko tetã koápe, che ha ne memby kuéra romba'apo vaekue romoi haguã ndéve ne rekotevẽ, che señora . . .* 'Don't even say that! Since we came to this country, your children and I have worked to give you everything you need, ma'am . . .'
SERAFINA:	(**Suplicante**) *Aikuaáko, aikuaáko . . .* '(Begging) Yes, I know, I know . . .'
JOSE MARIA:	*Anichéne ere ore mo'opihá nendive . . . Ko'ága niko añete ndaha'evei iporãiteva ko* **Argentina***-pe. Sa'ive ñamba'apo haguã ha tekove repy ojupi ko'ẽre . . . Jepevénte upéicha, Ñandejára ñande rovasa ha ndaha'éi ñaikotevẽteíva . . .* 'Don't say we are stingy with you. It is true that now here in Argentina things aren't good. There is little work, prices go up . . . but even so, God blesses us and there is nothing that we need.'
SERAFINA:	*E'ána,* **Josemariá***! Cheko ndajeruréi mba'eve . . . !* 'Well, José María, I am not asking for anything!'
JOSE MARIA:	*Jaju vaekue ñande po ñane akã ári, ne mandu'ápa, ojehapypa rire ñande rógami ha heta oñeñembosarái rire ñanderehe . . . Ñaguãhẽ ko'ápe jaikuaa'ỹre mamó jaháta, mitã tavy mimi ñande rapykuéri. Mokõivéva ñañemoi ñamba'apo oimeraẽva mba'epe . . . Ha upéicha,*

	*mbegue mbeguépe ñañakarapu'ã. Ñandejára ome'ẽ jey ñandéve mokõi mitã. Ko'ágã, ha'ekuéra ome'ẽma ñandéve **niéto** . . . Mba'épo jaipotave!* 'We came with our hands on our heads, remember? After they burnt our house down and tortured us so much. We arrived here not knowing where to go, with our little children behind us. We both took up any kind of work. And that way, little by little, we reared our heads. God gave us two more children. Now they give us two grandchildren. What more can we want!'
SERAFINA:	*Ha'éma niko ndéve, **Josemariá** . . . Chéko ndaipotái mba'eve!* 'I already told you, José María . . . I do not want anything!'
JOSE MARIA:	*Mba'é katu piko aiporõ!* 'Then what?!'
SERAFINA:	*Ndavy'ái reínteko . . . Oimé nune che añoitereígui mba'e . . . Ndé niko resẽ reho ko'ẽ mboyve ha rejevy pyharéma. Nañañe'ẽmírinte jepé niko! Che memby kuérare katu niko, reí ajekóta. Omendapáma ha mombyry mbyry jaiko ojuehegui . . .* 'I am not happy, that's all. Maybe because I am always alone or something. You leave at dawn and come back already at night. We don't even talk! I cannot rely on my children either. They are all married and live really far from us.'
JOSE MARIA:	*E'a! Ha mba'e piko reipota, che áma! Tamba'apove'ỹ ha tapyta ko'ápe piko . . . Nañaiméi aveí niko upeicharãicha . . . Umi mitãre katu piko, mba'e ja'éta . . . . Guyra ipepo mbarete vove, oveve, ha ndojevyvéima haityguépe . . .* 'Jeez! And what do you want, honey? Do you want me to not work anymore to stay here with you? That is not what we are here for. And what can we say about the children? When birds get their strong wings, they fly, and they do not return to the nest anymore.'
SERAFINA:	*Ha nei, **viejo**, ani repena cherehe . . . Añe'e reipáko . . . Oime vaerã niko che guãiguĩgui reí mba'e . . .!* 'Well, honey, do not worry about me, I am just talking for nothing. Maybe it is because I am old.'
JOSE MARIA:	*Mba'éiko jajapota, **Serafina** . . . Péa niko ñande rekove . . .* 'What can we do, Serafina? This is our life.'

16.5 Newspaper article

This is an article from the online edition of *ABC Remiandu*, published on 15 March 2019.[40] Spanish words and phrases appear in boldface.

*Oñepyrũ **periodo** pyahu **sesión del Congreso**-pe*
***Contralor**, **hierro** aku **agenda parlamentaria**-pe*

> *Opytu'u rire hikuái, oñembyaty ko árape **mesa directiva** ko'ã mokõi **cámara** orekóva **tema pendiente**. Noñeakãngetái mba'épa pe ipúva **Enrique García**-gui, **juicio político** oñemombytáva **Senado**-pe. Osẽ tesape ombohapéva oikévo **seriamente contralor enriquecimiento ilícito** ha viru johéi rehe. Jepénte omotenonde **conexiones políticas**, hasýta ichupe oipykúi jesareko ko'ã mba'e ivaietéva ha umi mba'e pyahu opo jeýva.*

A new period in the session of Congress begins
The Comptroller, a "red-hot iron" (i.e., a thorny subject) in the legislative agenda

> After the break, with unfinished business, the governing boards of both legislative houses meet today. They didn't imagine what would blow up regarding Enrique García, whose impeachment has been stopped in the Senate: clues that seriously point to the Comptroller's involvement in illicit gain and money laundering. In spite of his political connections, it will be hard for them to look the other way faced with these new serious facts that have come to light.

---

[40] Available at http://www.abc.com.py/especiales/remiandu/onepyr-periodo-pyahu-sesion-del-congreso-pe-1792361.html.

17 Paradigms

17.1 List of circumfixes

n(d)(a/e/o)-... -(r)i	negation
n(d)e-... -va	superlative
ja-... -ma	completive aspect

17.2 List of prefixes

a-, (r)e-, o-, ja-/ña-, ro-, pe-	active person prefixes
e-	second-person singular imperative
ro-	portmanteau first-person agent, second-person singular patient
po-	portmanteau first-person agent, second-person plural patient
che-, n(d)e- i-, ij-, iñ-, hi- ñan(d)e-, ore-, pen(d)e-	inactive person prefixes
mba'e-	antipassive voice, non-human patient
poro-	antipassive voice, human patient
m(b)o-	causative voice for intransitive roots
gue-/re-	verbal increments (interfixes)
(gue)ro-	sociative causative voice
jo-	reciprocal voice
je-	agent-demoting voice (reflexive, passive, middle, impersonal)
-eko-	nominalizer (qualities)
-em(b)i-	nominalizer (resultative, instrumental)

t-	optative mood
t-/h-/r-	relational prefixes

17.3 List of postpositional particles

As elsewhere in the book, in the following table, a dash (-) identifies a suffix and an equals sign (=) an enclitic. These are used where there is enough evidence to decide on the correct characterization of each particle. Where the status of a particle is unclear, I present the postposition as an independent word (a free morpheme), and no dashes or equals signs are used. Suffixes are presented first, then enclitics, then putative independent words. For each postposition, I indicate whether it attracts stress or not (according to the rules in **2.2.2**).

Guarani morpheme	Stress properties	Meaning
-(e)te, -(i)te	stressed	intensifier
-(e)terei, -(i)terei	stressed	elative superlative
-ha	stressed	ordinal number
-ha	stressed	nominalizer; subordinator
-hára	stressed	agentive nominalizer
-harã	stressed	future agentive nominalizer
-hare	stressed	past agentive nominalizer
-je	unstressed	hearsay marker
-ke	unstressed	forceful imperative
-kue/-ngue	stressed	post-stative (cf. English 'ex-')
-kue/-ngue	stressed	abstract nominalizer
-ma	unstressed	'already' (completive aspect)
-mante	unstressed	'only'
-mi	stressed	habitual aspect
-mi	stressed	pleading, affectionate imperative
-mi	stressed	diminutive
-mo'ã	stressed	quasi-eventive aspect
-na	unstressed	requestative imperative, 'please'
-ne	unstressed	dubitative marker
-nga'u	unstressed	desiderative mood
-nte	unstressed	'only'; focus marker

-pa/-mba	stressed	'all'; totalitive aspect
-pavẽ	stressed	elative superlative
-pota/-mbota	stressed	immediate future
-py	unstressed	urging imperative
-py/-pýra/-mby/-mbýra	stressed	passive nominalizer
-pyrã/-mbyrã	stressed	future passive nominalizer
-pyre/-mbyre	stressed	past passive nominalizer
-rã	stressed	destinative aspect/nominal future tense
-rasa	stressed	elative superlative
-re	stressed	post-stative (cf. English 'ex-') (very infrequently used)
-rei	stressed	frustrative marker
-se	stressed	'want'
-ta	unstressed	future tense
-t(e)i	unstressed	imperative negation, prohibitive
-tee	stressed	exclusive possession
-ty/-ndy	stressed	collective plural
-uka	stressed	causative voice for transitive roots
-va	unstressed	habitual aspect
-va	unstressed	nominalizer/adjectivizer, relativizer
-va(')erã	unstressed	future relativizer; deontic future
-va(')ekue	unstressed	past relativizer
-ve	stressed	'more'
-vete	stressed	elative superlative
-vo	unstressed	simultaneity marker
-vusu	stressed	elative superlative
-vy/-ngy	stressed	attenuative
-'i	stressed	diminutive
-'o	stressed	resultative denominal verbalizer
-'ỹ, -'ỹre(he), -rehe'ỹ	stressed	'without'
=ári	stressed	'upon, on top of'
=eta, =ita	stressed	multitudinal plural
=guarã	stressed	'for'

=gui	unstressed	'from; because of'
=guive	stressed	'from a starting point; since'
=guýpe	stressed	'below'
=haguã	stressed	purposive subordinator
=(i)cha	unstressed	'like, as'
=katu	unstressed	'but; just'
=kuéra	stressed	plural enclitic
=ndi	unstressed	'with' (comitative)
=ndi(v)e	stressed	'with' (comitative)
=(n)got(y)o	stressed	'towards'
=(ni)ko, =(ni)ngo	unstressed	emphatic veridical enclitic
=(ni)mbo	unstressed	interrogative dubitative marker
=pa	unstressed	interrogative enclitic
=pe/=me	unstressed	'in, on, at, to; with (instrument)'
=peve/=meve	stressed	'to an endpoint; until'
=pi(k)o	unstressed	interrogative enclitic
=ramo	unstressed	conditional
=re	unstressed	'at, about; with (instrument)'
=rehe	unstressed	'at, about; with (instrument)'
=rehehápe	stressed	'for the sake of; on behalf of'
=rõ	unstressed	conditional
=rupi	unstressed	'around, through; because'
=(y)gua	stressed	'from, of' (provenance, origin)
aja	stressed	'during'
anga	unstressed	'poor thing' (commiserative)
gua'u	stressed	simulated or non-realized action
hína	unstressed	progressive aspect
jave	stressed	'during'
jeko	unstressed	hearsay marker
jepi	unstressed	habitual aspect
jerére	stressed	'around'
káusa	stressed	'because of (a negative cause)'
kuri	unstressed	direct evidence, usually past event
mboyve	stressed	'before'

ndaje	unstressed	hearsay marker
pópe	stressed	'with' (manner)
pype	stressed	'with' (instrument)
pýpe	stressed	'inside'
ra'e	stressed	inferential evidence, recent event
raka'e	stressed	inferential evidence, distant event
ramo	stressed	'when; instead of; just now'
rapykuéri (relational)	stressed	'behind'
rehegua	stressed	'about, in relation to'
rendápe	stressed	'next to'
renondépe	stressed	'facing'
rire	unstressed	'if'
rire	stressed	'after'
rõ	stressed	'when'
rovake	stressed	'in front of, in the presence of'
rupi	stressed	'because, thanks to, by means of'
rupive	stressed	'by means of'
voi	unstressed	emphatic marker
vove	stressed	'during'

17.4 List of morphemes with consonant allomorphs conditioned by nasal harmony

17.4.1 Affixes and clitics

Regressive nasalization on prefixes

Meaning or gloss	Non-nasal allomorph	Nasal allomorph
1PL.INCL.ACT	*ja-*	*ña-*
1PL.INCL.INACT	*ñande-*	*ñane-*
2SG.INACT	*nde-*	*ne-*
2PL.INACT	*pende-*	*pene-*
negation	*nd-* . . . *-i*	*n-* . . . *-i*
superlative	*nde-* . . . *-va*	*ne-* . . . *-va*

PARADIGMS

3.INACT	i-	iñ-
AGD	je-	ñe-
RECP	jo-	ño-
NMLZ.REL	-embi-	-emi-
'make'	mbo-, mby-, mbu-	mo-, my-, mu-

Progressive nasalization on suffixes and enclitics

Meaning or gloss	Non-nasal allomorph	Nasal allomorph
'in, on, at, to'	=pe	=me
'until'	=peve	=meve
'completely'	-pa	-mba
PL	=kuéra	=nguéra
POST	-kue	-ngue
COLLECTIVE PLURAL	-ty	-ndy
NMLZ.PASS	-py	-mby
NMLZ.PASS (PAST)	-pyre	-mbyre
NMLZ.PASS (FUTURE)	-pyrã	-mbyrã
IMMEDIATE FUTURE	-pota	-mbota
'towards'	-got(y)o	-ngot(y)o

17.4.2 Roots

As mentioned in **2.2.3**, the first voiceless stop /p/, /t/ or /k/ for some oral roots exceptionally becomes a nasal-oral consonant in combination with the nasal variant of the intransitive causative prefix *mo-* or (very rarely) with the nasal variant of the nominalizing (relational) prefix *-emi-*. It is important to know that some of these also have "regular" derivations where the voiceless stop does not change.

Cases with the causative prefix *-m(b)o*

Oral root	Meaning	Causative derivation	Meaning
ike	'to enter'	moinge	'to make enter'
iko	'to be, to exist'	moingo	'to give life; to activate'

kakuaa	'to grow (intransitive)'	mongakuaa	'to raise'
karai		mongarai	'to bless; to become initiated in something'
karáu	'sprain, dislocation'	mongaráu	'to sprain (something)'
karu	'to eat (intransitive)'	mongaru	'to feed'
ka'u	'drunkenness'	monga'u	'to get someone drunk'
ke	'to sleep'	monge	'to put to sleep'
kora	'corral'	mongora	'to enclose; to siege'
kuera	'to get healthy'	monguera	'to heal'
kuerái	'boredom, annoyance'	monguerái	'to bore someone'
kúi	'to fall; to become detached'	mongúi	'to make fall; to tear off'
kurusu	'cross'	mongurusu	'to crucify'
ku'e	'to move (intransitive)'	mongu'e	'to move (transitive); to loosen'
ku'i	'dust'	mongu'i	'to grind'
ky	'to rain'	mongy	'to make rain'
kyhyje	'fear'	mongyhyje	'to intimidate'
kyra	'fat, grease'	mongyra	'to fatten; to put oil on'
ky'a	'dirty'	mongy'a	'to make dirty; to stain'
páy	'awake'	mombáy	'to wake someone up'
pe	'flat'	mombe	'to flatten'
pi	'to cease'	mombi	'to make stop'
po'o	'to tear out'	mombo'o	'to wean'
pu	'sound'	mombu	'to burst'
tyky	'(a) drop'	mondyky	'to make drip; to distil'
tyryry	'to crawl'	mondyryry	'to break violently'

PARADIGMS

In only one case, an initial bilabial voiceless stop /p/ does not change into a bilabial nasal-oral /ᵐb/ but into the bilabial nasal /m/:

porã   'beautiful; good'   *momorã*   'to admire'

Cases with the nominalizing prefix *-embi-/-emi-*

There are only a couple of examples of nasalization with the nominalizer *-embi-*, mostly found in older Guarani texts.

Oral root	Meaning	Nominalization	Meaning
kuai	'direction, government'	*chereminguai*	'my servant'
pota	'to want'	*cheremimbota*	'my will'
porara	'passion, ire'	*cheremimborara*	'my passion'

17.5 List of relational roots and morphemes

Note: this is a non-exhaustive list. The roots are given in their absolute or non-relational form. If no irregularities are noted, the expected inflectional pattern is *t-/r-/h-*.

óga	'house'	
okẽ	'door'	
ovetã	'window'	
ta'anga	'image'	
ta'arõ	'wait'	
ta'ã	'attempt; effort'	
tague	'hair'	
tai	'line; writing'	
tái	'tooth'	
tãimbíra	'gingiva, gum'	
tãimbiti	'teeth-clenching'	
tãitarara	'teeth-chattering'	
taity	'nest'	
tajýra	'daughter.of.father'	(*rajý* POSSM, *itajýra* POSSM3)
takã	'tree branch'	
tako	'vagina'	

taku	'warmth'	
takua	'pointy'	
takuãi	'penis'	
takuvo	'sun glare'	
takuvy	'lukewarm'	
tañyka	'jaw, chin'	
tape	'road'	
tapo	'root'	
tapy	'burn'	
tapykue	'behind'	
tapypa'ũ	'lap (front part of lower trunk and thighs when seated)'	
tasa	'to pass, to cross'	
tasẽ	'cry'	
taso	'become full of maggots'	
tasy	'sickness; pain'	
tata	'fire'	
tatatĩ	'smoke'	
tatypy	'cheek'	
taviju	'fuzz, down, plush'	(cf. non-triform *aviju* 'fuzz')
tayhu	'love'	
ta'ỹi	'testicle'	
ta'ýra	'son.of.father'	(*ra'ý* POSSM, *ita'ýra* POSSM3)
techa	'sight'	
techagi	'neglect'	
techakuaa	'understanding'	
techambi	'suspicion'	
techaramo	'admiration'	
techavoi	'foreboding'	
teindy	'sister.of.male'	
teja	'abandonment'	
teka	'search'	
teko	'nature; essence; being; culture'	
tekove	'life, existence'	
tekovia	'replacement'	
tekua	'current; canal'	
tekuaty	'cavern'	
tekýi	'taking away'	
tembe	'lip'	

tembiporu	'utensil, tool'	
tembi'u	'food'	
tembo	'penis'	
temby	'surplus, excess, leftover'	
temiandu	'visit'	
tenda	'place'	
tendu	'listen'	
tendy	'saliva; fire; flame'	
tendysyry	'drool'	
tendyva	'beard'	
tenimbe	'cot'	(cf. non-triform *inimbe* 'cot')
tenimbo	'thread'	(cf. non-triform *inimbo* 'thread (not in relation to the creator of it)')
tenói	'call'	
tenonde	'in front of'	
tenyhẽ	'fullness'	
tenymy'a	'knee'	
tenypy'ã	'knee'	
teñói	'birth; sprout'	
te'o	'death'	
te'õ	'humid'	
te'ongue	'corpse'	
tepy	'price, value'	
téra	'name'	
tero	'nickname'	
tesa	'eye'	
tesãi	'health'	
tesapara	'difficulty'	
tesape	'light, clarity, illumination, ray of light'	
tesarái	'oblivion'	
teta	'quantity; many'	
tetã	'nation, country'	
tete	'body'	
tetia'e	'good humour'	
tetũ	'smell; kiss'	
tetyma	'leg'	
tevi	'anus'	
teviro'o	'buttocks'	

te'ỹi	'to scratch'	
togue	'leaf'	
toky	'sprout'	
tope	'(pea) pod; petal; eyelid'	
topea	'eyelash'	
topehýi	'sleepiness'	
topepi	'eyelid'	
tory	'bliss, joy'	
tova	'face'	
továi	'forehead'	
tovaja	'brother-in-law/sister-in-law'	
tovasa	'blessing'	
tovy	'blue'	
to'o	'meat'	(cf. non-triform *so'o* 'meat (alienable)')
to'y	'cold'	
to'ysã	'coolness'	
tu'ã	'summit'	
tuguy	'blood'	
tumby	'hip'	
tupa	'bed'	
tupã	'god'	
tupi'a	'egg'	
túva	'father'	(*ru* POSSM, *itúva* POSSM3)
tuvicha	'leader'	
ty'ái	'sweat'	
tye	'abdomen, belly'	
tyjúi	'bubble, froth'	
tykue	'juice; wet'	
tymba	'animal'	(cf. non-triform *mymba* 'domesticated animal')

Points to note:
- The postposition *rehe* 'at' takes the second form *hese* 'at him/her/it' for the third person. There are no forms **tehe* or **tese*.
- The verbal root *-upi* 'to lift' lacks an absolute form **tupi*.
- Similarly, the nominal root *-upi* 'truth' uses *rupi* or *hupi* as absolute forms.

17.6 List of aireal verbs

Note: this list is not exhaustive.

ko'õ	'to itch'
korocho'o	'to smooth out'
kotevẽ	'to need'
kuaa	'to know'
kuatia	'to write'
kutu	'to pierce'
ky'o	'to delouse'
kyra'o	'to degrease'
kytĩ	'to cut'
nupã	'to beat'
papa	'to count'
pete	'to slap'
pichãi	'to pinch'
pire'o	'to skin'
poepy	'to reward'
pohano	'to cure'
pohéi	'to wash (one's) hands'
poka	'to twist'
pokua	'to tie (someone's) hands'
pokuaa	'to get someone used to something'
popete	'to clap'
porangareko	'to esteem, to respect, to admire'
poravo	'to choose'
poriahuvereko	'to feel pity'
poru	'to use'
pota	'to want'
pyhy	'to grab'
pyso	'to extend, to stretch'
pysyrõ	'to save'
pyte	'to suck'
pytyvõ	'to help'
sambyhy	'to guide, to govern'
su'u	'to bite'
typei	'to sweep'
tyvyro	'to shake'

18
Common phrases and expressions

Heẽ.	'Yes.'
Nahániri.	'No.'
Maitei.	'Hello.'
Mba'éichapa.	'How are you?'
Mba'éichapa reiko.	'How are you?'
Iporã.	'Fine.'
Iporãnte.	'Just fine.'
Aiko porã.	'I am fine.'
Iporãiterei.	'Very well.'
Iporãrasa.	'Super.'
Ha nde?	'And you?'
Iporã avei.	'I am fine too.'
Mbaetekópa.	'What's up?'
Mbaetépio.	'What's up?'
Mba'éichapa neko'ẽ.	'How are you this morning?' (That is, 'Good morning', used immediately after getting up.)
Cheko'ẽ porã, ¿ha nde?	'This morning, fine. And you?'
Mba'éichapa nde pyhareve.	'How are you this morning?' (That is, 'Good morning', used a little later and throughout the morning.)
Chepyhareve porã.	'This morning, fine.'
Mba'éichapa ndeasaje.	'How are you this afternoon?' (That is, 'Good afternoon', used between noon and 2 p.m., roughly.)
Cheasaje porã.	'This afternoon, fine.'
Mba'éichapa ndeka'aru.	'How are you this afternoon?' (That is, 'Good afternoon', used a little later and throughout the afternoon.)
Cheka'aru porã.	'This afternoon, fine.'

321

Mba'éichapa ndepyhare.	'How are you this evening?' (That is, 'Good evening'.)
Chepyhare porã.	'This evening, fine.'
Aguyje.	'Thanks.'
Aguyje mante ndéve.	'Thank you.'
Aguyjevete. / Aguyjetaite.	'Thank you very much.'
Aguyjevete chepytyvõhaguére.	'Thank you for your help.' / 'Thank you for helping me.'
Avy'aiterei.	'I am very glad.'
Aháma.	'I'll get going now.'
Jaha. / Jahápy.	'Let's go.'
Jajohechapeve. / Jajuechapeve.	'See you later.'
Jajuecha jeýta upéi.	'See you later.'
Jajuechάta ko'ẽrõ.	'See you tomorrow.'
Japyta upéicha.	'That's the plan.'
Rejútapa orendive.	'Are you coming with us?'
Ejútapio.	'Will you come?'
Aháta aju.	'I go and come back.'
Añua kakuaa ndéve.	'Hugs.'
Tereğuahẽ porãite.	'Welcome.' (To one person.)
Tapeğuahẽ porãite.	'Welcome.' (To more than one person.)
Vy'apavẽ.	'Congratulations.'
Vy'apavẽ nerembiapóre.	'Congratulations on your work.'
Terehupyty vy'apavẽ.	'Best wishes.'
Cheñyromi.	'Sorry.'
Añembyasyiterei.	'I am sorry.'
Marãve ndoikói.	'It doesn't matter.'
Ndaipóri probléma.	'No problem.'
Ñembyasy.	'Condolences.'
Che ñembyasy.	'My condolences.'
Mba'éichapa nderéra.	'What is your name?'
Mba'éichapa nderérajoapy.	'What is your last name?'
Cheréra . . . / Cheréra hína . . .	'My name is . . .'
Péina ápe che . . .	'This is my . . .'
. . . ména	'. . . husband'
. . . rembireko	'. . . wife'
. . . irũ	'. . . friend'
. . . ru	'. . . father'
. . . sy	'. . . mother'

Avy'a roikuaahaguére.	'Pleased to meet you.'
Maitei nderúpe.	'Say hi to your father.'
Maitei ndesýpe avei.	'Say hi to your mother too.'
Karai.	'Sir.'
Kuñakarai.	'Madam.'
Kuñatai.	'Miss.'
Ndépa moõgua. / Moõguápa nde.	'Where are you from?'
Moõpa reiko hína.	'Where do you live?'
Che aiko . . .	'I live . . .'
. . . Paraguaýpe	'. . . in Asunción'
Moõpa nderóga.	'Where is your house?' / 'Where do you live?'
Moõpa opyta . . .	'Where is . . . ?'
Mbovy arýpa reguereko.	'How old are you?'
Mboy año ereko?	'How old are you?'
Aguereko . . . ary.	'I am . . . years old.'
Areko . . . año.	'I am . . . years old.'
Ndépa reñe'ẽ . . .	'Do you speak . . .'
ingléspe.	'. . . English?'
castellánope	'. . . Spanish?'
Che nañe'ẽi guaraníme.	'I don't speak Guarani.'
Che nañe'ẽporãi guaraníme.	'I don't speak Guarani well.'
Che nañe'ẽporãi gueteri guaraníme.	'I don't speak Guarani well yet.'
Astudia hína guarani.	'I am studying Guarani.'
Mba'éichapa ere. / Mba'e ere?	'What did you say?'
Nantendéi hína.	'I don't understand.'
Norontendéi hína.	'I don't understand you.'
Ikatúpa reñe'ẽ mbeguemive chéve.	'Could you speak a little slower to me?'
Mba'épa he'ise . . .	'What does . . . mean?'
Mba'éichapa oje'e . . . guaraníme?	'How do you say . . . in Guarani?'
Ajavýramo, chekorrehimína.	'If I make a mistake, please correct me.'
Cherasy.	'I am sick.'
Chekane'õ.	'I am tired.'
Chekaigue.	'I am feeling lazy.'
Chekangy.	'I am weak.'
Chekuerái.	'I am bored' / 'I am fed up.'
Chero'y.	'I am cold.'

Chevare'a.	'I am hungry.'
Chey'uhéi.	'I am thirsty.'
Chesogue.	'I am broke.'
Hi'ã chéve . . .	'It seems to me . . .'
E'a!	'Rats!' / 'Oh heck!'
Ich!	'Good grief!'
Anína! / Aníkena!	'God forbid!'
Néike!	'Go on!'
Tove!	'Let it be so!'
Opa.	'All gone.' / 'Finished.'
Péicha ha'e. / Péa ha'e.	'That's it.' / 'It is so.'
Ha upéi?	'So?' / 'And then?'
Rohayhu.	'I love you.'
Vai-vai.	'So-so.'
Mbore.	'No way.'
Nambré(na).	'Leave me alone.' / 'I am fed up.'
kape / kapelu	'buddy'
lo mitã	'guys'
lo pérro	'guys' (from Spanish *los perros* 'the dogs')
Ani ndepochy(tei).	'Don't get mad.'
Hendy kavaju resa.	'Times are tough.' (Literally, 'The horse's eyes are flashing.')
Terehóna embojahu pira mba'e.	'Get lost.' / 'Leave me alone.' / 'Stop talking nonsense.' (Literally, 'Go bathe the fish or something.')

Some sayings (*ñe'ẽnga*)

These sayings were mostly collected from Aguilera Jiménez (2007) (see Data sources).[41]

Cherehe jeýnte opẽ, he'i ipo'a'ỹva.
che=rehe   jevy-nte   o-pẽ   he'i   i-po'a-'ỹ-va
I=because again-only 3.ACT-break(intransitive) says 3.INACT-luck-PRIV-ADJZ
'It is again my fault that it broke, says the unlucky person.'

---

[41] These are also freely accessible at http://paraguayway.blogspot.com/.

(This is an expression used by someone complaining about yet another misfortune.)

Tapeho peho mandi peẽ, he'i ikasõ revi soróva.
ta-pe-ho~pe-ho   mandi   peẽ   he'i   i-kasõ
OPT-2PL.ACT-go~2PL.ACT-go once.and.for.all you.PL says   3.INACT-pants
r-evi   soro-va
POSSM-anus   break(intransitive)-ADJZ
'You all start leaving, says the one with the seat of his pants ripped.'
(This is used by somebody who does not want make others late.)

Ndokýiramoko ndotykýi, he'i hóga soropáva.
nd-o-ky-i=ramo=ko   nd-o-tyky-i   he'i   h-óga
NEG-3.ACT-rain-NEG=if=VERD   NEG-3.ACT-drip-NEG   says   3.INACT-house
soro-pa-va
break(intransitive)-all-ADJZ
'If it doesn't rain, it doesn't leak, says one with a house in ruins.'
(This is used by somebody who has made peace with an enduring problem.)

Mbokaja ha mboriahúrenteko aratiri ho'áva.
mbokaja   ha   mboriahu=re-nte=ko   aratiri   ho-'a-va
coconut.palm   and   poverty=at-only=VERD   lightning   3.ACT-fall-ADJZ
'Lightning only strikes coconut palms and the poor.'
(This expression is used to highlight the lack of protection for poor people. It can also be used to comment on a misfortune that is unlikely to happen.)

Ñaniháme aiko, jagua inambi rasóvaicha.
ñani-ha=me   a-iko   jagua   i-nambi   r-aso-va-icha
run-NMLZ=in   1SG.ACT-be dog   3.INACT-ear POSSM-become.full.of.maggots-ADJZ-as
'I am always running around, like a dog with maggots in its ear.'
(This is said by somebody who is very busy and harried.)

Pytũ ha ake, ryguasu kurúicha.
pytũ   ha   a-ke   ryguasu   kuru-icha
dark   and   1SG.ACT-sleep   hen   broody.hen-as
'(As soon as) It gets dark, I go to sleep like a broody hen.'
(This is used as an excuse not to go out late.)

Omanóta ijuru rupi, piráicha.
o-mano-ta   i-juru   rupi   pira-icha
3.ACT-die-FUT   3.INACT-mouth   through   fish-as
'By his/her mouth s/he will die, like a fish.'
(This is said of someone who cannot keep their mouth shut.)

Sambo sambo, ñanduguasu nanicha.
sambo~sambo   ñanduguasu   ñani-cha
big.stride~big.stride   ostrich   run-as
'By skips and jumps, like an ostrich's run.'
(This expression is used when something was done in a hurried manner.)

Kururúicha, typychápe oñemosẽ.
kururu-icha   typycha=pe   o-ñe-mo-sẽ
frog-as   broom=with   3.ACT-AGD-MAKE1-go.out
'He was kicked out with a broom like a frog.'
(This is said when somebody was unceremoniously kicked out of a place.)

Che sogueve kurusu léguagui.
che-sogue-ve   kurusu   légua=gui
1SG.INACT-broke-more   cross   league=from
'I am more broke than a burial cross a mile away.'
(This is used to excuse oneself from buying something or spending money on something.)

Vúrro ha kate ndopiávai.
vúrro   ha   kate   nd-o-pia-va-i
donkey   and   elegant   NEG-3.ACT-detour-ADJZ-NEG
'The donkey and the dandy do not change course.'
(This is said of somebody who stubbornly persists in an idea.)

Ojekuaave vúrro rasẽgui.
o-je-kuaa-ve   vúrro   r-asẽ=gui
3.ACT-AGD-know-more   donkey   POSSM-cry=from
'S/he is more famous than the cry of the donkey.'
(This is said when somebody is very easy to recognize from their tics or habits.)

References

Data sources

In addition to collected fieldwork data and publicly available data (from social media, web pages and so on), the following literary and academic works were consulted as primary sources of examples:

Aguilera Jiménez, Domingo. 2007. *Ñe'ẽnga. Dichos populares paraguayos*. 7th ed. Asunción: Servilibro.

Burckett-Picker, Jenifer, and Rosalba Dendia. 1999. *Ka'aguy mba'e mombe'upy. Cuentos de la selva guarani. Stories from the Paraguayan Jungle*. Asunción: Centro Editorial Paraguayo S.R.L.

Correa, Julio. 2012. *Sandía yvyguy*. Asunción: Servilibro.

Delgado, Susy. 2004. *Tataypýpe. Junto al fuego*. Asunción: Editorial Arandurã.

Ferrer, Renée. 1996. *La mariposa azul y otros cuentos. Panambi hovy ha ambue mombe'urãnguéra*. Trans. Mario Rubén Álvarez (into Guarani). Asunción: Intercontinental Editora.

Galeano Olivera, David A. 2002. *Antropología. Avakuaaty*. Asunción: Ateneo de Lengua y Cultura Guarani.

Guarania, Félix de. 2001. 'Techaga'u rei opáma'. In *Teatro paraguayo de ayer y de hoy (Tomo I A–G)*, edited by Teresa Méndez-Faith, vol. I, 352–6. Asunción: Intercontinental Editora.

Martínez Gamba, Carlos. 1971. *Pláta yvyguy*. Asunción: El Lector.

Meza, Miguel Ángel. 2010. *Perurima pypore. Las huellas de Perurimá*. Trans. Mauro Lugo (into Spanish). Asunción: Servilibro.

Quino (Joaquín Salvador Lavado). 2017. *Mafalda guaraníme 1*. Trans. María Gloria Pereira de Jacquet (into Guarani). Asunción: Servilibro.

Zarratea, Tadeo. 2010. *Kalaíto Pombéro*. Asunción: Marben. First edition 1981.

Suggested resources

Even though Paraguayan Guarani is among the two or three most widely spoken indigenous languages in the Americas, and it is the only one spoken by a non-indigenous majority, no book-length works on the language exist that are accessible to a broad English-speaking audience. For example, currently, there is no book-length general introduction to Guarani language and culture that is accessible to a non-specialist English-speaking audience. For that reason, I give below a few resources, some in languages other than English, that readers interested in learning more about Guarani may find useful.

General introductions

Palacios Alcaine, Azucena. 1999. *Introducción a la lengua y cultura guaraníes*. Valencia: Universitat de València. [In Spanish].

Zajícová, Lenka. 2009. *El bilingüismo paraguayo: usos y actitudes hacia el guaraní y el castellano*. Madrid: Iberoamericana. [In Spanish].

Phrasebooks

The only phrasebook I know of for Paraguayan Guarani is the following:

Lustig, Wolf, and Michael Blümke. 2013. *Guarani für Paraguay Wort für Wort* (Reise-Know-how Series 34). Bielefeld: Kauderwelsch/Verlagsgruppe Reise Know-How. With Audio CD. [In German].

Textbooks and online courses

Blair, Robert W., Charles R. Graham, Delbert H. Groberg, Carlos Z. Gomez, and Carlos R. Espínola. 1968. *Guarani Basic Course. Part I*. Washington, DC: Peace Corps. Online. https://files.eric.ed.gov/fulltext/ED200014.pdf.

Blair, Robert W., Charles R. Graham, Delbert H. Groberg, Carlos Z. Gomez, and Carlos R. Espínola. 1968. *Guarani Basic Course. Part II*. Washington, DC: Peace Corps. Online. https://files.eric.ed.gov/fulltext/ED200015.pdf.

Melià, Bartomeu, Luis Farré, and Alfonso Pérez. 1997. *El guaraní a su alcance*. 14th ed. Asunción: Centro de Estudios Paraguayos "Antonio Guasch" (CEPAG). [In Spanish].

Ortiz, Diego, Domingo Aguilera, and Elda Marecos. 1991. *Hablemos el guaraní. Curso completo en cuatro niveles para extranjeros. Segundo nivel*. Asunción: CEPAG. With Audio CD. [In Spanish].

Ortiz, Diego, Domingo Aguilera, and Elda Marecos. 1995. *Hablemos el guaraní. Curso completo en cuatro niveles para extranjeros. Segundo nivel*. Asunción: CEPAG. With Audio CD. [In Spanish].

Ortiz, Diego, Domingo Aguilera, and Elda Marecos. 1995. *Hablemos el guaraní. Curso completo en cuatro niveles para extranjeros. Tercer nivel*. Asunción: CEPAG. [In Spanish].

Ortiz, Diego, Domingo Aguilera, and Elda Marecos. 1995. *Hablemos el guaraní. Curso completo en cuatro niveles para extranjeros. Cuarto nivel*. Asunción: CEPAG. [In Spanish].

Verón, Miguel A. 2006. *Curso Práctico de Lengua Guarani*. San Lorenzo, Paraguay: Fundación Yvy Marãe'ỹ. [In Spanish].

Dictionaries

Ávalos Ocampos, Celso. 2017. *Ñe'ẽryruguasu (Gran diccionario) Guaraní-Español Español Guaraní*. Asunción: El Lector. [In Spanish].

Britton, A. Scott. 2005. *Guaraní Concise Dictionary*. New York: Hippocrene Books.

iGuarani. Online. http://www.iguarani.com/ (Guarani-Spanish).

Krivoshein de Canese, Natalia, and Feliciano Acosta Alcaraz. 2018. *Ñe'ẽryru avañe'ẽ-karaiñe'ẽ karaiñe'ẽ-avañe'ẽ. Diccionario guaraní-español español guaraní*. Asunción: Instituto Superior de Lenguas, Universidad Nacional de Asunción, Colección Ñemity. [In Spanish].

Professor Wolf Lustig's Interactive Guarani Dictionary. Online: https://www.uni-mainz.de/cgi-bin/guarani2/dictionary.pl (Trilingual Guarani-Spanish-German).

Grammars

Ayala, José V. 1996. *Gramática Guaraní*. Buenos Aires: Ministerio de Educación y Cultura de la Nación de la República Argentina. [In Spanish].

Krivoshein de Canese, Natalia, and Feliciano Acosta Alcaraz. 2007. *Gramática guaraní*. Asunción: Instituto Superior de Lenguas, Universidad Nacional de Asunción. [In Spanish].

Liuzzi, Silvio M. 2006. *Guaraní elemental: Vocabulario y gramática*. Corrientes, Argentina: Moglia Ediciones. [In Spanish].

Kallfell, Guido. 2016. *Cómo Hablan Los Paraguayos Con Dos Lenguas? Gramática Del Jopara*. Asunción: Centro de Estudios Antropológicos de la Universidad Católica (CEADUC). [In Spanish].

Kallfell, Guido. 2011. *Grammatik des Jopara: gesprochenes Guaraní und Spanisch in Paraguay*. Frankfurt am Mein: Peter Lang. [In German].

Linguistic overviews

Estigarribia, Bruno, and Justin Pinta. 2017. *Guarani Linguistics in the 21st Century*. Leiden: Brill.

Online resources

ABC Remiandu (Newspaper ABC's section on Paraguay). http://www.abc.com.py/especiales/remiandu/.

YouTube channels with content in Guarani:

- David Galeano Olivera
- PARAGUAY TV
- cafeterambarete
- ayvuguarani

Online bookshops

Guarani Raity. http://www.guarani-raity.com.py/.

Academic works consulted

Aikhenvald, Alexandra Y. 2012. *The Languages of the Amazon*. Oxford/New York: Oxford University Press.

Ayala, José V. 1996. *Gramática Guaraní*. Buenos Aires: Ministerio de Educación y Cultura de la Nación de la República Argentina.

Boidin, Capucine. 2006. 'Jopara: una vertiente sol y sombra del mestizaje'. In *Guaraní y "Mawetí-Tupí-Guaraní". Estudios históricos y descriptivos sobre una familia lingüística de América del sur*, edited by Wolf Dietrich and Haralambos Symeonidis, 303–31. Berlin: Lit Verlag.

Cadogan, León. 1970. 'En torno al "guaraní paraguayo" o "coloquial"', *Cahiers du monde hispanique et luso-brésilien* 14: 31–41.

Cadogán, León. 1987. 'Comentarios a la Gramática guaraní del padre Antonio Guasch', *Amerindia* 12: 113–32.

Carol, Javier, and Alicia Avellana. 2019. 'Tiempo, evidencialidad y miratividad en guaraní paraguayo y español de contacto: ra'e/había sido'. *Verba. Anuario Galego de Filoloxía* 46: 11–67.

Clopper, Cynthia G., and Judith Tonhauser. 2011. 'On the Prosodic Coding of Focus in Paraguayan Guaraní'. In *Proceedings of the 28th West Coast Conference on Formal Linguistics*, edited by Mary Byram Washburn, Katherine McKinney-Bock, Erika Varis, Ann Sawyer, and Barbara Tomaszewicz, 249–57. Somerville, MA: Cascadilla Proceedings Project.

Estigarribia, Bruno. 2017. 'A Grammar Sketch of Paraguayan Guarani'. In *Guarani Linguistics in the 21st Century*, edited by Bruno Estigarribia and Justin Pinta, 7–85. Leiden: Brill.

Estigarribia, Bruno, and Zachary Wilkins. 2018. 'Analyzing the Structure of Code-Switched Written Texts: The Case of Guaraní-Spanish Jopara in the Novel *Ramona Quebranto*', *Linguistic Variation* 18 (1): 121–44. Special issue "Romance (Parsed) Corpora" edited by Christina Tortora, Beatrice Santorini, and Frances Blanchette.

Gómez Rendón, Jorge A. 2017. 'The Demographics of Colonization in Paraguay and the Emergence of Paraguayan Guaraní'. In *Guarani Linguistics in the 21st Century*, edited by Bruno Estigarribia and Justin Pinta, 131–57. Leiden: Brill.

Guarani Ñe'ẽ Rerekuapavẽ (Academia de la lengua guaraní). 2018. *Guarani Ñe'ẽtekuaa* (Gramática guaraní). Asunción: Servilibro.

Gynan, Shaw Nicholas. 2017. 'Morphological Glossing Conventions for the Representation of Paraguayan Guaraní'. In *Guarani Linguistics in the 21st Century*, edited by Bruno Estigarribia and Justin Pinta, 86–130. Leiden: Brill.

Gynan, Shaw Nicholas, and Ernesto López Almada. 2014. Metodología de enseñanzas de lenguas: Teoría y práctica. Unpublished manuscript. Accessed 5 January 2020 at http://myweb.facstaff.wwu.edu/sngynan/methods.pdf.

Hamidzadeh, Khashayar, and Kevin Russell. 2014. 'The Phonology of Reduplication in Paraguayan Guaraní'. In *Proceedings of the Workshop on Structure and Constituency in the Languages of the Americas 19* (University of British Columbia Working Papers in Linguistics 39), edited by Natalie Weber and Sihwei Chen, 95–108.

Krivoshein de Canese, Natalia, and Feliciano Acosta Alcaraz. 2007. *Gramática guaraní*. Asunción: Instituto Superior de Lenguas, Universidad Nacional de Asunción.

Liuzzi, Silvio M. 2006. *Guaraní elemental: Vocabulario y gramática*. Corrientes, Argentina: Moglia Ediciones.

Penner, Hedy, and Dora Bobadilla de Cazal. 2010. *Guía de estilo para una ortografía razonada del guaraní. Un instrumento práctico para profesionales.* Asunción: Ministerio de Educación y Cultura.

Pinta, Justin, and Jennifer L. Smith. 2017. 'Spanish Loans and Evidence for Stratification in the Guarani Lexicon'. In *Guarani Linguistics in the 21st Century*, edited by Bruno Estigarribia and Justin Pinta, 285–314. Leiden: Brill.

Rodrigues, Aryon Dall'Igna, Ana Suelly Arruda Câmara Cabral, and Beatriz Carretta C. da Silva. 2006. 'Evidências lingüísticas para a reconstrução de um nominalizador de objeto **-mi- em Proto-Tupí', *Estudos da Língua(gem)* 4 (2): 21–39.

Salanova, Andrés, and Javier Carol. 'The Guaraní Mirative Evidential and the Decomposition of Mirativity'. In *NELS 47: Proceedings of the 47th Annual Meeting of the North East Linguistic Society, vol. 3*, edited by Andrew Lamont and Katerina Tetzloff, 63–76. Amherst: Graduate Linguistic Student Association of the University of Massachusetts.

Velázquez-Castillo, Maura. 1995a. 'Noun Incorporation in Guaraní: A Functional Analysis', *Linguistics* 33 (4): 673–710.

Velázquez-Castillo, Maura. 1995b. 'Noun Incorporation and Object Placement in Discourse: The Case of Guarani'. In *Word Order in Discourse*, edited by Pamela Downing and Michael Noonan, 555–579, Amsterdam: John Benjamins.

Velázquez-Castillo, Maura. 1996. *The Grammar of Possession: Inalienability, Incorporation, and Possessor Ascension in Guaraní.* Amsterdam: John Benjamins.

Walker, Robert S., Søren Wichmann, Thomas Mailund, and Curtis J. Atkisson. 2012. 'Cultural Phylogenetics of the Tupi Language Family in Lowland South America', *PLoS ONE* 7 (4): e35025. Online. https://doi.org/10.1371/journal.pone.0035025.

Zarratea, Tadeo. 2013. *Gramática elemental del guaraní paraguayo.* Asunción: Servilibro.

Glossary

A (argument)	the agent argument of transitive predicates, often but not always a subject
ablative	a morpheme indicating separation
absolute superlative	indicates a high degree of some property without comparing it to a standard
active	generally speaking, the term **active** is used when a word or construction expresses the agent of an event
active-stative split	see **split intransitivity**
active voice	a verb whose subject is (prototypically) the agent that controls an event; by extension, the clause that has such a verb as predicate is said to be in the active voice
addressee	also **hearer**, the person or persons being addressed or spoken to
adjectivization	turning a word of a different category into an adjective
adverb	an independent word that modifies a verb
adversative conjunctions	a coordinating conjunction used to signal the addition of information that opposes or contrasts with the information in the main clause
affectee	a participant in a causative event that is affected by the action of the participant that is made to act (the causee)
affix	a morpheme that always attaches to a base and can never appear separate from it
agent-demoting	any process that eliminates the agent of an event or makes it less important in some way
agentive	that which has properties of the agent of an event; that is, has control over the event and volition, and often initiates and/or stops the event

agent-oriented	referencing the agent of an event
agglutination	see **agglutinative language**
agglutinating	see **agglutinative language**
agglutinative language	also called **agglutinating**, such a language forms words and sentences by attaching together morphemes that have a single, well-identified meaning, with small or no changes in shape
alienable possession	a relation where the possessed participant is possessed only transitorily or contingently, and where this relation can stop
allophone	one phone (sound) from a group of different phones that are used to pronounce a phoneme category; these can be thought of as variants in the pronunciation of sounds
allomorph	one linguistic form from a group of different linguistic forms that are used to instantiate a morpheme category; these can be thought of as variant shapes of morphemes (for example, the English regular plural has allomorphs '-s' ('cat-s') and '-es' ('class-es'))
alveolar consonant	pronounced with the tip or blade of the tongue approaching or making full contact with the alveolar ridge behind the upper front teeth
analytic language	a language where sentences are composed of many separate words as in English (compare **polysynthetic language**)
antipassive voice	a sentence with a verb whose object is expressed by a prefix with the generic meaning 'people' or 'things'
antonym	a word that is in some sense the opposite of another word
apheresis	omission of the first sound or sounds of a word
apposition	a construction where two noun phrases are used side by side, referring to the same thing or participant, so that the second element adds information about the first
approximant	a consonant produced with very little constriction in the mouth, without creating friction or noise

argument	each one of the expressions that complete the meaning of a verb or, more generally, of any predicate, by designating the participants of the event described by the predicate (for example, subjects, objects and so on)
article	a morpheme that accompanies a noun and indicates if this noun has a definite or indefinite interpretation, or if the noun's referent is being newly introduced in the discourse or already old in the discourse
aspect	a grammatical category of markers that help describe how an event unfolds
aspirated consonant	pronounced with the release of a "puff of air" at the end
asyndetic coordination	a coordination of two (or more) clauses without a coordinating conjunction, by simple juxtaposition
atelic	said of a verb/predicate whose meaning does not imply that the event it describes has an endpoint
attenuative	a morpheme indicating less intensity of an event or less instantiation of a quality or property (cf. English '-ish' in 'green-ish')
back vowel	a vowel pronounced with the body of the tongue towards the back of the mouth
backchanneling	responses that are used mainly to signal the hearer's attention or agreement without interrupting a speaker's turn
bare noun	a noun used without a determiner in front of it
base	when discussing a specific affix, the morpheme or group of morphemes this affix is added to
beneficiary	the participant for whom an event happens, whether the event is advantageous or disadvantageous to the participant
bilabial consonant	pronounced with the lower lip approaching or making full contact with the upper lip
calque	an expression that is a copy word-for-word of an expression in another language
cardinal number	a number that denotes quantity

case	the marking of a noun or noun phrase to indicate whether it has the function of a subject, direct object, indirect object or possessor, among others
case marking	see **case**
castení	a mixture of Guarani and Spanish that is mostly Spanish
causal clause	a clause that expresses content interpreted as the cause of the event in the main clause
causative	a verb form that expresses a meaning of the type 'become something' or 'make someone do something'
causee	the participant in an event that is caused by another participant to act or be in a particular way (see **causer**)
causer	the participant in an event that causes another participant to act or be in a particular way (see **causee**)
central vowel	a vowel pronounced with the body of the tongue in neutral position in the centre of the mouth
circumfix	a morpheme that has two parts that must be used together: one part that precedes the base it attaches to and modifies it and one that follows it, thus "surrounding" the element it modifies
clause	the group of phrases including a single verb and its arguments or dependents (this is very similar to the concept of a simple sentence)
clitic	a morpheme that cannot appear by itself (like affixes) but that can attach to whole phrases, not to words
close vowel	also **high** vowel, a vowel pronounced with the lower jaw in a high position
clusivity	a language shows clusivity if it has first-person plural forms that include the hearers/addressees explicitly and other first-person plural forms that exclude them explicitly
coda	the consonants that come after a vowel in the same syllable and end this syllable

code-switch	the use of a word or expression from another language that is recognized as foreign
collective plural	a kind of plural that expresses not 'more than one' but rather 'a group of something'
comitative	an expression that denotes accompaniment (for example, phrases with the English preposition 'with')
common ground	the set of beliefs and knowledge common to both speaker(s) and hearer(s) in a situation of communication
complement	a required argument of a verb (excluding the subject) or a required noun phrase that accompanies a postposition
complement clause	a clause that is the required complement of a verb and hence fulfils the functions of a noun phrase, usually being the object of the verb
complex sentence	a sentence with more than one clause; that is, with more than one predicate and their associated arguments
composite nucleus (of a syllable)	a syllable nucleus with more than one vowel in it, a focal vowel plus one glide (diphthong) or two glides (triphthong)
compositional meaning	the situation where the meaning of a whole (word, phrase, etc.) can be calculated by combining the meaning of its parts
compound	a word that is composed of more than one lexical root (for example, noun + noun or noun + verb)
completive aspect	a kind of **perfective aspect**, it expresses that an event has been completed
concatenation	see **concatenative language**
concatenative language	a language that forms words by taking a root and adding a chain of "parts" with additional meanings to it
concessive clause	a clause that expresses content in opposition to the content of the main clause, but that still allows the main clause to be true
conditional clause	a clause that expresses content interpreted as a condition for the event in the main clause to be true

consonant	a speech sound produced with some measure of impediment to the passage of air through the mouth
continuous aspect	here used as synonymous with **progressive aspect**, it highlights that an event is continuing
conversion	a word's change from one word class to another without changing its shape
co-present demonstrative	used to refer to people or objects physically present in the situation of communication
copulative conjunction	a coordinating conjunction used simply to signal the addition of information to a main clause
coronal consonant	pronounced with the tip or blade of the tongue approaching or making full contact with the roof of the mouth
countable noun	also called **count noun**, it denotes something that can be found in a single countable piece and can be grouped, keeping each individual piece separate
counterfactual conditional	also called **contrary-to-fact**, it expresses what would have occurred if something that did not happen had happened
covert prestige	the fact that speakers have a positive evaluation and identification with a language that is not overtly prestigious in their society
creole language	a natural language that develops from mixing different languages that come into contact at a point in time, often showing universal or "default" grammatical characteristics
deadjectival noun	a noun created from an adjective root (for example, in English, 'weak-ness' from 'weak')
deixis	the ways in which a language locates persons, objects or events in space or time, generally with reference to the position of speaker and hearer, or to some other reference point
demonstrative	a morpheme that helps to locate a person, object or event in space, generally with reference to the position of speaker and hearer
denominal noun	a noun created from another noun (for example, in English, 'friend-ship' from 'friend')

dental consonant	pronounced with the tip or blade of the tongue approaching or making full contact with the upper front teeth
deontic modality	related to or indicating the possibility or necessity of an event
derivation	adding affixes to a word to form new words, generally to change the part of speech of a word
derivational morphology	addition of affixes that creates a new word from a given word; see **deadjectival noun, denominal noun, deverbal noun**
desiderative	a mood that expresses desires
destinative	an aspect marker for noun phrases that tells us that a noun phrase refers to something in the future
determiner	a morpheme that accompanies a noun and helps build a noun phrase by expressing whether it is definite or indefinite, or quantifying the noun, or locating it in space and time
deverbal noun	a noun created from a verb (for example, in English, 'driv-er' from 'drive')
diacritic mark	a mark added to a basic letter to signal some specific change in sound
digraph	a group of two letters that represent a single sound (for example, English <sh>)
diminutive	a morpheme that expresses smallness, and often also, by extension, affection
diphthong	a sequence of two vowels that belong to the same syllable
direct evidence	cases where the speaker's basis for an assertion is having directly witnessed the relevant event
direct object	the non-subject argument of a transitive verb, the one that is usually a patient; that is, that receives or is affected by the event
direct-inverse system	a system where a verb takes different markers depending on the relative positions in the person hierarchy of the subject and object
discourse context	the information in previous sentences and other information in the world (including information about the speakers and what they know) that is used to interpret a sentence in an actual communication situation

disjunctive conjunction	a coordinating conjunction used to signal alternatives to the information in the main clause
dissimilation	a sound that changes to become more distinct from surrounding sounds
distal demonstrative	a demonstrative that locates a person, object or event far from the position of both speaker and hearer (compare **medial demonstrative, proximal demonstrative**)
distributive number	a number that expresses how a quantity is divided or distributed
ditransitive verb	a verb (or more generally, any predicate) that has three arguments, a subject, a direct object and an indirect object
dorsal consonant	also called **palatal**, a consonant pronounced with the centre of the tongue approaching or making full contact with the roof of the mouth
double negation	also called **negative concord**, languages that have this property require the appearance of multiple negative words in a negated sentence, even though negation is interpreted only once (for example, in many varieties of English, 'I don't know nothing' = 'I don't know anything')
dubitative	a marker that expresses doubt about an event occuring
durative	said of a verb/predicate whose meaning conveys the idea that the event described lasts in time
effected object	the object of a verb when it designates something that will come into being as a result of the event expressed by the verb
elative superlative	indicates a very high degree of some property
elicitation questionnaire	a questionnaire designed to allow native consultants to produce specific linguistic forms that the researcher is seeking
emphatic	a marker that conveys emphasis on some part of a sentence

enclitic	a clitic that attaches to the end of its host
endonym	a name that the speakers themselves use for their own language
epenthesis	the addition of an extraneous sound to facilitate pronunciation of a word or phrase or make it more regular according to the rules guiding the syllable structure of a language
epenthetic consonant	a consonant added to facilitate pronunciation of a word or phrase or make it more regular according to the rules guiding the syllable structure of a language
epenthetic vowel	a vowel added to facilitate pronunciation of a word or phrase or make it more regular according to the rules guiding the syllable structure of a language
epistemic modality	related to or indicating the knowledge state of a speaker
equative clause	a clause that establishes identity of reference between two noun phrases
evidential	a morpheme that expresses the degree of certainty speakers have and the source and kind of evidence they have for their statement
exclusive pronoun	see **clusivity**
expressive language	speaking or writing
extralinguistic knowledge	knowledge participants in a conversation have that refers to the world outside of the linguistic discourse
filler	sounds or small words or phrases that are used during hesitations to signal that the speaker is not finished talking and intends to hold the floor
flap	a consonant produced by a quick tap of the tongue tip against the roof of the mouth
focal vowel	in a diphthong or triphthong, the vowel that is not a glide, is pronounced fully, and can be stressed
focus	the most relevant, most important contribution and foregrounded information in a sentence

fossilized	a language form (word or phrase) that historically was composed of different parts, but that now is perceived and used by speakers as a single unit (compare **lexicalized**)
free variation	the situation where speakers can choose freely among a set of variant sounds or morphemes with the same meaning
frequentative aspect	presents an event as happening with some frequency
fricative	a consonant produced with some constriction in the mouth that creates friction and noise
front vowel	a vowel pronounced with the body of the tongue towards the front of the mouth
frustrative mood	conveys a negative evaluation of an action, or its fruitlessness
generic	a noun phrase that refers to a class of individuals or a species
glide	in a diphthong or triphthong, the vowel or vowels that are not pronounced fully (they are usually shorter), and cannot be stressed
gloss	also called **interlinear gloss**, a series of lines added to an example to clarify its internal structure and composition
glottal consonant	pronounced with the vocal cords approaching or making full contact with one another
government	conditions that a predicate imposes on its arguments; for example, how they must be marked
grammar	body of structural rules that speakers use unconsciously to formulate and understand words, phrases and sentences in their language
grammatical morpheme	a morpheme that has a meaning related to specific categories of the grammar of the language under study, not to the observable, non-linguistic world
grapheme	a letter or group of letters used to represent a sound
guaraniete	literally, 'true Guarani', it is a mostly academic register of Guarani devoid as much as possible of Spanish influence

guarañol	a mixture of Guarani and Spanish that is mostly Guarani
habitual aspect	portrays an event as occurring regularly or customarily
head	also called **nucleus**, it is the most important word in a phrase, in the sense that it is the only obligatory word and it determines what the phrase refers to
hearer	see **addressee**
hearsay	the fact that the content communicated by a speaker is known to the speaker from a third-party report, or is generally known, but not known from first-hand experience or reasoning
helping vowel	see **epenthetic vowel**
hiatus	a sequence of two vowels that belong to different syllables
homophonous	morphemes or words that have distinct meanings but have the same pronunciation
hortative mood	used to exhort a group including oneself to carry out an action
host	the word or phrase a clitic attaches to
imperative modalizer	a suffix that conveys nuances of force, coercion, mitigation or politeness when used with the imperative mood
imperfective aspect	highlights that an event is continuing or not fully completed, or that the endpoint is absent or not important
inactive	generally speaking, the term **inactive** is used when a word or construction expresses an event participant that is not an agent
inalienable possession	a relation where the possessed participant is necessarily possessed, and where this relation cannot stop: body parts and kinship terms use inalienable possession
inclusive pronoun	see **clusivity**
indefinite quantification	use of a quantifier meaning 'some', 'a few' or other indefinite quantity

indirect object	a non-subject argument of a verb (usually ditransitive) that expresses the recipient of a transfer or a goal
indirect question	a question that appears subordinated to a main clause
inflection	adding affixes to a word to express different grammatical categories such as number, gender, tense, and so on
information structure	the organization of phrases in a sentence according to whether they are new or old information, or whether the information is foregrounded or backgrounded
instrumental	referring to the instrument used to carry out an action
integrated loanword	a loanword that is pronounced and used following fully the conventions of the recipient language
interfix	an increment or linking element that appears arbitrarily between a root and an affix and that contributes no meaning to the word
interlinear gloss	see **gloss**
intermittent aspect	portrays an event as occurring at intervals, not continuously
intonation	variations in pitch while speaking that can convey sentence meanings; for example, whether a sentence is a question or a statement, or whether the speaker is saying it emphatically
intonational phrase	a part of a sentence that has its own recognizable intonation contour and is pronounced as an intonation unit
intransitive verb	a verb (or more generally, any predicate) that has only one argument, its subject
IPA	International Phonetic Alphabet, a conventional system of symbols used by linguists worldwide to represent accurately and unambiguously the sounds of any human language
irregular verb	a verb whose root or person prefixes change for different persons; that is, a verb where the root or the person prefix have different allomorphs

iterative aspect	portrays an event as repeating
jopara	any sentence or discourse that includes mixed elements of both Guarani and Spanish
juxtaposition	establishing a relation between two nouns, phrases or clauses by simply putting them one after the other, without adding any morphemes or words to mark the relation
kinship term	a term describing a family relationship
labial consonant	pronounced with articulation of the lips
labiodental consonant	pronounced with the lower lip approaching or making full contact with the upper front teeth
language contact	the geographical contact between communities that speak different languages
language family	a grouping of languages that share traits that suggest they descend from a common ancestor
language mixing	all the phenomena that result from including sounds, words or rules from one language into another language
language stock	a larger grouping of language families, putatively descending from a common ancestor
language typology	the study and classification of languages according to a cross-comparison of their structural features
lateral	a consonant produced by letting air flow around the sides of the tongue
lengthening	making a syllable last longer, usually by making the nucleus vowel longer
lexeme	a unit of the language that has lexical meaning (for example, *door, run, pretty, never*), as opposed to grammatical meaning (for example, *the, -'s, -ness*)
lexical morpheme	a morpheme (usually a word) that has a meaning related to the observable, non-linguistic world (these are usually nouns, verbs, adjectives and adverbs)
lexicalized	said of an expression that has entered the language as a single word and is not "built on the fly" anymore by speakers (compare **fossilized**)
lexicon	the inventory of lexemes

lingua franca	a language that is adopted as a common language between speakers whose native languages are different
loanword	also called **borrowing**, a word adopted in a language that comes from another language
locative	that which has a meaning related to location in space
locative clause	gives some information that is relevant to the place at which the event in the main clause occurs
main clause	the group of a main predicate in a sentence with its arguments, when it subordinates another clause in a complex sentence
manner clause	expresses the way in which the event in the main clause unfolds
manner of articulation	indicates how much the flow of air is modified by the tongue or lips to produce a consonant, and how the air escapes through the mouth or nose
medial demonstrative	a demonstrative that locates a person, object or event not too far from the position of speaker and hearer, especially if close to the hearer (compare **distal demonstrative, proximal demonstrative**)
mid vowel	a vowel pronounced with the lower jaw in a position that is neither high nor low
minimal pair	a pair of words that differ in only one sound and therefore serve to prove that the differing sounds are different phonemes of the language (as opposed to merely pronunciation variants of a single phoneme)
mirative	a marker that indicates that something is surprising or counter to expectation
modal deixis	see **notional deixis**
modality	the expression of speaker intent or speaker attitudes, as well as the expression of the possibility, necessity, reality or desirability of an event
modifier	any item that "adds meaning" to a word it relates to

mood	the grammatical ways in which a language expresses modality
morpheme	in one sense, a part of a word that has a discernible meaning it contributes to the whole word; prefixes, suffixes and roots are all kinds of morphemes that come together to form words (more broadly, any language item that has a discernible meaning and is not composed of inner parts is a morpheme, including affixes, clitics, particles and independent words)
morphology	the study of how words are formed by a combination of the meaning of their parts (see **morpheme**)
morphological typology	the classification of languages in terms of how they form words and sentences
morphosyntactic alignment	the pattern shown by all possibilities that a language has to mark subjects of intransitive verbs compared to subjects and objects of transitive verbs
multitudinal plural	a kind of plural that expresses not 'more than one' but rather 'a large quantity of something'
nasal	a vowel or consonant produced allowing the passage of air through the nose
nasal harmony	also **nasal spread** or **nasalization**, the fact that nasal sounds in a word tend to spread their nasality to other sounds in the same word
nasalization	see **nasal harmony**
nasal-oral consonant	also called **prenasalized consonant** or **postoralized consonant**, a kind of consonant that begins with a nasal articulation and ends in an oral articulation
nasal spread	see **nasal harmony**
naturalistic data	language used to illustrate grammatical points that comes from natural native speakers' usage; that is, not planned or edited for "correctness"
negative concord	see **double negation**

neologism	a newly created word or expression
nominal	referring to nouns and their properties, more broadly including adjectives and their properties, by opposition to **verbal**
nominalization	turning a word of a different category into a noun
notional deixis	also called **modal deixis**, deixis that refers to the way something is done (cf. English 'thus', 'this way', 'that way')
noun incorporation	the attachment of a noun to a verb forming a compound that functions as a single verbal unit
noun phrase	a phrase that has a noun as its head
nucleus (of a phrase)	see **head**
nucleus (of a syllable)	the vowel or group or vowels in a syllable
object	the function of a noun phrase in a sentence that is usually a patient that receives an action or is created or destroyed or changed in some way (in this sense, also **direct object**)
object drop	leaving out an understood object noun phrase in a sentence
object incorporation	the attachment of a direct object noun to the verb it depends on to form a compound that functions as a single verbal unit
object relative clause	a relative clause whose object is understood as the noun the relative clause itself modifies (for example, 'the man who(m) I saw')
oblique	an argument of a verb that is not a subject or direct object, but is marked in some special way; for example, via a preposition (in English) or postposition (in Guarani)
onset	the consonant or group of consonants that come before a vowel in the same syllable
open question	a question that cannot be fully answered by saying 'yes' or 'no', but instead must be answered with a content phrase
open vowel	also **low vowel**, a vowel pronounced with the lower jaw in a low position
optative	a mood that expresses wishes and hopes

oral	a vowel or consonant produced with no passage of air through the nose
ordinal number	a number that denotes order
overt prestige	the fact that the standard dialect of a language is usually considered to be more correct and desirable and is highly valued socially
P (argument)	the patient argument of transitive predicates, often but not always an object
palatal consonant	see **dorsal consonant**
paradigm	a set of linguistic forms that contain some common element and cover a whole domain of meaning
part of speech	also called **word classes**, the classification of words or roots according to their meaning and how they are used in a sentence (for example, noun, verb, adjective, and so on).
particle	a more generic name for any kind of morphological marker that cannot be clearly identified as an affix or a clitic
partitive	that which refers to part of a whole
passive	generally speaking, a term used when a word or construction expresses the patient of an event
passive voice	a verb whose subject is the patient that receives or is affected by an event; by extension, the clause that has such a verb as predicate is said to be in the passive voice
patient	the participant that suffers an action, or is otherwise changed or affected by an event
patient-oriented	referencing the patient of an event
patrimonial word	a word that is part of the historical lexicon of a language, not borrowed from another language or (re)introduced artificially
perfect aspect	also called **perfective aspect**, it focuses on and highlights the end or full completion of an event, rather than focusing on the course of the event

person hierarchy	the realization that not all persons of a verb have the same status, and that (usually) the first person is in some sense more important than the second person, which is in turn more important than the third person
phone	a sound used in language
phoneme	a category of sounds that are perceived by speakers as being the same and that serve to differentiate words by opposing themselves to other categories of sounds
phonetic transcription	a representation of the pronunciation of a word, phrase or sentence, using the conventional symbols in the International Phonetic Alphabet (IPA)
phonetics	the study of how sounds and other acoustic properties (pitch, volume, rhythm) are produced and heard in a given language
phonology	the study of how sounds and other acoustic properties (pitch, volume, rhythm) are used in a given language to form words, phrases and sentences and convey meaning
phrase	a grouping of words that function as a unit
pitch	the degree of highness or lowness in the frequency of a tone
pitch fall	an intonation curve that goes from higher pitched syllables to lower pitched syllables
pitch rise	an intonation curve that goes from lower pitched syllables to higher pitched syllables
place of articulation	indicates where in the mouth the flow of air is modified by the tongue or lips, by constriction or complete closure, to produce a consonant
plural	referring to more than one single person, object, place, event and so on
polysynthetic language	a language where sentences are often single words (or a few words) composed of many parts, rather than many separate words as in English (compare **analytic language**)
portmanteau morpheme	a morpheme that simultaneously expresses two or more distinct meaning components

possessor	the "thing that possesses" in a possessive construction
possessum	the "thing possessed" in a possessive construction
postoralized consonant	see **nasal-oral consonant**
postposition	a word or morpheme placed after the noun phrase it modifies
postpositional complement verb	a verb (or more generally, any predicate) that has two arguments, one a subject and the other an oblique complement marked by a specific postposition required by the verb
post-stative	an aspect marker for noun phrases that tells us that a noun phrase refers to something in the past (actual, or past with respect to another event)
predication	the attribution of a quality or state to the subject
predicative clause	a clause that assigns some property to a referent
prefix	a morpheme that precedes the root it attaches to and modifies
prenasalized consonant	see **nasal-oral consonant**
preposition	a word or morpheme placed before the noun phrase it modifies
primary stress	the highest prominence peak on a given syllable in a word, in pitch, volume or length (compare **secondary stress**)
privative	expressing the absence of a property
proclitic	a clitic that attaches to the beginning of its host
proform	a free-standing morpheme that has the function of a specific part of speech (pronouns, pro-verbs, pro-adverbials)
progressive aspect	see **continuous aspect**
prohibitive	a negated imperative

prosodic boundary	a place in a sentence where the phrasing changes because of a change in intonation, the introduction of a pause, a change of rhythm and so on
prosody	pronunciation phenomena that include syllable structure, stress placement in words, nasal harmony, intonation (pitch contours), pauses and rhythm
prospective	an aspect marker for noun phrases that tells us that a noun phrase refers to something in the future (actual, or future with respect to another event)
pronoun	a free-standing morpheme that has the function of a noun phrase
protractive aspect	presents an event as continuing longer than what is expected, reasonable or normal in the context
proximal demonstrative	a demonstrative that locates a person, object or event near the position of the speaker (compare **distal demonstrative, medial demonstrative**)
psych-verb	a verb expressing a psychological state such as an emotion, a thought or a feeling that is experienced
purposive clause	a clause that expresses the purpose of the predicate in the main clause
quantifier	a morpheme that indicates a quantity of something (English 'all', 'half', 'none', 'some', 'a few', 'many', and so on)
quasi-eventive aspect	presents an event as almost having happened, but not having happened
reasoned evidence	when the speaker's communicated content is the result of an internal reasoning process
receptive language	listening or reading
recipient	the participant in an event that receives something
reciprocal	an event where several agents act on several patients, and these patients in turn act on the agents (cf. English 'each other' or 'one another'); by extension, applied to the verbs or the voice used to describe the event

reduplication	a repetition or "doubling" of a root or part of a root
referent	something a speaker refers to with a linguistic expression; for example, a person or an object being referred to with a noun phrase
reflexive	referring to a situation where an event affects its initiator, or in other terms, where a participant accomplishes an action unto itself
relational prefix	a prefix that serves to indicate that the word is to be interpreted in construction with another, often a possessor
relational root	a root that must be used in conjunction with a relational prefix
relexification	a historical development where a language's lexicon is replaced completely or almost completely with words borrowed from a foreign language, but without changing the grammar of the recipient language (cf. English, which was partially relexified by French during the Norman Conquest, and therefore has a high percentage of Latinate words)
resultative	a word or construction that expresses the meaning of the result of an event
resyllabification	the reorganization of sounds that belong to one syllable to be pronounced as if they belonged to different syllables
retroflex consonant	a consonant produced with the tip of the tongue curved inwards to meet the roof of the palate
root	a single morpheme that provides a basic lexical meaning to which affixes can be added
S (argument)	the single argument of intransitive predicates, which can usually be identified as its subject
schwa	a mid-central vowel like the first vowel in English 'ago', represented in the IPA as [ə].
secondary stress	any prominence peak on a given syllable in a word, in pitch, volume or length, which is not the highest in the word (compare **primary stress**)

segmental phonology	the area of phonology that concerns properties associated with individual sounds
sentential nominalization	a process that allows a whole sentence to function as a noun phrase, for instance by the addition of an affix
serial verb construction	a construction where two or more lexical verbs occur in sequence and are understood to have the same subject and to denote a single event
set partitive	refers to a subset of members of a set
sibilant consonant	a consonant that makes a hissing sound by directing air towards the teeth
singular	referring to a single person, object, place, event and so on
sociative causative	a verb form that expresses a meaning of the type 'make someone do something and do it with them'
sociolinguistic interview	a method of linguistic data collection that allows linking the use of specific forms to social and sociolinguistic variables, and the collection of natural data in different contexts of use, styles and registers
split intransitivity	a language has this property if intransitive verbs can be classified into distinct classes according to how their subjects appear in a sentence
standard of comparison	in a comparative sentence, the thing that something is compared to
stop	a consonant produced by completely stopping the flow of air in the mouth
stress	the relative higher prominence of a given syllable in a word, in pitch, volume or length
subject	the function of a noun phrase in a sentence that is usually (but not always) the agent of an action or the person or animal experiencing a sensation
subject drop	leaving out an understood subject noun phrase in a sentence
subject relative clause	a relative clause whose subject is understood as the noun the relative clause itself modifies (for example, 'the man who saw me')

subordinate clause	the term used to call the group of a predicate in a sentence with its arguments, when it is subordinated to another clause in a complex sentence
suffix	a morpheme that follows the root it attaches to and modifies
suprasegmental phonology	the area of phonology that concerns properties associated with units larger than single sounds
symmetric verb	a verb describing an action that applies to the object and to the subject in the reverse direction
syntax	the study and description of how words and phrases are arranged in sentences and how the meaning of a sentence is derived from an understanding of this arrangement
target	a sound that becomes nasal due to the spread of nasalization in a word
telic	said of a verb/predicate whose meaning implies that the event it describes has an endpoint
temporal clause	gives some information that is relevant to the time at which the event in the main clause occurs
tense	a grammatical category of markers that help place an event in time
tone	a way of differentiating words by changes in pitch (Guarani does not use tone)
topic	the information in a sentence that serves as background to understand what the focus talks about
toponym	a place name
totalitive aspect	a kind of **perfective aspect**, expressing that an event applies to the whole subject or object
transitive verb	a verb (or more generally, any predicate) that has two arguments, a subject and a direct object
transparent	a sound that is neither affected by nasal harmony nor stops its spread

trigger	a nasal sound that generates the spread of nasalization in a word
trill	a sound produced by multiple quick vibrations of the tongue
unaspirated consonant	pronounced without the release of a "puff of air" at the end
uncountable noun	also called **mass noun**, it denotes something that cannot be separated in countable pieces, like substances or qualities, for example
universal quantification	use of a quantifier meaning 'all'
urheimat	the original homeland of speakers of a language or language family
utterance	a complete unit of talk, preceded and followed by the speaker's silence (not necessarily a complete sentence)
velar consonant	pronounced with the back of the tongue approaching or making full contact with the roof of the mouth at the velum (soft palate)
verbal	referring to verbs and their properties, by opposition to **nominal**
verbalization	turning a word of a different category into a verb
veridical	a marker that indicates that the truth of a statement is known
voice	a specific pattern that indicates what role the subject of a sentence has (agent, patient and so on), what role the object has, and so on
voiced	a language sound that is produced with concomitant vibration of the vocal cords
voiceless	a language sound that is produced without concomitant vibration of the vocal cords
volitive mood	used to express wants
vowel	a speech sound produced without impediment to the passage of air through the mouth
vowel harmony	the fact that vowels in a word tend to resemble other vowels in the same word in the position in the mouth (front, central, back), height (close, mid, low), or lip roundness (rounded, unrounded)

word classes	see **part of speech**
word order	refers to the order of words, or better, phrases, in a sentence; most commonly it refers to the relative ordering of subjects (S), verbs (V) and objects (O) in a sentence
yes/no question	a question that can be fully answered by saying 'yes' or 'no'
zero derivation	see **conversion**

Index

Note: Page numbers in italics indicate figures

ability, expressing, 178–9
ablative pronouns, 106
academic works consulted, 327
achegety, 46–7
active personal markers. *See* active prefixes
active prefixes, 13, 127–8, 136–40
active-stative languages, 14. *See also* active/stative split
active/stative split, 2, 130. *See also* active-stative languages
active verbs, 127–30, 203–4, 207
addressees, 107
adjective clauses, 263. *See also* relative clauses
adjective compounds, 85
adjectives, 15
    adjectival modifiers of nouns, 87–9
    adjective compounds, 85
    word order and, 58–9
adjectivizers, 74
adverbial clauses, 263, 271–9
    causal clauses, 273–4
    concessive clauses, 272–3
    conditional clauses, 274–5
    locative clauses, 278–9
    manner clauses, 276
    purposive clauses, 271–2
    temporal clauses, 277–8
adverbial proforms, 115
adverbs, 15, 190–2
adversative conjunctions, 260–3
affectees, 215, 220–1
affixes, 10, 25, 58, 128, 285–9, 313–14. *See also* circumfixes
agent-demoting prefixes, 140, 210–11
agent-demoting voice, 207–8
agent-oriented nominalizations, 78
agents, 132, 207
agglutinative morphology, 2, 10–11, 24
aireal verbs, 132–5, 211–12, 320
alienable possession, 66–7, 236
allomorphs, 313–16
    affixes, 313–14
    clitics, 313–14
    irregular verbs and, 146–8
    nasalization and, 40
    roots, 316–19
allophones, 9

alphabet, 46–56
analytic construction, 12
Anchieta, Joseph de, 5
animals, 294–5
animate objects, 140
antipassive voice, 211–15
antipassive voice suffixes, 128
antonyms, 85
apheresis, 100, 152–4
approximants, 33–4
approximation, 87
Aragona, Alonso de, 5
arguments, 13, 126–7
articles, 89–94
aspect, 57, 121–2, 163–70
    completive aspect, 163
    continuous aspect, 163–5
    frequentative aspect, 170
    habitual aspect, 167
    imperfective aspect, 163
    incompletive aspect, 169–70
    intermittent aspect, 166
    iterative aspect, 168–9
    nominal temporal-aspectual inflection, 2
    nominal temporal-aspectual markers, 121–5
    perfect (perfective) aspect, 163
    post-stative aspect, 121–2
    progressive aspect, 163–5
    prospective aspect, 121–2, 128
    protractive aspect, 170
    quasi-eventive aspect, 169–70
    totalitive aspect, 163
atelic predicates, 158
attenuatives, 86–7

bases, 10, 119–20
basic clauses, 230–40
beneficiaries, 196
body parts, 291–3
bookshops, online, 330
Brasiliano, 1–2
Brasílica, 1–2

cardinal numbers, 100, 102
Castení, 17
causal clauses, 273–4

causative voice, 215–22
  intransitive causative, 215–18
  sociative causative, 218–20
  transitive causative, 220–2
causatives
  causative affixes, 25
  causative voice suffixes, 128
  morphological, 2
  See also causative voice
causees, 220–1
causers, 215, 220–1
circumfixes, 2, 36, 154–5, 178, 309
clauses
  adverbial clauses, 271–9
  basic, 230–40
  complement clauses, 267–70
  coordinated clauses, 259–63
  equative clauses, 231–2
  existence clauses, 232–5
  location clauses, 232–5
  non-verbal possessive sentences, 235–7
  predicative clauses, 231–2
  questions, 237–40
  relative clauses, 263–8
  sentences expressing possession, 235–7
  simple clauses, 230
  subordinate clauses, 263–79
  verbal possessive sentences, 236–7
  word order in simple, 230–1
clitics, 10, 285–9, 313–14
clusivity, 2, 24
colonization, European, 1–5, 19, 46
colours, 298
comitative verbs, 152
commands, 170–6
common expressions, 321–6
common phrases, 321–6
comparatives, 246–9
complement clauses, 263, 267–70
  interrogative/exclamative, 270
  by juxtaposition, 269–70
  with subordinator -ha/-hague, 267–9
complements, 194–6
  of postpositions, 70
completive aspect, 163
complex sentences, 259–79
compound words, orthography and, 51–3
comprehension, 21
concatenative languages, 9–11
concessive clauses, 272–3
conditional clauses, 274–5
conjunctions
  adversative, 260–3
  coordinating copulative, 268
  disjunctive, 268
consonants, 9, 30–3
  approximants, 33–4
  consonant allomorphs, 313–16
  consonant phonemes, 9
  English closest equivalent, 30–2
  fricatives, 33
  manner of articulation, 30
  nasal-oral, 34
  place of articulation, 30
  postoralized, 9
  prenasalized, 9, 34
  pronunciation of, 8, 30–3
  sibilants, 34
  verbs with loss of initial, 152–4
  voiced alveolar lateral, 34
  voiced labiodental approximant, 33
  voiced palatal fricative, 33
  voiced velar approximant, 33–4
  voiceless glottal fricative, 33
  voiceless postalveolar fricative, 33
continuous aspect, 163–5
contrastive focus, 281
contrastive topics, 283–4
conversion, 16
coordinated clauses, 259–63
  with adversative conjunctions, 260–3
  with coordinating copulative conjunction, 268
co-present demonstratives, 94–6
copulative conjunctions, 268
counterfactual conditionals, 275–6
courses, 21–2
  online, 22

data sources, 327
days of the week, neologisms for, 296
deadjectival nominalizations, 75
Decoud Larrosa, Reinaldo, 99
definite articles, 89–94
degree expressions, 246–54
  comparatives, 246–9
  superlatives, 249–54
deixis, 94, 97–8
Delgado, Susy, 304–5
demonstrative pronouns, 115–16
demonstratives, 89–90, 94–9
  co-present, 94–6
denominal nominalizations, 75
deontic modality, 161
dependent-marking, 12
depreciation, 87
desire, expressing, 181–5
determiners, 58, 89–105
  articles, 89–93
  demonstratives, 89–90, 94–9
  determiners, 89–104
  numerals, 99–105
  quantifiers, 89–90, 99–105
deverbal nominalizing affix, 128
deverbal nouns, 71
diacritic marks, 46
dictionaries, 329
digraphs, 46
diminutives, 86
diphthongs, 29–30
Dirección General de Estadística, Encuestas y Censos (DGEEC), 6
direct evidence, markers of, 226–7
direct-inverse systems, 14–15
direct object pronouns, 106
disjunctive conjunctions, 260
distal events, 94–5
distributives, 102–3
distributivity, over predicative argument, 245
ditransitive verbs, 140–1
double negation, 155–6
dubitative future tense, 163

dubitative particles, 240
durative events, 159–60
dwelling, 297–8

effected object, 121–2
elative superlatives, 252–3
emphatic markers, 110–11, 223–5
enclitics, 42, 57–8
   interrogative, 25
   orthography and, 50–1
   plural marking and, 59–61
   stress and, 36
   verb enclitics, 25
English language, 19
Enlhet/Maskoy family, 20
epenthesis, 148, 154–5
epenthetic vowels, 154–5
epistemic markers, 160
epistemic modality, 161
equative clauses, 231–2
European colonization, 1–5, 19
events, expressing properties of, 157–8
evidentiality, 223–9
   direct evidence, 226
   hearsay, 225
   reasoned evidence, 227–9
evidentials, 25
exclamation, 239–40
exclamative complement clauses, 270
exclusive prefixes, 129
existence clauses, 232–5
expressions, common, 321–6

fixed stress, 2
focus, 280–2
food vocabulary, 290–1
frequentative aspect, 170
fricatives, 33
frustrative modality, 186–8
future tense, 126, 159–62
   dubitative future tense, 160
   immediate future tense, 161

gender agreement, 24
general introductions, 328
generic voice, 207–10
German language, 20
glossary of high-frequency vocabulary
   animals, 294–5
   body parts, 291–3
   colours, 298
   dwelling, 297–8
   food, 290–1
   kinship terms, 293–4
   numbers, 293
   senses, 293
   thematic, 290–8
   time, 294–7
glottal stops, 33, 34
graphemes, 32, 46
Guaicurú family, 20
Guarani, 1–3
   agglutinative morphology of, 10
   apps for learning, 22–3
   coexistence with Spanish, 6
   as concatenative language, 9–11
   contact with other languages, 16–20
   courses in, 20–1
   covert prestige of, 8
   declared national language, 6–7
   as defining Paraguayan language, 6
   disadvantageous position relative to Spanish, 7–8
   history since European colonization, 3–5
   intergenerational transmission of, 7–8
   as most widely spoken indigenous language in Americas, 7
   official indigenous language of MERCOSUR, 7
   overview of the language, 1–3
   polysynthesis and, 10–12
   resource for learning, 20–5
   as second or foreign language, 20–5
   sociolinguistic information, 6–8
   survival of, 5–6
   traits from Tupi-Guarani family, 2–3
   typological information, 9–16
   word order in, 3
Guarania, Félix de, 305–7
Guaraniete, 16–17
Guarani-Portuguese-Spanish trilinguals, 20
Guarani-Spanish bilinguals, 5–7, 19
Guarañol, 17, 19

habitual aspect, 167
head, 13, 58
heading-marking, 12–13
hearsay, markers of, 226
helping vowels, 154–5
hortative mood, 183–5
hypothetical conditional clauses, 274–6

immediate future tense, 161
imperative modalizers, 172–5, 177
imperative mood, 170–7
imperatives, 170–7
   negative imperatives, 176–7
imperfective aspect, 163
impersonal voice, 207–11
inactive prefixes, 13, 136–8
inactive verbs, 127
inactive voice, 204–7
inalienable possession, 66–7
inanimate objects, 140
inclusive/exclusive distinction, 24, 107, 129
inclusive prefixes, 129
incompletive aspect, 169–70
increments, verbs with, 150–1
indefinite articles, 89–94
indefinite pronouns, 113–15
indefinite quantification, 244
indigenous languages, 20
indirect object pronouns, 106
indirect questions, 238
inflection, nominal temporal-aspectual, 2
information structure, 280–2
   focus, 280–2
   topic, 283–4
instrumental meaning, 77
interfixes, 150–2
intermittent aspect, 166
interrogative complement clauses, 270

interrogative dubative particles, 240
interrogative enclitics, 25
interrogative pronouns, 111–13
interrogative sentences, 55. *See also* questions
interrogative words, 112–14
interview, text samples, 299–302
intransitive causative, 215–18
intransitive predicates
    active voice and, 203–4, 207
    inactive voice and, 205–6
    intransitive relational predicates, 149
intransitive verbs, 13–14, 126–32
    active verbs, 128–30
    inactive verbs, 130–2
    passive/reflexive/impersonal voice with, 207–10
intransitivity, split, 2, 14, 130
IPA (International Phonetic Alphabet) symbols, 9, 26, 30
irregular verbs, 146–8
iterative aspect, 168–9

Jesuits, 5–6, 46
Jopara, 16–19, 23
juxtaposition, 269–70

kinship terms, 293–4

lengthening, 45
lexical negation, 85
lexical nominalizations, 71
lexicalized nouns, 78
linguistic overviews, 330
listening, 22
literacy, 21
loanwords, 17–19, 34, 36
    integrated, 17
    orthography and, 53–5
    from Spanish language, 17–18, 34, 36
location clauses, 232–5
locative clauses, 278–9
locatives, 194–5

main clauses, 259, 263
manner clauses, 276
    dependent-marking, 12
    heading-marking, 12–13
    no marking, 12–13
Mataco Mataguayo family, 20
Mayan language, 7
Mbyá Guaraní cosmogony and mythology, 65
MERCOSUR, 7
minimal pairs, 27
mirative markers, 227–8
modal deixis, 97–8
modality, 170–87
    deontic modality, 161
    epistemic modality, 161
modalizers, imperative, 172–5, 177
modifiers, 58–9
months of the year, neologisms for, 297
mood, 170–87
    expressing possibility and ability, 178
    hortative, 183–5
    imperative, 170–5
    optative, 184–6

prohibitive, 176–7
volitive, 181–3
mood and modality
    expressing commands, 172–5
    expressing desire and volition, 181–5
    expressing negative evaluationism, 186–8
    expressing obligation and permission, 180–1
    expressing possibility and ability, 178–9
morphemes, 9, 24, 313–16
    relational, 316–19
    stress and, 36–8
morphology, 2, 24
    agglutinative morphology, 2, 10–11, 24
    morphological causatives, 2
    morphological typology, 9
    nasal spread and, 40
morphosyntactic alignment, 14
multiform verbs. *See* relational (multiform) nominal roots
multilingualism, 7, 19–20

narrative, text samples, 302–4
nasal harmony, 2, 9, 39–44, 313–16
nasal-oral segments, 34
nasal-oral stops, 9
nasal spread, 40
nasal tilde, 8
nasal vowels, 2
nasality, orthography and, 48–9, 53
nasalization, 39–44
nasals, 8, 34
negation
    double negation, 155–6
    lexical negation, 85
    negative imperatives, 176–7
    nominal/adjectival negation, 85–7
    six different types, 25
    verbal negation, 154–7
negative concord, 155–6
negative evaluations, expressing, 186–8
negative pronouns, 113–15
newspaper article, text samples, 308
no marking, 12–13
nominal/adjectival negation, 85–7
nominal case marking suffixes, 3
nominal temporal-aspectual inflection, 2
nominal temporal-aspectual markers, 121–5
nominalizations, 71–84
    abstract -*kue*, 74
    adjectival -*va*, 74
    agent- *vs.* patient-oriented, 78
    deadjectival, 75
    denominal nominalizations, 75
    general nominalizer -*ha*, 71–2
    lexical, 71
    passive -*py*, 73
    sentential, 71, 263
nominalizers, 209
nominalizing prefixes, 77–82
    abstract *mba'e-*, 82
    abstract *t-eko-*, 81–2
    reciprocal *jo-*, 80–1
    reflexive/passive/impersonal *je-*, 79–80
    resultative/instrumental *t-embi-*, 77–9
nominalizing suffixes, 71

abstract -*kue*, 75–6
adjectival -*va*, 74–5
general nominalizer -*ha*, 71–3
passive -*py*, 73–4
nominals, 57–125
   adjectival modifiers of nouns, 87–9
   determiners, 89–104
   forming nouns from other words, 70–86
   nouns, 57–85
   pronouns, 106–16
non-compositional meaning, 78
notional deixis, 97
noun clauses. *See* complement clauses
noun compounds, 82–5
noun incorporation, 11–12
   into the verb, 255–8
noun phrases, 58
   functions of, 69–70
   possessive, 117–21
nouns, 57–85
   adjectival modifiers of, 87–9
   determiners and, 89–105
   deverbal, 71
   forming from other words, 70–87
   functions of noun phrases, 69
   gender agreement and, 24
   gender marking, 62
   lexicalized, 78
   modifiers of, 58–9
   noun compounds, 82–5
   noun incorporation into the verb, 255–8
   noun phrases, 58
   number agreement and, 24
   plural marking, 59–62
   possessive noun phrases, 117–21
   relational (multiform) nominal roots, 63–9
   See also pronouns
nucleus, 13, 58
numbers, 99–103, 293
   cardinal, 100, 102
   number agreement, 24
   ordinal, 102
numerals, 99–103

object drop, 15, 230
object incorporation, 11–12
object pronouns, 106
object relative, 264
objects of predicates, 69–70
obligation, expressing, 180–1
oblique object pronouns, 106
Old Guarani, 2, 10
Old Tupi, 1–2, 19
open questions, 239
optative mood, 184–6
oral comprehension, 21
oral vowels, 2
ordinal numbers, 102
orthography, 32, 46–56
   compound words and, 51–3
   enclitics and, 50–1
   history of orthographic conventions, 46
   inconsistencies in rendering of, 55–6
   interrogative sentences and, 55
   loanwords and, 53–5
   nasality and, 48–9, 53

   postpositions and, 50–1
   prefixes and, 49–50
   questions and, 55
   recommended, 46
   reduplications and, 52–3
   stress and, 47–8, 53
   suffixes and, 50–1

paradigms, 318–20
   affixes, 313–14
   of aireal verbs, 320
   allomorphs, 313–16
   circumfixes, 309
   clitics, 313–14
   common expressions, 321–6
   common phrases, 321–6
   consonant allomorphs, 313–16
   morphemes, 313–19
   postpositional particles, 310–13
   prefixes, 309–10
   relational morphemes, 316–19
   of relational roots, 316–19
   roots, 314–19
Paraguay
   1967 constitution of, 6–7
   founding of, 6
   multilingualism in, 7, 19–20
   other indigenous languages spoken in, 20
   vibrancy and viability of, 7
Paraguayan Academy of the Guarani Language, 46
particles
   order of, 285–9
   in the predicate, 285–9
   verb particles, 25
parts of speech, 15–16
passive/reflexive/impersonal voice, 207–11
   generic meaning, 207–10
   impersonal meaning, 207–10
   with intransitive verbs, 207–10
   with transitive verbs, 209–11
passive voice, 209–11
past tense, 157–9, 163
patient-oriented nominalizations, 78
patients, 132, 207
patrimonial words, 18
perfect (perfective) aspect, 163
permission, expressing, 180–1
person hierarchy, 135–6
personal pronouns, 105–6
phonemes, 27
   consonant phonemes, 9
   vowel phonemes, 9
phonology, 26–45
   phonological contrast, 27
   pronunciation, 26–33
   segmental phonology, 26–34
   sound inventory, 26–33
   suprasegmental phonology, 34–45
phrasebooks 328–9
phrases, common, 321–6
pitch rises, 45
place, postpositions of, 197–8
plural marking, 59–62
   suffixes and, 61–2
poem, text samples, 304–5

polysynthesis, 2–3, 10–12
portmanteau person prefixes, 2, 138–9
Portuguese colonization, 1–2, 19
Portuguese language, 19–20
possession, 25, 58, 70
  alienable possession, 66–7, 236–7
  inalienable possession, 66–7
  non-verbal possessive sentences, 235–7
  possessive noun phrases, 117–21
  possessive pronouns, 116–17
  possessor possessum relationship, 58, 60, 70
  sentences expressing, 235–7
  verbal possessive sentences, 236–7
possibility, expressing, 178–9
postoralized consonants, 9
postpositional complement verbs, 127, 141–6
postpositional particles, list of, 310–13
postpositions, 2, 12, 24, 109, 127, 141–6, 194–202
  complements of, 70
  locative, 194–5
  marking a predicate's complements, 194–7
  orthography and, 50–1
  of place, 197–8
  of time, 199–200
post-stative aspect, 121–2
predicates
  objects of, 69–70
  order of affixes in, 285–9
  order of clitics in, 285–9
  order of particles in, 285–9
  postpositions marking complements of, 194–7
  subjects of, 69
predication, 205–6
predicative clauses, 231–2
prefixes
  active, 13, 136–8
  active voice and, 203–4, 207
  agent-demoting prefixes, 140, 207–8, 210–11
  deverbal nouns and, 71
  exclusive prefixes, 129
  homophonous, 49
  inactive, 13, 136–8
  inactive voice and, 205–7
  inclusive/exclusive distinction, 24, 129
  intransitive predicates and, 203–6
  intransitive verbs and, 127–32
  irregular verbs and, 146–8
  list of, 309–10
  nasalization and, 43
  as nominalizers, 209
  nominalizing, 77–82
  orthography and, 49–50
  passive/reflexive/impersonal voice and, 207–11
  portmanteau person, 2, 138–9
  possessive, 118–20
  prohibitives and, 176–7
  reciprocal voice and, 211–12
  relational, 2
  stress and, 36
  transitive verbs and, 132
  verbal negation and, 154–7
  verbs and, 25

prenasalized consonants, 9
prenasalized segments, 34
present tense, 157–9
privatives, 85
probability, 161
production, 21
progressive aspect, 163–5
progressive nasalization, 42
prohibitive mood, 176–7
prohibitives, 176–7
pronouns, 105–17
  ablative pronouns, 106
  addressees and, 107
  demonstrative pronouns, 115–16
  direct object pronouns, 106
  emphatic markers and, 111–13
  inclusive/exclusive distinction and, 24, 107
  indefinite pronouns, 113–15
  indirect object pronouns, 106
  interrogative pronouns, 111–13
  negative pronouns, 113–15
  object pronouns, 106
  oblique object pronouns, 106
  personal pronouns, 105–6
  possessive pronouns, 116–17
  postpositions and, 109
  reflexive pronouns, 109–10
  separative pronouns, 106, 109
  subject pronouns, 106
pronunciation, 24, 26–33
  consonants, 30–3
  diphthongs, 26–9
  nasal harmony, 39–44
  phonology, 34–45
  practical considerations for, 45
  pronunciation, 8, 45
  prosody sketch, 45
  stress, 36–8
  suprasegmental phonology, 34–45
  syllable structure, 35
  vowels, 26–9
  See also phonology
prosody, 34, 45
prospective aspect, 121–2, 126
Proto-Tupian homeland 3, 4
protractive aspect, 170
proximal events, 94–5
purposive clauses, 271–2

quantification, 241–5
  indefinite, 244
  universal, 244–5
  See also quantifiers
quantifiers, 89–90, 99–105
quasi-eventive aspect, 169–70
Quechua, 7
questions, 247–50
  indirect questions, 238
  open questions, 239
  orthography and, 55
  in subordinate clauses, 238
  yes/no questions, 237–40

reading, 22
reasoned evidence, markers of, 227–9
recipients, 199

364 INDEX

reciprocal verbs, 145, 211–12
reduplications, 102–3
   orthography and, 52–3
   as superlatives, 253
referents, 90–4
reflexive events, 142
reflexive pronouns, 109–10
reflexive voice, 209–11
regressive nasal assimilation, 42
regressive nasalization, 42
relational (multiform) nominal roots, 63–9
relational (multiform) verbs, 148–9
relational morphemes, 316–19
relational prefixes, 2
relational roots, 25, 63–9
   list of, 316–19
relative clauses, 263–8
   that function as an adjective, 264–6
   that function as a noun, 265–7
resources, suggested, 327–32
   academic works consulted, 330–2
   dictionaries, 329
   general introductions, 328
   grammars, 329–30
   for learning Guaraní, 20–5
   linguistic overviews, 330
   online bookshops, 330
   online courses, 328–9
   phrasebooks, 328–9
   textbooks, 328–9
Restivo, Paulo, 5
resultative meaning, 77
resyllabification, 34
retroflex, 34
rhythm, 45
roots, 316–19
   adjectival use of, 15–16
   malleability of, 206
   nasal-oral, 44
   nasalization and, 43–4
   as nouns, 57–8
   relational, 25, 63–9, 316–19
   stress and, 36
   verbal/predicative use of, 16
Ruiz de Montoya, Antonio, 5

schwa, 8
secondary stresses, 39
segmental phonology, 26–34
senses, 293
sentences, complex, 259–79
sentential nominalizations, 71, 263
separative pronouns, 106, 109
serial verb constructions, 169
sibilants, 34
simple clauses, word order in, 230–1
sociative causative, 218–20
   verbs, 152
   voice suffixes, 126
sociolinguistic information, 6–8
sound inventory, 26–33
sounds. *See* pronunciation, phonology
Spanish, contact with, 16–20
Spanish colonization, 1–5, 19, 46
Spanish language, 3–8, 36
   loanwords from, 17–18, 34, 36

mixing with, 16–19
   words borrowed from Guaraní, 19
speech, 21
split intransitivity, 2, 14, 130
spoken production, 21
standard of comparison, 246–8
stative verbs. *See* inactive verbs
stops, 35–6
   glottal, 33, 35–6
   unaspirated, 32
   voiced, 9
   voiceless, 32–3
stress, 9, 36–9
   acute, 8
   fixed, 2
   orthography and, 47–8, 53
   secondary stresses, 39
students, pointers for, 21–5
subject drop, 15, 230
subject pronouns, 106
subject relative, 264
subjects of predicates, 69
subordinate clauses, 263–79
   adverbial clauses, 271–9
   causal clauses, 273–4
   complement clauses, 263, 267–70
   concessive clauses, 272–3
   conditional clauses, 274–5
   hypothetical conditional clauses, 274–6
   locative clauses, 278–9
   manner clauses, 276
   purposive clauses, 271–2
   questions in, 238
   relative clauses, 263–8
   temporal clauses, 277–8
suffixes
   antipassive voice suffixes, 126
   attenuatives and, 86–7
   causative voice suffixes, 126
   deverbal nouns and, 71
   diminutives and, 86
   nasalization and, 40, 43–4
   nominal case marking suffixes, 3
   nominalizing, 71
   orthography and, 50–1
   plural marking and, 61–2
   prohibitives and, 176–7
   sociative causative voice suffixes, 126
   stress and, 36
   verb suffixes, 25
   verbal negation and, 154–7
superlatives, 249–54
   elative, 252–3
   reduplications as, 253
suprasegmental phonology, 34–45
syllable structure, 35–6
symmetric verbs, 145

talking, 23
targets, 40
telic verbs, 158
temporal clauses, 277–8
tense, 157–62
   dubitative future tense, 160
   future tense, 126, 159–62
   immediate future tense, 161

past tense, 157–9, 163
present tense, 157–9
tense/aspect markers, 57, 121–2
text samples, 299–308
  interview, 299–302
  narrative, 302–4
  newspaper articles, 308
  poetry, 304–5
  theatre, 305–7
tilde, use of, 8
time, 294–7
  postpositions of, 199–200
topic, 283–4
toponyms, 61
totalitive aspect, 163
transitive causative, 152, 220–2
transitive relational predicates, 150
transitive verbs, 126–7, 132–40, 209–11
transparency, 40
triggers, 40, 42
Triple Alliance War, 6
Tupi-Guarani family, 1–3, 20
  nasal harmony in, 9
  Portuguese language and, 19
  spread of, 5
  voiced stops in, 9
Tupinambá, 1–2, 19
typological information, 9–16

uncertainty, 161
universal quantification, 244–5

verb compounds, 192–3
verbal negation, 154–7
verbal possessive sentences, 236–7
verbalizations, 188–90
verbs, 126–93
  active verbs, 127–30
  aireal verbs, 133–5, 211–12, 320
  aspect, 163–70
  comitative verbs, 152
  ditransitive verbs, 140–1
  expressing properties of events, 157–8
  inactive verbs, 127
  with increments, 150–1
  intransitive verbs, 13–14, 126–32, 215–17
  irregular verbs, 146–8
  loss of initial consonant, 152–4
  main classes of, *127*
  modality, 170–87
  modifiers of, 190–2
  mood, 170–87
  noun incorporation into, 255–8
  postpositional complement verbs, 127, 141–6
  prefixes and, 25
  reciprocal verbs, 145
  relational (multiform) verbs, 148–9
  serial verb constructions, 169
  symmetric verbs, 145

tense, 157–62
transitive verbs, 126–7
verbal negation, 154–7
verbalizations, 188–90
veridical markers, 223–5
voice, 203–79
  active voice, 132–40, 203–4, 207, 220–2
  antipassive voice, 211–15
  causative voice, 215–22
  impersonal voice, 207–11
  inactive voice, 204–7
  passive voice, 209–11
  reciprocal voice, 211–12
  reflexive voice, 209–11
voiced sounds, 32
  voiced alveolar lateral, 34
  voiced labiodental approximant, 33
  voiced palatal fricative, 33
  voiced velar approximant, 33–4
voiceless sounds, 32
  voiceless glottal fricative, 33
  voiceless postalveolar fricative, 33
  voiceless stops, 32–3
volition, expressing, 181–5
volitive mood, 181–3
vowels, 9, 26–9
  back, 27
  central, 27–8
  epenthetic, 154–5
  front, 27
  helping, 154–5
  high, 27–8
  low, 27–8
  mid, 27
  nasal, 27–8
  open, 28
  oral, 2, 27–8
  oral *vs.* nasal, 2
  pronunciation of, 8, 28
  unrounded, 28
  vowel harmony, 184, 154–5
  vowel phonemes, 9

wants, expressing, 181–3
word classes, 15–16
word order, 3
  noun-adjective, 58–9
  noun-relative clause, 58
  possession and, 58
  in simple clauses, 230–1
writing, 22–3
written comprehension, 21
written production, 21

yes/no questions, 237–40

Zamuco family, 20
Zarratea, Tadeo, 302
zero derivation, 16